cultural studies and political theory

Edited by Jodi Dean

cultural studies & political theory

CORNELL UNIVERSITY PRESS

Ithaca & London

First published 2000 by Cornell University Press
First printing, Cornell Paperbacks, 2000

Printed in the United States of America

Library of Congress Cataloging-in-Publication Data

Cultural studies and political theory / edited by Jodi Dean
p. cm.
Includes index.
ISBN 0-8014-3602-8 (cloth : alk. paper) — ISBN 0-8014-8578-9 (pbk. : alk. paper)
1. Culture—Study and teaching—United States. 2. Political science—United States. I. Dean, Jodi, b. 1962
HM623 .C85 2000
306'.071'073—dc21

00-009220

Cornell University Press strives to use environmentally responsible suppliers and materials to the fullest extent possible in the publishing of its books. Such materials include vegetable-based, low-VOC inks and acid-free papers that are recycled, chlorine-free, or partly composed of nonwood fibers. Books that bear the logo of the FSC (Forest Stewardship Council) use paper taken from forests that have been inspected and certified as meeting the highest standards for environmental and social responsibility. For further information, visit our website at www.cornellpress.cornell.edu.

Cloth printing 10 9 8 7 6 5 4 3 2 1
Paperback printing 10 9 8 7 6 5 4 3 2 1

contents

III. Generating Politics

IV. Haunting Affiliations

introduction: the interface of political theory and cultural studies

JODI DEAN

"It is clear today that culture and economy have both so thoroughly transformed politics that it becomes difficult to recall when they did not."

SHELDON WOLIN, "What Time Is It?"

Questions

Political theory takes as one of its central questions, "What is the political?" The essays collected here, most of which were written expressly for this volume, address a variation of this question, namely, "What does it mean for something to be political?" In affirming that there are different answers to questions of the political, these essays expand and reconstitute the domain of politics in light of transformations in globally networked, consumer-driven, mediatized technoculture. They try to understand how the political is produced.

These essays are at the interface of two fields of contemporary theoretical work, political theory and cultural studies. In some respects this interface is already quite seamless, part of the way we think about and experience everyday life in late capitalism's barrage of media, entertainment, and consumption. We expect cultural analysis to highlight the workings of power. Since Ronald Reagan became president, making the office a role like one in any Hollywood movie, since Vice President Dan Quayle had an argument with a fictional television character, and since Jesse "The Body" Ventura became governor of Minnesota, we have become accustomed to seeing national politics through the windows of popular culture.[1] Similarly, we presume that political theory will appreciate the complexities of representation and mediation, that it will recognize and help us understand the impact of imagery and desire on political principles. Especially in light of the contributions of identity politics, of analyses of sexism, racism, and homophobia, we often think of successful political theories in terms of their attunement to cultural diversity and their capacity to contest a variety of forms of domination, from those that produce subjectivities or limit available subject positions to those that territorialize sites through violence, technology, corporate control, and regulation.

Despite the apparent obviousness of political and cultural interconnection, how political theory and cultural studies work together as academic practices is more complex. Their institutional sites are not analogous. Their disciplinary histories and commitments are, in fact, strikingly different. The premise of this collection is that these differences make the interface of political theory and cultural studies especially useful for thinking about politics at a time when the political and the cultural can no longer be decoupled, at a time when we cannot know in advance who "we" are.

Political theory takes as its central question the relations between subjects, rationalities, and practices that have been subsumed under the name of the political. This question is generally figured as the topic of a discussion whose significance is connoted by its duration across millennia. In the origin stories that helped establish normative political theory as a subfield of political science at a time when behavioral approaches were dominating the discipline, for example, political theory is presented as a vocation with a long and venerable history. Sheldon Wolin writes, "Testimony that such a vocation has existed is to be found in the ancient notion of the *bios theoretikos* as well as in the actual achievements of the long line of writers extending from Plato to Marx."[2] Although Wolin is careful not to reduce political theory to a tradition of textual analysis—and, indeed, he asserts the importance of "epic" political theories that address problems in the world—he conceptualizes it nonetheless in terms of a line of thinkers, all of whom sought to "reassemble the political world."[3]

In contrast, cultural studies rejects the idea of a single line of thinkers or a central(ized) discussion. The work that presents itself as cultural studies—a loose affiliation of interdisciplinary research initiatives and political projects that rarely claim a history much earlier than Gramsci—spans a wide variety of subjects and concerns. Its origin stories emphasize this diversity, linking cultural studies to an appreciation of popular cultural productions as well as to the field's avowedly political intentions. "Cultural studies is not one thing," Stuart Hall asserts; "it has never been one thing."[4] Cultural studies presents itself, then, as less a conversation than an intervention.[5] It is an engaged mode of inquiry committed to understanding the complex terrain of the cultural in connection with relations of power.

Work at the interface of political theory and cultural studies brings together the disciplinary focus of political theory with the commitments and range of cultural studies. I use the term "interface" because this work, as the essays here demonstrate, does not simply combine the two fields in a partnership where each brings its own specific strength to the table. Rather, it configures thinking about the contemporary world through framings that are accessible in each mode but particularly productive when used together to understand the meaning of the political. I want to emphasize four methods of framing questions about the fields and terms of the political.

The first way work at the interface tries to think about the political is by *problematizing* it. Foucault describes problematization as "the development of a domain of acts, practices, and thoughts that seem . . . to pose problems for politics."[6] A form of critical reading, problematization rejects the idea that there is *one* answer that politics will provide to a given question, one just solution or right arrangement. It also rejects the notion that politics can provide *all* the answers to a given set of concerns, that it will tell "us" what to do. Instead, the extent, role, and meaning of politics are what have to be explained. Problematization works to question the "we" that political questions take for granted by challenging the terms in which the presumption that something is political is formulated. Foucault writes: "The problem is, precisely, to decide if it is actually suitable to place oneself within a 'we' in order to assert the principles one recognizes and the values one accepts; or if it is not, rather, necessary to make the future formation of a 'we' possible by elaborating the question."[7] To problematize the political, then, is to ask why and how a political formation comes to have a particular shape. It is to appreciate the contingency present in any conception of politics and to use this appreciation to think better about how arrangements might be otherwise.[8]

The second way interfacial work addresses the production of the political is by *pluralizing* it. It does not presume from the outset that politics is centered in the state or can be summed up with analyses of voting behavior. Nor does it presume that cultural theorizing is or has been "largely dissociated from social theorizing."[9] Rather, inspired by Marx's focus on the economy, critical race scholarship on ethnicity, feminist accounts of privacy, and queer theory's attention to sexuality, work at the interface of political theory and cultural studies multiplies the sites and categories that "count" as political. It acknowledges the complex of interlinked relations, fields, and effects whose traversals and flows produce the networks of politics. William Connolly's compilation of a list designed to stimulate further pluralization gives a sense of the ongoing surplus of political possibilities. He includes a micropolitics of action, a politics of disturbance, a politics of enactment, a politics of representational assemblages, a politics of interstate relations, and a politics of nonstatist, cross-national movements.[10] Not surprisingly, pluralization is a way to frame questions of the methods as well as the contents of political analysis. Different modes of politics will suggest different protocols of research.[11] Pluralization, then, is an engaged process, one that looks for new paths and makes new links in the interests of opening up the terms and terrain of the political. This makes it a particularly useful approach for theorizing the complex networks of mediatized technoculture.[12]

Interfacial work also frames questions of the political by *contextualizing* them. Some political theories claim to provide an Archimedean point or "view from nowhere" that can set out universal principles of justice or the basic tenets of that consensus about justice common to late-capitalist democracies.[13] This is not the path taken by work at the interface of political theory and cultural studies. Instead, this work situates political questions in the contexts of the present, appreciating the fact that there will always be excesses that escape and subvert the concepts through which the political is formatted. Thus, what contextualization involves is the effort to clarify the various elements linked together in a given political constellation.[14] It is a way of thinking about politics through the variety of connections traversing a political and cultural formation. Importantly for politics in the information age, contextualization enables political and cultural analyses to take depoliticization seriously, to address the means through which spaces, issues, identities, and events are taken out of political circulation or are blocked from the agenda—or are presumed to have already been solved. Catriona Sandilands, for example, documents the demise of the environment as a site of political contestation through changes in patterns of consumption. Focusing on Canada, she observes: "Environmental concern can be relatively unproblematically expressed in such actions as recycling, paying deposits on aluminum cans, buying cute little green key chains, and condemning polluters and forestry practices."[15] Attuned to the contexts within which citizens express their environmentalism, she analyzes how their concerns are co-opted into corporate support, into a complacency that lulls consumers into thinking that the ecological problem has already been redressed and hence discourages them from more direct engagement.

The fourth way of framing questions of the political that the interface of political theory and cultural studies contributes is *specification*. By this I mean not simply an attunement to difference, but to the relations through which differences are produced, through which generalities and specificities are measured, demanded, replicated, and understood to exist.[16] Because specification puts contexts in relief, it helps contextualization avoid the flattening effects that result from the assumption that all elements in a context are equally available for deployment or utilization in a given cultural formation. Without it, for example, reverse discrimination seems like a harm as in need of redress as discrimination; hurting someone's feelings by calling them a racist becomes a problem as significant as racism.[17] Slavoj Žižek observes, "In the good old days of traditional *Ideologiekritik*, the paradigmatic critical procedure was to regress from 'abstract' (religious, legal . . .) notions to the concrete social reality in which these notions were rooted; today it seems more and more that the critical procedure is forced to follow the opposite path, from pseudo-concrete imagery to abstract (digital, market . . .) processes which effectively structure living experience."[18] Through specification, work at the interface of political theory and cultural studies theorizes the connections between immediate images and events and larger structures, relations, processes, and assemblages of power. As with the other three framings, specification is a vehicle for contestation, for politicization through the acknowledgment of different registers of significance, violation, harm, and need.

As it affirms the importance of understanding *how* something is political, interfacial work attends to the risks of presuming in advance that a specific site is already or necessarily political or that an analytical intervention is political enough. These are risks that accompany political theory and cultural studies as they try to think about the present. To put it bluntly, political theory risks oversimplifying its accounts when it fails to acknowledge the multiplicity of political domains. Cultural studies risks non-intervention by presuming its political purchase in advance. The essays here respond to these risks as they consider what is at stake, what is gained or lost, when the political is constituted.

Politics Isn't Everything

Raising the question of what makes something political is important because of the depoliticizing effects of the pervasive sense that, today, *everything* is political. Voices raised from a variety of sectors join in the observation that our whole culture has become political and our politics cultural. Sheldon Wolin writes, "It is hard to think of an action, much less a relationship, that someone has not declared to be 'political' or involve 'politics' or, its shorthand, 'power.' It is not at all clear today what would not count as politics."[19]

The observation, of course, is not neutral; it is a complaint, a lament, a critical diagnosis of the times. That politics is everywhere is considered a problem. It presumes that we need a respite from politics, that "too much" politics "drives out" other important human practices or modes of being.[20] Amy Gutmann, for example, treats efforts on behalf of multicultural education in terms of the "deconstruction" of intellectual life into "a political battlefield of class, gender, and racial interests." Moreover, she accuses "deconstructionists" of reducing "every answer to an exercise of political power."[21]

The lament that everything is political is a strange one. If everything is political, why does it seem as if our fields and opportunities have narrowed, dwindled, and become confining? Why does it seem as if there is no room to act? These questions point to the depoliticizing effects of the lament itself. The claim that everything is political makes action seem, if not impossible, then at least pointless—there's no need to bother with organizing, consciousness raising, or critique if everything is already political. Under the overwhelming weight of a political *everything*, we become mired in world-weary knowingness and cynicism.[22]

The cliché that everything is political occludes *how* things are political. It does not tell us what makes an event or text, for example, a matter of politics. It does not give us any insights into the way disconnected figures and themes become linked together into a particular power formation. In assuming the fact of politics, the totalizing shorthand of "everything" neglects the *how* of politics, the ways concepts and issues come to be political common sense and the processes through which locations and populations are rendered as in need of intervention, regulation, or quarantine.

Some of the same people who use the charge that everything is political to evoke nostalgia for a time before politics are themselves highly politicized.[23] Organizations such as the Traditional Values Coalition, Concerned Women of America, and the American Family Association, for example, mobilized during the eighties and nineties in opposition to changes in cultural norms governing gender and sexuality.[24] Conservatives campaigned in national elections and went directly to state and local voters with referenda and ballot initiatives. Toting an agenda built around decency, security, and basic values, activists targeted museums, school districts, entertainment, workplaces, and the Internet.

In the United States, the right-wing has been smart about political action. They have operated in a variety of domains. They have also reaffirmed (while redirecting) the political messages of the sixties, namely, the centrality of raced and sexed identity and the importance of culture as tool and terrain of struggle. A number of the essays here address this point, in particular those from Lauren Berlant, William Connolly, Barbara Cruikshank, Paul Passavant, and Michael Shapiro. Taking up incidents in right-wing culture war, they specify the moves through which fundamentalists configure the political terrain around and with values like responsibility and decency. As they make clear, when American conservatives make the politicization of "everything" an issue, they are displacing attention from their own activism and, more importantly, from issues of equity, inclusion, and harm. Indeed, Cruikshank extends the argument to suggest that, in asserting the "naturalness" of their values even as they politicize them, those on the right back themselves into a corner from which they can only escape through violence.

With the accusation that "everything is political," contemporary American fundamentalists blame academic "deconstructionists" and "multiculturalists" for widespread cultural dislocations resulting from movements in transnational corporate capital; shifts to information, consumption, and distribution-based economies; expansions in entertainment media and content; and the violence of urban decay and rural despair.[25] Conservative organizer Paul M. Weyrich makes this point explicitly:

> It is impossible to ignore the fact that the United States is becoming an ideological state. The ideology of Political Correctness, which openly calls for the destruction of our traditional culture, has so gripped the body politic, has so gripped our institutions, that it is even affecting the Church. It has completely taken over the academic community. It is now pervasive in the entertainment industry, and it threatens to control literally every aspect of our lives.
>
> Those who came up with Political Correctness, which we more accurately call "Cultural Marxism," did so in a deliberate fashion. I'm not going to go into the whole history of the Frankfurt School and Herbert Marcuse and the other people responsible for this. Suffice it to say that the United States is very close to becoming a state totally dominated by an alien ideology, an ideology bitterly hostile to Western culture. Even now, for the first time in their lives, people have to be afraid of what they say. . . . You can't approach the truth about a lot of different subjects. If you do, you are immediately branded as "racist," "sexist," "homophobic," "insensitive," or "judgmental."[26]

Weyrich analyzes the experience of unfreedom in terms of ideology, an ideology that fails to establish a subject position for those to and for whom he speaks. He doesn't connect this ideology to economic conditions, although he does see it as exerting a strong influence on media. Disruptions in traditional culture, in his view, are not connected with corporate capital, consumerism, or globalization. Instead, he sees the alien ideology of political correctness as a product of academia, and as extending out from universities with a controlling, gripping, dominating power.

What is striking about Weyrich's analysis is its assertion of the political centrality of academic discourse. He confirms the efficacy of theoretical work, of critique. In fact, faced with such vehement, hostile attacks, those of us committed to combating racism, sexism, and homophobia often feel emboldened, empowered. We want to defend what we know is right. Under these conditions it seems to us very clear that our work is making a difference—it combats discrimination, exclusion, oppression.

We might even start to think that it is making all the difference or the very difference that matters. That is to say, our political stance or intention may come to dominate our own understanding of our theoretical work, reinforcing the flattening sense of the political everything. A problematization becomes reduced to a position. For example, few Americans—especially in the wake of the Lewinsky affair—would deny that the personal is political. But fewer still would accept the analyses of power relations, of distributions of work and responsibility, productions of gendered subjectivity, and separations of domestic and public spheres that feminists have offered. Moreover, most are likely to reject as well the notion that, if the personal is political, then perhaps there are personal practices that should be changed through organized collection action.

This flattening is manifest in university politics as sides are taken and solidified. Not only is analytical work reduced by one's critics to a kind of soundbite or line, but in the wake of this reduction one is tempted to respond in kind, contributing one-liners and enabling this contribution to substitute for more organized, mundane collective action. As George Lipsitz says in his contribution to this collection, however, "Taking a position is not the same as waging a war of position; changing your mind is not the same as changing society." The presumption of a political everything in effect eliminates politics; it deletes struggle, contestation, and argument from the cultural terrain.

In the face of the enervating effects of the political everything, studies of how the political is produced, or, more precisely, of how particular sites become political, might contribute to energies affiliated around diversity, freedom, and equity. Such studies, themselves contestable and contingent, might restore conflict and energy to thinking about culture and politics, not by taking "politically incorrect" or simply contrary positions, but by problematizing, pluralizing, contextualizing, and specifying the political.

But Everything Can Be (Made) Political

Despite the depoliticization the claim perversely effects, the notion that everything is political marks a change in the political situation of late capitalism, namely, the decentering of the state.[27] In other words, everything seems political because the political is not confined to one specific location or set of actions. The new social movements of the sixties and seventies, for example, targeted families, media, churches, schools, medicine, consumption, identity, and sexuality.[28] They opened up specific economic, cultural, and social practices, making them political.

One of the strengths of cultural studies has been its connection with these movements. It has continued these battles, extending them into universities and supporting research and analysis. The formation of Women's, Ethnic, and African-American Studies Departments, as well as the opening up of traditional disciplines to the study of non-traditional populations, texts, arrangements of living, and cultural productions, has been a political struggle. For cultural studies, the political everything marked by the decentering of the state has been a stimulus, provoking critical accounts of media, subcultures, consumption, leisure, popular science, and the rich variety of experiences, resistances, exclusions, alignments, subordinations, and pleasures inscribed into the life of the ordinary.

One might think that political theorists would have jumped on the opportunity to consider expansions and pluralizations of the political. For the most part, this has not been the case. Political theory has seemed overwhelmed by the political everything. Sheldon Wolin worries that the dispersion of politics is part of political theory's failure of political sensibility, its "inability or refusal to articulate a conception of the political in the midst of widely differing claims about it, some issuing from nontraditional claimants."[29] David Held responds by invoking the specter of totalitarianism, the risk that widespread politicization opens up the door to an intrusive state.[30] Jeffrey Isaacs also responds by trying to limit the political; delineating a particular set of issues as those proper to political theory, he attacks those who fail to address these issues for irrelevance.[31]

Political theory and theorists have had a difficult time coping with the excesses of the political everything because they have operated under the general terms of a state-centered conception of the political. As Thomas Dumm explains,

> This perspective on power, which reduces it to state power, informs the recent detente between the followers of Habermas and Rawls. Advocates of procedures that would somehow ensure communicative action and their counterparts who embrace a liberalism of fear recently have found a common ground in the slogan 'procedural democracy.' That form of democracy has as its exclusive site of struggle the contemporary state. Moreover, it is a state that is itself understood to be largely devoid of struggle and is presented as a place where through adequate procedures, all differences might be successfully negotiated.[32]

The state-centeredness of mainstream political theory results in a reductive dismissal of alternative forms of and sites of politics that treats them as pathologies rather than contestations. If, to echo Foucault, politics is analyzed on the basis of the state, then the political subject can only be conceived as the subject of law.[33] The possibility of politics in other fora starts to sound invasive, an invitation to massive state intervention, or naive, a misunderstanding of what politics is. Under the presumption that the state remains the political center, the idea that politics is everywhere sounds like an alarmist rant; the presumption that culture is a terrain and tool of politics evokes the propagandistic machinations of the Soviet Union, Nazi Germany, and for some (particularly those who irresponsibly map political correctness onto McCarthyism, thereby erasing the histories of each) Cold War America. Presuming that politics necessarily targets the state, in other words, contributes to the depoliticizing effects of the claim that everything political. It makes non-state centered action, and, more specifically, cultural politics, seem at best ineffectual or irrelevant and at worst paranoid. It also allows those ready to mobilize on a variety of terrains to proceed without a fight.

For the most part, the focus on the state has been a characteristic of liberal political theories and rights-based conceptions of democracy. Nonetheless, communitarian accounts, precisely because they have emerged as alternatives to liberalism, have retained a state-centered structure. Their evocations of shared values, of common understandings, of traditions that give meaning and sense to the community, rely on a presumption of knowing who "we" are and endorsing rather than criticizing that "we."

Briefly put, in the 1970s, communitarian theorists such as Michael Sandel challenged the liberalism of John Rawls for the inadequacy of its account of personal identity. Selves are embedded in their contexts, they argued. Hence, community is not properly thought of as the result of individual choices; it is not merely a dimension of an individual's disposition. Rather, a community is marked by "a common vocabulary of discourse and a background of implicit practices and understandings within which the opacity of the participants is reduced if never fully dissolved."[34] Because they have endorsed community in their critique of what they perceive as liberalism's atomism, communitarians have tended to foreground commonality. That is to say, they have embraced the "bed" of the embedded self uncritically. Conflicts, exclusions, and contradictions in cultural traditions are either resolved through the dividing up of society into various spheres, as in the work of Michael Walzer, trumped through an account of reconciling progress, as in the work of Charles Taylor, or left outside the scope of the theory altogether.[35] This latter path is found in most communitarian work, as its accounts of "we" are generally homogeneous and disconnected from popular forms of consumer-oriented, entertainment-driven technoculture. Folks in communities seem not to watch much television (and of course they rarely bowl alone). So, although communitarians have emphasized the political importance of personal identity and emphasized the cultural terrain of politics, as Mark Reinhardt makes clear in his chapter, they have done so in a way that eliminates contingency, that fails to problematize culture and identity.

As liberals and communitarians have concurred that selves are encumbered and that rights matter in the nineties, they have consolidated in opposition to "post-modern" and "neo-Nietzschean" theories attuned to the excesses and exclusions in cultural traditions, the contradictions whose suppressions enable presumptions of an overlapping consensus and a rational public sphere.[36] It is these theories, an assortment of post-this and critical-that, that have affiliated most readily with cultural studies. Informed by similar archives—those that have built up around Marx, Adorno, Althusser, Foucault, Derrida, Lacan, and Deleuze, on the one hand, and in alliance with feminist, race, queer, and multicultural concerns, on the other—this heterodox or alternative political theory explores multiple possibilities of political engagement. It questions efforts to reassert the proper boundaries of politics, as well as the prior status of theory.[37]

Questionings

There are multiple paths through these essays, only one of which is the chapter ordering presented here. Readers interested in the political costs accompanying cultural forgetfulness, to give one example, might start with Connolly's essay and then jump to those by Zerilli, Hozic, and Stewart. Concern with how cultural politics reconfigures political subjectivity and action, to give another example, links the essays from Lipsitz, Passavant, Grant, Apostolidis, and Shulman. Although no single essay claims a specific identity category as its point of departure or primary object of concern, some thematize issues of race, class, sex, and sexuality directly; each incorporates insights from the last thirty years of critical multicultural work into its analysis.

In sorting the essays collected here, I have tried to highlight the way they frame questions about the meaning of the political. Those in the first section contextualize the culturalization of politics in late-capitalist America, locating this process in the nation's increased conservativism. The second set of essays problematizes the terms through which culture has been politicized. The third section attends to specific generations of politics, the contingencies forgotten in national(ist) enthusiasm. The fourth group of essays pluralizes the sites of politics, thinking through the links of association that enable sites, themes, and relations to be territorialized in the name of the political. Thus, the first two sections establish the political and institutional framework that informs the essays in the last two sections.

The essays in "Warring Maneuvers" analyze some of the tactics and strategies deployed during the culture wars of the eighties and nineties. At issue are the ways in which cultural conflict during this period constricted the space of politics. For William Connolly, this constriction is an effect of the drives to purity and revenge that empower demands for the death penalty. Discussions of capital punishment employ notions of the will, responsibility, and punishment as if these notions were stable, forgetting the cultural and corporeal uncertainties that complicate them. In these discussions, Connolly explains, the will is "above" culture, rather than produced within it. Punishment can thus be meted out unproblematically: because the criminal act was freely willed, punishment is deserved. Culture is relieved of responsibility for criminality at the same time that the will becomes transparent, knowable. Connolly argues that social practices of law, social science, journalism, and electoral politics displace the ambiguities of the will into a compensatory politics of vengeance. This politics of vengeance has been particularly effective because of the resentment, unfreedom, and desire for release on the part of various constituencies grappling with changes in the transnational economy. In contemporary American culture wars, he explains, the neoconservative deployment of the death penalty reasserts the strength of the state weakened by globalization and the ultimate responsibility of individuals for their own fates. It channels the pleasures of killing and violence into state service.

Lauren Berlant also considers the deployment of feeling in American politics. Problematizing the theorization of privacy in the line of cases beginning with *Griswold v. Connecticut*, she argues that the sentimental politics of the national moment reduces society to a space free from struggle and the home to a space free from pain. In this sentimental nation, people want public figures to "care." Visions for social equity are less significant. If I hurt, law can "feel my pain"—and make it go away. Traumatized subjectivity, Berlant explains, has become the index for personhood in the sentimental nation. National sentimentality reduces politics to experience, to the close-up of personal suffering rather than the larger view of systematic violence. The sympathetic identification that anchors national unity establishes the elimination of pain as the limit of political responsibility. Berlant conveys the necessity of risking the sense of belonging that national sentimentality makes possible so that questions of equity and value can be struggled over as issues of power, rather than limited to questions of sincerity.

Barbara Cruikshank takes issue with the presumption that neoconservatives have constricted the political, suggesting that their politicization of the boundaries between culture and politics in fact pluralizes it. She demonstrates the ways neoconservative discourse challenges three postulates of "traditional political wisdom" regarding the relationship of politics to culture. Traditional political wisdom holds, first, that the stability of government is founded on the commonality of culture; second, that culture operates as the limit of politics (that it is impervious to law); and, third, that America's exceptional political consensus and continuity were neither guided by a theory of government nor rent by conflict. Although these three tenets are often espoused by cultural warriors, and although efforts to impose cultural unity and political boundaries may well lead to violence (a claim born out by the ongoing assassinations of abortion providers and the murder of Matthew Shepard, to give but two examples), Cruikshank argues that they are performatively contested in neoconservative discourse. "Cultural warriors take the 'givenness' of culture to be an absolutely necessary foundation for democratic politics," she writes. "Cultural politics, on the other hand, is a practice that takes the contingency and alterability of the borders between the cultural and the political to be a measure of democracy." Through their politicization of previously "given" and natural assumptions about family, nature, culture, and the values of Americans, neoconservatives help create a space for cultural politics.

Finally, in the last essay in this section, George Lipsitz addresses the constriction of the political stemming from the contradictory consciousness under which many artists and intellectuals live. His essay situates the militant posturing and desire for political purity sometimes found in campus politics in the context of contradictions that arise when one works in the elitist and closed institutions of the academy while believing in the importance of struggles for social change. Lipsitz argues that acknowledging the contradictory consciousness that arises out of the contradictory contexts of middle-class life is particularly important to combat the gains made by the American right over the past thirty years. Not only have neoconservatives succeeded in encouraging "everyone to see as the ruling-class mythmakers want them to see," but they have also rewritten the history of American political struggle to obscure the long history of radical democratic politics. Recovering this history, Lipsitz suggests, can direct attention to opportunities for political alliance and engagement, to possibilities for action and change, that may reconnect intellectuals and communities in organized social movements.

The essays in the second section, "Shifting Culture," problematize thinking about culture in some specific theoretical locations. Mapping recent debates in political theory, Mark Reinhardt highlights the points of contact between the preoccupations of communitarians and those of cultural studies scholars. Although he acknowledges some of the reactionary positions held by communitarians, Reinhardt prefers to read them generously. He credits communitarians with placing political subjectivity on the agenda of mainstream political theory through their critique of liberalism's "unencumbered self." Moreover, he takes seriously their efforts to provide an inclusive account of shared cultural attachments attentive to diverse concerns of a multicultural populace. Nonetheless, through a close reading of some representative communitarian texts, Reinhardt finds that communitarians obscure the harms committed in the name of community. He concludes that cultural studies within and without political theory provides a better opportunity to conceive of more robust and emancipatory democratic practices.

Paul Passavant problematizes the communitarian critique of liberalism, pointing out that the unencumbered liberal self is not as abstract and disembodied as the critics claim. Taking issue with the "repressive hypothesis" that liberalism rests on a vision of rights as trumps for selves disconnected from their bodies, communities, and constitutive beliefs, "The Governmentality of Discussion" uses the imbrications of civility and race, decency and sex in free speech law to specify how "the rights of subjects necessitate the production of subjects for rights." Passavant argues that the communitarian critique of liberalism fails because it does not understand rights as a form of cultural production. His close reading of first amendment law highlights the way it culturally constitutes and regulates the citizen who can claim a right to speak freely.

Judith Grant also looks at shifts in the place of culture in debates in political theory. She focuses on Marxist cultural theory and the critical theory of the Frankfurt school. Because of the collapse of reason into technocratic rationality, a collapse made particularly visible in the horrors of National Socialism and the dropping of the atomic bomb, critical theorists looked elsewhere for imaginative resistance and dissent. For them, as Grant points out, "culture had the potential to reinvigorate the moribund critical elements in reason and to move humanity away from the totalitarian impulse and back towards democracy." Grant links this turn to culture to earlier divisions within Marxism, in particular the one between Lenin's emphasis on the economy and Lukacs's stress on consciousness. Influenced by Lukacs's account of totality, Horkheimer and Adorno began from the premise that the world and human subjectivity constitute each other. For them, understanding the place of ideology in the production of human subjectivity was politically crucial: it could help explain why Europe devolved into totalitarianism and war instead of, as the champions of enlightenment would have it, into democracy and peace. Grant thus reads the emphasis on culture in critical theory as a space for hope, for "the freedom which did not come to pass" (Adorno) and the "protest against that which is" (Marcuse), situating debates over the commodity form and the place of the audience in this context. She concludes with allusions to contemporary debates in cultural studies, viewing it as the study of "human possibility and political inaction" at the level of consciousness.

Like Grant, Paul Apostolidis is concerned with the political purchase of cultural studies, and, more specifically, with its link to political action. Cultural studies must be more than a set of political convictions sampled into mixed segments of late-capitalist consumer entertainment culture. Apostolidis argues that what has been missing, and what political theory can provide, is a more adequate account of leadership. "Action or Distraction? Cultural Studies in the USA" sees the film *Primary Colors* and cultural studies' sidestepping of crucial questions of political method and purpose as two sides of the same coin: neither addresses the criteria of successful political leadership in the face of culturalized politics.

The contributions to "Generating Politics" work through some of the complexities of political production in the context of the nation. Through what sorts of representations, myths, fears, and technologies are nations imagined? How do these imaginings produce the conditions for some kinds of political engagement while blocking opportunities for others? The essays in this section problematize the icons, boundaries, and desires of the nation, looking specifically at replicated monuments in consumer culture, anxiety over infection and disease in popular culture, stories of race and rebirth in literature, and televised images of war, violence, and refugees in global communications' representations of ethnic violence in the former Yugoslavia.

Linda Zerilli's "Democracy and National Fantasy: Reflections on the State of Liberty" rethinks American democracy's representations of uniqueness and originality. Zerilli interrogates American accounts of the Chinese Goddess of Liberty that see the statue as a copy of the Statue of Liberty. She contextualizes this interrogation through a genealogy of the Statue of Liberty's coming to prominence as a national icon. In a thoughtful application and extension of Hannah Arendt's discussion of the American revolution, Zerilli construes the statue as the site of an argument over the meaning of the American founding. Debates over the place and significance of the monument reiterate the complicated tensions between revolution and stability, original and copy, exception and replication imbricated in the nation's efforts to legitimize its revolutionary past. The statue's semiological plasticity, a plasticity resulting in part from its feminine incorporation, has facilitated its deployment in the service of causes that include feminism, civil rights, nativism, and consumerism. But this versatility makes the statue vulnerable as well as powerful. Any use can be derided as a misuse, a corruption, debasement, or "inappropriate appropriation." For Zerilli, the fact of replication, one she illustrates through the story of a Queens factory that produces miniature Statues of Liberty, points to that "strange global economy of national identity in which mimesis is at once demanded and forbidden." America desires yet denies its imitators.

In a study of the generation of community through disease, Priscilla Wald takes up the way nations need their imaginers. Whereas most comments on Benedict Anderson's *Imagined Communities* have focused on community, Wald attends to the imaginings that enable such community. She concentrates on those imaginings stimulated by contacts among strangers and understood through vectors of contagion and disease. To this end, she reads "carrier narratives" as epidemiological detective stories, as stories of community and contagion where what secures us, what keeps us healthy, always threatens to morph into what can kill us. This threat becomes especially clear in genetic narratives that undermine the distinction between the transmission of disease and "catching" something. Wald writes: "The balance of the stable community marked by immunity is always precarious, with the requisite number of strangers—those required to ensure a healthy and diverse gene pool—weighing constantly against the threat of too many strangers (hence social breakdown or anarchy in politics and germs)." Seen from the perspective of shared immunities, our common susceptibility to disease marks us as a community even as it turns each of us into strangers bearing contagions, into carriers of death.

Whereas Wald looks at the ways disease generates imaginings of community, George Shulman addresses the kinds of politics generated within the racist practices of a democracy with universalist pretensions. Put somewhat differently, if Wald is attending to the nation made vulnerable through imaginings of diseased bodies, then Shulman is thinking through a national politics sustained and disavowed through imaginings of raced bodies. Speaking in America is made possible through the symbols, narratives, and bodies that inform its history. Shulman makes this point with reference to the Warren Beatty film *Bulworth*, in which Senator Bulworth supports leftist political issues only after embracing African-American culture. Indeed, he voices his support by rapping, able to speak only through rap. Shulman uses this contemporary version of Mailer's "white negro" to understand the regeneration and redemption racialized discourse offers America, even as America uses race to dominate and exploit those within its compass. Although the country has upheld white supremacy, American nationhood has been idealized as a democracy. This creates a dilemma for struggle against racist oppression: resistance to white supremacy depends on refusing connection with a national (democratic) community. Reading the narratives of rebirth offered by King, Mailer, and Baldwin, Shulman specifies their efforts to retell stories of the nation when all alternatives are problematic, when there is no possible story, no course of action that can escape the entanglements of America's racism, but when confronting and combating this racism is necessary nonetheless.

Aida Hozic theorizes the entanglements of media and desire in the warfare in Bosnia and Kosovo. Her essay argues against dominant strands in postcolonial theory as it challenges the claim that the other is desired. It argues against strands in communications theory as it rejects the notion that the media intervenes violently in specific locations. In voyeuristic capitalism, she counters, the violence comes from economies based on watching. Hozic's analysis focuses on the "unwanted colonies" that have emerged to haunt postcolonial "economies of desire." In the imaginary space structured, fractured, and reconstructed through global media, "a zone of ethnic violence haunts the cosmopolitan center as a repugnant specter, an unpleasant reminder of its own violent past and present, a drawback in the age of digitality, transnationalism, and hybridity." The former Yugoslavia operates as such a specter. Hozic explains that it was able to secure media attention because of the media infrastructure built for the 1984 Winter Olympics in Sarajevo. Not only was the infrastructure superior to that more often available to war correspondents, but the city provided a "picture-perfect war-torn landscape" for film and video as well as an operative base for reality-based television programming. In this context, Sarajevo could function as a content-machine, generating a variety of important media stories. It could confirm the importance of watching.

The last essays, "Haunting Affiliations," pluralize the sites of politics as they take up connections that create political space. Like Hozic, Kathleen Stewart is concerned with the repugnant remainders that haunt contemporary society's economic successes. And, like Hozic, Stewart theorizes threatened and threatening spaces, spaces that are "too local," that are strange, dangerous, vast, and unknowable, just past the limit of the safely disciplined spaces on the other side. But in the inverse of Hozic's position, Stewart inquires into that which escapes public attention but remains nonetheless political (rather than that which is watched). "Real American Dreams (Can Be Nightmares)" listens to voices from the Appalachian hollers. Stewart hears eruptions of resistance, elements of a politics of everyday life and a political imagining not yet incorporated into the legitimate practices of the public sphere. These eruptions are from "beyond the pale," that is to say, they are the fears and anxieties of the losers and the poor left out of the American dream and outside the domains of its myriad enclosed and separated publics and counterpublics. Such anxieties often posit conspiracies, finding there an explanation for the forces that seem to block them at every turn. Stewart recounts the speculations of some West Virginian women, their suspicions regarding news of the dangers of salt, their discovery that food labels do not even mention salt, referring instead to sodium. It is a world of odd, unassimilated moments, where something funny is going on, but no one knows quite what it is. For Stewart, cultural politics is activated by these eruptions of the uncanny, by the skirmishes at the border that challenge the terms of the dream by evoking the nightmares that haunt it.

Thomas Dumm also looks to the ordinary and the everyday for possibilities of resistance. Like Stewart's essay, "Wild Things" specifies an eruption of the ordinary, an unassimilated moment where the terms of thinking and acting shift. Dumm, too, thinks about wild spaces at the edge of the normal, describing a scene in Montana, at a conference on Baudrillard, in the context of a post-punk performance. The engagement here is between Baudrillard and a wild instance of pop-cultural elation when the crowd begins to sing spontaneously while Baudrillard is left sitting. For Dumm, this eruption of the ordinary suggests an inspiration that resists Baudrillard's simulated indifference in the face of postmodern apocalypse. Something happened, something unexpected. In the context of what Baudrillard theorizes as a larger collapse of meaning, singing together unsettles cynical anomie with wit, wonder, and something like delight. Like Thoreau's nature, Dumm suggests, experiences of mediated uncanniness can inspire us with their unpredictability, responding to the overwhelming forces of nihilism with mystery and surprise.

Although his investigations also traverse wild, uncertain spaces, Michael Shapiro analyzes contingency less in terms of eruption of possibilities of resistance than with respect to the very institutional assemblages that produce bonds of sociality. "The Politics of the 'Family' " begins by juxtaposing a journey "out west" taken by Shapiro's grandfather and Jim Jarmusch's film *Dead Man.* What links the two, Shapiro explains, is the radical contingency of the family, their elucidation of the forces and events that create and dissolve family structures. For Shapiro, Jarmusch's film counters the political mythology of America that has become particularly useful to the contemporary right, that is to say, the mythology that posits the family at the moral foundation of the nation. The America in *Dead Man* is an organization of violence where connections are made and broken almost anarchically, where the ties that bind are contingent. Shapiro uses this contingency to critique the universalizing claims of the Hegelian account of the family and to introduce the impact of changing economic structures on the family-state nexus. As Shapiro argues, the mythologized, universalized family continues to serve as a vehicle for the nation, a move often made via the evocation of decency. He writes: "The evocation of 'decency' has been articulated during the past decade with a more general family values right wing political initiative, aimed at essentializing the conventional family and locating it in a mythic story in which the dissolution of traditional family structures is a threat to a previously vital national character." Shapiro concludes with a reading of Paul Thomas Anderson's film *Boogie Nights*, a film about the porn industry that reverses the presumption that the nuclear family is necessarily the decent family.

The book closes with my essay, "Declarations of Independence." Like Stewart, I am concerned with the conspiratorial haunting of the public. Like Dumm and Shapiro, I take up the wild spaces outside the bounds of the normalized political. Why would someone as politically astute as Hillary Clinton blame a "vast right-wing conspiracy" for the troubles that afflicted her husband's presidency? Didn't she know that such an accusation sounds crazy? To answer this question, I look at how the political space of America has been drawn in the course of the nation's historical imagining of conspiracy. Conspiracy, I argue, is not at the margins of politics. Rather, it is central to Americans' efforts to conceive themselves as a public.

The essays collected here demonstrate some of the possibilities for thinking about politics available at the interface of political theory and cultural studies. As they problematize, pluralize, specify, and contextualize the sites, practices, and affiliations of the political, they repeat some of the key insights available from political and cultural work in recent years, resignifying them through particular examples, remixing them through other archives. The repetition matters. It is important to say things again. In consumer-driven global technoculture, newness tends to be overrated, the specifics of reappearances in different contexts lost in the stultifying effects of the "been there, done that" attitude of the political everything.[38] Not only is there no "we" who already knows it all, not only is the presumption of such a "we" dangerous in its exclusivity, but the flux and flow of generations, the contingencies of reading, thinking, watching, and desiring create shifting networks of possibility and realization that themselves need to be fostered. This volume, then, attempts to provide a portal through which these possibilities might be accessed and expanded.

I. Warring Maneuvers

the will, capital punishment, and cultural war

WILLIAM E. CONNOLLY

A Brief History of Forgetfulness

The will, we are told, forms a hinge of western civilization because it is so crucial to our practice of individual responsibility. And murder is often said to deserve capital punishment because it is a *willful* act. But what if the very hinge upon which these judgments turn has always been creaky and unstable? What if the highest moral case for capital punishment rests upon cultural *forgetfulness* of instability in this category itself? Let us, then, review a forgotten history, condensing long stretches of time into brief summaries so that the shifting terms of instability persistently stalking western conceptions of the will can stand out vividly.

1. "Father, forgive them, for they know not what they do" (Luke, 23:34). It is uncertain, according to scholars, whether Jesus said this on the Cross or the words were attributed to him later by others. Part of the case for the latter judgment is that the statement asserts a difference between Son and Father that Jesus did not express intensely elsewhere. Either way the sentence prefigures an interminable struggle within Christianity. The father, on this reading, is a vengeful god with a soft spot in his heart, while the son is a gentle soul whose forgiveness expresses appreciation for the uncertainty and ambiguity in which violent action occurs. The son's sentiment, however, is not entirely independent of the father's passion: forgiveness becomes appropriate only after an injustice has been recognized. The language of will, in relation to responsibility, desert, and punishment, is not highly developed in the Gospels. The killers of Jesus, for instance, are considered by the one who uttered that sentence to have acted as much out of ignorance as out of willfulness. For four centuries, before the will became crafted into a cultural instrument of punishment, many Christians opposed the death penalty. The exemplary sacrifice of Jesus on the Cross spoke against such a spirit of revenge.

2. "Mind gives orders to itself, and it is resisted. . . . Mind commands mind to will . . . , but it does not do so. Whence comes this monstrous state? Why should it be?"[1] Augustinian (and Pauline) Christianity places

the will front and center, setting the stage for the displacement of Jesus/Christianity by a more punitive Christianity. It demands the will, first, to create conceptual space between its omnipotent, benevolent god and responsibility for evil in the world; second, to deepen human responsibility for vice while on earth (virtue, at this stage, is due solely to the grace of God and not to the will of the do-gooder); and, third, to connect the image of humanity itself to the God who willed the world into being. The divided will performs these three historical functions for Augustine. It appears in the world only after Adam, who was initially endowed with a pure, undivided will, disobeyed a divine command willfully. Henceforth, the "monstrous state" of the will arises recurrently when "mind gives orders to itself and it is resisted" . . . by itself. This volatility of the will is part of the punishment visited upon humanity for that first, free, and original sin. Division is both constitutive of the Augustinian will and extremely problematical to it. So Augustine introduces grace to soften the experience of injustice haunting this very instrument of justice.

The theme of division also threatens to throw Augustinianism back into the arms of those devils and heretics, the Manicheans. The latter treat monstrosity in the will to be a manifestation of the cosmic contest between the forces of good and evil. They dismantle the omnipotence of God to make sense of evil. Augustine must thus retain the division while doing whatever is necessary to ward off the loss of divine omnipotence that threatens to accompany it. He responds to this internal uncertainty in a punitive way:

> Let them perish from before your face, O God, even as vain talkers and seducers of men's minds perish who detect in the act of deliberation two wills at work, and then assert that in us there are two natures or two minds, one good, the other evil. They themselves are truly evil, when they think such evil things. . . . Thus they are made into a deeper darkness, for in horrid pride they have turned back further from you, from you who are "the true light which enlightens every man that comes into this world."[2]

"Let them perish before your face. . . ." The Augustinian will is grounded in equal parts on, first, its role in protecting an omnipotent god from evil, second, its indispensability to individual responsibility, *and*, third, the bullying of opponents (such as Manicheans and pagans) who point to paradoxes in the very projection of it. Might it have been possible for Augustine to appreciate the indispensability of the will to his faith and then to soften its role in life by emphasizing its uncertain character? Perhaps. But Augustine refuses such a combination. He emphasizes the mysterious character of the will while also asserting its primacy with fervor. He eventually lands on a mix of ecclesiastical discipline and divine grace to civilize a will that is otherwise unruly in its very constitution. The severity of the divine punishments he imagines—including the threat of an eternal "second" death for those who willfully rebel against faith in his god—reveals how precarious and militant the idea of free will is at the inception of organized Christianity.

3. In Augustinian Christianity disciplinary practices and the exercise of the will coalesce in an uncertain mixture. By the time of the Enlightenment—to abbreviate radically—disciplinary practices and the exercise of the will become separated more actively, partly because of uncertainty about the stability of the will itself. Beccaria, for example, first elevates the will above a level susceptible to human knowledge of it; he then becomes an advocate of disciplinary punishment for crime. Since the god who created the human will is the only one qualified to read its tangled text, the intentions and motives of offenders are to be judged by him alone:

> If he has established eternal punishments for anyone who disobeys His omnipotence, what insect will dare to supplement divine justice? What insect will wish to avenge the Being who is sufficient unto Himself. . . . Who alone among all beings acts without being acted upon? The one Who cannot receive impressions of pleasure and pain from objects . . . ? The seriousness of sin depends upon the unfathomable malice of the human heart, and finite beings cannot know this without revelation. How, then, can a standard for punishing crimes be drawn from this?[3]

Beccaria thus puts the will on ice. Human punishment for crimes of the will is translated into disciplines of the body designed to subdue the perpetrator and deter others from copying him. Capital punishment now becomes out of the question. It does not deter either those who kill out of momentary rage or those who do so out of a persistent disposition to revenge. And it hardens the hearts of those already disaffected from society by demonstrating to them how profoundly the law is founded on a "war" of the well-connected against the deeply aggrieved. Besides, the attempt to punish in proportion to the degree of evil in the will is futile.

Beccaria is not, however, a gentle soul like Jesus. He applies closely monitored punishments to the body and mind of the offender by apportioning punctual and sustained disciplines to the seriousness of the crime.

> The most powerful restraint against crime is not the terrible but fleeting spectacle of a villain's death, but the faint and prolonged example of a man, who deprived of his liberty has become a beast of burden, repaying the society he has offended with his labors. Each of us reflects, "I myself shall be reduced to such a condition of prolonged wretchedness if I commit similar misdeeds." This thought is effective because it occurs quite frequently, and it is

> more powerful than the idea of death, which men always see in the hazy distance.[4]

Beccaria's focus upon the effects of repetitive discipline on the mind takes him to the edge of concluding that the will itself is not a supersensible, master faculty, but a complex corporeal/cultural formation that always bears the specific imprint of the particular experiences from which it is crafted. His disciplinary conception of society points toward such an insight, while the confidence with which he apportions penalties to crimes in the interests of deterrence and reform expresses a scientific image of conduct verging on the fantastic. In general, those who place a timeless will at the center of freedom, responsibility, and punishment are inclined to assert an overweaning confidence in their ability to ascertain the right proportion between offense and penalty in the practice of retribution, and those who elevate social causality above attributions of willful responsibility express a corresponding confidence in the ability to devise disciplinary systems geared to the degree of protection, deterrence, and reform needed. Each party joins confidence in the precision of its own perspective to a dismissal of the other's ability to establish the proportionality it seeks. Each, therefore, is insightful about the other and blind about itself.

4. The will and capital punishment soon combine in a new way within the Enlightenment. To act morally, according to the moral purist Kant, is to *obey* "autonomously" a moral law each recognizes in itself. A crime thus *deserves* punishment because it is willed against the moral law anyone is able to recognize and to obey; the level of punishment must be proportioned to the degree the will's disobedience contradicts its own essence. Punishment is something the will brings upon itself by contradicting its own essence.

> Accordingly, whatever undeserved evil you inflict upon another within the people, that you inflict upon yourself. If you insult him, you insult yourself; if you steal from him, you steal from yourself; if you strike him, you strike yourself; if you kill him, you kill yourself . . . If he has committed murder he must *die*. Here there is no substitute that will satisfy justice. There is no *similarity* between life, however wretched it may be, and death, hence no likeness between the crime and the retribution unless death is judicially carried out upon the wrongdoer, although it must still be freed from any mistreatment that could make the humanity in the person suffering it into something abominable.[5]

A miracle has occurred. The will, previously uncertain, divided and opaque, has now become pure and rational. Now human punishment can be proportioned to the evil of the offense. Retribution becomes a moral obligation. And note how gentle and painless the image of capital punishment has become by comparison to the judgment of Beccaria. The offender is to be killed by the state only because he brings death upon himself; but this dead man with a beating heart is to be treated decently right up to the point of gentle termination because he also remains a *person*, a rational agent of free will. Punishment now becomes pure and purged of that drive to spectacular revenge the sovereign had only recently invested in it. Augustinian cruelty is surpassed while the will is redeemed. Bells chime and trumpets sound. Freedom, desert, and punishment now fuse together through the medium of the will.

But how does this pure will so often develop a "propensity" to will evil maxims, anyway? How could "radical evil" (consenting to sensual desires that go against the moral law) be such a *regular* effect of action emanating from "the will"? Could the eruption of violence sometimes be an aftereffect *within the will itself* of childhood terrors and abuses experienced before the will matured? Kant almost concedes such a possibility but recovers in time to reconcentrate all responsibility within the will. For to accept that dangerous thesis would be to admit worldly, sensuous elements into the very formation of the will. It would be to jeopardize again the purity, universality, and supersensibility Kant had worked so hard to install within the will. And retribution in the name of the will would now look too much like a form of cultural revenge. Kantian morality itself would begin to take on the appearance of immorality. And yet, for Kant the source within the will of the will's own perversion eventually becomes a profound and unanswerable question. We cannot answer it with confidence "within the limits of reason alone" even though our inability to do so threatens to recoil back upon the confidence we invest in our own conception of the will. Let us pray.

> Now if a propensity to this does lie in human nature, there is in man a natural propensity to evil; and since this very propensity must in the end be sought in a will which is free, and can therefore be imputed, it is morally evil. This evil is *radical* because it corrupts the ground of all maxims; it is, moreover, as natural propensity, *inextirpable* by human powers, since extirpation could occur only through good maxims, and cannot take place when the ultimate subjective ground of all maxims is postulated as corrupt; yet at the same time it must be possible to overcome it, since it is found in man, a being whose actions are free.[6]

Man is a free being, but it now becomes less certain just how this freedom is exercised and what impels it so often to compromise itself. Augustinian mystery and division return to haunt the will through the back door. For a "propensity" to evil must reside within the will itself or the will sacrifices its independent standing in a world where evil is so common. Moreover, the propensity to evil of the will is often not "extirpable" by will power alone. The source of this propensity is "inscrutable" to the agent, and "yet at the same time it must be possible to overcome it" in a being "whose actions are free." Thus speaks Kant, the pure defender of the pure will.

To escape this impasse Kant is moved to reinvoke—but this time around merely as a "hope"—a divine grace that might enter the will and help to drive its evil maxims away. Such help cannot be assumed or presupposed "within the limits of reason alone," and yet the integrity of the will depends upon the hope that such a supplement will be forthcoming. Grace is both necessary to the integrity of the Kantian conception of freedom and problematical within it. Even as mere hope it creates unwelcome paradoxes. Suppose grace were forthcoming for some and not for others. What becomes of the human capacity to judge what retribution requires after grace returns to secure and haunt Kantian morality from the inside?

The Kantian recourse to grace corrupts the autonomy of the person. And the Kantian will eventually stumble upon those paradoxes that introduced perplexity into the Augustinian conception. But Augustine, recall, offered a less definitive doctrine of human punishment than Kant advances. How do Kantians retain confidence in the morality of retribution, just measure, and capital punishment after they have (re)encountered difficulties internal to the will? Kant does not return to this issue. But, to put the point as bluntly as Kant presents the imperative to capital punishment, after these complexities are introduced you are pressed either to *forget* the complexities of the will to justify capital punishment or to relinquish a *Kantian* justification of capital punishment.

5. The attribution of free will is an uncertain projection often infused with a drive to revenge that its proponents seldom acknowledge. Neither the free will *nor* scientific determinism, according to Nietzsche, can stabilize itself in the domain of human action, crime, and punishment. Nor with respect to nature for that matter. Every preceding perspective now becomes confounded.

> Our usual imprecise mode of observation takes a group of phenomena as one and calls it a fact: between this fact and another fact it imagines in addition an empty space, it *isolates* every fact. In reality, however, all our doing and knowing is not a succession of facts and empty spaces but a continuous flux. Now, belief in freedom of the will is incompatible precisely with the idea of a continuous, homogeneous, undivided, indivisible flowing: it presupposes that *every individual act is isolate and divisible* . . . Through words and concepts we are still continually misled into imagining things being simpler than they are, separate from one another, indivisible, each existing in and for itself. A philosophical mythology lies concealed in *language* which breaks out again every moment, however careful one may be otherwise. Belief in freedom of the will—that is to say in *identical* facts and in *isolated* facts—has in language its constant evangelist and advocate.[7]

Kant and Beccaria are both unconscious evangelists of language, the first on behalf of purity of will and the second on behalf of the transparency of causal relations. The rest of us, including Nietzsche, are its evangelists as well, though we do have some capacity to tame those evangelical tendencies. Forgive us, for we know not what we do in the realm of punishment.

Nietzsche has a grudging respect for Jesus, who, he thinks, died on the cross too early to develop the implications of his own thinking. Nietzsche himself struggles to find ways to loosen the hold of these two dominant models of punishment. Such is the ethical task of the immoralist. He does eventually *recover* another, corporeal conception of the will. But this will is implicated in the messiness of the world itself rather than elevated above it. The Nietzschean will becomes a complex cultural/corporeal formation; the cultural elements that enter into its formation turn out to be too disparate, variable, and finely grained to be captured entirely either by the crude categories of explanation or the purity of a free will. Responsibility now becomes a social practice that is both indispensable and inherently problematical. An element of tragedy attaches to it. Punishment may be necessary to protect some from the violent dispositions of others, to deter potential criminals, and even occasionally to restore to the commmunity those who have committed crimes against it. But since the question of desert is fraught with uncertainty, since judgments about the will of others and oneself are haunted by undecidability, the territory of criminal responsibility is now recognized to be one in which "necessary injustice" contaminates the practice of justice. For a culture generally participates in engendering the violences it opposes. Nor can justice and punishment confidently be left to a god; for it is Nietzsche's subtraction of a god from his picture of the self and the world that encourages him to engage the labyrinth of the will and the cruelties attaching to the morality of retribution. Our hallowed conceptions of agency and explanation are themselves human, all too human. So says Nietzsche, while acknowledging the contestability of the assumptions through which *this* judgment is formed.

If you suspect a drive to revenge enters into the very conceptions of will, freedom, responsibility and punishment that define your own culture, you may be in a better position to fish more of that revenge out when called upon to judge in concrete cases. Generosity and forgiveness now become invested with new energy. To overcome resentment against the absence of fit between the clarity justice demands and the opacity of the actual cases before us is to fold *generosity* into assessments of the responsibility of others, *hesitation* into cultural explanations of violent conduct, and *forbearance* into the practice of punishment. As I read Nietzsche in writings subsequent to *Human All Too Human*, the practice of judgment cannot be eliminated. But it might be rendered a little less all too human by those who experimentally apply Beccarian-like tactics *to themselves* to subdue the ressentiment in which the most pure and hallowed conceptions of will, freedom, explanation, and punishment are set. With such "arts of the self" we step onto the stage of a post-Nietzschean ethic. It may be because the very Nietzsche who fights against purification of our fundamental moral categories is also so forbearing and subtle when it comes to punishment that so many carriers of cultural forgetfulness are eager to label *him* the consummate agent of nihilism.

Capital Punishment and Forgetting

With the advent of *Dead Man Walking*,[8] first a book and then a 1996 film of the same title, capital punishment returned as an intense topic of cultural debate. The recent upsurge of state executions excites horror in some, a sense of vindication in others, a strange recollection of uncertainty in many, and a differential mix of these feelings in most. But, for the most part, the labyrinthine history of the will, responsibility, and punishment we have reviewed is squeezed out of the discussion. Most parties treat these to be the pillars of "our Judeo-Christian tradition" rather than sites of uncertainty and persistent instability within it.

Dead Man Walking offers a cultural barometer of sorts in this domain. Do "we" have the right to kill those who murder? The book brings out superbly the awful suffering on death row, and it effectively dramatizes several considerations against state execution. Thus: (1) this ultimate act of finality might (and often does) condemn innocent men to death, and the mistake cannot be taken back if new evidence of innocence is found; (2) we never know for certain whether even a hardened criminal might not reform in the future; (3) if murder is wrong, so is killing by the state, which sends a message of revenge to hardened criminals and hardens the hearts of citizens; (4) many condemned killers have life histories filled with abuse, violence, deprivation, and neglect, and these "mitigating" factors cry out against the death penalty; (5) relatives of the deceased, who (often) press for execution to gain relief from the loss they have suffered, seldom actually experience that much relief after the execution. During a time when the feelings of the aggrieved play such a prominent role in the sentencing of murderers, this last experience is particularly pertinent.

Consider Vernon Harvey, who could not wait for his daughter's ruthless murderer to "fry." He is talking to Sister Prejean, the "sob sister" who opposes capital punishment and has nonetheless become a confidant of sorts a few years after the execution of "Willie":

> "Know what they should've done with Willie?" he says. "They should've strapped him in that chair, counted to ten, then at the count of nine taken him

> out of the chair and let him sit in his cell for a day or two and then strapped him in the chair again. It was too easy for him. He went too quick." He says he's been thinking of a much more effective way. . . . "What we do is fry the bastards on prime-time TV, that's what we oughta do. Show them dying in the electric chair, say, at eight at night, and see if that doesn't give second thoughts to anybody thinking of murder. . . . We really oughta do to them exactly what they did to their victim. Willie should've been stabbed seventeen times, that's what we oughta do to them."[9]

Harvey's rage has not diminished; "this chapter" has not been "closed" by Willie's execution as he had anticipated. So he fumbles for an act of revenge proportionate to the pain he suffers. And the language of "oughta" suggests that he seeks to enclose these feelings in a moral perspective. His rage and his morality become mixed together, understandably so.

Prejean summarizes her conversation with Harvey on another occasion while he is convalescing in a hospital: "He just can't get over Faith's death, he says. It happened six years ago but for him it's like yesterday, and I realize that now, with Robert (Willie) dead, he doesn't have an object for his rage. He's been deprived of that too."[10]

Harvey is not unique. The promise of relief through revenge generally exceeds the experience of it after the unrepeatable deed has been done. If only murderers could be executed several times, or, lacking that, if only the single act of execution were rendered more slowly, agonizingly and in public. Would crucifixion work? What about burning in oil? In the current political context, the public demand to vindicate grieving family members through punishment combines with the unstated impossibility of fully satisfying that desire to place opponents of the death penalty in a position of permanent defensiveness. Their very act of opposition seems to reveal that they do not care that much about mothers, children, lovers, and spouses devastated by the murder of their loved ones.

Sister Prejean poses these issues effectively, then. But a couple of counterdispositions also infiltrate quietly into the book and the film. First, the basic categories through which we judge murderers and assess penalties are themselves treated as stable and untouchable. The harsh childhood of a killer, for instance, is taken to "mitigate" the crime or to provide "extenuating" circumstances; these experiences are not treated as violences that enter into the very crystallization of the perpetrator's will. Such a reflection would throw our most cherished concepts of crime and punishment into uncertainty. It would insinuate culture, with its global divisions along the lines of class, race, and gender and its more finely grained variations in the life of each particular individual, into the very practices of action, judgment, and punishment. Many supporters of the death penalty would rather sacrifice the lives of killers than sacrifice the purity of the concepts through which they are judged and sentenced. And even opponents are hesitant to subject the categories to critical review.

Second, as the film reveals, the suspense intensifies pressure upon the condemned man, his loved ones and supporters, the family of the victim, and engaged spectators as the execution clock ticks away and pleas for reversal or delay are rejected. At the end, when the penalty is executed, a certain relief or release accompanies its finality, even among many who resist the death penalty. A decision has been executed as well as a human. A guttural element of authority attaches itself to the act through its very irreversibility. The uncertainty surrounding the right of the state to kill a killer—an uncertainty circulating within many of us, as well as between us—becomes muted. We can now turn to other things. At least those not intimately involved in that particular case can. And the suffering of those most closely connected to the executed man? Or those who have just witnessed the execution of one who killed someone they love? These both recede from the public eye. Two elements deposited in the authoritative background of capital punishment—cultural forgetting of the instability haunting categories of punishment and the strange sense of release attending the finality of execution—work upon one another, each adding a note of silence to the other.

Forgetfulness with respect to the unstable history of the will is lodged in the tangled relations between social science, court decisions, journalistic reporting, electoral campaigns, jury selection, and jury deliberations. These practices form a set of intertexts. Consider the domain of social science. In *Crime and Human Nature: The Definitive Study of the Causes of Crime*,[11] James Q. Wilson and Richard J. Herrnstein work hard to align the dominant cultural mood with respect to punishment with their empirical findings as social scientists. To accomplish this feat the social *explanation* of crime in the interests of deterrence and prevention must be rendered compatible with *retribution* in punishment—this because Wilson and Herrnstein, in accord with most members of the culture in which their research is set, explicitly support both. To accomplish this effect they adopt a compatibilist account of social causation and will formation.

> Scientific explanations of criminal behavior do, in fact, undermine a view of criminal responsibility based on freedom of action. And . . . this book has taken pains to show that much, if not all, criminal behavior can be traced to antecedent conditions. Yet we view legal punishment as essential, a virtual corollary of the theory of criminal behavior upon which the book is built. . . . An act deserves punishment, according to the principle of equity, if it was committed without certain explicit *excusing conditions*. . . . For the purposes of the law, behavior is considered "free" if not subject to those excusing conditions. One such condition is insanity, but there are others, such as duress,

> provocation, entrapment, mistake and accident. . . . By proving that excusing conditions are absent and then punishing, the criminal justice system sharply outlines for its citizens the choice between crime and non crime. . . . To the extent such excusing conditions can be demonstrated, punishment should be mitigated or totally suspended.[12]

That's it! The definitive 639-page study on crime and punishment condenses the most momentous and perplexing issue into one fuzzy paragraph. Though people's lives hang in the balance, no uncertainty is allowed to find explicit expression. These guys force Beccaria and Kant together while forgetting the troubles that haunt each theory on its own terms. Deterrence and retribution are both legitimate because, somehow, the people demand the compatibility of will and social causation. How is this sleight of hand accomplished? In a society riven by class and race divisions, "the will" is first moved from a position above culture to a place within it (the site of "free" acts). But then deadly dispositions within culture that deviate from an accepted standard of normal conduct are judged to be deserving of retribution by quietly treating them *as if* they were the product of the free will of the agent prior to acculturation. That relieves the culture of apparent implication in the acts it punishes. The authors can count on most readers sliding over this shift because they never truly endorsed the relocation of the will inside culture in the first place. The authors were the ones pressed to do that, in the interests of fostering a science of criminality.

But what has retribution now become? If the difference between "will" and "excuse" has now become the difference between motives that "society" places beyond appeal and those "it" allows to excuse, ameliorate, or attenuate responsibility, retribution now slides from an act of equitable compensation tied to an unstable doctrine of the will to an act of revenge tied to the level of outrage felt by normal people. Can Wilson and Herrnstein, for instance, reiterate Kant's claim that the killer has willed his own execution by murdering another? They cannot. They can only draw implicit sustenance from a broader cultural belief in a model of retribution their own theory calls into question. They get away with this ruse to the extent that the earlier model of the will and retribution was itself fueled by a drive to revenge. Execution no longer punishes murderers according to a standard they themselves are reputed to have willed (the Kantian ideal of retribution); it enacts the desire for revenge which, understandably enough, follows acts of murder.

The Supreme Court joins the cultural cascade of forgetting in the way it frontloads murder cases. The most consequential way it does so, perhaps, is its determination that only those who are "death qualified" can serve as jurors in murder cases where the death penalty is at issue. This injunction disqualifies at least 20% of potential jurors from the start. It also affects the way the prosecution and the defense proceed in making their cases before a death-qualified jury. For death-qualified juries are demographically distinctive. "They are more likely to be male, to be white, to be well off financially, to be Republican, and to be Protestant or Catholic"[13] than the general population. With such a jury in place a defense lawyer would be foolish to pose difficult questions about attributions of the will. No juror is apt to pick such a theme up during jury deliberation and most will be hostile to its articulation. A prosecutor, on the other hand, is encouraged to use problematic conceptions of responsibility and the will as a whip to beat down the defense during the sentencing hearing. In such constrained contexts—repeatedly set before the public as a trial by peers who embody "the conscience of the community"—cultural immunity against public excavation of self-doubts about the relation between will, action, responsibility, and retribution is assured from the start. The following interrogation by a prosecutor against a social worker who has presented mitigating considerations in a murder case is doubtless repeated in capital sentencing hearings daily.

> Q: Do you believe in the Christian principle of free moral agency? Do you believe that God gave us the capacity to choose right from wrong?
>
> A: Yes, that can happen if one has a nurturing environment that would support that capacity and allow it to be used.
>
> Q: Do you believe that Almighty God gave us the capacity to know right from wrong?
>
> A: Almighty God gave us the potential . . .
>
> Q: How do you explain why some people who come from bad homes do well in life?
>
> A: We all have different innate endowments and ability to tolerate frustration. One can't just look at people and know who will turn out good and who will turn out bad. . . .
>
> Q: Are you saying that people are not responsible for what they do?
>
> A: What William Brooks did was the product of interaction between himself and his environment. . . .
>
> Q: Can someone be just plain mean?
>
> A: No, not without reason. Children aren't born mean. Children are responsive to their environment.[14]

In such a predetermined context of legal argument, the prosecutor appears to be a clear thinker with coherent categories while the social worker emerges as a fuzzy idealist trying to force two opposing conceptions of the world into one story line. The first agent appears to embody the clarity of "our culture," while the second struggles to twist that clarity to save the life of a defendant. But in fact *our* culture is marked by fundamental instability in its basic categories of responsibility and punishment, and it is administered by legal/political practices that translate this instability into a vengeful model of responsibility. To say some people are "just plain mean" is to infantilize the judgment of criminal cases by purging the image of the will of the mysteries and ambiguities that haunt it. Dominant practices of social science, court decision, jury selection and deliberation, prosecutorial presentation, media reporting, and citizen predisposition coalesce to organize this politics of displacement. Capital punishment sacrifices the lives of killers to reassure a culture that would otherwise be perplexed and troubled by the constitutive uncertainty haunting some of its most cherished categories of self-interpretation.

The Death Penalty and the Forgetfulness of Death

Powerful cultural demands for categorical integrity foster political pressure for the death penalty, even when a politics of cultural forgetting is needed to meet those demands. That is the thesis so far. These demands set an authoritative set of intertexts in which legal practice, journalism, social science, and public opinion support one another. And they infiltrate into the judgment of opponents of the death penalty as well as the supporters. But how could this be? The categories, according to my story, have been unstable since their inception; and yet sentiment about the death penalty changes century by century and decade by decade. It seems to me that two major shifts in contemporary life combine with a couple of more specific changes to intensify support for the death penalty. The profound shifts include the *globalization* of so many aspects of life in a world organized politically around the presumption of sovereign nation-states and the radical acceleration of *tempo* in several domains of life. The specific changes revolve around the concentration of an African-American underclass in inner cities where the most visible acts of violence occur.

The globalization of economic life compromises the nation-state as the highest site of citizen sovereignty. According to the logic of democratic sovereignty *I* am free when I can choose among several life options in a variety of domains; *we* are free when the state formally accountable to us through elections can act to protect both its standing in the world and the institutional conditions of nationhood. But the globalization of economic life deflates the experience of a sovereign, democratic state by imposing a variety of visible effects upon it that the state is compelled to adjust to in one way or another. The state can most easily respond to many of these by shifting their most onerous burdens to its least powerful constituencies. The tendency to shift burdens to the most vulnerable constitutencies is accentuated by the widespread tendency to blame the state for the limits it faces while celebrating the market as a potential site of freedom. That combination, in turn, further depletes the sense of efficacy attributed to the one agency whose actions are accountable in principle to citizens. It deflates again our sense of collective freedom. A compensatory site of efficacy and accountability is thereby needed.

The capacity to execute is a visible and awesome public power, one able to divert attention from the state's limited efficacy in other domains. The "failure" of capital punishment, from the vantage point of deterrence, then, is trumped by its success in symbolizing the state as a potent agent of public revenge in a world of high anxiety. The perverse equation is that *we* feel free as a public under unfavorable conditions of citizen confidence and state efficacy when the primary unit of democratic accountability displays the power to wreak revenge against those who it targets as the most visible threats to personal freedom. These internal and external limits to state power then work in rough coordination with the refusal by suburban dwellers to address the conditions of life in the inner cities. The high visibility of black violence in the inner city adds another potent element to the mix, then, making capital punishment the one act that can represent the power of the state while retaining collective unwillingness to invest in extensive programs of job creation, education, and urban renewal in the cities. We now feel free as a people when the state captures, tries, and kills the internal enemies it helps to render most visible to us.

These pressures combine with the accentuation of tempo in population migration, cultural communication, military mobility, tourism, and entertainment. With the sharp acceleration of tempo in so many domains of life, more people more often encounter ideas and relationships that call into question cherished aspects of their own identities heretofore treated as fundamental, immovable, natural or sanctified. Christians encounter diverse theistic and nontheistic faiths; established ethnic groups encounter strange new ethnicities; heterosexuals encounter gays and lesbians who have come out of the closet; males encounter feminists who call into question traits of masculinity previously marked as natural; and so on. The acceleration of tempo renders it more difficult to confirm the natural or transcendental character of what you are; and the tactical advantage such confirmation traditionally carries with it in the domain of moral judgment now becomes jeopardized. What you *are* in the domains of gender, ethnicity, religion, sensuality, and so on no longer so easily becomes translated into a set of moral commands you and everyone else are obligated to *obey*. You are placed under pressure to desanctify elements of your own subjectivity even as they help to define who you are.

The unstable practice of individual responsibility becomes even more difficult to fix under these conditions; for now the persistent instabilities inside are activated by contact with alternative interpretations outside. This categorical insecurity presses a variety of constituencies to insist more fervently upon fundamentalizing traditional dictates of morality, responsibility, normality and punishment. For how can those constituencies on the margin of the economy and educational system receive recognition for their insecure achievements and self-restraint unless those who break the code are held entirely responsible for their failures?[15] This may be why it is common to find many in this culture who support the death penalty aggressively to insist with equal fervency about the naturalness of heterosexuality, the moral superiority of Christianity, the irresponsibility of welfare recipients, the vacuity of liberalism, and the nihilism of deconstruction.

Under such conditions the death penalty performs a set of intercoded functions. It first confirms through its rhetoric of retribution a conception of will and responsibility through which a variety of insecure constituencies ratify desert for the precarious social standing they have attained and the difficult self-restraint they exercise at work, in the home, and on the street. It then allows selective release from this difficult logic of self-restraint by allowing vicarious participation in the legal killing of murderers. Finally, it deflects attention from the state's failure to respond to other grievances of those same constituencies and to the larger contexts in which both their grievances and criminal violence are set. Execution becomes simultaneously a theatrical demonstration of state power (amidst a general sense of state inefficacy), a violent vindication of individual responsibility (amidst life in interdependent institutional complexes subjected to feeble coordination), a momentary release from the dictates of self restraint (in a world where its practice elsewhere is demanded), and an opportunity to express strains of fascination and secret identification with outcasts whose acts of violence might be taken to symbolize repudiation of this entire complex of power, responsibility, and restraint. The very aura of finality that accompanies state executions helps to silence questions about the categories of will and responsibility that vindicate the actions.

Capital punishment thus becomes a major front in cultural war. It mobilizes political divisions between one set of partisans who seek to return to a fictive world in which the responsible individual, retributive punishment, the market economy, the sovereign state, and the nation coalesced and another set who seek to respond in more generous ways to new experiences of the cultural contingency of identity, the pluralization of culture, the problematical character of traditional conceptions of agency and responsibility, and the role of the state in a new world order.

The propagators of cultural war augment the first set of dispositions by attacking carriers of the second set of questions. The politics of forgetting is crucial to their success. William Bennett, in *The Devaluing of America: The Fight for Our Culture and Our Children*, connects a variety of right-wing campaigns in education, media programming, and drug wars to a more general "fight for our culture and our children." And his celebration of a virulent form of capital punishment forms a key part of that campaign. Bennett himself summarizes a piece of his CNN interview on "Larry King Live" when a listener calls in to press him to up the ante against drug dealers: "Why build prisons?" the caller asks. "Get tough like [Saudi] Arabia. Behead the damned drug dealers. We're just too damned soft." Bennett:

> "One of the things that I think is a problem is that we are not doing enough that is morally proportional to the nature of the offense. I mean, what the caller suggests is morally plausible. Legally, it's difficult."
>
> I could see King's eyes light up. He asked for a clarification. "Behead?"
>
> "Yeah. Morally, I don't have anything wrong with it," I said.
>
> "You would behead. . . ." King began again.
>
> "Somebody selling drugs to a kid?" I said. "Morally, I don't have any problem with that at all. I mean, ask most Americans if they saw somebody out on the streets selling drugs to their kid what they would feel morally justified in doing—tear them limb from limb. . . . What we need to do is find some constitutional and legally permissible way to do what this caller suggests, not literally to behead, but to make the punishment fit the crime. And the crime is horrible." During the program I strongly rejected calls for drug legalization and endorsed capital punishment for major drug dealers.[16]

Bennett's rhetoric is potent. He unites in one act of identification forgetfulness of instability in a culture's own categories of will and punishment, the theatricality of the state power to kill, and the promise to make state punishment "morally proportional" to the act. The enunciations of "morally proportional," "morally plausible," and "feel morally justified" do much of the work. They invest intense feelings of outrage and vengeance in the blue chip stock of morality, covertly debasing the latter until it becomes a container into which selective energies of revenge can be poured. Moral proportionality retains the appearance of equivalence between responsibility and punishment, but that uneasy equation is now translated into proportionality between the intensity of public outrage and the amount of agony to be endured by the targets of public punishment. The Bennett synthesis of beheading and moral proportionality both drowns out liberal questions about the morality of capital punishment and recruits new soldiers to a cultural war in the name of morality.

Once the recruitment pitch is delivered, Bennett moderates the message just enough to paint a veneer of deniability between him and those who fret about the constitutionality or barbarism of beheading. The veneer must be thin because Bennett, as he himself indicates, *seeks to incite* liberal elites to outrage against his virulent proposals in order to make them the primary targets of cultural war. Bennett binds his image of morality to a harsh form of capital punishment to insist that what is truly moral is also hard, efficacious, and satisfying to its perpetrators. Morality is severe and simple; if your brand lacks either quality it falls into the class of subjectivism or relativism. Public objections by liberals miss the point unless we are able to challenge the line of associations between morality, simplicity, revenge, and death. Until we do, the agents of cultural war will succeed in using our opposition to associate us with moral softness toward murderers, drug dealers, welfare cheats, and pornographers.

Bennett *converts* the liberal ripostes he calls forth into energies of cultural war against liberalism. Thus: "Many of the elites ridiculed my opinion. But it resonated with the American people because they knew what drugs were doing, and they wanted a morally proportionate response."[17] Why must these "elites" be targets? Because so many hold "our Judeo-Christian tradition" in "contempt" and are "so riven with relativism that they doubt the preferability of civilization to savagery."[18] What is the "morally proportionate" response? One that meets every act of criminal violence with an awesome act of state violence. *That* proportionality preserves the state as an instrument of punitive power and covers its depletion as an instrument of social welfare and education.

Lurking inside the most fervent demands for execution by the state may be a floating resentment against the obdurate fact of mortality in search of an acceptable outlet. To blame God would be too disturbing. To blame the world would be pointless. So concentrate on those who "deserve to die." This gives the semblance of control over an element in the human condition unsusceptible to evasion in the last instance. The pronouncement of radical difference between you and them obscures, if only partially and temporarily, a more profound similarity of condition. Part of the profound cultural resentment against liberal and secular elites may involve resentment against those whose perspective on the death penalty challenges this unstated equation between death and penalty.

My interpretation, as with others of its type, has no certainty attached to it. It tries to read subterranean currents of anxiety and desire at work in those who affirm the death penalty with the greatest intensity, doing so in order to think about the registers of being that must be engaged by those who oppose capital punishment. The interpretation is limited in its application. It may fit some of the most urgent activists in favor of capital punishment well enough, while it misses others who support capital punishment less urgently, out of frustration with high rates of crime.

Capital punishment has become a weapon of cultural war on several levels: it coarsens broad sections of the population, preparing them to accept punitive campaigns against a variety of disturbing constituencies; it foments political divisions favorable to the Right by associating liberal "relativism" and "weakness" with the "savagery" of implacable killers; it fosters the politics of forgetting by translating "moral proportionality" from an uncertain attempt to match penalty to crime into a politically potent equation between the level of social resentment felt by disaffected constituencies and the level of violence taken by the state against convicted murderers; it displays the state as an awesome theater of force in one domain during a time when its effective accountability is otherwise shaky; and it organizes a set of cultural anxieties about the place of death in life.

Sister Prejean and Albert Camus have faith that if only more people saw what actually happens on death row and at executions they would reconsider their abstract commitments to capital punishment. Camus dramatizes how the death penalty, often represented publicly as a brief, surgical event, actually involves a long, arduous "premeditation" and "organization . . . which is in itself a source of moral sufferings more terrible than death"; how it engenders a "devastating, degrading fear that is imposed on the condemned for months or years"; how futile appeals for official reprieve create a "horror parceled out to the man who is condemned to death." So, by the time a captive of the state has reached the time of execution, "He is no longer a man but a thing waiting to be handled by the executioners. He is kept as if he were inert matter, but still has a consciousness which is his chief enemy"; and "he travels along in the intricate machinery that determines his very gesture and eventually hands him over to those who will lay him down on the killing machine."[19] Sister Prejean exhibits the essence of this state utopia of violence in a phrase: "I can hear the words San Quentin guards used to yell when a death-row inmate was let out of his cell: 'Dead man walkin'.' "[20]

In the light of evidence from Vernon Harvey and William Bennett, though, the situation appears to be more divided. It may well be that capital punishment—exalted by some as "noble" in public rhetoric and hidden behind closed doors in practice—both diverts the eyes of humanists from its degrading effects and feeds the passions of those who celebrate the state's role in inflicting degradation upon available targets. To satisfy *this* latter demand for "proportionality" between the drive to revenge and state action is what it takes to save "our" culture, according to some. The imagination of an absolute power delivering a defeated and silenced enemy to a vengeful public focuses upon the long-term suffering of "mad dog" killers who await their own execution. But it also includes somewhere in its compass a punitive fantasy about liberals, secularists, and deconstructionists. The immediate prey of state execution pay a heavy price for their second status as surrogates for a larger enemy that cannot be reached so easily. But then the stakes in the war for "our culture" are high. Liberal and deconstructive elites (these two warring factions within the democratic left are treated as the same by many on the right) might play into the game of supporters of capital punishment by focusing merely on its cruelties. They themselves are targets because they expose things too disturbing to hear by members of the execution brigade. Liberal elites function as imaginary targets of the capital punishment regime because their "moral nihilism" is already associated by cultural warriors with the savagery of murder.

Under these circumstances, familiar critiques of capital punishment, taken alone, are insufficient. They may even contribute something to the politics of resentment they strive to surmount. That, anyway, is the hypothesis entertained here. To the extent it is true, it remains pertinent to show the least intense devotees of capital punishment how the politics of cultural forgetting proceeds in this domain, how support for capital punishment grows out of that politics, how such a practice imposes immense degradations on its prey while they are on death row and during the moments of execution, and how it diverts the state from other projects needed to sustain the general conditions of democratic pluralism. But these engagements are insufficient, and even liable to backfire, unless they are linked to a broader, more difficult agenda. To engage capital punishment at its cultural source we require interpretations that expose cultural sources of the intense social resentment in circulation today, and we need to probe more carefully the politics by which it so readily becomes shifted onto a selective set of targets. It then becomes incumbent upon us, first, to teach each other how to translate *existential* dimensions of resentment (including resentment over the fact of mortality) into a reaffirmation of life itself. And, second, to join political movements that speak to those economic, educational, and social circumstances that encourage so many to resent their place in a democratic culture. When we address each of these dimensions in relation to the others we might begin to reduce the huge fund of cultural resentment invested in capital punishment.[21]

the subject of true feeling: pain, privacy, and politics

LAUREN BERLANT

"Liberty finds no refuge in a jurisprudence of doubt."

Planned Parenthood of Southeastern Pennsylvania v. Casey
112 S. Ct. 2791 (1992), at 2803

Pain

Ravaged wages and ravaged bodies saturate the global marketplace in which the United States seeks desperately to compete "competitively," as the euphemism goes, signifying a race that will be won by the nations whose labor conditions are most optimal for profit.[1] In the United States, the media of the political public sphere regularly register new scandals of the proliferating sweatshop networks "at home" and "abroad," which has to be a good thing, because it produces *feeling* and with it something at least akin to *consciousness* that can lead to *action*[2] Yet even as the image of the traumatized worker proliferates, even as evidence of exploitation is found under every rock or commodity, it competes with a normative/utopian image of the U.S. citizen who remains unmarked, framed, and protected by the private trajectory of his life project, which is sanctified at the juncture where the unconscious meets history: the American Dream.[3] In that story one's identity is not borne of suffering—mental, physical, or economic. In the American dreamscape, identity is private property, a zone where structural obstacles and cultural differences fade into an ether of prolonged, deferred, and individuating enjoyment that one has earned, and that the nation has helped one to earn. Meanwhile, exploitation only appears as a scandalous nugget in the sieve of memory when it can be condensed into an exotic thing of momentary fascination, a squalor of the bottom too horrible to be read in its own actual banality.

The exposed traumas of workers do not generally induce more than mourning on the part of the state and the public culture to whose feeling-based opinions the state is said to respond. Mourning is what happens when a grounding object appears irretrievably lost. It is an experience of irreducible boundedness; it takes place over a distance. But what if the object who induces this feeling of loss and helplessness is neither dead nor at any great distance from where you are?[4] Mourning can also be an act of aggression, of social death-making: it is common to see the complexity of someone's existence reduced and distorted through pedagogic exemplification. Even progressives do it, one might say, when "others" can be ghosted for a good cause.[5] The sorrow songs of scandal that sing of the exploitation that is always "elsewhere" (even a few blocks away) are in this sense aggressively songs of mourning. Play them backwards and the military march of capitalist triumphalism (*The Trans-Nationale*) can be heard. Its lyric, currently crooned by every organ of record in the United States, is about necessity. It exhorts citizens to understand that the "bottom line" of national life is neither democracy nor freedom but survival, which can only be achieved by a citizenry that eats its anger, makes no unreasonable claims on resources or control over value, and uses its most creative energy to cultivate intimate spheres while scrapping a life together flexibly in response to the market-world's caprice.[6]

In this particular moment of expanding class unconsciousness that looks like consciousness emerges a peculiar, though not unprecedented, hero: the exploited child. If a worker can be infantilized, pictured as young, as small, as feminine or feminized, as starving, as bleeding and diseased, and as a (virtual) slave, the righteous indignation around procuring his survival resounds everywhere. The child must not be sacrificed to states or to profiteering. His wounded image speaks a truth that subordinates narrative: he has not "freely" chosen his exploitation; the optimism and play that are the "right" of childhood have been stolen from him. Yet only voluntary steps are ever taken to try to control this visible sign of what is ordinary and systemic amidst the chaos of capitalism, in order to make its localized and exposed nightmares seem uninevitable. Privatize the atrocity, delete the visible sign, make it seem *foreign*. Return the child to the family; replace the children with adults who can look dignified while being paid virtually the same revolting wage. The problem that organizes so much feeling then regains liveable proportions, and the pressure of uncomfortable feeling dissipates, like so much gas.

The central concern of this essay is to address the place of painful feeling in the making of political worlds. In this I affiliate with Wendy Brown's concern about the overvaluation of the wound in the rhetoric of contemporary U.S. identity politics.[7] Brown argues that the identification of minority identity with a wound—a conventional story about the particular and particularizing injuries caused by domination—must lead to the wound becoming fetishized evidence of identity, which thereby awards monumentality and value to the very negativity that would also be overcome. As a result, minority struggle can get stuck in a groove of self-repetition and habituated resentment, while from the outside it would appear vulnerable to the charge of "victim politics." In my view, however, what Brown locates in minority discourse generally has a longer, more specific, and far more privileged genealogy than she suggests. In particular, I would like to connect it to something I call national sentimentality, a liberal rhetoric of promise historically entitled in the United States, which avows that a nation can best be built across fields of social difference through channels of affective identification and empathy.

A current of feeling that circulates in and shapes a political world, national sentimentality transects a longstanding incongruity between two models of U.S. citizenship. In one, the classic Constitutional model, each citizen's value is secured by an equation between abstractness and freedom: an individual cell of national identity provides juridically protected personhood for citizens regardless of anything specific about them. Here, national subjectivity tends to be imagined first as an identification with the law and then with the nation that protects and administers it. In the second model, which emerged from the labor, feminist, and abolitionist struggles of the nineteenth-century United States, a very different version of the nation is imagined as the index of collective life. In this version, the nation is said to be peopled by suffering citizens and noncitizens whose structural exclusion from the utopian-American dreamscape exposes the state's claim of virtuous universality to an acid wash of truth-telling that makes the dominant culture's disavowal futile, at least at certain moments of political pressure.

Feminism in particular participated in establishing the trumping power of suffering stories in the United States, since abolition and suffrage worked to establish the enslaved Other as someone with subjectivity, which indicated not someone who thinks or works, but someone who has endured violence intimately. Women's traditional identification with suffering on behalf of virtue in the family, and feminism's extension of that structure into the rights talk of national and international public spheres, both enabled the political consensus that situates narratives of trauma on the ethical high ground above interest politics and established the precedent for exaggerating the value of transformations that happen primarily within individual consciences. I do not mean to say that testimonial discourse derived from subordination is invariably a shallow or cynical contribution toward building political worlds. Sometimes it helps to produce genuine social and political transformation and sometimes not. In the liberal tradition of the United States, in any case, it is not simply a mode of particularizing and puncturing self-description by minorities, but a *rhetoric of universality* located not in abstract categories but in what was thought to be, simultaneously, particular and universal experience.

Indeed, it would not be exaggerating to say that sentimentality has long been the more popular rhetorical means by which pain is advanced, in the United States, as the true core of personhood and political collectivity. It operates when relatively privileged national subjects are exposed to the suffering of their intimate Others, so that to be virtuous requires feeling the pain of flawed or denied citizenship as their own pain. Theoretically, those with power will do whatever is necessary to eradicate the misery they now feel vicariously, returning the nation once more to its legitimately utopian odor. Identification with pain, a universal true feeling, would thereby lead to structural social change. In exchange, populations emancipated from the pain of failed democracy would then reauthorize universalist notions of citizenship in the national utopia, which involves believing in a redemptive notion of law as the guardian of public good. The object of the nation-state in this light is to eradicate systemic social pain, the absence of which becomes the definition of freedom.

Yet since these very sources of protection—the state, the law, patriotic ideology—have traditionally buttressed traditional social hierarchies, and since their historic job has been to protect universal subject/citizens from feeling vulnerable in their own cultural and corporeal specificity, the imagined capacity of these institutions to assimilate to the claims of subaltern counterpolitics suggests some weaknesses or misrecognitions in these tactics. For one thing, it may be that the aura of sudden piercing injury implied by the traumatic model of pain implicitly mischaracterizes what a person is as what a person becomes in the experience of concrete social negation, thus potentially oversimplifying the historical field; this model also falsely promises a sharp picture of structural violence's source and scope, in turn promoting a dubious optimism that the law and other conspicuous regimes of inequality can be made accountable (the way persons are) to remedy their own taxonomizing harms. It is also possible that counterhegemonic deployments of pain as the measure of structural injustice actually sustain the utopian image of a homogeneous national metaculture, which can look like a healed or healthy body in contrast to the divergently scarred and exhausted ones. Finally, it might be that the tactical use of trauma to describe the effects of social inequality so overidentifies the eradication of pain with the achievement of justice that it enables various confusions: for instance, the equation of pleasure with freedom, or the sense that changes in feeling, even on a mass scale, amount to substantial social change. Sentimental politics makes these confusions credible and these violences bearable, as its cultural power asserts the priority of interpersonal identification and empathy for the vitality and viability of collective life. This sanctified mentality also gives citizens an outlet, something satisfying to do in response to overwhelming structural violence. Meanwhile, by equating mass society with that thing called "national culture," the important transpersonal linkages and intimacies created by calls to empathy all too frequently serve as proleptic shields, as ethically uncontestable legitimating devices for sustaining the hegemonic field.[8]

What does it mean for the struggle to shape collective life when a politics of true feeling organizes so much analysis, discussion, fantasy, and policy? When feeling, the most subjective thing, the thing that makes persons public and marks their location, takes the temperature of power, mediates personhood, experience, and history, takes over the space of ethics and truth? When the shock of pain is said only to produce *clarity* when shock can as powerfully be said to produce panic, misrecognition, the shakiness of perception's ground? Finally, what happens to questions of managing alterity or difference or resources in collective life when feeling *bad* becomes evidence for a structural condition of injustice? What does it mean for the theory and practice of social transformation when feeling *good* becomes evidence of justice's triumph? As many historians and theorists of "rights talk" have shown, the beautiful and simple categories of legitimation in liberal society can bestow on the phenomenal form of proper personhood the status of normative value, which is expressed in feeling terms as "comfort"; meanwhile, political arguments that challenge the claim of painful feeling's analytic clarity are frequently characterized as causing further violence to already-damaged persons and the world of their desires.[9]

Our first example, the child laborer, a ghost of the nineteenth century, taps into a current vogue to read the nation's moral and economic decline in the premature exposure of children to capitalist publicity and adult depravity, citing it as a scandal of citizenship, something shocking and un-American. Elsewhere I have described the ways the infantile citizen has been exploited, in the United States, to become both the inspiring sign of the painless good life and the evacuating optimistic cipher of contemporary national identity.[10] During the 1980s a desperate search to protect the United States from what seemed to be an imminently powerful alliance of parties on the bottom of so many traditional hierarchies—the poor, people of color, women, gays and lesbians—provoked a counterinsurgent fantasy on behalf of "traditional American values." The nation imagined in this reactive rhetoric is dedicated not to the survival or emancipation of traumatized marginal subjects, but to freedom for the American innocent: the adult without sin, the vulnerable child, and above all, and most effectively, the fetus. Although it had first appeared as a technological miracle of photographic bio-power in the mid-1960s, in the post-Roe era the fetus became consolidated as a political commodity, a supernatural sign of national iconicity. What constituted this national iconicity was an image of an American, perhaps the last living American, not yet bruised by history: not yet caught up in the excitement of mass consumption, or ethnic, racial, or sexual mixing, not yet tainted by knowledge, by money, or by war. This fetus was an American to identify with, to aspire to make a world for: it organized a kind of beautiful citizenship politics of good intention and virtuous fantasy that could not be said to be dirty, or whose dirt was attributed to the sexually or politically immoral.

By citizenship I refer here both to the legal sense in which persons are juridically subject to the law's privileges and protections by virtue of national identity status, but also to the experiential, vernacular context in which people customarily understand their relation to state power and social membership. It is to bridge these two axes of political identity and identification that Dr. Bernard Nathanson, founder of the National Abortion Rights Action League (NARAL) and now a pro-life activist, makes political films starring the traumatically post-iconic fetal body. His aim is to solicit *aversive identifications* with the fetus, ones that strike deeply the empathetic imaginary of people's best selves while creating pressure for the erasure of empathy's scene. First, he shows graphic images of abortion, captioned by pornographic descriptions of the procedures by which the total body is visibly turned into hideous fragmented flesh. He then calls on the national conscience to delete what he has created, an "unmistakable trademark of the irrational violence that has pervaded the twentieth century."[11] The trademark to which he refers is abortion. He exhorts the public to abort the fetal trademark so as to save the fetus itself, and by extension the national identity form and its future history. In this sense the fetus's sacred national being is the opposite of any multicultural, sexual, or class-marked identity: the fetus is a blinding light that, triumphant as the modal citizen-form, would white out the marks of hierarchy, taxonomy, and violence that seem now so central to the public struggle over the material and cultural resources of contemporary national life.

I have elaborated these basic Freudian dicta about mourning, the theory of infantile citizenship, and this account of U.S. political culture to make a context for four claims: that this is an age of sentimental politics in which policy and law and public experiences of personhood in everyday life are conveyed through rhetorics of utopian/traumatized feeling; that national-popular struggle is now expressed in fetishes of utopian/traumatic affect that over-organize and over-organicize social antagonism; that utopian/traumatized subjectivity has replaced rational subjectivity as the essential index of value for personhood and thus for society; and that, while on all sides of the political spectrum political rhetoric generates a high degree of cynicism and boredom, those same sides manifest, simultaneously, a sanctifying respect for sentiment.[12] Thus, in the sentimental national contract, antagonistic class positions mirror each other in their mutual conviction about the *self-evidence* and *objectivity* of painful feeling, and about the nation's duty to eradicate it. In the conjuncture "utopian/traumatized" I mean to convey a logic of fantasy reparation involved in the therapeutic conversion of the scene of pain and its eradication to the scene of the political itself. Questions of social inequity and social value are now adjudicated in the register not of power, but of sincerity: concerns about whether public figures seem "caring" subordinate analyses of their visions of injustice; subalternized groups attempt to forge alliances on behalf of radical social transformation through testimonial rhetorics of true pain; people believe that they know what they feel when they feel it, can locate its origin, measure its effects.

This essay will raise uncomfortable questions about what the evidence of trauma is, and what it means to try to administer society as a space ideally void of struggle and ambivalence, a place made on the model of fetal simplicity. I am not trying to posit feeling as the bad opposite of something good called thinking: as we will see, in the cases to follow politicized feeling is a kind of thinking that too often assumes the obviousness of the thought it has, which stymies the production of the thought it might become. My larger aim is to return to the question of the centrality of "the subject" who so powerfully animates much feminist, antiracist, and queer work but whose recent critical life has tacitly imaged society as a space that should be void of struggle and ambivalence.

In particular our cases will derive from the field of sexuality, a zone of practice, fantasy, and ideology whose standing in the law constantly partakes of claims about the universality or transparency of feeling, a universality juridically known as "privacy." We begin by addressing the work of feeling in Supreme Court decisions around sexuality and privacy. But the tendency to assume the nonideological and unmediated status of feeling is shared by opponents to privacy as well, with consequences that must equally, though differently, give pause: the following section interrogates the anti-privacy revolution legal radicals have wrought via the redefinition of harm and traumatized personhood. The paradoxes revealed therein will not be easily solved by ignoring or condescending to the evidence of injustice provided by the publicized pain of subordinated populations: but the way they inhabit politics, publicness, personhood, and power is instructive for thinking what it would mean, and what kinds of changes it would bring, to induce a break with the sentimental contract of U.S. citizenship.

Privacy

It would not be too strong to say that where regulating sexuality is concerned, the law has a special sentimental relation to banality. But this is not to accuse the law of irrelevance or shallowness. In contrast to the primary sense of banality as a condition of reiterated ordinary conventionality, banality can also mark the experience of deeply felt emotion, as in the case of "I love you," "Did you come?" or "O' Say, Can You See?"[13] But for an occasion of banality to be both utopian and sublime, its ordinariness must be thrust into a zone of overwhelming disavowal. This act of optimistic forgetting is neither simple nor easy: it takes the legitimating force of institutions—for example, the nation form, or heterosexuality—to establish the virtue of forgetting banality's banality. Take a classic instance of this process: an entirely forgettable moment in *The Wizard of Oz* that precedes an unforgettable one. Auntie Em says to Dorothy, who has been interfering with the work on the farm (no child labor there: Dorothy carries *books*): "Find yourself a place where you won't get into any trouble." Dorothy, in a trance, seems to repeat the phrase, but misrepeats it, sighing, ". . . a place where there isn't any trouble," which leads her then to fantasize "Somewhere Over the Rainbow." Between the phrase's first and second incarnations the agency of the subject disappears, and is transferred to the place: the magic of will and intention has been made a property of property.

The unenumerated relation between *the* place where *you* won't get into trouble and *a* place where, definitionally, *there is no trouble* expresses the foggy fantasy of happiness pronounced in the Constitutional concept of privacy, whose emergence in sexuality law during the 1960s brought heterosexual intimacy explicitly into the antagonistic field of U.S. citizenship. Privacy is the Oz of America. Based on a notion of safe space, a hybrid space of home and law in which people will act legally and lovingly toward each other free from the determinations of history or the coercions of pain, the Constitutional theorization of sexual privacy is drawn from a lexicon of romantic sentiment, a longing for a space where there is no trouble, a place whose constitution in law would be so powerful that desire would meet moral discipline there, making real the dreamy rule. In this dream the zone of privacy is a paradigmatic national space too, where freedom and desire meet up in their full suprapolitical expression, a site of embodiment that also leaves unchallenged fundamental dicta about the universality or abstractness of the modal citizen.

Much has been written on the general status of privacy doctrine in Constitutional history, a "broad and ambiguous concept which can easily be shrunken in meaning but which can also, on the other hand, easily be interpreted as a constitutional ban against many things other than searches and seizures."[14] Sexual privacy was first conceived as a constitutionally mandated but unenumerated right of sexual citizenship in *Griswold v. Connecticut*. The case is about the use of birth control in marriage: a nineteenth-century Connecticut law made it illegal for married couples to use contraceptives for birth control (oral arguments suggest that the "rhythm method" was not unconstitutional in that state);[15] they were only allowed prophylaxis to prevent disease. To challenge this law, Esther Griswold, director of Planned Parenthood in Connecticut, and Lee Buxton, the chief physician there, were arrested, by arrangement with the District Attorney, for giving "information, instruction, and medical advice to *married persons* as to the means of preventing conception."[16]

The arguments made in *Griswold* stress the Due Process clause of the Fourteenth Amendment, because denying the sale of contraceptives "constitutes a deprivation of right against invasion of privacy."[17] This kind of privacy is allotted only to married couples: Justice Goldberg quotes approvingly a previous opinion of Justice Harlan (*Poe v. Ullman*) which states that "Adultery, homosexuality, and the like are sexual intimacy which the State forbids . . . but the intimacy of husband and wife is necessarily an essential and accepted feature of the institution of marriage, an institution which the State not only must allow, but which always and in every age it has fostered and protected."[18]

We can see in Harlan's phrasing and Goldberg's citation of it the sentimental complexities of making Constitutional law about sexual practice in modern America. The logic of equivalence between adultery and homosexuality in the previous passage locates these vastly different sexual acts/practices in an unprotected public space that allows and even compels *zoning* in the form of continual State discipline (e.g., *laws*); in contrast, marital privacy is drawn up here in a zone elsewhere to the law and takes its authority from tradition, which means that the law simultaneously protects it and turns away its active disciplinary gaze.[19]

The banality of intimacy's sentimental standing in and above the law is most beautifully and enduringly articulated in the majority opinion in *Griswold*, written by Justice William O. Douglas. Douglas argues that a combination of precedents derived from the First, Fourth, Fifth, Ninth, and Fourteenth Amendments support his designation of a heretofore unenumerated Constitutional right for married persons to inhabit a zone of privacy,[20] a zone free from police access or the "pure [State] power" for which Connecticut was arguing as the doctrinal foundation of its right to discipline immorality in its citizens.[21] The language Douglas uses both to make this space visible and to enunciate the law's relation to it shuttles between the application of *stare decisis* (the rule of common law that binds judicial authority to judicial precedent) and the traditional conventionalities of heteronormative Hallmark-style sentiment:

> Would we allow the police to search the sacred precincts of marital bedrooms for telltale signs of the use of contraceptives? The very idea is repulsive to the

> notions of privacy surrounding the marriage relationship. We deal with a right of privacy older than the Bill of Rights—older than our political parties, older than our school system. Marriage is a coming together for better or for worse, hopefully enduring, and intimate to the degree of being sacred. It is an association that promotes a way of life, not causes; a harmony in living, not political faiths; a bilateral loyalty, not commercial or social projects. Yet it is an association for as noble a purpose as any involved in our prior decisions.[22]

Douglas bases his view that sexuality in marriage must be constitutionally protected—being above the law, prior to it, and beyond its proper gaze—on a sense that "specific guarantees in the Bill of Rights have penumbras, formed by emanations from those guarantees that help give them life and substance."[23] A *penumbra* is generally a "partial shadow between regions of complete shadow and complete illumination," but I believe the sense in which Douglas uses this dreamy concept is more proper to its application in the science of astronomy: "the partly darkened ridge around a sunspot." In other words, privacy protections around even marital sexuality are the dark emanations from the sunspot of explicit Constitutional enumeration; and the zone of privacy where marital sexuality thrives is the shadowland of the "noble" institution of marriage, with its sacred obligational emanations of social stability and continuity, intimate noninstrumentality, and superiority to the dividedness that otherwise characterizes the social. To back him up, Justices Harlan's and Goldberg's opinions remind of the state and the Court's propriety in pedagogically bolstering the institutions of traditional American morality and values: after all, the theater of marital intimacy is "older than our political parties, older than our schools."

After sexual privacy is donated to the U.S. heterosexual couple in *Griswold* by way of the sentimental reason the Court adopts—through the spatialization of intimacy in a bell jar of frozen history—a judicial and political nightmare over the property of sexual privacy ensued, whose mad struggle between state privilege and private liberty is too long to enumerate here. We can conclude that the romantic banality that sanctions certain forms of intimacy as nationally privileged remains hardwired into the practice of sex privacy law in the United States. However, almost twenty years later *Planned Parenthood of Southeastern Pennsylvania v. Casey* recast the force of its machinery remarkably, replacing the monumentality of sexual privacy *Roe* established as a fundamental condition of women's liberty with the monumentality of *Roe* itself as evidence of the Court's very authority.

In their majority opinion, Justices O'Connor, Souter, and Kennedy recognize the sovereignty of the zone of privacy as a model for freedom or liberty, returning explicitly to the method of penumbral enumeration and *stare decisis* introduced in *Griswold.* But the real originality of *Planned Parenthood v. Casey* is in the extent to which it supplants *entirely* the utopia of heterosexual intimacy on which sexual privacy law was based in the first place, putting *women's pain* in heterosexual culture at the center of the story of privacy and legal protections. In this sense the legitimating force of deep juridical feelings about the sacred pleasures of marital intimacy are here inverted and displaced onto the woman, whose sexual and political trauma is now the index of the meaning and value of her privacy and her citizenship.

Briefly, *Eisenstadt v. Baird* extended *Griswold* to unmarried women through the equal protections clause, transforming sexual privacy from its initial scene—the two-as-one utopia of coupled intimacy—into a property of individual liberty. This muted the concretely spatial aspects of the "zone of privacy," dismantling the original homology between the marital/sexual bedroom and the citizen's sense of self-sovereignty. It placed the focus on the space of the woman's body, which includes her capacities, passions, and intentions. But the shift from reframing contraception to adjudicating abortion required the discovery of more emanations from Constitutional penumbra: in *Roe v. Wade* the right of privacy remains the *woman's* right, but here one that has internal limits at the juncture where State interest over potential "life" and social self-continuity overtakes the woman's interest in controlling her sexual and reproductive existence. Gone, from that decision, is *Griswold's* rhetoric of the Court's moral pedagogy or its chivalry toward sexually sacred precincts: indeed, Justice Blackmun writes that because of the "sensitive and emotional nature of the abortion controversy" he wants to adhere to "constitutional measurement, free of emotion and predilection."[24] (There is not a sexuality/privacy case where such a caveat against emotion is not passionately uttered.) *Roe* attempts to achieve its post-emotionality by deploying knowledge, plumbing the juridical and historical archive on abortion: its emphasis is not on expanding liberty by thinking the contexts of its practice but rather by massaging precedent and tradition.

Planned Parenthood v. Casey was widely seen as an opportunity for a new set of justices to overturn *Roe*. The Pennsylvania Abortion Control Act of 1982 (amended in 1988–89) did not abolish abortion in the state but intensified the discursive contexts in which it happened, seeking to create around abortion a state-sanctioned, morally pedagogical *zone of publicity*. Provisions included a twenty-four hour waiting period, notification of parents by minors and of husbands by wives, and intensified standards of "informed consent" (including a state-authored brochure condemning abortion). The majority opinion has two explicit aims: to affirm the fundamental holdings of *Roe* on behalf of the sovereignty of women's citizenship, the unity of national culture, and the status of the Court's authority; and to enumerate what it felt was underenumerated in *Roe*, the conditions of the state's sovereignty over the contexts of reproduction. In other words, as Justice

Scalia's dissent argues, the Court's majority opinion seeks to affirm Roe while also significantly dismantling it. Its technical mechanism for achieving this impossible feat is the substitution of an "undue burden" rule for a whole set of other protections *Roe* provides: especially by dismantling the trimester framework that determined the woman's sovereignty over reproduction in a pregnancy's first six months, and substituting for it a rule that favors the state's right to place restrictions on the woman's reproductive practice (restrictions that can then be weighed by courts that will determine whether a given law mounts unduly burdensome obstacles to the woman's exercise of her constitutional right to abortion).

Scalia claims that the majority pulls off this impossible feat (in its claim to refuse a "jurisprudence of doubt" while making equivocal legal judgements) by disguising its own muddy impulses in a sentimental and "empty" rhetoric of intimacy:

> . . . the best that the Court can do to explain how it is that the word "liberty" *must* be thought to include the right to destroy human fetuses is to rattle off a collection of adjectives that simply decorate a value judgement and conceal a political choice. The right to abort, we are told, inheres in "liberty" because it is among "a person's most basic decisions," *ante*, at 2806; it involves a "most intimate and personal choic[e]," *ante*, at 2807; it is "central to personal dignity and autonomy," *ibid.*; it "originate[s] within the zone of conscience and belief," *ibid.*; it is "too intimate and personal" for state interference, *ante*, at 2807; it reflects "intimate views" of a "deep, personal character," *ante*, at 2808; it involves "intimate relationships," and "notions of personal autonomy and bodily integrity," *ante*, at 2810. . . .[25]

Correctly, Scalia goes on to point out that these very same qualities meant nothing to the justices when they heard *Bowers v. Hardwick*, "because, like abortion, they are forms of conduct that have long been criminalized in American society. Those adjectives might be applied, for example, to homosexual sodomy, polygamy, adult incest, and suicide, all of which are equally 'intimate'. . . ."[26]

But Scalia's critique is trivial, in the sense that the majority opinion does not seek to rethink sexual privacy or intimacy in any serious way. The rhetoric of intimacy in the case partly extends from the justices' need to derive their decisions from precedent.[27] But the majority justices' most ingenious originality is located in their representation of the specificity, what they call the "uniqueness," of the material conditions of citizenship for women in the United States. Because the right to sexual privacy has been individuated by *Roe*, privacy no longer takes place in a concrete zone, but a "zone of conscience"—the place where, as Nietzsche tells us, the law is painfully and portably inscribed in subjects.[28] The justices refer to women's "anxieties," "physical constraints," and "sacrifices [that] have since the beginning of the human race been endured by woman with a pride that ennobles her": they contend that a woman's "suffering is too intimate and personal for the State to insist . . . upon its own vision of the woman's role."[29] Therefore abortion definitively grounds and sustains women's political legitimacy: their "ability to participate equally in the economic and social life of the Nation has been facilitated by their ability to control their reproductive lives."[30]

The justices here indicate that heterosexual femininity in the United States is an undue burden, however ennobling it might also be. The deutopianization of sexual privacy established in *Griswold* and the installation of female citizenship at the juncture of law and suffering is further reinforced by the one part of the Pennsylvania law that the majority finds unconstitutional: the clause that commands women to notify their husbands of their intention to abort. The segment in which this happens exposes women's suffering in the zone of privacy where, it turns out, men beat their wives. They cite evidence, supported by the American Medical Association, that men are raping their wives, terrorizing them (especially when pregnant), *forcing* them to inhabit a zone of privacy that keeps secret men's abuse of women. In short, the "gruesome and torturous" conditions of marital domesticity in battering households requires the Court *not to protect privacy* for the couple, but to keep the couple from becoming the unit of modal citizenship where privacy law is concerned.[31]

Catharine MacKinnon deems privacy law a tool of patriarchal supremacy: "Women in everyday life have no privacy in private. In private, women are objects of male subjectivity and male power. The private is that place where men can do whatever they want because women reside there. The consent that supposedly demarcates this private surrounds women and follows us everywhere we go. Men [in contrast], reside in public, where laws against harm exist. . . . As a legal doctrine, privacy has become the affirmative triumph of the state's abdication of women."[32]

MacKinnon's arguments in these essays—which purport to be about "women" and "men," but which to my ear are more profoundly about heterosexuality as a virtual institution and a way of life—derive from Court practice through the late 1980s, and do not consider the work jurists like O'Connor have done to deprivatize privacy. But it should be no surprise that the modal citizen imagined by even moderates these days is no longer a complex subject with rights, needs, reciprocal obligations to the state and society, conflicting self-interests, or prospects for happiness in realms beyond the juridical: the modal citizen now is a trauma-effect who requires protection and political reparation. The opinion of the Court in *Casey* answers the dissenters' argument—which asserts that so few women are battered in the United States that the husband notification principle stands within Constitutional norms—by arguing that "the analysis does not end with the one percent of women upon whom the statute operates: it begins there."[33] Here their jurisprudence is not so far from Mari Matsuda's, when she claims that "looking to the bottom" of social hierarchy and making reparative law from there is the only politically ethical thing to do.[34]

In the twenty years between *Roe* and *Planned Parenthood v. Casey*, the general scene of public citizenship in the United States has become suffused with a practice of making pain count politically. The law of sexual privacy has followed this change, registering with symptomatic incoherence a more general struggle to maintain the contradictory rights and privileges of women, heterosexuality, the family, the state, and patriarchalized sexual privilege. The sheer ineloquence of this jumble of categories should say something about the cramped space of analysis and praxis to which the rhetoric and jurisprudence of sexual privacy has brought us. A place where there *is* much trouble: a utopia of law.

Politics

Central to the legal emergence of the politics of trauma against the scene of liberal-patriotic disavowal has been a group of activists from within (mainly academic) legal studies who speak from feminist, gay and lesbian, anti-racist and anti-exploitation movements. They take their distinctively painful experiences of social hierarchy in the United States to require a radical expansion of the law to accommodate the contradictions between abstract justice and "subjectivity of perspective." This involves coming to terms with the transpersonal nature of subject formation and refuses traditional liberal notions that organize the social optimism of law around relatively unimpeded individuality, privacy, property, contract, and conventional "community" values.[35] Since liberal law has long recognized a particular and traditionally sanctioned form of universal personhood as that around which society, theory, forms of discipline, and class-aspirational pedagogies should be organized, anti-liberal activism has strategically had to ground law in the collectivizing experience of particular identities.

In this sense, critical legal praxis opposes national sentimentality, which pursues collective cohesion by circulating a universalist currency of distress within a field presumed to be populated by abstract individuals. At the same time, if subaltern pain is not considered *universal* (the privileged do not experience it, do not live expecting that at any moment their ordinarily loose selves might be forcibly arranged into a single humiliated atom of subpersonhood), subaltern pain is deemed in this context universally *intelligible*, constituting objective evidence of trauma reparable by the law and the law's more privileged subjects. In other words, the universal value is here no longer a property of political personhood, but a property of a rhetoric that claims to represent not the universal but the true self marred by an unfair barring of itself from the universal.

In this political model of identity the trauma stands as truth. Happiness cannot be relied on as a guide to aspirations for social change, for the feeling of it might well be false consciousness, boredom, or the hoarded pleasure of privilege. Pain, in contrast, is something quick and sharp that simultaneously specifies you and makes you generic: it is something that happens to you before you "know" it, and it is intensely individuating, for surviving its shock lets you know it is your general survival at stake. Yet if the pain is at the juncture of you and the stereotype that represents you, you know that you are hurt not because of your relation to history but because of *someone else's* relation to it, a type of someone whose privilege or comfort depends on the pain that diminishes you, locks you into (a collective, and therefore subuniversal) identity, covers you with shame, and sentences you to a hell of constant potential exposure to the banality of derision.

Pain thus organizes this specific experience of the world, separating you from others and connecting you with others similarly shocked (but not surprised) by the strategies of violence that constantly regenerate the bottom of the hierarchies of social value you inhabit. In this sense subaltern pain is a public form because its outcome is to make you readable, for others. This is, perhaps, why activists from identity politics generally assume pain as the only sign readable across hierarchies of social life: the subaltern is the surrogate form of cultural intelligibility generally, and negated identities are pain-effects. Know me, know my pain, you caused it: in this context paranoia would seem adaptive, and would make understandable a desire for law to be both the origin *and* end of my experience of injustice. It might even make a wish I have—to see even a political world organized by suffering as something more ambivalent—seem perhaps cold, or an effect of the leisure of privilege. Who has time, after all, to query violence between shock and the moment it becomes true meaning?

These dicta ground much current countertraditional legal argument. Take, for example, an original and impassioned work like Robin West's *Narrative, Authority, and Law*, which sees as its task the production of moral criticism and transformation of the law from the point of view of its and a society's victims.[36] West powerfully wields narratives throughout the book that reveal the law's fundamental immorality (and therefore its fundamentally immoralizing effect on the subjects who are educated to its standards) where women's lives are concerned, and her powerful feminist arguments for the need to deprivatize women's structurally induced pain testify to the radical changes in the law and other institutions of intimacy that would have to happen if women are to attain legitimacy as social subjects. But West assumes that women's pain is already available as knowledge. To her, it *is* meaning, and the material for radical pedagogy. To think otherwise is to be either misogynist or guilty of shallow and overacademic postmodernism. Empathy is an ethical rule. Not surprisingly, as it happens, one example of pain's pure force she uses to summarize her argument comes from a child: "We must be able to say, to quote my two-year-old, 'don't do that—you're hurting me,' and we must be able to hear that utterance as an ethical mandate to change course."[37]

Not all radical legal theorists so simplify pain as to make the emblem of true wisdom about injustice and its eradication something as sentimental and fictive (to adults) as a child's consciousness:[38] yet the desire for an unambiguous world in West's vision of justice's clarity is not all that idiosyncratic. Would the child build a just world from the knowledge she or he gleans from her hurt? What would the child need to know for that to happen? How could it learn to think beyond trauma, to make a context for it? It seems hard for this group of legal theorists to imagine the value of such questions, for a few reasons. One may be due to the centrality of "pain and suffering" to tort law, which endorses a construction of the true subject as a feeling subject whose suffering disables a person's ability to live at his or her full capacities, as she or he has been doing, and thus requires reparations from the agents who wielded the force. New enumerations in this area are burgeoning: for example, feminist anti-pornography and anti-racist hate speech litigation borrows much of their legitimation from its archive.[39] Their tactic here is to challenge local purveyors of structural violence in order to make racism and misogyny *less profitable*, even symbolically, and meanwhile to use the law to debanalize violence by making illegal that which has been ordinary practice, on the model, say, of sexual harassment law or, even more extremely, using the Constitutional model of "cruel and unusual punishment" to revoke legitimation from social relations of violence traditionally authorized by the state and the law.

Kendall Thomas has made this latter point, in an essay on privacy after *Bowers*.[40] He takes up Elaine Scarry's model of torture as a vehicle for the legitimating fiction of state power and claims that the cruel-and-unusual-punishment clause of the Eighth Amendment should be applied to state discrimination against gays and lesbians. The strength and clarity of his vision and the sense that his suggestion seems to make bring us to the second reason it seems hard for theorists who equate subjectivity in general with legal subjectivity to work beyond the rule of traumatic pain in imagining the conditions for progressive social change. The law's typical practice is to recognize kinds of subjects, acts, and identities: it is to taxonomize. What is the relation between the (seemingly inevitable) authoritarianism of juridical categorization, and the other, looser spaces of social life and personhood that are not organized in categories of power, cause, and effect the way the law does? Is the "cruel and unusual punishment" tactic meant to be merely a reversal *in extremis* that points to the sublime banality of state cruelty, or is it a policy aspiration seeking a specific reparation for the specific violation/creation of gay and lesbian identities? Would the homeopathy of law against its own toxins in this domain of state cruelty work outside the identity form, for the working poor who are currently being economically disenfranchised from the resources state capitalism manages? Thomas's model only works if the agent of violence is the state or the law; it works only if the domain of law is deemed interchangeable with the entire field of injury and reparation; and if the subject of law is fully described by the taxonomies law recognizes. This position would look awkward if it were rephrased: subjects are always citizens. But the fact is that the notion of reparation for identity-based subordination assumes that the law describes what a person is, and that social violence can be located the way physical injury can be traced.

Without making a ridiculous argument that the nation-state is a mirage or a fetish standing in for a shapeless array of forces, it should be possible to say that radical counterpolitics needs to contend with notions of personhood and power that do not attain the clarity of state and juridical taxonomy, even across fields of practice and stigma. The desire to find an origin for trauma, and to rework culture at the violating origin, effectively imagines subjects only within that zone, reducing the social and subjectivity to that zone (in this case the state and the laws that legislate non-normative sex) and covertly reauthorizing the hegemony of the national. It is not only that lawyers see law as a mirror of the real. The desire to use trauma as the model for the pain of subordination that gets refracted into identity suppresses the difference between trauma and adversity: trauma takes you out of your life shockingly, and places you into another one, whereas structural subordination is not a surprise to the subjects who experience it, and the pain of subordination *is* ordinary life.

But to say that the traumatized self is the true self is to say that a particular facet of subjective experience is where the truth of history lies: it is to suggest that the clarity of pain marks a political map for achieving the good life, if only we would read it. It is also to imply that in the good life there will be no pain. Wendy Brown suggests that a replacement of traumatic identity ("I am") with a subjectivity organized by the agency of imagined demand ("I want") will take from pain the energy for social transformation beyond the field of its sensual experience.[41] For this to happen, however, *psychic pain experienced by subordinated populations must be treated as ideology,* not as prelapsarian knowledge or a condensed comprehensive social theory. It is more like a capital letter at the beginning of an old bad sentence that needs rewriting. To think otherwise is to assert that pain is merely banal, a story always already told. It is to think that the moment of its gestation is, indeed, life itself.

Coda: The Political Is Also Impersonal

The world I have tried to telegraph here in this story about privacy's fall from the utopia of normal intimacy finds the law articulating its subjects as public and American through their position within a hegemonic regime of heterosexuality, which involves coordination with many other normative social positions that are racially and economically coded in support of traditional matrices of privilege. Too often, and almost always in the work of legal radicals, the nation form remains sanctified as a political "zone of privacy" in *Griswold*'s sense: it holds out a promise that the law can relieve specific individuals of the pain of their specificity, even as the very project of liberal nation-formation virtually requires the public exposure of those who do not structurally assimilate to the national norm (so, if population *x* is relieved of the obstacles to full juridical and cultural citizenship, a given population *y* will almost inevitably come to bear the burden of surrogacy that expresses citizenship's status as *privilege*). The implicit logic of the national-social contract is constantly broken, and yet the nation-state insists that the contract remain in force for its disappointed subjects, who are told to conceive it as a promise of a contract rather than as an obligation they can fight for in the present. Seeking justice under the law in the face of these normative strategies is crucial, a tactic of necessity. If it means telling half-truths (that an experience of painful identity shocks a minoritized subject) in order to change juridical norms about that kind of subject, it still must be a good thing. But thinking that the good life will be achieved when there is no more pain but only (your) happiness does nothing to alter the hegemonic structures of normativity and mourning whose saturation of the diminished expectations for liberty in national life I have sketched out in this essay. The reparation of pain does not bring into being a just life.

Usually this point is made in studies of testimony and the Holocaust, the unspeakable national violence which generates horrific evidence that will always fail to represent the brutal totality of its referent, and which can never be repaired, remunerated.[42] The situations (heterosexual couplehood, marriage, sex acts, and reproduction) addressed in this essay, in contrast, are ever so common, cruel but not unusual. Such a difference advises replacing the model of trauma I have been describing critically as inadequate material for world or nation-building with a model, say, of *suffering*, whose etymological articulation of pain and patience draws its subject less as an effect of an act of violence, and more as an effect of a general atmosphere of it, peppered by acts to be sure but not contained by the presumption trauma carries, that it is an effect of a single scene of violence or toxic taxonomy. Thus where certain ordinary identity forms are concerned, the question of suffering's *differend* might be drawn differently without resulting in the analytic diffusion of any population's subordination into a fuzzy equivalence with that of any other. (But even "suffering" can sound too dramatic for the subordinated personhood form I am reaching toward here: imagine a word that describes a constantly destabilized existence that monitors, with a roving third eye, every moment as a potentially bad event in which a stereotyped someone might become food for someone else's hunger for superiority, and connect that to a term that considers the subjective effects of structural inequalities that are deemed inevitable under national and transnational conditions. "Suffering" stands in for that compound word.)

The binary trauma/reparation would not satisfy the conditions of genuine hardship that women in the United States endure. "Their" issues are not as (dis)located in time as trauma is, because these issues are central to what normative feminine aspirations are: a world where women are responsible for sustaining conditions of intimacy and of sexual desire; where they are made radiant by having more symbolic than social value (derived from their expertise in realms of intimate feeling and sexuality); where their anger is considered evidence of their triviality or greed and lack of self-knowledge. Having no place for and therefore only an ambivalent commitment to their anger, it pulsates instead in the muffled tone of resignation or the passionate aversion of resentment as a matter of ordinary life. Their case reminds us that the heavily symbolized are always supposed to take whatever social value is accorded them and find a way of being within it; and to spin negative value into the gold of an always deferred future, meanwhile coping, if they can, in the everyday.

Sentimental culture takes its strength from this configuration of contradictions and, in this case, by framing normative femininity and reproduction, as the hardwired work of expressive femaleness gender praxis becomes established as a ground of solidarity. But because this labor is so mixed up with intimacy, and therefore with the grounds of feminine optimism, political responses threaten the very domain of pleasure that has come to represent fantasies of the good life: contemporary national/capitalism has made a bargain with "the personal," after all, which is that people can have dignity in its domains only insofar as they inhabit the world passively, living through negativity on behalf of the optimism held out by that Oz over the mountaintop, a (nation-) state of amelioration. The liberal-radical solution to such positioning has recently been to deploy an ethics of storytelling about trauma against the normative world of the law, to change the conditions of what counts as reliable evidence and argument, and thereby to make something concrete happen in response, something that pays for the past that is ongoing. In this view, legal discourse represents the real, is a rhetoric of realism: and melodrama is the realism of the oppressed. But the *particularity* of suffering, its historicity, suggests the limitation of this trend in witnessing, with all of its presumptions that pain is the only prelapsarian knowledge there is, more eloquent than and superior to the law, which cannot overcome its universalist norms.

It is in this sense that trauma transcodes heterosexuality in the genealogy of taken-for-granted "universal" norms that hinge the political with the fantasy of spaces beyond politics in the U.S. political imaginary. As Derrida has recently argued, the dialectic between situated expression that challenges universalist norms and the categorical universalism of law itself constitutes an incommensurateness already within the law that cannot be overcome by law.[43] This is why the reparative use of the law on behalf of subordinated identities is sentimental. The subject of sentiment is the "I" who suffers in a way that seems to surmount these differences.[44]

Political optimism requires a future, any future that might not be more drowning in the present. More than anything, this is the lure of the sentimental contract, the mechanism by which consent is secured to a variety of long term subordinations. But the cost of the contract is the muffling of an analytically powerful and political rage, an equivocation of demand and radical critique, and a concession to short-term coalition building of a politics of the long haul. To interfere with the contract leads to attempts to humiliate the left into silence by charges of "irrelevance" to policy and to "common sense" in an era of transnational capitalist triumphalism, class-bound racism, and sentimental misogyny. Meanwhile, the real is located in the seeming rationality of diminished expectations. This is why it is imperative to risk the sense of belonging that national sentimentality promises—not because the sympathy that anchors identification across the nation is false or harmful, but because so often it represents the imaginable limit of political responsibility in the face of pain's claims. The everyday of citizenship is a ground that must be fought for: but the struggle must be expanded to include technologies of the impersonal, remote experience, and destabilizing knowledge as a part of any "personal" story, aspects of living one may not encounter concretely but which shape one's conditions of possibility nonetheless.

This is what was meant by "the personal is the political," a sentence virtually impossible to understand at the present moment. It did not mean that there is only the personal, only a zone of intimate politics, and no such thing as the political. It meant to say that the feelings we acknowledge having are unreliable measures of justice and fairness, not the most reliable ones; and that new vocabularies of pleasure, recognition, *and* equity must be developed and debated. I would add to this that the everyday of struggle is a ground on which unpredicted change can be lived and mapped—but the new maps will not reveal a world without struggle, or a world that looks like the opposite of the painful one.

Who gave anyone expertise over the meaning of feelings of injustice? I was sympathetic to the cultural politics of pain until I felt the violence of sentimentality: presented as a horror at momentous mass trauma that unifies a fractured society, national sentimentality is too often a defensive response by people who identify with privilege yet fear they will be exposed as immoral by their tacit sanction of a particular structural violence that benefits them. I was a wholly sympathetic participant in practices of subaltern testimony and complaint, until I saw that the different stories of trauma wielded in the name of a population's political suffering not only tended to confirm the state and its law as the core sites of personhood, but also provided opportunities to further isolate dominated populations by inciting competitions over whose lives have been more excluded from the "happiness" that was Constitutionally promised by national life. Meanwhile the public recognition by the dominant culture of certain sites of publicized subaltern suffering is frequently (mis)taken as a big step toward the amelioration of that suffering. It is a baby step, if that. I have suggested in contrast that the pain and suffering of subordinated subjects in everyday life is an ordinary and ongoing thing that is underdescribed by the (traumatic) identity form and its circulation in the state and the law. If identity politics is a literacy program in the alphabet of that pain, its subjects must also assume that the signs of subordination they feel also tell a story that they do not feel yet, or know, about how to construct the narrative to come.

cultural politics: political theory and the foundations of democratic order

BARBARA CRUIKSHANK

Alexis de Tocqueville is famous for his argument that the solid foundation of Protestant political culture in America made it possible to have democratic politics, a politics that was unpredictable and full of contention yet did not fall into chaos. "What keeps a great number of citizens under the same government is much less a reasoned desire to remain united than the instinctive and, in a sense, involuntary accord which springs from like feelings and similar opinions."[1] In other words, a people who see the same things from different cultural perspectives cannot live in harmony under the same government. One of the things that made America exceptional according to Tocqueville was the absence of class conflict. He did predict that America would be divided by racial conflict, but in the 1830s, that conflict had not yet taken place to the extent that the political culture was destabilized. Presumably, then, American political culture united people across class, providing the foundation of democratic political order.

In Tocqueville's view, the grounding of American political culture in a shared religion and feeling provided for unity even in the context of political turmoil. Consider his account of the relation between American politics and culture:

> Thus, in the moral world everything is classified, coordinated, foreseen, and decided in advance. In the world of politics everything is in turmoil, contested, and uncertain. In the one case obedience is passive, though voluntary; in the other there is independence, contempt of experience, and jealousy of all authority. Far from harming each other, these two apparently opposed tendencies work in harmony and seem to lend mutual support.[2]

American morality and culture were fixed but in politics anything was possible. Today, one could argue that the relationship of American culture and politics is reversed. Government seems fixed, particularly elections, yet in culture anything is possible. For example, whereas the canon of political theory is concerned with "political culture," today we speak in reverse of "cultural politics." In the political world, everything is decided in advance, foreseen, and stable. Polls can accurately predict elections in advance; mass opinion determines election campaigns and even foreign policy. In the political world, obedience is passive, yet voluntary; low voter turnouts are routine and the highest political virtue belongs to the candidate who stands forthright in the middle of the road. In the cultural/moral world, however, everything is contested. From language to religion, education, to American history and identity, in each there is independence, contempt of experience, and jealousy of all authority.

While Americans at present are said to be generally uninterested in Washington politics or representative government, cultural politics touches everyone. In addition to the culture war, think of "identity politics," "family values," La Raza, Operation Rescue, English-only movements, "sex wars," V-chips, and the New York City mayor's highly contested attempt to "civilize" the city. In America today it is culture, not government, that is in turmoil and where all is uncertain. According to traditional political wisdom, such as Tocqueville's above, we should be experiencing a breakdown of political order. Yet the American culture war is, so far, largely a war of contending discourses. As murderous as discourse can be,[3] the provocation for this essay is the relative stability of the American state despite the rages of war over the terrain of culture. Governmental stability does not typically incite political theory, yet I will point out why the stability of American government in the midst of cultural warfare calls for revisiting some of the traditional problematics in political theory regarding the relationship of culture and politics.[4]

My purpose is to challenge the traditional political wisdom on "political culture" only insofar as culture is held to be both mutually constitutive and the limit of government. The point is not to debunk canonical political theory, but to illustrate the danger of repeating traditional political wisdom in the context of the American culture war. As a case in point, I will argue that the theory of American exceptionalism is a source of disorder rather than a source of political stability.

Neoconservative cultural warriors, I will argue, are cornered by traditional political wisdom. Without a thorough rethinking of the political itself and the role of political theory, I suggest that the war may yet amount to more than a discursive tirade. To defend the natural and the traditional, as we shall see, neoconservative discourse must continually circle back upon the repetition that such and so is best because it is natural and traditional. Backed into a tautological corner, the only way for neoconservatives to win the culture war is by violence. I fear the escalation of violence in the battle to reterritorialize the borders of nature, culture, and politics. By reading the canon (Tocqueville and Machiavelli, in particular) against neoconservative warriors such as Robert Bork, Newt Gingrich, Gertrude Himmelfarb, and

Samuel Huntington, I suggest that cultural politics and culture war require a reconceptualization of the political, made possible, in part, by neoconservative discourse. I also suggest the possibility that the traditional problematics of political theory could be settled by cultural politics rather than by reterritorialization.

Political Culture and Cultural Politics

My argument turns on three postulates of traditional political wisdom regarding the relationship of culture and politics. The first comes as a pairing: a common culture provides the *foundation* for stable (and in some cases, free) government; culture and politics are mutually dependent for the *maintenance* of political order. Second, culture is impervious to the law; culture is the limit of governmental and legislative reach. That is, a corrupt or divisive political culture cannot be restored or stabilized by governmental and legislative action. The third postulate concerns the exceptionalist wisdom that American democracy necessarily operates without a political theory; theory cannot help to restore or stabilize American political culture and government.

1. Political Culture

First, political theorists as diverse as Plato, Hobbes, Machiavelli, and Tocqueville held that a common political culture (language, religion, history) was the foundation of stable governments and that culture and political order existed in a mutually dependent relationship. To put it a bit too straightforwardly, the traditional wisdom is that a stable and homogeneous political culture provides the foundation, as well as for the maintenance, of stable government. In large part, culture provides for the regular reproduction of citizens who are unified, coherent, predictable, and obedient. Political culture reproduces a governable population, a job that government cannot do itself unless it is willing to impose a unified culture upon a people by force, as both Plato and Hobbes were willing to concede in *The Republic* and in *Leviathan.*

Machiavelli, for example, held that it was religion that gave the Roman republic its good laws and good fortune. He understood culture and government to be mutually dependent upon one another for sustaining the liberty of a republic: "For as good habits of the people require good laws to support them, so laws, to be observed, need good habits on the part of the people."[5] One cannot flourish without the other. Once the people and their culture in a republic became corrupt, Machiavelli warned, the hope that good government or new laws could redeem them was in vain. (It is according to the same reasoning, as we shall see, that contemporary neoconservatives fear the worst for America.)

It is tempting to read the present condition of culture war and cultural politics as a reversal of traditional political wisdom regarding the relationship of politics and culture: perhaps now it is the stability and homogeneity of the liberal state that makes it possible to have a culture war going on with no drift into general violence. What keeps the American people united under the same government is their general indifference to the government, not "like feeling" and "similar opinions." Indeed, that is the argument made by pluralists such as Robert Dahl. On that reading, the relationship of culture and politics is still mutually dependent, but now it is politics that provides a stable foundation for cultural turmoil.

Or, it is equally possible to read the present quite differently yet still remain consistent with the terms of conventional wisdom. A Tocquevillian observer might say, for example, that the "involuntary accord" that made it possible to remain united under one government has eroded in America. The inculcation of instinct, like feelings and similar opinions, is no longer compulsory. Because Americans no longer see the same things from the same cultural perspective, multicultural perspectives pose a threat to political order. On that reading, the relationship of culture and politics has not been reversed; rather, the "decline" and "corruption" of American culture into cultural politics is tearing the (necessary) foundation out from under democratic institutions. That is, in fact, the way that neoconservatives read the present and why they have declared a culture war, as we shall see.

Another possible reading of the present is neither a reversal of traditional wisdom nor a tale of corruption and decline, but as a new beginning. Those who declare that the "postmodern" age is upon us, for example, might reject the "grand narrative" of conventional political wisdom altogether, and give up on reading canonical political theory altogether as something relevant to the present. Also, fundamentalist and apocalyptic readings of the present as "the beginning of the end"—for example, Frances Fukuyama's declaration of the present as "the end of history"—are strangely consistent with prefixing "post-" onto modernism.[6] I do not mean to say that postmodernists and fundamentalists are alike, only that their readings of the present are given in relationship to the past, be it revivalist or rejectionist.

Finally, and now obviously, the present might be read as a time in which all these possible readings are contested, a time, that is, in which the borders and proper relationships between culture and politics are contested and confused. I explore this last reading of the present more below. For the moment, I leave aside the question of how to characterize the present, whether the traditional wisdom on the relationship between culture and politics is infallible, reversed, or irrelevant in terms of the present culture war. So far, I have concentrated on the conventional wisdom that culture and politics are mutually dependent, with one providing the necessary foundation for the other. I now turn to the ways they are held to be distinct.

2. Culture and the Law

A second bit of traditional political wisdom is that the law is powerless to change culture. While culture and politics are mutually dependent, culture operates as the limit of politics. For example, Machiavelli believed that once a people became corrupt, short of instituting a whole new constitution, it was impossible for the law to "check a general corruption." "Besides, the constitution and laws established in a republic at its very origin, when men were still pure, no longer suit when men have become corrupt and bad. . . . New laws do not suffice, for they are not in harmony with the constitution, that has remained intact."[7] So long as the old constitution survives, the law is powerless to redeem a corrupt people.[8]

Similarly, Tocqueville predicted in the 1830s that the American political culture of racism might stabilize only by one or another cultural adaptation: sexual/racial miscegenation or apartheid. The latter was more likely, he believed, but a race apart could spell nothing but violent conflict in the long run. Tocqueville held that in the ancient world, the difficult thing was to change the law. In a modern democracy, however, the legal emancipation of slaves was a relatively simple matter. But the culture of racism would not end along with legal prejudice. "When they have abolished slavery, the moderns still have to eradicate three much more intangible and tenacious prejudices: the prejudice of the master, the prejudice of the race, and the prejudice of the white."[9] Tocqueville's line of argument appears to be consistent with the fact that civil rights gains and the formal political equality of blacks in America ended neither racial segregation nor racial conflict. If the law cannot change culture, then culture operates as a defining limit of governmental power. Perhaps traditional wisdom rings true; while political culture and political order are mutually dependent, culture is impervious to the law.

The recent "Republican revolution" may well illustrate the wisdom of the traditional view. Neoconservative Newt Gingrich led the "Republican revolution" with an understanding of revolution in the antiquated sense (that of Machiavelli) of a turning back or revolving rather than as an abrupt break and a new beginning.[10] His goal was to "renew American civilization" by returning to the principles of the Founding Fathers. While drafting the "new" Contract with America, however, Gingrich ignored Machiavelli's warning that the law is powerless to redeem a corrupt people. The American people are, according to Gingrich, thoroughly corrupt. The people are characterized in the Republican Party's Contract with America as dependent on drugs and welfare, yet fearful and powerless in the face of the violence taking over their streets; people who disrespect the law and escape justice by hiring fancy lawyers, people who sue each other in court rather than handle their own problems, people who are quick to divorce an unhappy marriage rather than honor their vows, or avoid the obligations of marriage altogether, irresponsibly begetting illegitimate children. How can a people so thoroughly corrupt be brought back from the abyss?[11]

With his characteristic apocalyptic twist, Gingrich writes, "I'm a history teacher by background and I would assert and defend on any campus in this country that it is impossible to maintain civilization with twelve-year-olds having babies. . . . What is at issue is literally not Republican or Democrat or liberal or conservative, but the question of whether or not our civilization will survive."[12] The self-reproduction of American civilization ground to a halt, according to Gingrich, because the countercultural movements of the sixties successfully overthrew the American value system of hard work. Great Society social welfare programs produced "dependence" instead of an independent and responsible citizenry. How is it now possible to turn back the decline of American civilization?

The Contract sets out to renew the faith of the American people in their government by reviving "traditional American values" of family, hard work, and personal responsibility through legislation. It says "[to] the counterculture: Nice try, you failed, you're wrong." And it proclaims the importance of "simply, calmly, methodically reassert[ing] American civilization." For Gingrich, this reestablishment of American values "starts with the work ethic."[13] The question of whether the work ethic or "traditional American values" are winning rally cries now that capitalism is global is not important here.[14] What matters is that the failure of the "Republican revolution" appears to serve as a perfect illustration of the traditional wisdom that culture is impervious to the law. Republican legislation failed on both counts to "renew American civilization" and to restore "the deeper underlying cultural meanings of being American."

Despite the very real consequences of the 1994 "Republican revolution" in Congress (the Defense of Marriage Act, the further erosion of civil liberties, the "devolution" of welfare provision, and a yet more draconian and privatized criminal justice system, to mention but a few), there is yet no revolution of any kind, no fundamental transformation of American government and no restoration of "traditional American values."[15] Remaining bound to a liberal Constitution that does not suit their illiberal and "revolutionary" aims, Republicans failed even to convince the majority that America is going to hell in a handbasket.

Rhetorically, Gingrich actually mobilized the same political strategy used to forge the Great Society programs he blames for the current crisis. Gingrich, echoing community action rhetoric, proposes a "government that works *with* the poor rather than *for* and against the poor." The dismantling of the welfare state, Gingrich writes, "should be done in cooperation with the poor. The people who have the most to gain from eliminating the culture of poverty are people currently trapped in a nightmare."[16] The five principles laid out in the Contract are familiar liberal principles: individual liberty, economic opportunity, limited government, personal responsibility, security at home and abroad. The Republican Contract is a traditionally liberal technique for uniting the American people with their government. It was bound to fail, according to traditional political wisdom, because American political culture and the people are no longer, so to speak, traditional. Gingrich says this himself, that the countercultural movements and governmental reforms of the 1960s undermined the "traditional American values" of family, hard work, Jim Crow, and political quietude. The people, in other words, no longer conform to the liberal political culture of individualism and so liberal remedies will be unable, as Machiavelli said, to "check a general corruption."

More in tune than Gingrich with traditional political wisdom, most neoconservatives are ready for a modern revolution that would overthrow rather than attempt to mobilize liberal institutions to save American civilization. Neoconservatives fear the worst: it is too late to reform the liberal government because American culture is no longer capable of reproducing a uniform, quiescent, and governable population.

This fear has driven neoconservatives to declare a culture war. In response to the successes of the counterculture and social movements, neoconservative Samuel Huntington argued in 1975 that there are "potentially desirable limits to the indefinite extension of political democracy. Democracy will have a longer life if it has a more balanced existence."[17] Without limits on where it is appropriate to apply the standards of democratic accountability, the population becomes ungovernable. Huntington declared a "crisis of governability" in the face of the politicization of the family, military, universities, and race relations. The political activism of women, blacks, and students was dangerous not because those groups overran the political realm, but because they took politics out of the governmental realm into previously settled cultural terrain. Huntington argued that the "arenas where democratic procedures are appropriate are, in short, limited."[18] Indeed, the countercultural challenge to traditional cultural authorities threatened to bring democracy to the street, into the family, university, military, and the shop floor. "Too much democracy," Huntington argued, was not a good thing. Only a reterritorialization of culture and politics, a return to a bounded democratic system conducted by political elites, would safeguard democracy against the crisis of cultural authority.

More recently, neoconservatives meet "the crisis of democracy" with talk of violence and authoritarian rule. There is little faith among neoconservatives that the cultural "crisis" has a political or legal solution. Under the tutelage of the American Enterprise Institute, a neoconservative think tank, Robert Bork summarized the failings of the "Republican revolution":

> But it is well to remember the limits of politics. The political nation is not the same as the cultural nation. . . . However many political victories conservatives may produce, they cannot attack modern liberalism [egalitarian and countercultural] in its fortresses. . . . Conservative political victories will always be tenuous and fragile unless conservatives recapture the culture.[19]

The culture war is a war of last resort to mobilize, in Gertrude Himmelfarb's phrase, a "counter-counter-revolution." For example, Himmelfarb (a more formidable historian than Gingrich) believes that the sexual revolution was truly revolutionary: "What is striking about the 1960s 'sexual revolution,' as it has properly been called, is how revolutionary it was, in sensibility as well as reality."[20] Moreover, the sexual revolution is symptomatic of the more general "de-moralization" of America. A "de-moralized" culture is one in which culture replaces the social and economic causes of crime: "Today in inner cities there is a correlation between unemployment and crime, but it is not a causal one. Or if it is causal, it is not unemployment that causes crime so much as a culture that denigrates or discourages employment, making crime seem more normal, natural, and desirable than employment."[21] If culture is a causal factor, then culture itself, not the law, must be the terrain of a counter-offensive.

To restore the moral foundation of liberal and democratic institutions, many neoconservatives hold that strong governmental action is required to enforce personal responsibility, marriage, legitimacy and sexual abstinence, prohibit abortion, and to condemn homosexuality, child pornography, and dead-beat dads. Himmelfarb argues that it is not enough to remove the obstacles of governmental intrusion to free the individual to act on his or her own moral sense of personal responsibility. The individual is already corrupt, so to enlarge their freedom is to enlarge the scope of corruption. The liberal state relied upon cultural conditions of reproduction that no longer exist. Contra Gingrich, less governmental intervention will not remedy the fact that the social and moral conditions for the exercise of individual responsibility and freedom can no longer be assumed.

Himmelfarb cites two kinds of revolution in the 1960s. "The first was a social revolution [Great Society programs] intended to liberate the poor from the political, economic, and racial oppression that kept them in bondage. The second was a cultural revolution liberating them . . . from the moral restraints of bourgeois values."[22] If there was a moment for turning back the social revolution by scaling down the size of government and allowing the market to discipline the poor, as Gingrich proposed, according to Himmelfarb, that moment is now past. The impact of the cultural revolution was to undermine the culture and values upon which democratic government rested. Those values will not be restored by a new liberal contract, but only, Himmelfarb suggests, if strict moral (bourgeois) judgment guides policy making. A corrupt people cannot be expected to know what is best for them. Himmelfarb proposes a return to the (in her reading) stern and strict morality of the Victorians who were willing and able to impose their own bourgeois morality upon the demoralized.

Quite unlike the Victorians, however, Himmelfarb believes that it is necessary to resort to using state power to inculcate Victorian values. In other words, neoconservatives find themselves in the awkward position of calling for a strong state and authoritarian measures in order to reproduce a citizenry capable of existing under a liberal and limited state. "Those who want to resist the [counterculture] cannot merely opt out of it. . . . They may be obliged, however, reluctantly, to invoke the power of the law and the state, if only to protect those private institutions and associations that are the best repositories of traditional values."[23] Rather than try to elicit the consent of a corrupt people to liberal and voluntary forms of government, Himmelfarb is ready to impose a moral order on an unwilling people by means of an authoritarian state. (Below, I explain why neoconservatives are pushed into going to war by the logic of their own discourse rather than the strength of the counterculture.)

James Kurth upped the ante with a call to arms published in the neoconservative journal, *The National Interest*.[24] Kurth does not hearken back to the constitutional founding, but to the "second founding" or the "Golden Age" of the American nation-state (1890s–1960s). The Golden Age came with "the arrival of wide-spread, multi-class literacy in a common language, especially in a common literature" that united Americans.[25] The decline of the Golden Age began in the 1960s with the celebration of multiculturalism, the rise of the mass media, the post-conscription army, and, most importantly, the ruling elite's coming to consciousness of themselves as "the Establishment." Once, the "American political class was confident and cohesive enough to impose not only literacy but Americanization by means of mass education," military conscription, and wage production.[26] To recharge contemporary elites who are unwilling to do what is necessary, Kurth attempts to rally their willingness to use force to impose a common culture upon the American people. Kurth calls for a civil war to restore America's once-dominant position on the world stage. "The central actors of history have been great Leviathans who have been rich, civilized, brutal, and big."[27] Kurth places no confidence in liberal institutions to stem the decline. His faith rests on a powerful ruling elite, physical strength, violence, money, and cultural unity.

Is America headed for a civil war if the culture war escalates? If it is to be, is it merely ironic that the instigators of radical measures are those who hold tight to tradition? Next, I will argue that it is not ironic but inevitable that neoconservative discourse, by mobilizing the tenets of traditional political wisdom, corners its own advocates. Boxed in by their own logic, the only way out is to fight. Cultural warriors are prepared to impose an "involuntary accord" and cultural unity upon the people, if necessary by force. That is, perhaps, unless a third and final postulate of traditional political wisdom is reconsidered.

3. American Exceptionalism

The third postulate of traditional political wisdom is that America is an exception to the rules of European political thought.[28] Taking their lead from Tocqueville, exceptionalists believe that American history and political development proceeded according to a general consensus and continuity rather than ongoing class and racial conflict. Although I cannot give a full account of exceptionalism here, suffice it to say that even the American Civil War was, in the words of one exceptionalist, an occasion "to reinforce our sense of the continuity of our history."[29]

Here, I want to concentrate on the American exceptionalist conviction that political theory is un-American. For example, Daniel Boorstin, a former Librarian of Congress and historian, wrote in 1953 that ideology, propaganda, and political theory are foreign to America. Boorstin is a "consensus historian"; he holds that American history is guided by the consensus of the American people. Consensus history was opposed to "conflict history" and "social history," the view that American history is not built upon a consensus, but upon the repression of class conflict, slavery, the colonization of American Indians, and the subjugation of women. Boorstin, we would say today, is on the side of monoculturalism as opposed to multiculturalism. He believed, like Tocqueville, that America was truly exceptional among western democracies because it was not guided by a theory of government or divided by ideological and class differences.

Boorstin wrote with the goal of curing the "cultural hypochondria" of Cold Warriors and McCarthyism. To quell the fear that something was amiss in America, that there were Communists in our midst or that socialism presented a genuine alternative to liberal capitalism, Boorstin argued that American values were implicit in the landscape, history, and values of Americans. "Some Americans, however—and they are probably increasing in number—make the un-American demand for a philosophy of democracy. They believe that this philosophy will be a weapon against Russia and a prop for our own institutions. They are afraid that, without some such salable commodity, they may not be able to compete with Russia in the world market."[30] Disappointed and embarrassed by the fact that they had no theoretical defense of capitalism and democracy in their arsenal, Cold Warriors called upon intellectuals to lay down a philosophy of democracy. To defend those values, however, to make them explicit, to provide a theory of American values was, Boorstin believed, downright un-American and a threat to the stability of democratic institutions. Nevertheless, the ultimate failure of intellectuals to draft such a theory, Boorstin insisted, was itself an expression of "the genius of American politics." The incapacity for articulating "American values" clearly in defense of democracy, said Boorstin, was evidence that those values were "given," expressions of the natural landscape of America.

In a chapter titled "How Belief in the Existence of an American Theory Has Made a Theory Superfluous," Boorstin argues that it is enough for Americans to believe that they have a theory, despite the fact that they do not. That is "because we already somehow possess a satisfactory equivalent, I propose the name 'givenness.' 'Givenness' is the belief that values in America are in some way or other automatically defined: given by certain facts of geography or history peculiar to us."[31] Boorstin's origin myth, as he understands it, is no myth: Americans agree on their values not because they discuss them and are able to articulate those values, but because their agreement is implicit in the fact that those values are shared.

The Cold Warriors were actually putting American values at risk by making them explicit, Boorstin warned. To extract a theory from the given is, he feared, to call the given into question. "When people already agree, the effort to define what they agree on is more likely to produce conflict than accord. Precise definitions are more often the end than the beginning of agreement."[32] A political theory of American democracy would be dangerous to the American consensus. Better to supply a fact than a theory, the principle of "givenness," that in itself implicitly presupposes agreement.

Nevertheless, although he claims there is no and should be no theory of American democracy, Boorstin cannot defend what is "given," or even articulate that it is given without recourse to theory, or, at the very least, an interpretive "principle." Why is a principle any less dangerous than a theory? With "givenness," Boorstin proposes a principle that needs no theoretical justification, no argument. It just is. As his own argument goes, the lack of an explicit theory of American democracy is due to the fact that American institutions grew up without one. There is a circularity to Boorstin's argument, to be sure, making it seem, at least to him, unnecessary to draft a theory. Echoing Tocqueville, Boorstin writes that "what has held us together as a nation has been no explicit political theory held in common but rather *a fact of life* (what Whitman properly called 'adhesiveness')."[33]

Is Boorstin, like an uneasy parent, avoiding the revelation of some unspeakable or awful truth? Is "givenness" an ironic political myth, an expression of the inexpressible? American exceptionalism is "a fact of life"? Like death and taxes? Could this Librarian of Congress and keeper of the faith be cynically espousing a noble lie like Plato's philosopher-kings? I don't know. I will suggest, however, that whereas Boorstin called for leaving well enough alone and hoped to suppress the urge to theorize, he did something far more dangerous than theorizing. Boorstin hoped to defer theory and political conflict, but in so doing he illustrated the fact that American exceptionalism works to exclude political contestation of the "given." "We Americans are reared with a feeling for the unity of our history and an unprecedented belief in the normality of our kind of life to our place on earth."[34] The "American consensus," then, is somehow compulsory, perhaps akin to the "involuntary accord" that Tocqueville described. It is not normal, according to Boorstin, for an American to see things otherwise, to theorize, challenge, or to resist living "our kind of life." "Givenness," as it turns out, is a principle of rule and "normality" its regulative method, the point at which a governable population is reproduced.

Boorstin hoped to reassert the discourse of the given in order to make it, again, a given. But his own discourse leaves him chasing his tail, insisting that our kind of life is normal because we believe that how we live is normal. American exceptionalism, in effect, begs the question. To reconstitute the "fact" that American culture is based upon a consensus, even when in the 1950s new facts were flying in the face of it, Boorstin let slip that the "facts" and the "given" were, all along, constituted as such. The "facts of life" in America were undergoing an intense challenge within from socialists and the civil rights movement, and from without from the alternative of socialism.

Boorstin was not entirely unaware of the risks he was taking. As the quote above indicates, he was aware that calling for agreement on the principle of "givenness" might produce disagreement. However, he believed the greater risk was that a theory would be drafted and the "American consensus" would end in the rise of an empty nationalism and ideological conflict. He failed to anticipate (or perhaps he inadvertently helped to instigate) that countercultural movements of the 1950s and 1960s would call the constraints of the given and the normal—heterosexuality and marriage, work,

American supremacy, patriotism, racial segregation, and the gendered division of labor—into question. When the counterculture held these cultural "givens" up to a standard of democratic accountability, the American landscape was fundamentally altered. While seeking to foreclose the possibility that American democracy could be theorized, Boorstin made that foreclosure over into the foundational premise of American democracy and political thought. But he risked making the very cultural foundation of the "given" vulnerable by making it explicit.

To theorize American democracy, he believed, is automatically to undermine it.[35] It is theory, not culture, which operates here as the limit of American government. It is true that theory can change our world and our vision of it, and so it is dangerous. But political theory only calls that which can be changed into question. If something cannot be changed by human action, then it is a thing of nature or an act of God, and not political. Boorstin brought something formerly fixed and unalterable, that which is "given," "normal," and "natural" into the domain of politics and contestation. In short, he inadvertently politicized that which he held to be a "given": the idea that American history is founded upon consensus.

Boorstin hoped to avoid conflict by avoiding theory; but he did something much more dangerous than theorize. He brought the very constitution of cultural "givens" into question, making them appear changeable and so making them political. Even "the facts of life," even what is "given" by nature and by God, might be otherwise.[36]

Boorstin made it explicit that what held America together was the discourse of exceptionalism. As Samuel Delany put it, discourse tells us, out of all that we see, what is important and what is not. Discourse, writes Delany, is "material, educational, habitual."[37] Discourse is the manner by which the facts of life are established and maintained, how we do things as a matter of course or habit, because it feels right or normal. In other words, discourse comprises what Boorstin calls "givenness."

Delany offers an ordinary example: girls pee sitting down, he explains, not because they are incapable of peeing standing up but because that is what girls do. Girls are taught to sit and boys are taught to stand. Indeed, that is one of the ways children learn the difference between a boy and a girl. Of course, girls can pee standing up (and with remarkable accuracy, he adds), the same way boys do, by manually pointing their genitals in the direction of the toilet. But men's restrooms are often equipped with urinals and toilets; women's rooms are not. Discourse is made material in the architecture of gender difference. Discourse is material also in the sense that girls might not only find it hard to believe that they can pee standing up, but they may not want to pee "like a boy." Discourse does not make it impossible for a girl or a woman to pee standing up, as Delany observes, but it does make it likely that she will voluntarily not do so. (Recall here Tocqueville's phrase, "involuntary accord.")

Discourse is not the same thing as ideology or political theory, although they are all related concepts. The discourse of American exceptionalism is more than an ideology or a myth. "Ideology" is most often used to explain that how one sees is determined by the worldview of another. "Ideology" gets into your head. Discourse does, too; it is learned, but discourse does not *determine* the possible. Discourse *both* enables and constrains what it is possible to do, think, say, be, or feel. That is how Tocqueville could make sense of American culture with an oxymoron, "involuntary accord." Discourse makes it a normal "fact of life" that girls sit and boys stand to pee. Girls can and do, of course, pee standing up, and boys do pee sitting down. But witnessing such anomalies does not usually make us pause and wonder about the social construction of gender. The limits of the possible are routinely transgressed without erupting into conflict. Yet those limits are always matters of power relationships.

Discourse, like power, is everywhere. But that is not to say that politics is everywhere, only that we should not be surprised to find either power or politics in the toilet. Relations of power are not essentially contested; they are contingently contested.[38] Many relations of power solidify in the discourses of our material lives, our habits and our traditions. Here, I cannot give a complete explanation of the conditions under which discourse, or the given, gets politicized. What I can say is that the discourse of American exceptionalism presumes that "givenness" is uncontestable. To avoid theorizing American democracy, Boorstin hoped to reconstitute its status as a discourse, the kind of material and conventional constraint on the possible that he calls the "given." As I have shown, what he actually did was draw attention to the ways that what is "given" is in fact constituted by power. This is not to say that Boorstin caused the decline of the "American consensus" or generated a reaction in the form of multiculturalism. Rather, my account of Boorstin is meant to explain how the discourse of American exceptionalism has itself become dangerous and destabilizing in the context of the culture war.

Discourse, unlike theory, is not something that more readily survives by its defense. If discourse, or the "natural," "traditional," and the "given" cannot be reconstituted by their defense, then they must be imposed by force. For neoconservatives, imposing a unified culture on Americans by authoritarian means is necessary because, according to traditional wisdom, for democracy to survive, it must rest upon a foundation of cultural certainty. Traditional political wisdom and the three postulates that continue to instruct neoconservative culture warriors are dangerously misleading in this transformed American landscape. In fact, there are two possible outcomes of the culture war. One is the escalation of violence due to the fact that neoconservative discourse cannot reconstitute culture back into the stable foundation for democracy. So long as neoconservatives cling to traditional wisdom regarding the relationship of culture and politics, I see no way out for them but violence. On the other hand, cultural politics itself might offer a solution to the traditional problematics of culture and politics.

Cultural Politics

Like Boorstin, neoconservatives are trapped by traditional political wisdom. For example, when neoconservatives call attention to and defend "traditional family values," they actually make discourses of "the family" plural; neoconservatives transgress the limits of the possible precisely by trying to galvanize those limits. In the neoconservative understanding, cultural politics, or the contestation of cultural givens, can only represent a sign of decline and an anathema to political order. The rhetoric of returning to "traditional" American values, however, appeals to the naturalness of those values at the price of undermining their givenness. Again, one reason that the culture war may become more violent or lead to an actual revolution is that neoconservatives cannot win a battle of discourses.

On my reading, however, neoconservative discourse actually aids in opening up the possibility that the culture itself might be democratically ordered, that we might democratically decide what kind of families are best and what sort of values should be instilled in children. To make what is given explicit is to create a new possibility: cultural politics.

Culture war is not cultural politics by other means. Whereas cultural politics are aimed at transforming the discursive conditions of possibility, the culture war is mobilized to re-territorialize the confused and contested borders between culture and politics. Culture warriors take the "givenness" of culture to be an absolutely necessary foundation for democratic politics. Cultural politics, on the other hand, is a practice that takes the contingency and alterability of the borders between the cultural and the political to be a measure of democracy.

The culture war could as easily go the way of a violent re-territorialization as it could go the way of cultural politics. However, the latter course will be adopted only if traditional political wisdom undergoes a thorough rethinking. The three postulates of traditional political theory, that culture and politics are mutually dependent and mutually constitutive, that culture is the limit of governmental or legal intervention, and that America is founded upon a consensus, are all dangerous in the present context because they foreclose the possibility that cultural conflicts might be settled by cultural politics rather than by war.

Concerning the first postulate, while I suggested at the beginning of this essay that cultural politics might signal a reversal of traditional wisdom, that is not the case. Rather, cultural politics contests the discursive constitution of the boundaries between culture and politics. Cultural politics is about altering the boundaries that order American democracy. We might say today, for example, that the personal is political, we have sexual politics, health politics, family politics, racial politics, and so on. The iterability of these new forms of politics, I believe, signals a transformation of the political and the cultural altogether, not a simple reordering of two exclusive but mutually dependent domains.

The second postulate, that culture is the limit of the law is also eclipsed in the present. By holding onto traditional wisdom, neoconservatives can see the attempts to change culture through legal means—affirmative action, civil rights—only as sources of corruption. But the law no longer operates over and above culture. Cultural politics recognizes that the law is, like any discourse, potentially constitutive of the given. And that means, of course, that it will be contingently contested, and rightly so. The territory of the law cannot be analytically separated from culture without shutting down the possibility that the law might be made democratically accountable.[39]

The third postulate of traditional political wisdom, that American democracy is exceptional in that it is governed by a consensus that is essential to its stability, implies that democracy cannot withstand cultural politics. In effect, I argued above that Boorstin and neoconservatives laid the constraints of "givenness" and "normality" at the door of the counterculture. However, if cultural politics is to be supressed at all costs, those costs will be very high indeed and will include missing the opportunity to settle cultural conflicts by political means.

A revolution that would overthrow American democracy and impose an authoritarian state is certainly possible. So far, the culture war hasn't come to that. My question remains, why hasn't the culture war spilled over into the domain of government? How it is possible that the liberal state remains relatively stable at a time when the extent to which discourses and culture have been politicized may be unprecedented? On the one hand, there may be no "crisis of governability" because Americans, in general, remain under one government without being united.[40] Or, it is also possible that the practices, rhetorics, and changes in American government are so routine, so utterly irrelevant to politics, that they operate as givens. If the liberal state is a given, however, we cannot depend on the fact that it will remain so.

Political Theory

I have tried to show the ways in which the traditional political wisdom regarding the relationship of culture and politics makes it impossible to see that cultural politics is a novel political form that contests the boundaries between culture and politics, between the given and the governmental, the facts of life and the political. Social movements and countercultural politics, in particular, have confused the boundaries between culture and politics. Cultural politics cannot be mapped out by analytically distinguishing between what goes on in the House of Congress and in the domain of culture, precisely because cultural politics reconfigure the relationship of public to private, the personal and the political, the cultural and the governmental. Rather than solidifying new boundaries, cultural politics recasts the boundaries themselves as terrains of contestation.[41]

Settlement of the analytical confusion produced by cultural politics is unlikely to come from political theory unless, contra Boorstin, it is reconstituted along with politics itself. Political theory will be relevant to the resolution of the culture war only insofar as it transgresses the limits of the possible ways to theorize.[42] The traditional focus in political theory on the foundations and maintenance of sovereign political orders is a discursive trap. The stability of American democracy can no longer be understood to rest on cultural foundations that theory should not and cannot touch without destroying. Our analytical confusion will be settled in the same way as the culture war, by either cultural politics or from a reterritorialization of academic disciplines.

The solution to the culture war I hope for is not the reconstitution of the given or the reterritorialization of culture and politics, but a voluntary accord that the facts of life in America will be democratically derived.

academic politics and social change

GEORGE LIPSITZ

> It's a tremendous responsibility—responsibility and honor—to be a writer, an artist, a cultural worker . . . whatever you call this vocation. One's got to see what the factory worker sees, what the prisoner sees, what the welfare children see, what the scholar sees, got to see what the ruling-class mythmakers see as well, in order to tell the truth and not get trapped.
>
> TONI CADE BAMBARA from *Black Women in America: An Historical Encyclopedia*

Many contemporary intellectuals and artists feel a sense of responsibility to relate "cultural work" to struggles for social change, to communicate ideas through arguments and art and serve as a bridge between different communities and experiences. Notwithstanding Toni Cade Bambara's screed on this noble "vocation," it may be more difficult today to understand how the obligation she cites is an honor rather than simply a burden. Intellectuals and artists today often live disconnected from active social movements in a way that would have been difficult to predict two decades ago. They work within hierarchical institutions and confront reward structures that privilege individual distinction over collective social change.

It may not seem like much of an honor for contemporary intellectuals and artists to have to think one way and live another, to believe in a more egalitarian and open society while working within increasingly elitist and closed institutions, to conceive of intellectual work as social and collective while feeling cut off from collectivity and immersed in sustained surveillance and individual evaluation, to believe deeply in the need to build a different kind of society while feeling compelled to struggle for resources and power within the one that actually exists. Living with contradictions is difficult, and, especially for intellectuals and artists employed in academic institutions, the inability to speak honestly and openly about contradictory consciousness can lead to destructive desires for "pure" political positions, to militant posturing and internecine battles with one another that ultimately have more to do with individual subjectivities and self-images than with disciplined collective struggle for resources and power.

The painful contradictions confronting socially conscious artists and intellectuals in our society are most often experienced individually, but they stem from the systematic and structural imperatives that give cultural workers contradictory social roles. By their very nature, creative and critical endeavors allow and encourage identification with others. Intellectuals often work in solitude, but rarely in isolation. Empathy emerges within artistic and intellectual work as a crucial way of knowing, as a tool for understanding things outside our own experience. In times of tumult and change, artists and intellectuals can often experience their connections to others as both an honor and a responsibility. On the other hand, the routine conditions of training, employment, and evaluation in jobs that rely on "mind work" encourage a competitive individualism rooted in the imperative to distinguish oneself from others and to surpass others in accomplishment and status. Artists and intellectuals who have never experienced directly the power of social movements in transforming social relations can easily become isolated in their own consciousness and activity, unable to distinguish between their own abstract desires for social change and actual social movements. Taking a position is not the same as waging a war of position; changing your mind is not the same as changing society.

Artistic and intellectual work in our society takes place in a contradictory context and it produces people with a contradictory consciousness. Many intellectual and cultural workers appear to have the privileges of professionals, receiving yearly salaries rather than hourly wages and controlling many decisions about the nature, purpose, and pace of their jobs. Yet these workers lack the prerogatives of professionals in many ways; they do not control the supply of new labor, their reliance on institutions limits their mobility, and many of them are part of large units of employees whose compensation and working conditions are collectively set with only small variances for individual achievement. Intellectuals and artists are sometimes allowed and even encouraged to take positions in opposition to prevailing power relations, but they are also pressured to segregate themselves from aggrieved communities and to work within the confines and ideological controls of institutions controlled by the wealthy and powerful.

This contradictory social position often leads to a contradictory consciousness. As John Dos Passos argued during the 1930s, professional "mind" workers often have interests and ideas that place them in opposition to the people who pay their salaries and on the side of aggrieved groups in the broader community. Yet Dos Passos noted that these workers can easily become defined by their jobs, and consequently fail to take advantage of "the technical education that makes them valuable to the community," because in the course of their training "they have taken in a subconscious political education that makes them servants of the owners."[1] This "subconscious education" does not usually take the form of simple acquiescence to ruling ideology, but manifests itself in reluctance to work cooperatively and collectively with others, in a cynicism about the ability of ordinary people to change their own conditions, in a stoical fatalism resigned to the powerlessness and isolation of intellectuals as an immutable condition, and in a working definition of politics as symbolic and self-referential gestures rather than coordinated and collective mass struggle.

What passes for politics on college campuses can be especially frustrating and futile. Academics need to take the written and spoken word seriously as a basic condition of their labor. Yet excessive preoccupation with political expression and analysis, with finding the right word for the right situation and the correct context for one's own thought can lead academics away from the kinds of thinking and action needed for social change. On the other hand, in a desire to escape this contradiction, many swing to the other extreme, to a glib anti-intellectualism that privileges any action over critical thinking, that ignores the very important structural role that educators can play through their teaching and writing by expressing, validating, disseminating, and legitimating oppositional ideas with direct relevance for oppositional political action.

Proclamations and position papers can be found in abundant supply on campuses, but the actual practice of politics often remains limited to the written and spoken word, to the expression of opinions, ideas, and attitudes. Under these conditions, it is easy for moral posturing to take the place of social analysis, for conclusions to count because they conform to people's desired self-images of themselves as "radical" or "political" rather than because of their actual utility in bringing about transformative social changes. Minor disagreements over tactics and strategy easily escalate into mutual recriminations and condemnations. Even when the content of academic discussions concerns life and death issues, their form still seems to flow from more prosaic considerations about who gets the last word and who gets to be the center of attention. Repeated failures and frustrations rarely lead to reassessments of the nature of academic politics, because each instance can be blamed on the moral or intellectual imperfections of individuals (preferably from the opposing camp) rather than on the structural context in which the actions of individuals occur. Moreover, people not participating in political struggles of their own become ill-attuned to the struggles of others, writing books and articles that concentrate on personal alienation as the problem of politics instead of examining the prospects for collective and coordinated movements for change. A discourse of personal injury and alienation that could be the starting point for transformative collective action all too often becomes an end in itself in academic life.

Students involved in campus politics experience similar contradictions, but in different ways. As Danny HoSang, organizer of People United for a Better Oakland, points out, at the student level, "political" organizing emphasizes educational events that replicate many of the practices of the classroom, confidence-building confessions and dialogues that replicate therapeutic practices, and cultural events aimed at building unity and pride that replicate the practices of commercialized leisure.[2] Only rarely does student activism take the form of efforts to exercise collective control over institutions that affect student lives or to connect students to aggrieved groups off campus engaged in direct action struggles. Student politics on campus entails endless preparation for struggles that never happen because they so rarely move from talk to action. Sonia Pena, an activist with Denver Action for a Better Community, argues, "The goal of direct action organizing is not only to teach people that something needs to be done, but to show them that something can be done and that they can do it."[3] Students sometimes seem to feel that once they have changed *themselves* they have changed society, but for all the emphasis on student leadership training and development on campus, it is hard to see what these students will be able to lead if they have no practical experiences with collective strategic struggles for resources and power.

Yet for all of its pitfalls, academic politics still matters. Professors and students, like all artists and intellectuals, can play crucial roles in collective social struggles. Schools are important social institutions; their policies and procedures help influence broader social debates about what is forbidden and what is permitted, who is included and who is excluded, who speaks and who is silenced. Scholarly analysis of social conditions and social movements helps frame the political context in which activists work. It communicates activist concerns to new audiences, and brings to social movements greatly needed evidence, analysis, and arguments.

Many teachers, researchers, writers, and artists presently devote a great deal of attention to political questions, but too little effort to asking exactly how intellectuals fit into society or what roles they might play within struggles for social change. One reason for this imbalance stems from a point made by Toni Cade Bambara: "Of course it is difficult to maintain the faith and keep working toward the new time if you've had no *experience* of it, not *seen* ordinary people actually transform selves and societies."[4] It is difficult to believe in something you have never seen. For nearly three decades the decisive social movements in our society have come from the right, from mobilizations organized, funded, and guided by the wealthiest and most powerful people in our society. A series of "think tanks" and public relations operations masquerading as social movements have dramatically transformed the terms of political and cultural work in the United States, often by attacking and eclipsing the "expertise" previously vested in public educational and cultural institutions.[5]

The right wing has been successful in building organizations and institutions that give full time employment to intellectuals who devote all of their time to serving as "experts in legitimation" for the wealthy corporations and individuals who pay their salaries.[6] The John M. Olin Foundation, Heritage Foundation, American Enterprise Institute, and the Scaife Foundation provide a form of corporate welfare for intellectuals willing to turn out arguments that conform to the current political line. Charles Murray, Dinesh D'Souza, Abigail Thernstrom, and David Horowitz (among others) have secured lavish funding for producing research that does not pass the standards of scholarly peer review but which successfully serves the interests of "spin control" and public relations central to the aims of their employers. There is of course a delicious irony in the spectacle of these defenders of the free market subsisting on handouts from wealthy patrons, in the production by staunch anti-Communists of propagandistic pseudo-scholarship worthy of the crudest fabrications of Stalinist Russia, and in attacks on "politically correct" doctrinaire college teachers coming from corporate *apparatchiks* afraid to submit to the standards of academic peer review, afraid to face actual students, and dependent for their livelihood on adjusting their thoughts to meet the political imperatives of the moment as determined by the think tanks that employ them. Yet while incapable of producing generative intellectual work, the right-wing mobilization of intellectuals has proven itself very capable of obscuring the kind of vision necessary for oppositional intellectual and cultural work—the ability described by Toni Cade Bambara in the epigraph opening this essay—"to see what the factory worker sees, what the prisoner sees, what the welfare children see, what the scholar sees . . . what the ruling-class mythmakers see as well."[7]

Neoconservative intellectuals and other ruling-class mythmakers have disseminated ways of knowing that obscure "what the factory worker sees, what the prisoner sees, what the welfare children see, what the scholar sees" in order to encourage everyone to see as the ruling-class mythmakers want them to see. As Sidney Plotkin and William E. Scheuerman argue in their important book *Private Interest, Public Spending: Balanced Budget Conservatism and the Fiscal Crisis*, a key goal of conservative political work over the past three decades has been to hide public concerns while foregrounding private interests—to encourage people to think of themselves as taxpayers and homeowners rather than as citizens and workers, to depict private property interests and the accumulated advantages accorded to white men as universal while condemning demands for redistributive justice by women, racial and sexual minorities, and by other aggrieved social groups as the "whining of special interests."[8]

In addition, this dominant discourse aims to transform popular memory of the democratic movements for change that shook society from the 1930s through the 1970s into a temporary moment of madness described as "the 1960s," and comprised of two parts—a legitimate "civil rights movement" aimed only at *de jure* segregation whose gains were satisfied by the 1964 and 1965 Civil Rights Act, and an illegitimate collective of social movements including the women's movement, gay liberation, ethnic nationalism, and many of the mechanisms aimed at actually implementing the "victories" of the civil rights movement, including school busing, affirmative action, and integrated housing.[9]

By describing the civil rights movement as simply a struggle for desegregation and individual inclusion, neoconservatives erase the radical democracy basic to that movement, insulating the movement from its broader critique of U.S. society.[10] One core meaning of the anti-racist popular mobilizations that emerged under the broad term "civil rights" was that they did not view racism as an aberrant phenomenon in an otherwise just society. Rather, these mobilizations identified racism as one of the key social mechanisms for teaching, institutionalizing, legitimating, and naturalizing hierarchy, inequality, and exploitation. They saw that much of their society's mechanisms for social, political, and economic exclusion relied on racism for their deep structure and practical legitimacy. The movement produced integrationists to be sure, but it also nurtured and sustained broad social critiques—not just of racist hierarchies but of all hierarchies, not just of racist dehumanization but of the broader dehumanization integral to a society where the lives of humans count for less than the concerns of capital.

In a recent interview, Angela Davis identified the epistemological importance of political activism that incorporates perspectives from different identities and experiences.[11] She shows how the deep structural problems currently confronting African Americans become distorted by simplistic analyses based on single identities. To view the current crisis in the black community as a crisis about black manhood, for example, in some ways acknowledges the harm done to black male employment and black male wages by deindustrialization. But describing the crisis in terms of the declining value of black manhood mistakes consequence for cause and leads to "remedies" that privilege the private sphere. Rites of passage ceremonies, special schools for black males, and condemnation of black women for "succeeding" in ways that diminish the relative power of black males, all hide the broader structural causes of the crisis facing black men and the black community. They encourage black men to seek more power *within* their community but not outside it, to seek redress from other aggrieved groups rather than from those whose power has enabled them to engineer and profit from the decline in black male wages. This approach hides the ways in which black women and children have also been devastated by the effects of deindustrialization, and it renders invisible black gays and lesbians. Davis shows how a positive politics might still emerge from the experiences of black men. They could, she argues, support the reproductive rights of women in their communities, could help black lesbians adopt children, could lead a struggle against violence against women. But these actions would require an intersectional and multiply positioned perspective on identity and social power.

Similarly, Davis urges us to extend our definitions of class to take into account the entire social world of the worker. She praises the activist centers in Chinatown run by Asian Immigrant Women Advocates and other groups that combine lessons in literacy with legal advice about domestic violence, that address issues about hours, wages, and working conditions, but refuse to detach the workers' lives as workers from their other identities as women, as racialized subjects, and as family members. In addition, these cross-class coalitions linking the concerns of immigrants with the struggles of ethnic women born in the United States also lead to interethnic anti-racism, since issues like low-wage women's labor and domestic violence cut across racial lines. Davis's own role in mobilizing support among diverse populations for a garment-worker-instigated boycott against a prominent garment maker exemplifies the positive possibilities of this kind of coalition work. Women of color play prominent roles in these movements because their situatedness in relation to power has always required this kind of supple and creative thinker. As Lisa Lowe explains, "The Asian American woman and the racialized woman are materially in excess of the subject 'woman' posited by feminist discourse, or the 'proletariat' described by Marxism or the 'racial' or ethnic subject projected by civil rights and ethnoracial movements."[12]

Interethnic anti-racist struggles for social justice bring together diverse populations in a way that makes visible previously hidden aspects of social relations. Within the structure of business unionism that prevails in the United States, it is hard for workers to win gains that do not hurt other workers. The concessions made to workers within individual labor-management negotiations are often passed on to consumers in the form of higher prices or at the very least still force unorganized workers to experience a new disadvantage in relation to workers who are organized. Davis notes that the demand for a shorter work day offers an alternative to this process, that it presents one demand that helps *all* workers by relieving the toil of some and opening up new jobs to unemployed and undocumented workers. By coming to this conclusion about the kind of demand capable of forging a unified struggle out of diverse identities, Davis reconnects us with the experiences of the past and shows that the "new social movements" are very much like the old. The original struggle for the "eight hour day" in the late nineteenth century came about because of conditions very much like our own—a differentiated and divided work force looking for common ground. In the same fashion, the struggle to wage politics in the context of the contradictory consciousness of middle-class life today may be made easier if we position ourselves within historical precedent—the role of intellectuals in the great social upheavals of the 1930s.

The right-wing mobilization of corporate-sponsored intellectual *apparatchiks* has concentrated on winning resources and policy battles in the present, but it has also been aimed at erasing memories of the past—at making it seem as if aggrieved communities have never made alliances with oppositional intellectuals and artists in struggles for democratic social change. Precisely because of thirty years of right-wing mobilization against present and past organizing for egalitarian social change, it is imperative to recover and retheorize past instances of alliances between cultural workers and democratic social movements. Michael Denning's recent revisionist history of "the cultural front" of the 1930s makes a major contribution to that project by reminding us of things that the New Right would like us to forget. Denning's book offers indispensable evidence for thinking about intellectuals and social movements, both through his careful recovery of unexpected alliances in the past as well as through the things that those alliances can teach us about the prospects we face in the present and the future. Most important, his emphasis on the shared experience of "ethnic formation" as a radicalizing force in the lives of workers from diverse ethnic and racial backgrounds indicates that the kinds of interethnic anti-racism we require now actually have a long history within progressive struggles.

Denning refers to the 1930s as the "Age of the CIO," a term designed to call attention to a specific institution—the Congress of Industrial Organizations—as well as to the broader cultural and political ferment that found only partial representation in the establishment of that institution. For Denning the organizational history of the CIO is only a small part of a broader democratization of society achieved by coalitions of activists, artists, and academics in a plethora of institutional sites including college classrooms and adult evening education courses, literary magazines and trade union picket lines, amateur camera clubs and Hollywood studios, mass circulation magazines and discussion groups at neighborhood bookstores. He shows that cultural workers served strategic ends most effectively when they connected themselves to spaces, institutions, and organizations generated by social movements themselves. Perhaps most important, Denning shows how the work carried out by intellectuals and artists on behalf of social movements actually augmented rather than diminished their professional scholarly and creative work by connecting them with broad democratic currents that demanded a fundamental critique of the hierarchies, exclusions, and injustices of the cultural and social institutions in which they were embedded.

During subsequent periods of intense activism, social movements often brought to the surface suppressed aspects of social relations and called into question prevailing research paradigms in academia. Until the 1960s, generations of scholars in elite institutions identified black "passivity" and "deprivation" as the main consequence of slavery, but the self-activity of black masses in motion during the 1960s rendered that question moot, forcing scholars to "discover" that powerful currents of resistance and self-affirmation had existed among slaves and their descendants all along.[13] Similarly, during the 1930s, egalitarian mass movements influenced scholarship by exposing tensions between American capitalism and American democracy, by calling attention to long-standing injustices, and by revealing how hierarchical standards of evaluation obscured the dynamic ingenuity and originality of the masses. Consequently, the historical scholarship of Charles Beard at Columbia University interpreted much of the American past through the lens of 1930s struggles for power. The writings of Harvard scholar F. O. Matthiessen developed a new appreciation of the social criticisms advanced by writers during the nineteenth-century American Renaissance. At UCLA Kenneth MacGowan began to apply traditional methods of literary criticism to the mass medium of film. The egalitarian struggles for social change of the 1930s and 1940s emphasized the centrality of "ethnic formation" within the lives of ordinary people and enabled activists, artists, journalists, and scholars, including Ernesto Galarza, Carey McWilliams, and Richard Wright, to rethink the role of racism in shaping life chances and opportunities.

Not all of this work succeeded, and very little of it resolved some of the deep contradictions confronting middle-class intellectuals. F. O. Matthiessen exemplified one characteristic response to these contradictions; he made sharp distinctions between his radical activism and his increasingly conservative scholarship. Desires for pure identities and for foundational certainty led too many Popular Front intellectuals to support the Communist Party and the destructive Leninist vanguard politics that it embodied. The homogenized "America" celebrated by Popular Front politics during the 1930s manifested an uncritical attitude toward the nation state, inadequately theorized the role of race, and imposed a false uniformity on communities clearly divided by gender, sexual identification, and other identities.

The weaknesses of the 1930s Cultural Front described by Denning bear close similarity to the characteristic flaws of contemporary social movements; both originate in the contradictory conditions and contradictory consciousness confronting intellectuals and artists. Precisely because the old social movements were so much like the new social movements, Denning's work does us a great service in showing the links connecting Popular Front ideas and the broad social movements that created the spaces in which they flourished. Charles Beard taught adult education courses at an evening "Workers University" sponsored by the International Ladies Garment Workers Union in New York. F. O. Matthiessen served as a founder, trustee, and teacher at the trade union sponsored Samuel Adams School for adult education in Boston. Kenneth MacGowan joined with screen writer John Howard Lawson, composer Earl Robinson, and "People's Songs" activist Harry Hay teaching courses at the ILGWU's Los Angeles and Hollywood adult education schools.[14] After becoming the first Mexican American to receive a doctorate in economics from an ivy league university (Columbia), Ernesto Galarza joined forces with Guatemalan-born labor activist Luisa Moreno to organize mass movements of Spanish-speaking people through the Pan-American Union and the National Congress of Spanish Speaking People. Galarza then went to work for the CIO, editing a picture magazine aimed at telling labor's story to a mass audience. Novelist H. T. Tsiang joined with other writers in New York's Chinatown to build public support for the Chinese Hand Laundry Alliance. The John Reed Club in Carmel, California, sponsored lectures by radical intellectuals and labor leaders, but also mobilized popular support for trade-union organizing drives among farm workers, longshoremen, and cannery employees. The Socialist Party's Rebel Arts Group in New York City sponsored a drama club, camera club, chess club, and a puppet theater while also broadcasting dramas on radio station WEVD (a station using the initials of socialist leader Eugene Victor Debs as its call letters). Filmmaker Orson Welles, literary scholar F. O. Matthiessen, and music producer John Hammond served as co-chairs of the citizens committee protesting efforts to deport Harry Bridges, the Australian-born leader of the International Longshore Workers Union.[15]

It would be neither feasible nor desirable to imagine that the politics of the 1930s could be replicated in our own era. But the experiences of the 1930s as recuperated by Denning direct our attention to unrealized possibilities in the present about the possibilities of political work by artists and intellectuals. In direct contradiction to previous interpretations of the 1930s that gave either credit or blame for the politics of that decade to the Communist Party and its affiliated organizations, Denning describes the "cultural front" as broader than the "popular front" and presents the "age of the CIO" as more important than the CIO itself. In other words, while stressing the inescapable importance of organizations and institutions in a social movement, he identifies the ultimate "politics" of the decade as the politics of the masses, not of the institutions through which they worked. A crucially important quotation from Antonio Gramsci encapsulates Denning's argument and its ultimate implications: "A new social group that enters history with a hegemonic attitude, with a self-confidence which it initially did not have, cannot but stir up from deep within it personalities who would not previously have found sufficient strength to express themselves fully in a particular direction."[16]

Denning's view of the 1930s directs our attention to the possibility of politics (and to the politics of possibility) in our own day. Cultural workers capable of connecting with "new social groups" stirring up from within new personalities provide the best prospects for linking artistic and intellectual work with broad-based movements for social change. Despite the depressing isolation endemic to academic employment, scholars, students, artists, and activists on campuses across the country demonstrate the positive effects of campus-community alliances.

The same contradictions that create a core of characteristic behaviors in academic politics also enable many academic and artistic activists to engage in exemplary actions that draw productively on the specific skills and talents that intellectuals possess. Glenn Omatsu shows how scholarly research and community based activism mutually reinforce one another within the Asian-American activist movement. Community groups organizing among low-wage immigrant workers remain community-based in their mobilizations against racism, sexism, and class oppression, but they draw on the intellectual and material resources of Asian-American Studies programs, on theories of popular literacy and democratic pedagogy advanced by Paulo Freire and his followers, and on unexpected alliances and affiliations across class, race, and gender lines.[17] Important research by Laura Pulido, Robert Bullard, Clarice Gaylord, and Elizabeth Bell reveals how campaigns against environmental racism have entailed alliances among representatives of aggrieved communities of color, academic experts, and organized social movement groups.[18] Manning Marable heads a scholarly research center at a prestigious ivy league university and writes well-received books about racism and power, but he also writes a regular column syndicated in African-American newspapers across the country.[19]

Connections between academics and artists also play a vital role in the possible politics of the present moment. In his prophetic work, *The Wretched of the Earth*, Frantz Fanon described how artistic expressions sometimes anticipate political upheavals:

> Well before the political fighting phase of the national movement, an attentive spectator can thus feel and see the manifestations of a new vigor and feel

> the approaching conflict. He will note unusual forms of expression and themes which are fresh and imbued with a power which is no longer that of invocation but rather of the assembling of the people, a summoning together for a precise purpose. Everything works together to awaken the native's sensibility of defeat and to make unreal and unacceptable the contemplative attitude or the acceptance of defeat.[20]

In our time, evidence of this cultural creativity exists in abundance. Community-based cultural production in Los Angeles exemplifies this phenomenon; on one weekend in 1995, for example, college students from the California State University at Northridge chapter of the Moviemiento Estudiantil Chicano/a de Aztlan staged a "happening" to raise money to fund a suit against the University of California by a prominent Chicano professor. The evening's entertainment featured Chicano rap artists, comedians, musicians, and the Teatro Por La Gente (theatre for the people/community) performing what they described as "social/political/cultural Edu-drama-dies." On the same weekend, Chicano poets, visual artists, and singers joined with Japanese taiko drummers and the Watts Prophets, an African-American spoken word/hip-hop ensemble, to stage a benefit at a warehouse loft owned by Chicano heavy metal musician Zach de la Rocha of the musical group Rage Against the Machine and raise money for the Los Angeles chapter of the National Commission for Democracy in Mexico, the support arm of the EZLN rebels fighting the Mexican government in Chiapas. Writing for the hip-hop magazine *Urb*, journalist Gerry Meraz described the weekend's events as "a new culture with roots in the old and appreciation for the art of people who need to be heard whether anyone likes it or not."[21] The broader culture of performance art, graffiti writing, and hip hop from which these events emerged has been carefully catalogued and assessed in exemplary work by innovative scholars including C. Ondine Chavoya, Michelle Habell-Pallan, and Tricia Rose, among others.[22]

Scholarly analyses of how actual social movements work—why they win, how they lose, what legacies they leave—contain tremendous relevance for the politics of the present. Superb historical studies such as Robin D. G. Kelley's *Hammer and Hoe* and *Race Rebels*, Robert Fisher's *Let The People Decide*, David Gutierrez's *Walls and Mirrors*, Charles Payne's *I've Got the Light of Freedom*, and Vicki Ruiz's *Cannery Women, Cannery Lives* offer indispensable evidence and argument about the nature of contesting for power under unequal conditions.[23]

Our time does not lack for activists or activism. Three decades of neoconservative and neoliberal assaults on the victories of the egalitarian movements of the past insure that the communities we come from and the institutions we inhabit will remain in crisis for the foreseeable future. Efforts to create new sources of private profit within the educational system through privatization, charter schools, vouchers, patent sharing, technology-based instruction, and schemes to turn universities into research and development arms of private corporations threaten the institutional future of education at all levels. It may be that, rather than serving as crucibles for a more democratic future, educational institutions will be phased out as useless anachronisms in a society devoted to making maximum possible profits out of all social endeavors. Yet intellectual and artistic work will remain important even if they largely take place outside of existing institutions, even if it is the work of social movements to re-create them in new sites. Similarly, social movements will remain under assault in a society that allocates resources and opportunities along group lines yet insists on structuring legal, educational, and political debates along individualistic lines—as if sexism, racism, class subordination, and other collective axes of power suppress us individually rather than collectively. Yet social movements are proscribed in this culture precisely because they are so powerful, because we know more together than we know apart, because we are stronger collectively than we can ever hope to be as individuals. It is a burden—but also an honor and a responsibility to attach ourselves to social movements, to see what others see, to live out the dream of Toni Cade Bambara—"to tell the truth and not get trapped."

II. Shifting Culture

the song remains the same: communitarianism's cultural politics

MARK REINHARDT

"A person belongs to many communities. A 'self' identifies with only one."

—SAMUEL R. DELANY

"Oh, you don't know what you're missing now."

—LED ZEPPELIN

This essay is both an effort to draw a rough map of some of the landscape of recent political theory and a more sustained encounter with one portion of that landscape.[1] The more substantial engagement is with the body of work known as "communitarianism." The purpose of the map is to situate that body in relation not only to "liberalism," the neighbor with which communitarianism is generally associated and often locked into a kind of dependent rebellion, but also with "cultural studies," a large and diverse territory not usually thought to have much of a relationship to communitarianism at all.[2] The map highlights the points of contact, the common borders, between communitarian preoccupations and those of cultural studies scholars, but does so in order to frame my ultimate argument about a crucial point on which the two ways of thinking about the world differ. The argument is that, judged comparatively, communitarian theorists lack an adequate understanding of cultural struggle, with the result that communitarianism often becomes a politics of normalization and discipline. In the more egregious cases, this politics is overt, intentional, and some communitarians thus wage a kind of reactionary cultural struggle, even if the terms and workings of that struggle escape their explicit theoretical vocabulary and categories. But sometimes such a punitive politics is far from what is intended, and here my claim is that the most generous of communitarian thinking ends up defeating its best intentions; in these cases, a simplistic and reductive account of cultural politics obscures the harms done and constraints imposed in the name of building "community," thereby eliding possibilities for more emancipating practices. So broad a thesis about an entire school of thought is doubtless impossible to demonstrate conclusively in a brief essay, but perhaps by concentrating on a few representative examples it can be illustrated in suggestive ways. My task is thus primarily critical, to give an account of a project that I think should be resisted or overcome and to suggest some of the more obvious points for contestation, but my hope is that the criticism points toward a more analytically satisfying and robustly democratic way of understanding politics in this country. My search for that understanding begins with a joke.

Stop Me If You've Heard This One—

The joke dates back to the summer of 1994, when it circulated so widely through American society that I imagine even most political theorists heard it. It went like this:

—Knock-Knock.
—Who's there?
—O. J.
—O. J. Who?
—Congratulations. You're on the jury!

Popular jokes, even bad ones, inevitably reveal something about their time and place. This one illuminated some of the distinctive characteristics of American political culture in the nineties. It spoke knowingly about the layers of irony and loops of reflexivity that marked the increasingly intense mass-mediation of the nation's public life. The premise was not only that the listener had, like everyone else, been tuned in to the spectacle that seemed to hold the whole populace in thrall in the weeks after Simpson's arrest (more people saw the live, made-for-TV freeway chase sequence than watched any presidential debate in American history),[3] but that *everybody knew that everybody knew* about the Simpson case. The punch line thus registered a contemporary paradox: that which qualifies individuals as jurors in celebrity cases is also a kind of disqualification. Not only was it nearly impossible to find people oblivious to the alleged facts of the case, but the very ignorance of these facts demanded by prevailing standards of jury selection had become suspect when, amidst such complex forms of publicity, political competence depended upon precisely the kind of cultural knowledge that the joke presumed we all share and that courtroom standards require us to lack. To get the joke was to know too much, but to fail to get it was to demonstrate a profound disconnection from the public life of the nation.

Here, as elsewhere, progress marches on: after the nonstop, twelve-month run of what might as well be called the Bill and Monica show, the Simpson case now seems like a mere warm-up, a dress rehearsal. The irony and reflexivity keep adding loops and layers. While even those who profited by exploiting the earlier case often professed anxiety about the kind of commodity they were creating, it now seems that no celebrity journalist worth his or her seven-figure salary can consider passing up the chance to bemoan, on the air, the place of the sordid and invasive multimedia spectacular in American politics. (Think of Barbara Walters's feigned ignorance and embarrassed hesitation when asking Lewinsky to explain the meaning of "phone sex.") The O. J. joke's serious point about the terrain of contemporary politics and the knowledge needed to negotiate it has, a few years later, become not merely more compelling but completely obvious, self-evident.

Yet the passage of time has also underscored the politics of what the joke asked its audience to repress. The criminal and civil trials, and the commentary these generated during and after the events, proved, yet again, that the electronic "global village" is not without its contending clans and interminable feuds: though televised spectacles have changed the meaning of geographical locality and social location as they have disseminated certain kinds of knowledge and symbols throughout the land and across classes, they have hardly broken down politically salient differences among groups. Even from the beginning, what "everybody knew" about Simpson's guilt or innocence turned out, notoriously, to correlate substantially with the spectator's "race." As the case unfolded, the outraged responses of many whites to both real and imagined differences of perception offered a vivid reminder that one of the oldest and most powerful traditions of identity-formation in America, the use of black bodies as markers through which the contours of the national body politic are publicly negotiated (a tradition the joke at once extended and effaced), continues to flourish, under changing conditions, through new genres and technologies.

I resurrect an ephemeral joke, then, because—in both what it captures and what it obscures about the events to which it responds—it raises complex and increasingly pressing questions of cultural politics. In recent years, these questions have become central to the work of political theorists. The political production and accommodation of identity and difference, the problem of borders and boundaries, and the relationships between old theoretical narratives and contemporary modes of expression, traditional political antagonisms and new ways of establishing belonging, are the subjects of some of the most charged contemporary intellectual debates. The greatest energy and animosity currently run through the various arguments about the meaning, status, and legitimacy of "postmodernism," but these questions, or versions of them, entered academic political theory in the seventies in the works of communitarians. Communitarian theorists are largely responsible not only for placing the subject of community at the center of contemporary theory, but for doing so in a way that helped put questions of political subjectivity on the agenda for discussion: the communitarian critique of the most influential liberal work on rights and justice traced liberalism's alleged erosion of community health and moral order to both a denial of the authority of cultural tradition and a misconception of individual moral identity, a combination that Michael Sandel influentially, and emblematically, captured in criticizing "the unencumbered self."[4] How has that critique fared in the intervening decades?

The past few years should have been the best of times for communitarian theorists, both within and beyond academy's walls. Out in what students—like MTV—prefer to call "the Real World," prominent communitarians found themselves in paid positions or advisory roles in a Clinton administration that often spoke in a communitarian idiom. Calls for national service and complaints about a decaying social fabric that can be repaired only through a resumption of personal and community responsibility and the restoration of social discipline have issued from both parties and resonated through editorials and talk radio, sermons, and school board meetings. Inside the more rarefied precincts of political theory, the "liberal-communitarian debate" has continued to feature prominently in the conferences, journals, and academic publishing lists that structure the life of the mind as we late-twentieth-century professional knowledge workers know it. Of course, on the communitarian account, things have not gone well with America or the modern world. But ill health in the polity can be good business for political theory: diagnosing contemporary malaise appears to have brought communitarian critics prominence in the profession and real influence upon the *demos*. What more could a political intellectual ask for?

A more careful look, however, indicates that communitarianism, as both organized movement and philosophical program, is in shakier condition than the foregoing account suggests. Despite bestsellers and manifestos, sympathetic editorialists and photo opportunities with the president, it is not yet clear that reform-minded academic communitarians have left a lasting stamp on American social policy or political culture. Certainly the growing enthusiasm for school uniforms and community policing, and arguably such substantial changes as the passage of welfare reform and the Defense of Marriage and the Family Act, owe a debt to organized communitarianism. But neither these changes of law and policy, nor the rhetorical power of a few key communitarian tropes and phrases, nor the virtual collapse of left-liberalism as a significant force in American electoral life, add up to anything like the revival of the classically republican "second language" spoken about so fervently in popular communitarian works such as *Habits of the Heart*.[5] Nor is this surprising: the contemporary forms and sites of political struggle and the media and techniques through which communities are fashioned strain hard against the limits of older political languages. It is at least worth asking how the communitarian model of political identity can successfully encompass a public life powerfully conditioned by the forces of transnational capital, and articulated through not only the Clinton-Lewinsky spectacle and those like it, but such diverse events, institutions, and representational practices as, say, America Online, the Asian financial crisis, high-tech polling, telemarketing, Greenpeace, actuarial methods of constructing customers as subjects of risk, and the Gay.com Network.

Such phenomena can, as we will see, provoke anguished or angry calls for a refurbishing of older modes of living together. But the changing political-cultural landscape is making other theorists restive over the now familiar arguments about community and individualism, even as those arguments continue to occupy much time and attention. Current resistance is in part the result of previous success, of the degree to which the debate hegemonized the field of contemporary Anglo-American political theory in the eighties and the extent to which participants' positions converged through the give-and-take of reasoned argument. At this point, even John Rawls populates his theoretical speculations with selves "encumbered" by history and tradition, and just about every proponent of community this side of Alasdair MacIntyre concedes, at least in principle, that individual rights are among modernity's finer achievements. With the emergence of this "overlapping consensus," the intensity of the contest seems to have diminished, and at least some of the disputants may be beginning to wonder whether this particular conversation has reached the point of rapidly diminishing returns.

But if a degree of convergence has produced one set of problems, waning hegemony poses another: as the distance between parties to the debate narrowed, the ground outside it has changed rapidly. Feminism, postcolonial criticism, and poststructuralism—intellectual currents that have their most important origins outside of American academic political theory, narrowly construed—have swept through the field with increasing force. Though not necessarily convergent, these diverse currents have all borne questions about power, culture, and identity that had been shoved to the margins of the liberal-communitarian argument. Each of these bodies of work shares with that argument a concern with argument itself, with the scope and character of discourse about politics, and with the politics of discourse. But if there is a certain common territory of inquiry, the differences are at least as important: within political theory, now, there is seemingly irreconcilable disagreement over the role of the theorist, the vocabulary appropriate to theorizing, and the proper subjects and objects of theoretical reflection and political struggle. Just what is to *count* as political struggle or discourse is a particularly contentious topic these days. Writing done in the newer genres or areas can thus be seen as both a late entry into the debate over community and an attempt to displace its terms, if not to altogether replace the older conversation.

In political science, as in some other fields, "postmodernism" has become the heading under which many of these diverse newer writings and approaches are gathered together. I find this unfortunate. Whatever specificity and utility it once had, the word is now distinguished by a particularly low signal-to-noise ratio: whether used enthusiastically or dismissively, "postmodern" tends to carry a strong affective charge while offering only the fuzziest designation of its referents. Casual use of the term allows readers and writers to equate schools or movements that are fundamentally at odds with each other, and to treat each account of power, agency, and subjectivity as if it were also, necessarily, a periodizing thesis about modernity. These confusions render the whole field of contemporary positions difficult to map, but they are most likely to undermine those arguments that make careful use of one or another of the newer critical grammars (polemics *against* the postmodern often advance their cause through a calculated vagueness about the targets of criticism).[6] For these reasons, I propose a different rubric under which to read such work.

My suggestion is that the common project of many otherwise heterogeneous recent trends in political theory is, first, an approach to reading that takes the rhetorical and performative dimensions of texts seriously (viewing them as inescapably political and inextricably bound up with theoretical "content" or "argument") and, second, a broad extension of the concepts of "textuality" and "reading" so that they can be brought to bear on a wide array of social practices, performances, and institutions. Works of this type are thus serious, for example, about the implications and effects of the forms of publicity through which citizen-spectators have experienced such conventionally political events as the Gulf War, pondered such ostensibly peripheral matters as the existence of extraterrestrials, and participated, wittingly and unwittingly, in projects such as the social construction of whiteness. While "postmodern" work is often rejected as intolerably abstract or indicted for its dismissal of the world's reality, I suggest that recent works that try to make sense of the shifting forms of representation and to analyze the politics of signifying practices in everyday life—works that grapple with both the macropolitics and the micropolitics of contemporary cultures—are better treated as embodying an "empirical turn" in contemporary political theory. Yet despite this preoccupation with specific performances and practices, and *contra* the tendency of critics of postmodernism to decry it as a source of nihilistic moral paralysis, this work is often manifestly driven by a preoccupation with the venerable ethical question of how to live humanely and democratically with others. With some eccentricity, perhaps, I propose that we might bring this diverse body of work under the heading of "cultural studies," with the field understood in such a way as to apply equally well to such thinkers as, say, Paul Gilroy, Arjun Appadurai, George Lipsitz, Judith Butler, and Donna Haraway outside of political science departments, and Michael Rogin, Michael Shapiro, David Campbell, and Jodi Dean within them.

This approach not only tells us more about the works' purposes and procedures than could be learned by simply labeling them "postmodern," but also helps to account for the hostility that "postmodernism"—as both signifier and signified—has provoked within most of political science and from many quarters of political theory. The work commonly placed under that sign is not merely intended as contribution to one part of political science, an addition to a "subfield" with its own clear tasks and narrow boundaries, but as an alternative perspective on the whole enterprise. Employing methods peculiar to theoretical work in the humanities and the "soft" social studies, such works occupy turf that has long been reserved for other specialties within the discipline, contesting prevailing conceptions of both the empirical and the normative while retaining an explicitly political orientation toward the world. These acts of trespassing disrupt the tacit settlement that was established with the ebbing of the theory/science wars in the early seventies, a settlement that maintained a place for political theory within political science departments by consolidating a division of labor in which political theorists served as custodians of old texts, exhorted (often unheeding) citizens to care more about politics, and perhaps proposed some of the questions that could be "answered" by work in public policy and behavioral analysis, while otherwise leaving "the real world" to their "empirical" colleagues. Because that division offered at least some benefits to nearly all workers, it is understandable that recent transgressions of it have disturbed people accustomed to laboring on one or the other side of the divide. As should be obvious by now, the burden of my argument will be that the disturbance is all for the good.

It is revealing, I think, that communitarianism has not occasioned a comparable academic hostility. Now, it is certainly the case that the liberal-communitarian debate has at times grown heated, polemical; some liberal participants have clearly believed the stakes to be high and the communitarian critique both dangerous and misguided. But communitarians' own frequent forays out of the library of great books and into the world of policies, practices, and problems of political culture have not been labeled as subversions of either the desirable patterns of academic labor or the standards of legitimate theoretical inquiry. One obvious reason for this disparity is the fundamental difference in vocabularies and modes of interpretation: unlike much "postmodern" or "cultural studies" work, neither the terms nor the claims of most communitarian arguments pose challenges to conventional forms of social scientific analysis. This lack of challenge, and the corresponding legitimacy within the field of political science, I suggest, are intimately bound up with how communitarianism engages the problem of cultural struggle: what I take to be a fundamental source of its political limitations has been an enabling condition of its academic acceptability. Pursuing this suggestion requires, finally, a more specific and substantive encounter with communitarian projects.

Calling the Cops

In 1998, twenty-four intellectuals and leaders issued a report entitled *A Call to Civil Society: Why Democracy Needs Moral Truths.*[7] The work of the Institute for American Values' "Council on Civil Society," a group chaired by the communitarian theorist Jean Bethke Elshtain, this glossy, photo-filled document is obviously intended as a public intervention, an attempt to influence policymakers and the kind of journalists and commentators who shape legislative debates. *A Call to Civil Society* develops a dire account of the ethical and political condition of the United States today. The authors frame this account, which typifies a strong current in communitarian analysis, by suggesting that their own sense of urgency is essentially a reflection of American public opinion. The majority of citizens, they argue, have concluded that the nation is suffering from "fragment[ation]" and "moral decline." From the diminishing well-being of American children, to the "coarseness and harshness in popular culture," to the "loss of confidence in the possibility of moral truth," the symptoms of crisis are visible all around us. The basic consequence of this crisis is an undermining of democracy itself, for "we are using up, but not replenishing, the civic and moral resources that make our democracy possible."[8] The needed response is a strengthening of "civil society," that network of extra-state relationships and institutions such as "families, neighborhood life, and the web of religious, economic, educational, and civic associations" that nurture good character and citizenship.[9] Such "seedbeds of virtue," which are essential to self-governance, have been untended for too long because their importance has been obscured by an all too prevalent philosophy of "expressive individualism." To fully appreciate the importance and appropriate place of civil society in our democracy, we need to supplant that flawed philosophy with an understanding of the intrinsic connection between community health and individual flourishing.[10]

What kind of politics does this report propose to us? Some of the argument is virtually impossible to contest, which is to say that it is pitched at a level of abstraction too high to bear on any significant political controversy: surely education and "community" life, for instance, are important to the kind of people we become, but no particular policy or orientation follows from that general claim. Much of the argument is more contestable, of course, and some of it, to my mind, deserves assent: early on, the report flags "racism and sexism" as "serious problems" in contemporary society, and explicitly describes economic inequality as a problem deeply related to, and almost as important as, "moral decline."[11] A sustained and fundamental challenge to these forms of oppression might take the defense of community and civil society down a provocative path. Yet as the authors develop their analysis and move toward specific proposals for reform, it becomes clear that such matters are far from the center of their concerns. They offer no significant analysis of economic inequality, nor (aside from the endorsement of "flexible workplace arrangements") meaningful recommendations for economic policy.[12] And if race is a "problem," it is not one that the Council on Civil Society appears to consider worthy of any real scrutiny.

It soon becomes clear that home is where *A Call to Civil Society*'s heart is. When the authors seek to illustrate our moral crisis, they turn to examples like this one: "A pop star announces that she wants a baby but not a husband."[13] The example is not arbitrary, for the report's ultimate argument is that the dissolution of the two married parent family is "the leading propeller of our overall civic deterioration."[14] In response, *A Call to Civil Society* outlines a series of legal reforms designed to make divorce considerably more difficult and costly, proposes "that states establish preferences for low-income married couples in the distribution of limited, discretionary benefits such as public housing units and Head Start slots," and recommends that "students who become pregnant, or who impregnate someone, are thereafter ineligible for extra-curricular school activities."[15] Overcoming "civic deterioration" and restoring self-government would appear to require significant sacrifices, and the burden will fall particularly hard on poor, single parents and their children. Straight parents are targeted explicitly, gay parents by implication: indeed, as best as I can tell, there are no queer people in this report (unless we should count Madonna, the authors' unnamed metonym for scandalously irresponsible husbandless parenthood). Presumably, there is not much room for them in the authors' communitarian vision of democratic civil society, either.

Throughout *A Call to Civil Society*, the critique of expressive individualism persistently slides into an assault on individualities and relationships that deviate from an extremely narrow spectrum of normality and propriety. Unveiling the punitive politics at work in the text does not require an elaborate hermeneutics of suspicion: despite the authors' initial gesture toward inclusiveness and equality, their document exemplifies what I earlier characterized as communitarianism's more overtly reactionary struggle. Certain symptomatic features of the report's analysis are therefore worth highlighting. First, although "civil society" is used, promiscuously, to cover a diverse set of institutions, activities, and relationships, mass-mediated culture is constructed less as part of the terrain *of* civil society than as an alien force that bears a primary responsibility for doing destructive things *to* civil society. Conversely, while the capitalist enterprise *is* included as an integral part of civil society, the report develops no structural analysis of economic power inside or outside the workplace, and the authors pay minimal attention to the way economic relationships condition other "seedbeds of virtue." As for the text's sustained attempt to deploy the symbols of health and corruption to construct an image of the sexually normal and stably coupled virtuous citizen, these rhetorical maneuverings cannot be described within the terms the report provides, unless we can appropriately characterize these normalizing gestures as mere examples of the authors' pursuit of what they call "transmittable moral truth."[16] *A Call* to Civil Society frames "morality" in such a way as to make it a weapon of struggle, even as it denies that there is legitimate scope for contestation over the basic terms of ethical life.

To diagnose symptoms is not the same as to refute arguments, of course. One could say much more in replying to the report.[17] My intention, though, is not to develop a sustained counterargument to this reactionary face of communitarianism. Rather, I will presume that this face is unappealing and, having briefly sketched some of its features, explore in more depth the extent to which less conservative, more pluralistic communitarian projects can or cannot escape such a politics of discipline.

Must the Song Remain the Same?

One relatively recent version of such a project is Daniel A. Bell's *Communitarianism and Its Critics*. Though by no means the most prominent of communitarian analyses, the book is, I think, a particularly useful and illuminating example. One reason is its scope: it offers a survey of the past two decades of argument between communitarians and liberals, canvassing the most influential positions with both breadth and depth. Much of what Bell has to say will be familiar to anyone who has followed the evolution of the liberal-communitarian debate, but the book stands out for the degree to which it is reflective and genuinely instructive about that evolution. Like *A Call to Civil Society*, his, too, is a representative text, but of the most generous communitarian spirit. The presentation is exceptionally fair-minded: liberal positions are conveyed as forcefully as communitarian ones, and there are no straw men or women in Bell's arguments. His explicit goal is to move beyond the common, piecemeal critiques of liberalism to a substantive communitarian vision of contemporary political life.[18] As he elaborates and interrogates his vision, he makes it clear that his is a communitarianism concerned with the cultivation of respect for diverse ways of being. In all of these ways, Bell has, I think, crafted about as good a book as can be written on the liberal-communitarian debate from within its terms. That book enables us to think productively about where the larger debate has been, where it stands now, and what its potential for further work is likely to be: *Communitarianism and Its Critics* is thus an ideal vehicle for exploring the possibilities and limitations of communitarianism's cultural politics.

The author begins by voicing his worries about "unshackled greed, rootlessness, alienation from the political process, rises in the rate of divorce, and all the other phenomena related to a centering on the self and away from community in contemporary Western societies."[19] This is a familiar complaint—it could easily have found its way into *A Call for Civil Society*—and Bell acknowledges not only that contemporary communitarians have often made such points but also that the arguments have had noticeable effects on works by some liberal theorists. Even though he thus calls attention to the philosophical convergence that followed the initial rounds of debate, however, Bell also argues that important theoretical and political differences remain beneath the surface of the current agreement over the situated (time and place bound) character of individuality and political rationality. Liberal theorists have responded to the communitarian critique by "cleansing" their theories of atomism, excessive individualism, and indefensible universalism. But in order to do so, they have retreated from engagement with the actual conditions of politics, thus failing to understand "how traditional liberal institutions and practices have legitimized the uninhibited pursuit of interest characteristic of the Reagan/Thatcher years."[20] As a result, Bell insists, liberals cannot envision the kinds of cultural transformations and institutional reforms that must accompany a principled rejection of atomistic individualism. Nor is their theoretical change of heart thoroughgoing enough, for they do not grasp the full extent to which community membership is constitutive of identity or the ways in which an understanding of that constitutive role problematizes the fundamental liberal commitment to a self that can choose its own ends, its own vision of the good life.

This last claim is, I think, the core of philosophical communitarianism, and is itself therefore familiar. But Bell pursues the implications of that common idea in an uncommon form: in a move that, sadly, seems unusually daring today, he returns to political theory's inaugural genre, casting his investigation in the form of a dialogue. Two old Canadian acquaintances, Philip and Anne, are surprised to find each other in a Parisian cafe. Anne has just completed her dissertation, a defense of communitarianism. Philip, a liberal who has recently placed his own (unhappy) graduate career on hold, becomes the eager but highly skeptical audience for Anne's account of her work. As the subsequent dialogue pursues the communitarian account of and response to those putative ailments, Anne challenges liberal conceptions of individual agency and state neutrality, sketching an alternative social ontology, and arguing for the central importance of *national* forms of community. We are, on this account, inevitably shaped by our "constitutive attachments" to particular others, particular ways of life. Community provides the "*moral* space" within which we operate. We can become critical of our origins and our social context but we can never simply step outside of them. To try to escape what and where we have been is to do a kind of violence to ourselves.[21] Based upon these views, Anne also defends a model of social criticism as the use of "shared understandings" of a community's "deepest commitments" against contemporary policies or practices that violate them. Meeting strenuous and articulate objections from Philip at each note, she sounds these themes at length and with precision.

Anne's argument throughout the conversation, then, is that the communitarian account of the "encumbered" self is both more philosophically sound and more conducive to the establishment of psychologically nourishing social and political arrangements. Once we recognize that the self in control of its ends is an untenable fiction, that our well-being depends on the strength of those constitutive attachments that give shape and meaning to our lives, we should seek policies that actively strengthen such attachments and enable significant communities to flourish. We should support interventionist measures that mold individual choices, if such measures produce stronger and healthier individuals.[22] Liberal Philip resists this conclusion, of course; and as he and Anne debate these claims, there is an admirable movement back and forth between position and contending position, philosophical premise and practical political implication. Out of both her own convictions and in response to Philip's challenges, Anne moves the communitarian position away from some of its most conservative affiliations, insisting upon the multiple and at times conflicting memberships that constitute identities, and emphasizing the need for communitarians to embrace a pluralistic respect for individual and cultural differences.[23]

Indeed, through the example of gay rights, Anne argues that despite their emphasis on the plurality of goods, *liberals* are unable to sufficiently respect difference. While liberalism offers no more than neutral tolerance, the communitarian position can support an ethics and politics of robust affirmation. Liberalism can think politically about sexuality under the heading of preserving "choice," thus allowing "homosexual acts, in the same way that a society might tolerate Nazi rallies." Communitarianism allows us to recognize that sexual orientation is "a constitutive feature of one's identity" and, hence, cannot be reduced to a matter of individual choice; this recognition underwrites the more expansive principle that gay people "should have access to the structures that enable them to express their identity."[24] A sophisticated and open communitarianism, Bell suggests, gives self-expression more meaningful guarantees than does the liberalism that claims to do so much for individuals.

Clearly, such an argument brings Bell's communitarianism a substantial distance from the type of project elaborated in *A Call to Civil Society*. And if, as I will argue, there remain fundamental problems with his attempt to align a communitarian ontology and conception of shared understandings with the cultivation of individuality and the elaboration of a more politically generous pluralism, one of the notable qualities of *Communitarianism and Its Critics* is that it provides us with resources for identifying them. At a number of key points, Philip's criticisms are, to my mind at least, more persuasive than Anne's defenses. Anne's account of "constitutive attachments," to take a politically crucial example, assumes that healthy communities living up to their deepest commitments will bring individuals into harmony with the prevailing forms of order. That some selves inevitably will fit very badly into their social worlds, and that most selves will fit imperfectly, leading to painful external conflict and internal dissonance, is a possibility she—like *A Call to Civil* Society's authors—will not really engage. In Philip, the book provides a critic who helps us identify the costs of this refusal. He repeatedly marks Anne's tendency to treat selves that are not attuned to their communal origins as "damaged." He calls attention to the informal and institutional oppressions this act of labeling can sanction, and questions her faith that "shared understandings" provide us with standards that allow such labels to be applied accurately or fairly.[25] Philip is not answered effectively. The teleological certainties required by this communitarian approach to constraining individual choice and action are *never* given a convincing foundation in Bell's book, despite all of his reflections on epistemology and ontology, encumbrance and identity: Anne never shows either how to avoid or how to redeem the abusive language of damaged selfhood. I do not think this failure differentiates this representative book from the works of Michael Walzer, Michael Sandel, Robert Bellah, Charles Taylor, and others on whom Bell draws. What does distinguish Bell is the degree to which he works to make the fundamental problems with his position visible to his readers. This ability to argue outside the circle of his sympathies (or is it, rather, a willingness to stage his own ambivalence?) is an intellectual virtue, one that opens up possibilities for further dialogue and exchange, but it cannot make Bell's particular version of communitarian cultural politics fundamentally more compelling.

Further problems with the communitarian argument are brought out in the book's most unusual section, a section that further enables my symptomatic reading. As an appendix, Bell reprints a respectful but politically critical reader's report that liberal theorist Will Kymlicka wrote in response to an earlier version of the manuscript. This incisive report, also presented in dialogue form, not only sharpens the criticisms Philip had made of the constraints that could be imposed in the name of preserving "constitutive attachments," but also raises substantial questions about the way Bell frames the whole argument between his characters. In his most important line of criticism, Kymlicka notes that, by casting conventional academic liberalism as communitarianism's only critic, the dialogue overlooks highly relevant interlocutors. His example is feminism, a perspective that Bell co-opts (by insinuating that Anne's is the feminist viewpoint) even while marginalizing it through most of the book. Kymlicka's critique shows how the evasion of feminist work makes possible a communitarian account of gender politics that severely limits the targets and methods of appropriate political struggle. Bell would like to be an advocate of gender equity, but he cannot raise the possibility that what we currently experience as gender is itself inequitable. His framework cannot encompass the feminist argument that "domination and subordination were built into the social construction of masculinity and femininity."[26] I think this is an acute criticism, one that lets us begin, at least, to think about the problems with communitarianism's ways of conceptualizing and obscuring cultural struggle.

The problems become clearer in Bell's second appendix, in which he has Anne respond to these criticisms. Appealing to a simple dichotomy, Anne authorizes her refusal to politicize the very categories of masculinity and femininity: there is liberal feminism which, seeing inherited gender categories as political, aims at "nothing less than an androgynous society where sex differences no longer exist," and there is communitarian feminism, which accepts inherited identities and views the problem as "the devaluation of women's qualities and activities by a male dominated culture."[27] Anne, of course, stands in the latter camp, arguing that masculinity and femininity are just the kind of constitutive identities that we cannot challenge without "damaging" ourselves. This survey of contemporary feminist positions is deeply and paradigmatically problematic. It locates some stances—perhaps Susan Okin's liberalism and certainly Elshtain's communitarianism—but it ignores much of the most interesting work in contemporary feminist theory. Bell leaves no room for struggles that would problematize and *politicize* (not merely revalue) conventional gender identities without necessarily embracing androgyny. That such struggles might give rise to the destabilizing *proliferation* and radical *transformation* of genders—that the political arithmetic of gender can go beyond two—is not thinkable within this dialogue. There is no room, then, for the kind of questions asked by such theorists as Butler, Haraway, Nancy Fraser, Hortense Spillers, or Cindy Patton, by the kind of theorists I have lined under a certain (eclectic and inclusive) understanding of cultural studies. But the problem is by no means narrowly academic, for it is hard to see how Bell's communitarian strictures *could* accommodate the gender-bending self-presentations visible on the streets of any contemporary American city, or, for that matter, on television screens anywhere. In what useful sense can cross-dressing married men or transgendered women be said either to be abolishing gender as category or affirming the values and importance of conventional masculinity? Articulating a theory and politics of subversive disruption or parodic deconstruction would explode Bell's conceptual language.

What of that language? In arguing that dialogue enables a uniquely self-questioning form of theorizing, Bell invokes the example of the *Republic*.[28] But his is a *Republic* without Thrasymachus: there is no voice that provides a hostile or ironic commentary on the form of the conversation, none that explicitly questions this *kind* of theoretical enterprise. Kymlicka suggests as much, but the problem is more serious than he can afford to allow. Even the feminist contributions Kymlicka summarizes remain largely within a liberal orbit and, though his comments on the politics inscribed within conventional gender identities push that orbit to its outer limits, they still take us only so far: as my comments on the political arithmetic of gender and sexuality indicated, much of the material that must be confronted in order to come to terms with the intertwining of power and culture today lies in a space beyond that encompassed by the work of feminist liberals. The conclusion to be drawn from this, I think, is that while many of the virtues of the book are personal, the result of Bell's (and Kymlicka's) significant labors, the shortcomings are generic, categorical. *Communitarianism and Its Critics* does an outstanding job of charting the liberal-communitarian debate. When the book is lacking, then, it is because of the limitations of the debate itself.

The key limitation, which is plainly visible from the stances I've associated with cultural studies, is the failure to provide theoretical tools that can make sense of struggles over the basic terms of the cultural order, over specific signifying practices, and over the ways political differences originate and are negotiated. Like others in their respective schools, Kymlicka and Bell present an account of political criticism in which we must choose between an abstract universalism and the Walzerian form of "connected criticism" based on "shared understandings." Either we speak in the name of transcendent right, or we show that the target of our complaint is at odds with our community's deepest principles. Each of these appeals has its philosophical strengths and important political uses, but this stark binary choice is not adequate to the diverse spaces and forms of contemporary ideological contestation and cultural struggle. The categories it offers cannot fully come to terms with the role of force and the play of power in interpretation and disputation, with the work done by affect, myth, symbol, story, and performance—in short, by rhetoric—in the processes through which we make claims upon, about, and against each other. Though advocates of "shared understandings" complain about the arid rationalism of universalist doctrines, the "connected criticism" advocated in this debate is itself too narrowly cognitive and formalistic in orientation. Traditions are assumed to speak univocally, spheres of life are treated as if their boundaries were sharply delineated, and political argument is presented as if it took place entirely at the level of high philosophical principle. This model smells too much of the seminar and not enough like life.

The political costs of so constrained an approach to criticism can be further clarified by returning to Bell's arguments about gay politics and identity. He (Anne's position here is clearly his own) maintains that America's shared traditions can sustain an affirmation of gay relationships because our most important shared understanding is that families are "members responding to each other on the basis of freely expressed love." There is thus "no reason, in principle, why the family ought to be composed only of heterosexuals. In fact, among homosexuals the trend seems to be toward coupling in family-type cells characterized by intimacy, affection, unconditional acceptance, and loyalty." In a footnote, Bell adds that he thinks this may well be because "most gays prefer coupling in family-type cells to a life of random release of libido impulses in bathhouses."[29] Though Bell's comments on the elasticity of the family identifies a significant resource for arguments over sexual tolerance (surely, it often does make political sense to stretch conventional understandings to cover less conventional relationships), when placed together the three statements reveal some symptomatic limitations. The first two remarks display, I think, a bit of the generous academic communitarian's characteristic wishful thinking, an attempt to read the theorist's preference into the structure of social practices or shared understandings. The substantial ways in which these practices or understandings push in the opposite direction—and the degree to which any serious attempt to claim them will occasion intense forays into the politics of resignification—is obscured. The third of Bell's comments points to the problems faced by people whose goals or desires trespass against "shared understandings": what of those who—"community standards" be damned—prefer bathhouses? Bell seems to believe that gay people "should have access to the structures that help them express their identity" only when that identity (and the use of the singular here is revealing) looks a lot like the most socially sanctioned form of heterosexuality. What resources does communitarianism offer to defend sexualities that exceed or defy the gay version of a politics of "family values"?

Such problems are enough to restore some luster to the oft-maligned liberal conception of privacy and to universalist understandings of rights.[30] But though these concepts provide important political checks on the most conservative impulses at work in Bell's account, they do not tell us much about the nature or sources of those impulses. They reveal nothing about the desire for moral discipline that even Bell, like virtually all contemporary communitarians, voices so persistently. They don't help us to unpack the—highly political—rhetorical work performed by his invocation of bathhouse sex in the age of AIDS. Nor is it clear what they contribute to a political understanding of the theatrical *public* confrontations over sexual identity that occupied the national stage and shape our roles at the century's end. They give us little purchase on the ways that, say, ACT UP or Queer Nation (aimed to) bend received sex/gender categories, or the ways that Focus on the Family seeks to reinforce them. Despite their tactical merits, then, the standard liberal categories have analytical limitations. These have political consequences. Sticking within the confines of the mainstream liberal-communitarian debate makes it nearly impossible to see how socially constructed sexual (and other) identities can be meaningful and experientially "real"—and yet also be rent, fissured, formed at the intersection of a wide array of discourses and marked by political powers and struggles too complex to be squeezed into the vocabularies of universality, privacy, or community. Liberals defend a generalized "tolerance," but tend not to recognize the *politics* of these processes of identity-making. Communitarians view the collective fashioning of selves as important to politics, but tend to mask, dismiss, or seek revenge against the processes of self-fashioning that fall outside their nostalgic models of belonging.

Consider, as a final example of these forms of political refusal, Anne's distinction between the "Basque nationalist, the proud French speaker, the committed Catholic, and the true homosexual," on the one hand, and "the member of the Led Zeppelin Fan Club" on the other.[31] The distinction made here is between *real* communities/individuals and mere simulacra (e.g., the "false" homosexual?) or "lifestyle enclaves." There is something to this categorization: each of the identities invoked by Bell is enmeshed in distinctive practices and institutions, and each of these weighs differently in individual and collective life. While liberal political talk passes over such differences in the silence proper to "the private sphere," Bell seeks to engage them. Yet his mode of engagement is, in the end, another form of denial. If states, religions, and sexualities are produced and maintained through different—though often mutually entangled—organizations, that does not justify Bell's quest for the mother lode of authenticity, for that quest is nothing less than a flight from the thoroughly inauthentic terrain of contemporary politics. Though I have no doubt that, at this late date, Led Zeppelin is not a major generator of politically significant subject positions, the force for which the seventies' rock group substitutes synechdocically in Bell's drama—mass-mediated subculture—*is* a meaningful determinant of the idioms and affects of contemporary micro-politics. To remove this force from an account of the attachments that constitute identity, to dismiss it as frivolous, displays a remarkable but paradigmatic imperviousness to or resentment of some of the fundamental conditions of in our time life. The problem lies not only in Bell's conception of political criticism but in his understanding of membership: despite his passing acknowledgment of the multiplicity of communal attachments, the fact that virtually no one lives in a single, monolithic community proves very hard for him to sustain at the important moments of his argument.

Hip-hop, country, piercing, soap operas, tabloids, pick-up trucks, hunting rifles—though they lie outside the field of political vision for most students of political science, these genres and objects all number among the means through which contemporary selves are (re)made. Such forms of subjectivity inflect our everyday encounters with others, shaping our speech, helping us to map our social worlds, filtering and at times even producing the divisions that run through the polity. Of course, no one even minimally attuned to the structural inequalities of this society would claim that any form of fandom shapes American lives and self-conceptions with a force or gravity comparable to those exerted by "race." The often decrepit facilities and inadequate education found in poor urban schools is not due to funding schemes that allocate resources on the bases of musical preference! Yet, even here, cultural politics is more complex than communitarian accounts admit: just about any tense, heterogeneous high school offers instructive reminders of how the articulation of "race," its consolidation as an identity that takes shape in relationship to others, is bound up with acts of appropriating styles of popular music and other products of mass-mediated culture. In some instances (traveling clans of Deadheads come to mind), participation in a subculture may even bring with it such "authentically" communitarian experiences as "a common past and certain moral obligations that flow from [it]."[32] The point holds more generally. To put it in the most conventional of political science terms, which is to say electoral ones, there are political reasons why Ronald Reagan calculatedly referred to federal institutions as "Guvmint," why George Bush ate pork rinds, why Bill Clinton took aim at Sister Souljah, and why Lamar Alexander could not decide whether or not to launch his run for president in a plaid work shirt. Or, to put it yet another way, there was a politics to *Time* magazine's decision to present O. J. in blackface when it ran his picture on its cover. Neither the communitarian perspective exemplified by Bell nor the common categories of contemporary liberal political theory offer terms that are of much use in discussing how that politics—a politics central to the inquiries of cutural studies—works.

In our time, these silences matter. Though spectacles and mass-mediated subcultural identity markers are by no means all there is to politics, they are increasingly important parts of it, parts that change the character of the whole. Any perspective that cannot account for these changes is at best gratuitously disabling and at worst actively harmful. Entering the strange terrain of contemporary publicity does not require us to lose our sense of political direction, and the most punitive and reactionary policies for regulating relationships and identities are underwritten by nostalgic arguments born of rage against recent changes in the cultural landscape. (Even many of those whose rage is greatest take advantage of the changes that prompt their anger: think, to take two examples that capture an important dimension of nineties politics, of the technologically sophisticated activists of the Christian Right, or Newt Gingrich's combination of Victorian moral longing and millenarian cyberbabble.) Neither evasion nor *ressentiment* offer adequate bases for democratic intellectual work.

My criticisms of communitarianism have periodically indicated or implied that cultural studies within and without political theory are beginning to forge more satisfying means of doing the work. These studies reject and contest the destructive fantasy that a good or democratic society will harmonize differences and dissonances out of existence. Cultural studies scholarship is by no means uncritical of the global transformations wrought by contemporary capitalism, but the critique neither romanticizes the past nor ignores the distinctive democratic opportunities that are also, along with new forms of exploitation, emerging in the present. Recognizing the struggles and impurities that necessarily mark all forms of collective order not only enables more satisfying readings of the contemporary social text but pushes us toward more generous ethical and political practices. The times demand this generosity. Maybe they always have. In "America," state and nation, self and citizen have been carved out of encounters with otherness, each struggle to relax the boundaries of identity occasioning a countervailing policy of containment. Since its inception, America's cruelest acts and noblest aspirations have been bound together, the yearning for freedom and democracy entangled with fearful imaginings of threatening forces lurking without and within our borders. Today, our habits of mind, our structures of prestige, our distributions of wealth and opportunity, the length of our lives and the tenor of our days and nights, all fall under the shadow of that history. How long is the shadow? If there is no escape from history, there is, as a certain now disreputable theorist famously remarked, room for maneuver within the circumstances we inherit. Time after time, communitarians turn those circumstances into occasions for nostalgia. By identifying and embracing the democratic energies immanent in our novel condition we may open a more inclusive and ennobling path.

the governmentality of discussion

PAUL A. PASSAVANT

It is a commonplace of diverse forms of legal and political theory that the modern liberal subject is an abstract individual, unencumbered by social or cultural baggage. Critics since Marx have attacked liberalism for its seeming reliance upon a disembodied rights-bearing subject. They condemn liberalism for creating abstract, formalistic equalities among subjects. Critics argue that such fictions conceal or repress real differences among actually existing persons, the real social relations within which they are embedded, and the real bodies that they inhabit. The liberal rights-bearing subject, however, is not as abstract and disembodied as the critics claim.

Against the conventional criticisms of liberalism, I contend that rights are given meaning within a discourse that embodies subjects who can make legitimate rights claims. By staging my argument in the context of the First Amendment to the United States Constitution, I will argue that law is a system of meaning that enables some to be recognized as authorized subjects exercising their right of free speech, while the expressive acts of others are either lent no particular significance by this system or are constituted by it as social problems. Claiming a right within the discourse of American constitutional law rests, in part, upon claiming a subject position to which rights attach. By examining the way that the legal discourse of free speech deals with the problem of sexual expression, I will elaborate the type of subject demanded and reproduced by the First Amendment.

Today, controversies that involve the First Amendment, sexual expression, and the question of decency and civility seem ubiquitous. For example, federal and state courts have upheld Mayor Rudolph Giuliani's attempt to remove approximately 80 percent of the sex industry in New York City through various zoning regulations in order to promote "civility" in the city. This follows a pattern of Supreme Court decisions since the 1970s that give governments a great deal of leeway to regulate activities that are not even obscene, but merely "indecent."[1] The *New York Times* has described the sex wars in New York City as pitting civility against civil liberties.[2] Critics of liberalism would agree with this description of the conflict due to their argument that liberal legal rights draw boundaries around the individual, isolating this subject from external community norms. From this perspective, to enforce a right to free speech is to deny cultural values such as civility.

In contrast, by examining the central place of "civility" in the legal discourse forming the background of these controversies over the sex industry, I shall argue that these struggles are in fact constitutive of an American subject that derives from racialized understandings of the American people. Thus, these struggles help to embody, in a very particular way, the American subject who can claim its constitutional rights. The legal discourse that promotes a stricter regulation of sexual expression draws from a deep well of cultural meanings that distinguishes civilized subjects, who exercise their rights responsibly, from social problems that afflict the body politic. Therefore, civility is not the antithesis of rights (although those who argue that liberal rights are disembodied may misperceive civility to be a limit to rights), but is a mechanism by which subjects who are capable of exercising rights are produced. Indeed, even when public policies are found to violate a constitutional right to free speech, this finding does not follow from the anti-image of a disembodied holder of rights. It derives from understanding different commitments to follow from America's civilized identity.

Michel Foucault's perceptive analyses of the disciplinary interior to contemporary liberal societies and the normalization of "free" subjects who can be entrusted with the exercise of dispersed social powers heighten our attentiveness to the problems of governance faced by the American constitutional system. The U.S. Constitution decenters sovereignty from the state to the people. In so doing, it helps to inaugurate a form of politics to which Foucault refers in his essay on "governmentality." Governmentality is comprised of the three-way intersection of sovereignty—discipline—government that converges upon a "population."[3] As contemporary thought comes to invent and discern specific national and racial peoples, the interests and security of the nation-state come to focus heavily upon the population to which the state attaches itself. Acknowledging the decentered nature of contemporary mechanisms of power, the modern state becomes accomplished at governing "at a distance." It coordinates and cultivates the powers of the population. Through his studies of diverse social institutions, Foucault explores the dispersed, subtle, and mundane ways in which power is exercised to encourage the construction of subjects appropriate for a given social formation.

This attention to the production of subjects by the institutions comprising a given social formation is helpful to the project of understanding the practice of rights in a system that makes a national *people* sovereign. This paper examines legal discourse as one mechanism of social discipline that helps to produce subjects capable of exercising rights necessary to the government of the people. As the cultural mechanism that authoritatively represents the norms of the American nation-state, the circulation of constitutional law facilitates the project of governance at a distance.

The cultivation and reinforcement of the American people's civic qualities is a key concern within a constitutional context that entrusts to the people the power of self-government.[4] Additionally, these characteristics can be used as signs to pick out the American people and its interests from the confusing and heterogeneous flux of those factions that put forward interests deriving from other social identities. Throughout modernity, when analysts seek to understand better the American people in order to improve their government, be those analysts the framers of the Constitution or pundits decrying the crisis of the moment, very often the quality of self-government extolled or thought to be in danger is the *civility* of the American people.

Embodied Rights

Critics of liberalism frequently fault it for resting upon an inaccurate theory of the subject—the abstract, disembodied, isolated, or unencumbered individual. Michael Warner, for example, discusses the alienation caused by the bourgeois public sphere that derives public value through an inverse relationship with the substantive characteristics of one's body. The "we" of American constitutional law's subject "We the People," according to Warner, is a subject whose voice achieves validity by exiling its own positivity.[5] For Michael Sandel, the historical trajectory of American constitutional law is away from more communitarian and republican traditions and toward an embrace of the "procedural republic"—a neutral liberal state that puts into practice the concept of rights as trumps for unencumbered individuals. Because of this trend in American constitutional law, the nation is unable to address properly the problems that afflict it. As a result, the fabric of the community is unraveling. For Mary Ann Glendon as well, the liberalism of American constitutional law, resting as it does upon the unencumbered individual, erodes the social bonds that allow a community to address its collective problems.[6] While these scholars perceive the disjuncture between liberalism and their preferred concepts of the good life, they neglect the way that the practice of rights not only challenges certain modes of collective life, but also helps to reconstitute positive forms of social identity.

The foundational texts of the liberal tradition and American constitutional discourse should make us hesitate before claiming that the liberal subject is disembodied. Indeed, these texts attach cultural meanings to bodies, and prescribe different forms of government and freedom to those differently engraved bodies. We must be very deeply invested in the "repressive hypothesis" to fail to accord proper significance to J. S. Mill's introduction to "On Liberty." There, Mill contrasts a "civilized community," by which he means a community that is racially white, that is ready for the benefits of liberty to those "backward" societies where "the race itself may be considered as in its nonage." For those non-Western societies for which liberty is inappropriate, Mill states that "despotism is a legitimate mode of government in dealing with barbarians."[7] Furthermore, to the degree that the British working class seemed to approximate less the norms of civility and more the identity of the non-Western savage or barbarian, to that extent it lost its voice in the polity through his scheme of representative government with weighted votes. In Mill's work we can see how the rights of subjects necessitate the production of subjects for rights.[8]

Critics of liberalism rarely acknowledge how a discourse of rights can be productive of social formations that sustain the recognition of rights. In particular, critics of American constitutional law's liberalism fail to recognize how invoking legal rights not only disrupts, potentially, certain social relations, but also incites the production of the social basis that can lend authority to one's claim of right. This point becomes more clear as we examine the discursive rules of claiming rights in the specific context of American constitutional law.

Rather than locating sovereignty in the state, the U.S. Constitution is a reflection and creation of a new, governmentalized sovereignty—the American people. The rights guaranteed by the Bill of Rights are properly understood as the "rights of the people." The First Amendment, for example, protects the "right of *the people* peaceably to assemble. . . ." When one claims a constitutional right like freedom of speech, one is interpellated as an American. This is not, however, an instance of a passive subject being acted upon or repressed by power. One gains a subject position that allows conduct. One seeks to invoke this form of discursive power in order to gain recognition as one who exercises a right to free speech legitimately. In the moment of claiming a right, one also hails others as the American public with the aspiration that this call will incorporate a public that will recognize the practice in question as an instance of "free speech" rather than as a social problem that must be governed differently to promote the welfare of the people. In this process much depends upon which elements that might constitute America are constellated together, which are cast off, and if a given articulation can foster a self-recognition in one exercising judgment. Finally, much depends upon what sort of an identity the law fixes upon the one claiming a right.

To claim a right like freedom of speech is to seek to incorporate one's self into the American people. For example, Martin Luther King, Jr., mobilizes a national discourse in support of equal rights for black Americans. Speaking at the Montgomery bus boycott, King begins: "We are here . . . because first and foremost—we are American citizens—and we are determined to apply our citizenship—to the fullness of its means."[9] King continues: "If we were incarcerated behind the iron curtains of a *communistic* nation—we couldn't do this. If we were trapped in the dungeon of a totalitarian regime—we couldn't do this. But the great glory of *American* democracy is the right to protest for right."[10]

In the process of embodying an American people that will authorize a right to protest and the goals of the civil rights movement, King aligns his American identity through the construction of an outside—communist totalitarianism. Being branded with the identity of "communist" is perhaps the most effective way to delegitimate the claims of the civil rights movement during this period since communism is "un-American."[11] So, while the invention of the "American people" enables the possibility of claiming rights, "America" is distinguishable only by virtue of relations of difference—what is not American. American constitutional rights become recognizable through constitutive limits.

If constitutional rights are not as disembodied, abstract, or universal as they are sometimes theorized to be, then they cannot be as alienating or fragmenting as some communitarians fear.[12] Communitarians, construing rights as trumps for the isolated liberal individual, view rights as antagonistic to the social relations that hold together the community. Based upon an isolated individual, rights are hostile to the cultural make-up of actually existing persons. As an antidote to the detrimental effects of liberal rights, invocations of "our" tradition or current condition flow easily from the pens of communitarians. Privileged moral obligations constitute "us" as subjects and "we" must recognize this.[13] Somehow, these deep identities lie below the vagaries of cultural change and struggle. Failing to recognize or acknowledge the essential contestability of the image of community upon which their arguments rest, communitarians do not understand legal rights to be a form of cultural production in the context of a society that is internally incomplete.[14] To adjudicate a question of rights is, in some measure, to adjudicate the identity of the American people and the requirements that flow from this identity.

Thus, questions of rights are not opposed to the centrality of a national or racial "people" in contemporary politics. Indeed, the practice of rights under current conditions reproduces forms of national power. Therefore, rather than continuing to argue that rights alienate "us" from our fundamental social identity, we should borrow a page from foucauldian scholarship that challenges a narrowly repressive understanding of power with the insight that who we are is a contingent achievement that must always be reachieved in face of doubt. In relaying this insight to the arena of legal studies, we must comprehend law as one space within which such achievements are made, contested, and enforced. Moreover, we must be sensitive to the way that juridical rights have become thoroughly governmentalized in the American context. That is, legal rights have become a mechanism for the reachievment of national authority (in contrast to the conventional view of understanding individual rights as standing opposed to nationalism). While the constitution of a national people is the condition of possibility for American rights, this social entity is given new force whenever individuals cite their rights under constitutional law. As a form of power, claiming constitutional rights links a technology of the self with macro-level government, exemplifying Foucault's insight that the power of governance in contemporary society is both individualizing and totalizing.[15]

Social Discipline: Empowering Public Subjects

Although the U.S. Constitution is a critical intervention that shifts sovereignty and legal rights toward the people as their ultimate referent, the implications of this shift emerged gradually and unevenly. For instance, through the early twentieth century, U.S. constitutional law permitted governments to treat public places much as a homeowner would treat his living room. That is, if someone should say something that the owner did not like, the owner could kick the speaker off his property. This legal reasoning derived from the older perspective that the state is sovereign over public places much as the homeowner is sovereign over his place. During the 1930s, however, a change occurred. The Supreme Court's rulings began to recognize more fully the implications inherent in making the people sovereign.

In *Hague v. CIO* (1939), individuals associated with the Committee for Industrial Organization (CIO) complained that the government of Jersey City refused to allow any public meetings within the city to discuss the National Labor Relations Act. The individuals argued that these actions by the city government violated their rights of "free speech and peaceable assembly secured to them, *as citizens of the United States*." The Court ruled in favor of the CIO, and, in so doing, diverged from the line of legal precedent that had permitted state governments to exercise ultimate authority over public places. Instead, the Court argued that "[c]itizenship of the United States would be little better than a name if it did not carry with it the right to discuss national legislation and the benefits . . . to accrue to citizens therefrom." Marking this revolution, the Court argued that public places are "held in trust for the use of the public." Public places, Justice Roberts stated, are to be used for the purposes of "communicating thoughts between *citizens*, and discussing *public* questions. . . . The privilege of a *citizen* of the United States to use the streets and parks for communication of views on *national* questions . . . must not . . . be abridged or denied."[16]

Hague v. CIO continues the process of decentering sovereignty from the state to the people by empowering individuals to discuss national issues as citizens of the United States, and by empowering persons to claim these rights as American citizens. In this way, the Court opens up a subject position that enables these acts, although such conduct is constrained by the necessity of acting as an *American* subject. By entrusting government to the people, problems of discrimination and capacity emerge. That is, there must be some sign by which the American people can be identified and distinguished from other possible social identities. Additionally, the capacity of the American people for self-government must be cultivated while those social problems that endanger these powers must be regulated for the nation's security. In sum, relevant subjects must be produced.

Disciplinary institutions are key mechanisms by which national subjects are created, subjects who will be capable of self-government.[17] The 1986 case of *Bethel School District v. Fraser* displays the relationship between the production of national subjects and the exercise of constitutional rights. In this case a high school boy is punished by a public school for giving a speech laden with sexual innuendo. The Court rejects his argument that the school's disciplinary action, based on the content of his speech, violates the First Amendment. In *Bethel*, the Court argues that the "role and purpose of the American public school system . . . [is to] prepare pupils for citizenship in the Republic." To constitute these subjects, it "must inculcate the habits and manners of *civility* as values in themselves conducive to happiness and as indispensable to the practice of self government." The Court states that in order to educate America's youth for "citizenship," schools "must teach by example the shared values of a *civilized* social order. . . . The schools . . . may determine that the essential lessons of civil, mature conduct cannot be conveyed in a school that tolerates lewd, indecent, or offensive speech." The Court disposes of the student's contention that his right to free speech is violated with the argument that he is not yet an American subject who can make a legitimate claim to First Amendment rights.[18]

Tracking Mill's argument that savages have no claim upon inter*national* law or morality because they are not yet civilized, hence not *nations* properly understood, the Court indicates that education institutionalizes the civilizing process that leads to American national subjectivity as its *telos*.[19] The sexual nature of Matthew Fraser's speech merely proves his lack of civility or decency, and it constitutes him as a social problem that demands regulatory reform in a civilized social order. *Bethel* therefore presents the significance of decency or civility as a sign of American subjectivity. It is a form of self-governance that America demands of its subjects who are to be entrusted with a right of free speech. As we can see, being civilized is a necessary form of self-discipline for those seeking incorporation within the American body politic as a civilized social order. Civility thus plays the double role of being both a technology of self and a rule by which the American people governs itself. It links self-discipline with the regulation of a population.[20]

Government by Discussion

From within a society that fashions itself as civilized or decent, the meaning of civility or decency as social norms may appear neutral if not necessary for society's future. When placed in historical context, however, the racial content of these norms surfaces. The meaning of a civilized identity is given through its opposition to those who are savages or barbarians.[21]

Historically, the terms decency and civility or being civilized have been used interchangeably. The terms refer to the social importance of outward bodily propriety. Treatises on manners tell one how to govern every aspect of bodily relations in a way that conforms to the norms of civility or decency, from snot on the nostrils, to how to sit, greet, drink, dip one's fingers into the broth, how to fart, whether to greet a man taking a shit by the side of the road, how to share one's bed, or how to deal with questions of nudity and sexuality. Certain forms of self governance are cultivated for appearing in public, before the eyes of others, that are different from what one might do when not in public.[22] The treatises foster specific technologies of self, practices of the self that articulate with larger changes in the social order between the Middle Ages and modernity in Europe. Although a treatise like Erasmus's of the sixteenth century might use wolves or peasants as negative points of reference to inspire self discipline, by the eighteenth and nineteenth centuries, civilization gathers meaning in relation to those peoples the West is driven to colonize.[23] Thus, civility gives specific content to the norms by which American subjects like Fraser are disciplined and gives specific cultural meaning to the American body politic.

Civility in nations that interpret themselves as part of Western civilization thus becomes significant in its opposition to the savage or barbarian of the non-West. It is also intimately concerned with the regulation of the body; in particular, its sexual regulation. Decent sexual practices often act as a sign of the racial progress embodied by Western civilization. While civility and decency have long provided the context for the regulation of sexuality in the West, the particular prominence in American law and politics of sexual propriety today may be symptomatic of a national reformation since the end of the Cold War.[24] The American nation today may be haunted by different demons than at mid-century.[25] Instead of mapping its place in the world according to the logic of Communism and anti-Communism, America today seems to understand itself according to the more overtly racial logic of the West versus the Rest.[26] The ever-frequent sexual disputes that occupy the national attention are indicative of this reconstellation of the American national formation. This shift is both manifested and reproduced in contemporary legal discourse.

Legal scholarship has taken renewed interest in the conceptual break produced by the American Constitution regarding the question of sovereignty, and what this means for governance.[27] These interpretations of American constitutional law work to produce a particular culture of liberal rights. They incite technologies of self as they seek to educate their readers on the meaning of their rights and how they are to be exercised responsibly. The forms of social discipline that inhere in the liberties these texts extol emerge clearly through an examination of the hymns of praise recently sung to one element of the liberal tradition, the concept of "government by discussion." If we trace the genealogy of "government by discussion," we shall learn how rights adhere to specifically encultured subjects, rather than abstract individuals. That is, women must confine their sexuality to the patriarchal family while men and women must be heterosexual with moderate sex drives. These forms of decent self-control and civilized social organization are indicative of Western civilization's racial progress. They are the conditions that make for the productive exercise of speech rights.

Cass Sunstein is a leading constitutional scholar who has written extensively on free speech and has become a familiar face through his legal commentary on CNN during the impeachment of Bill Clinton. According to Sunstein, one "of the most important liberal innovations [is] the commitment to 'government by discussion.' " For Sunstein, the "placement of sovereignty in 'We the People,' rather than the government, may well have been the most important American contribution to the theory of politics." By locating sovereignty in the "People," the U.S. constitutional system "carried important lessons for freedom of speech. It created an ambitious system of 'government by discussion,' in which outcomes would be reached through broad public deliberation."[28]

Sunstein believes that current American law "protects much speech that ought not be protected. It safeguards speech that has little or no connection with democratic aspirations and that produces serious social harm." Sunstein advocates in favor of "distinctive protection to political speech," and a system that is "readier to allow regulation of nonpolitical speech." One example of the sort of contemporary free speech problem that the system must solve, and which he invokes repeatedly, is the problem of "nude dancing" at the "Kitty Kat Lounge."[29]

Sunstein refers his readers to Samuel Beer for a fuller understanding of what is meant by the concept "government by discussion." Beer, in *To Make a Nation*, argues that the American Constitution, and the Anglo-American constitutional tradition in general, is guided by rational deliberation or "government by discussion," a concept he borrows in turn from Walter Bagehot. Beer, paraphrasing Bagehot, argues that "government by discussion" is opposed to the

> typical "parley in a traditionalist society . . . which dealt with particular 'undertakings.' " In government by discussion the interchange took place on a higher plane of generality, dealing with "principles" under which many particulars could be classed. . . . In this process, Bagehot saw the central expression of the rational spirit of modernity. . . . In his Darwinian scheme, government by discussion greatly added to the survival power of a society, enabling it to surpass and overcome other societies still stuck in the "cake of custom."[30]

Walter Bagehot begins the chapter in *Physics and Politics* that introduces the concept "government by discussion" by stating that the "greatest living contrast is between the old Eastern and customary civilizations and the new Western and changeable civilizations." The passage that Beer paraphrases, when he distinguishes the "parley" of traditionalist societies stuck in the cake of custom from the principled discussion of modern and progressive societies, makes the racial division that constitutes government by discussion explicit through its devaluation of the speech of racial subordinates: "But the oratory of the *savages* has led to nothing, and it was likely to lead to nothing. It is a discussion not of principles but of undertakings."[31]

For Bagehot, one sign of racial backwardness is female sexual activity outside of patriarchal governance.[32] In fact, he places a premium upon harnessing female sexual agency to the patriarchal family. Bagehot makes the patriarchal family a precondition for government by discussion, which in turn leads to further progress. According to Bagehot, certain conditions can be "traced to the nation capable of a polity, which suggests principles of discussion, and so leads to progress." His primary condition is patriarchal marriage, which he argues makes home education and discipline both "probable and possible." For Bagehot, "while descent is traced only through the mother, and while the family is therefore a vague entity, no progress to a high polity is possible."[33] Nations are formed from this patriarchal base. The aggregation of patriarchal families makes clans, and the aggregation of clans makes nations.[34] Upon this foundation, the capacity for discussion arises.

Bagehot is concerned to regulate the sexual agency of women in order to serve the goal of nation-building, which in turn provides the social conditions for government by discussion. Sexuality, however, must be normal along potentially infinite additional dimensions according to this scheme. In particular, Bagehot argues that a specific economy of sexual desire indicates civilized progress. While in less civilized contexts the most successful races are those that can reproduce fastest, in the context of Western civilization the reverse is true. Bagehot states that where "exceptional fertility exists there is sluggishness of mind," and he goes on to argue that there is "only a certain quantum of power in each of our race; if it goes one way it is spent and cannot go in another." Furthermore, because "nothing promotes the intellect [as opposed to sexual desire] like intellectual discussion, and nothing promotes intellectual discussion so much as government by discussion," Bagehot argues with delightful Victorian indirection that "free government has . . . been shown to tend to cure an inherited excess of human nature." Thus, "two things which seemed so far off have been shown to be near."[35] The capacity for being a speaker and producing speech is created through a strict discipline of sexual desire, while discussion in turn regulates sexual desire, thus reproducing the conditions for free speech. In a broad sense, therefore, government by discussion describes a set of *economic* relations that reproduces a national people capable of exercising its rights of free speech. This liberal subject is hardly abstract. Indeed, Bagehot demonstrates great concern over the constitution of the rights bearing subject.

While Bagehot uses this economy of sexual desire as yet another proof of England's superiority over the savages of the "East," and seeks to instigate greater self discipline amongst its population, there are seeming differences even within the "West." Bagehot manages these by fixing such differences in a particular class of people and by locating this type of person within urban space.[36] He then uses these forms of difference to incite his audience to govern themselves properly through the haunting association of difference with the savage. Bagehot argues that "the lower classes in civilized countries, like all classes in uncivilized countries, . . . lack a *sense* of morality." He states that a "walk in London," to witness the "great sin of great cities," is all that is necessary to establish the truth of his argument.[37]

Government by discussion uses race to think social difference, sexual deviance to signify racial alterity, and sexual normality to represent the possibility of free speech. Sunstein's use of the term narrates the American people as part of Western civilization, an identity formation constituted in racial opposition to the savage or barbarian of the non-West. The semiotics of government by discussion represent who shall count as a speaker. As a system of governance, it seeks to cultivate the formation of subjects who will, in turn, produce the correct effects by their exercise of speech rights. Through normalizing strategies of comparison, Bagehot inspires technologies of self—practices upon one's self and knowledge of one's self—that make one's interpellation within this regulatory framework seem somehow reasonable.

As with Bagehot's representations of excessive sexuality, Sunstein's references to nude dancing that pepper his texts also serve to represent "ungoverned" sexuality inappropriate to a civilized society.[38] This legal discourse incites technologies of self similar to those incited by Bagehot. Indeed, Sunstein argues that "government should . . . be allowed to maintain a *civilized* society" by "guard[ing] against the degradation produced by . . . obscenity," and he endorses the Supreme Court's decision in *Barnes v. Glen Theatre* to uphold a public decency statute that forbids non-obscene nude dancing by Darlene Miller at the Kitty Kat Lounge.[39] In sum, Sunstein's free speech scheme furthers a strict discipline of signifying practices involved in the construction of subjectivities, and then provides for protection of the speech produced by authorized subjects.

Decency's Genealogy: Contemporary Legal Regulation

"A modern city can deteriorate into an urban jungle with tragic consequences to social, environmental, and economic values."

—Justice Lewis Powell, concurring in the Supreme Court's *Young v. American Mini Theatres* decision (1976) upholding the regulation of the sex industry

In light of the prominent attention in liberal legal discourse to the production of subjects who exercise rights, we must reject as "too easy" any analysis of constitutional jurisprudence on sexual expression that relies on the premise that liberalism fosters a repression of the body, and hence of sexuality. We would do better, I suggest, if we focus our attention on the specific socio-sexual subjects that American law constitutes. To this end, I will examine the patterns of justification for the regulation of sexuality.

Justice Stevens argues that the First Amendment reflects the "profound national commitment to the principle that debate on public issues should be uninhibited, robust, and wide-open." Yet he also argues that society's interest in protecting indecent sexual expression is of a "wholly different, and lesser, magnitude than the interest in untrammeled political debate." If we were to understand the liberal rights protected by the Constitution to refer only to an abstract individual, these statements of law might seem to contradict one another. On one hand, Stevens appears to protect the neutral principle of freedom of speech for anybody, while on the other he seems to advocate the repression of speech for those who wish to express themselves sexually. Former Chief Justice Earl Warren provides the key to understanding the compatibility of Stevens's assessments of First Amendment law in a way that links back to *Bethel*'s distinction between subject formation and freedom of speech, as well as the reemerging interest in government by discussion. As Warren argues, governments can regulate obscenity in order to maintain a "decent" society.[40] The right of free speech is protected for American subjects. American subjects, however, are identified by their decency. The regulation of decency cultivates subjects who can then exercise the rights of self government while controlling indecencies that threaten the body politic.

The problem with an indecent or obscene expression is not that it refers to sexuality. Nor is the problem one of maintaining a boundary between a disembodied public sphere and the private sphere to which the body's particularities are confined. As Justice Brennan puts it, "Sex . . . is one of the vital problems of human interest and *public* concern."[41] The problem is that indecency is a sexual practice that is improperly governed. The norms that define properly governed subjects are those of civility and decency, norms that are given content by the cultural context provided by Western civilization. The Supreme Court's opinion in *Ginzburg v. United States* demonstrates the importance of regulating sexuality to promote a civilized racial identity, and the important link between this racial identity and the right of freedom of speech.

In *Ginzburg v. United States* the Court upheld Ralph Ginzburg's obscenity conviction although the materials he distributed were not literally obscene in themselves. The materials, which included articles and photo essays on the subjects of love, sex, and sexual relations, were marketed to appeal beyond professional therapeutic and social science circles to the prurient interests of the general public. For soliciting interest in these publications without discrimination, Ginzburg was convicted under a federal obscenity statute. In other words, Ginzburg's crime was not to possess or to disseminate obscene materials. His crime was to incite the production of improperly governed subjects through a misuse of sexual expression that, if it had been used to reinforce the norms of civility, would have been perfectly legal.

Brennan sums up the Court's judgment:

> The works themselves had a place, though a limited one, in anthropology, and in psychotherapy. They might also have been lawfully sold to laymen who wished seriously to study the *sexual practices of savage or barbarous peoples, or sexual aberrations;* in other words most of them were not obscene per se. . . . However, in the case at bar, the prosecution succeeded . . . when it showed that the defendants indiscriminately flooded the mails.[42]

Brennan uses the discourse of Western civilization versus the savage or barbarian to describe and contain sexual difference. Insightfully, he also understands that a text receives its meaning and value through the economy of its circulation and use. In this case, the circulation of the texts does not discriminate—it is "indiscriminate." This lack of discrimination constitutes the social problem that demands regulation because it threatens to erode the difference that sustains the American people. Should the materials have circulated in a way that represented the sexual difference of savage or barbarous peoples as a deviation from the social norms that mark the progress of Western civilization, then they would not be found obscene. In other words, Ginzburg's crime is not that he engages in sexual expression. His crime is to threaten the constitution of civilized American subjects by inciting alternative sexual interests.

As we have seen, a close reading of First Amendment law demonstrates a great deal of concern for the American body politic. It culturally constitutes and regulates the national subject as the substantive referent for rights. Recent concern over public decency also shows that these contemporary struggles over legal rights do not pit an unencumbered individual against the social norms of the community so much as they present contrasting views of the commitments that follow from the embodiment of the American subject as decent and civilized.

Barnes v. Glen Theatre is a key Supreme Court precedent on public decency that supports Giuliani's sex war in New York City.[43] In *Barnes*, Darlene Miller, with several other women and clubs such as the Kitty Kat Lounge, challenged Indiana's public decency statute for preventing nude dance performances. The Court in *Barnes* overturns federal appellate decisions finding for the dancers and upholds the Indiana statute. Chief Justice Rehnquist's plurality opinion refers to the Indiana state supreme court decision *Ardery v. The State* as a source of meaning for the law.[44]

Ardery involves one Henry Ardery, who, in a public place, made an indecent exposure of his person. Decency, according to Indiana's supreme court, involves concealing from public gaze the sight of one's "privates." Adam and Eve's example of "covering their privates," the court goes on to argue, "has been imitated by all mankind since that time, except, perhaps, by some of the lowest grades of *savages*."[45] As we can see, decency refers to a proper governance of one's body and to the norms of the public. Thus, the genealogy of Indiana's legal interest evinces concern for the racial embodiment of the public subject.

Barnes was extensively discussed at the appellate level by two well-known judges, Judges Posner and Easterbrook. Although they disagreed on the question of whether nude dancing is protected by the First Amendment, they shared a common understanding of America as an instance of Western civilization while negotiating this landscape differently. Posner defends the dancers by linking nude dancing to the protection of Western high culture, while invoking America's difference from the "Orient." Posner reminds the

American people that "public performances of erotic dances debuted in Western culture in the satyr plays of the ancient Greeks." Additionally, Posner demonstrates a concern for Western high culture by stating that a "rule cannot be laid down that would excommunicate the paintings of Degas."[46] Posner recognizes the right claims for free speech at issue in the case by locating the American people within Western civilization.

In addition to establishing a vision of the public in which nude dancing fits, Posner argues that the regulation of nude dancing would be un-American if America is understood as an instance of Western civilization. He holds up a mirror to the public for it to recognize itself. The mirror is a reference to the "Islamic clergy," whom "most of us do not admire." He again holds up the mirror so that the American public can see "a morals police patrolling the streets of South Bend with knouts, like the Saudis."[47] By evoking incongruous images like a Saudi in South Bend, he encourages the American public to recognize the regulation of nude dancing as out of place within a civilized America.

Easterbrook dissents from the appellate court decision and argues that the state should be allowed to regulate nude dancing. During the mid-1980s, Easterbrook invoked the specter of "totalitarian governments" and located the right to propagate opinions as "one of the things that separates our society from theirs" in ruling against an anti-pornography ordinance.[48] With the waning of the Cold War, however, a new field of vision and new problems emerge. Easterbrook now territorializes America within Western civilization.

Using the category of class, Easterbrook differentiates reasonable and responsible citizens from undisciplined and ungovernable subjects. As did Bagehot, Easterbrook then links the tastes of the lower classes with the practices that Western civilization considers normal to other spaces, thereby justifying the demand for their regulation within America. He contrasts "sophisticates" who go to museums or the opera with "Joe Sixpack" who may want to see "naked women gyrate in the pub." Easterbrook articulates these class-based divisions of value to a racialized frame of reference in his concluding point: "Darlene Miller wants to impress the barflies so they will ply her with drinks. . . . We may doubt the wisdom of requiring women to wear more clothing in the bars of South Bend than in the *Folies Bergère* or on the beaches of Rio de Janeiro without concluding that Indiana has exceeded its powers under the Constitution."[49]

Easterbrook justifies constraining the performance of female sexual agency by arguing that the regulated dances would be more appropriate to places that signify exoticism, racial hybridity, and sexual licentiousness. In so doing, Easterbrook distances nude dancing from the norms of Western civilization. This makes the claims of the dancers upon American constitutional rights look anomalous and out of place. Moreover, he justifies the regulation of nude dancing by denying the patrons and dancers First Amendment standing by assimilating their existence to the social problem of excessive consumption of alcohol.

While Posner and Easterbrook differ over whether Darlene Miller has a right under the U.S. Constitution to dance nude, they agree that the norms by which the American people are recognized are those provided by Western civilization. They interpret differently the commitments that flow from this initial recognition, however. Thus, Posner's argument that Miller has a right to engage in nude performances does not depend upon an unencumbered rights-bearing individual. Both his arguments and Easterbrook's rely upon encumbering the American subject within the cultural predicament of Western civilization. The American people, empowered by the Constitution to claim a right to free speech, is embodied through the norms of Western civilization and its difference from the savage or barbarian.

Conclusion

Critics of America's liberal constitutional law and its radiating effects condemn this legal formation for its focus on legal rights that are said to function like trump cards for disembodied subjects against the rest of society. According to these critics, liberal legal rights force real persons to repress their fundamental identities, alienating themselves from their true selves, in order to play by liberalism's rules. Moreover, through a misconceived focus upon a disembodied individual, rights-claiming does not allow sufficient attention to the good of the community, the community that makes individuals who they are. Such formulations lead us to understand the problem of maintaining community norms such as decency as a distinct or opposed question to the individual right of freedom of speech.

These criticisms of America's liberal legal practices neglect the specific ways in which American subjects are substantively embodied within liberal legal law. As I have argued here, rights like freedom of speech are protected under the American Constitution as rights reserved to the people. Therefore, claiming a right protected by the U.S. Constitution requires one to invoke a specific American imaginary and claim it for one's self. By claiming a constitutional right, one incorporates one's self within the American body politic.

The American Constitution, by locating sovereign power within the people, trusts that the people will be able to exercise those rights necessary to its self-government. The capacity of the people to exercise its rights must be nurtured and threats to its civic qualities contained. This capacity is produced through a regulatory concern over the civility of the American people. Today, the public's heightened attentiveness toward sexuality as a social problem afflicting the body politic is manifested in an intense focus upon civility and decency. This calls up the racially significant discursive space of Western civilization to provide the means for understanding America's social problems and those values that are most at risk. Through the regulation of civility and decency, American subjects are produced who can claim their constitutional rights and are capable of self-government. As Matthew Fraser, Ralph Ginzburg, and Darlene Miller learned, civility is a capacity that is a necessary precondition to gain standing in the eyes of the First Amendment.

the cultural turn in marxism

JUDITH GRANT

In *Achieving Our Country*, Richard Rorty criticizes the Left for moving away from politics and activism, and moving toward cultural studies. He is particularly peeved by art and cultural criticism that inspires shame in America.[1] Rorty considers this a "disaster for the reformist Left,"[2] and attributes it to Marxism. He argues that Leftists should stop doing theory and begin to try to mobilize pride in America.[3] The Left should talk about "real" things again.[4] I think that Rorty is right to say that cultural studies began with Marxism; or at least, with a certain version of Marxism. I do not think he is right when he says that cultural studies is politically irrelevant or intellectually impoverished. I think he is wrong when he counterposes cultural studies to the "the real politics" of reformism. Herein I would like to show how and why Marxism turned to culture, and why cultural studies is an enterprise worthy of the attentions of political theorists.

The Frankfurt School and its fellow travelers are largely responsible for Marxism's turn to culture. I shall refer to these thinkers collectively using the term coined by Max Horkheimer, "Critical Theorists." Critical theory itself began as a response to historical events beginning with the Second International and culminating in World War II. Specifically, Marxism's cultural turn is related to totalitarianism (both National Socialist and Stalinist), and the rise of what was once termed the military-industrial complex in the United States (including the use of the atomic bomb and imperialism).

For Critical Theorists, totalitarianism triumphed even after the war to the extent that consciousness itself was successfully colonized by an ideology that supports the interests of the powerful. It does this by making them appear not as the interests of someone in particular, but as a universally true "reality," or as "common sense." As Marcuse wrote, " 'totalitarian' is not only a terroristic political coordination of society, but also a non-terroristic economic-technical coordination of society which operates through the manipulation of needs by vested interests."[5] From the point of view of this reality, any idea that challenges what is taken for "truth" is viewed as irrational. It is irrational not to reproduce the society, and only that which reproduces the society is taken as rational. "The movement of thought is stopped at barriers which appear as the limits of Reason itself."[6]

Reason thus collapses into what Marcuse called "technological rationality." In that mutilated system of thought, technological rationality masquerades as Reason. Thought comes to be defined only as an instrument of maintaining the status quo; i.e., thought becomes *techne*. In contrast, the progressive edge of Reason is fundamentally critical and linked to imagination, speculation, dissent, and justice.

The transformation of reason into technological rationality became visible in World War II through things such as the use of science in the development of the atom bomb, the utilization of bureaucracy, logistics (and so on) in the performance of the Final Solution, and the use of surveillance technologies in Germany, the United States, and the Stalinist USSR. While World War II becomes the occasion for Critical Theorists to reflect upon this transformation, Horkheimer and Adorno readily acknowledge that reason has always held the possibility of its opposite immanent within it. This is, of course, the famous dialectic of Enlightenment.[7] Ultimately, Critical Theorists looked to culture as a potentially uncolonized space where the most progressive aspects of reason might be stirred and alternatives might be imagined. Culture had the potential to reinvigorate the moribund critical elements in reason and to move humanity away from the totalitarian impulse and back toward democracy. This is, for them, the essence of what we now call cultural studies.

Totality and the Critique of Scientific Marxism

Marx and his contemporaries saw socialism as a natural outgrowth of the principles and politics of the Enlightenment. Marx, especially, understood socialism as a radical extension of the democratic principles of the bourgeois revolutionaries into the realms of economics and the life-world. Insofar as socialism could be brought about, the bourgeois promises of freedom, equality, and humanism would at last be concretized and universalized.

As is well known, Marx did relatively little in terms of making the moral or ethical case for socialism. He spent far more time in analyzing the features of economics, epistemology, consciousness, and politics that might make the transition away from capitalism occur. His readings of Hegel and Feuerbach led him to conclude that both materialist and idealist philosophies were flawed, each for not taking account of the world as described by the other. His solution was a materially grounded version of Hegelian dialectics. Only this would be capable of comprehending the world in its "totality."

As Martin Jay has argued, Critical Theorists relied heavily on the term "totality."[8] In their hands, it referred to that entity wherein subjects and objects interact dialectically. Totality is meant to describe the space wherein subjects (actors) and objects (that which is acted upon) mutually constitute one another in the context of an ongoing stream of time. Marx and the Critical Theorists use "subject" and "object" in the generic Kantian/Hegelian sense such that there is no fixed meaning for either term. Something that is a "subject" under one circumstance can be an "object" under another.

For the purposes of this chapter, the best example of the subject/object relation is Marx's explanation of the proletariat that is both a subject and an object. It is an "object" in the sense that workers are constituted as commodities in capitalist relations of production. One can know objectively who is a worker and who is not simply by determining whether or not one sells ones' labor power. Workers are objects in another sense as well in that they are constituted as such under conditions of capitalism. Marx writes that "labourers, who must sell themselves piece-meal, are a commodity, like every other article of commerce and are consequently exposed to all the vicissitudes of competition, to all the fluctuations of the market."[9]

The "subjective" side of the proletariat is manifested in consciousness when the worker knows herself to be a worker. In this instance, the subject refers to rational self-reflection, while object refers to the material and historical reality of the proletarian class. This example illustrates the way in which subject and object are fluid, each embodying elements of the other. Subjects need not be classes but can be individuals, groups, consciousness, and so on. Marx, of course, believed the proletariat to be *the* "Subject" of history in the sense that he believed it to be the single agent capable of truly changing history in that particular epoch. This does not mean that he did not speak of other kinds of subjects.

Critical Theorists read Marx to be saying that "subject" and "object," posited by Kant and others as irreconcilable dualisms, are actually implied in each other. We can take the reductivist example of the so-called "chicken and egg" question as a crude example. Which came first, the chicken or the egg? That is to ask, do subjects (say, chickens) create objects (eggs) or do objects yield subjects? The dialectical answer is that the question itself falsely poses a positivistic opposition between subject and object, as well as a linear and discrete relationship between cause and effect. The dialectical answer is that eggs presume chickens and vice-versa. That is, they exist in tandem, and one cannot conceptualize a chicken (which is, in reality, a bird that lays eggs) without conceptualizing an egg (and vice-versa). To do so is to engage in abstraction (i.e., to pose a world where chickens do not come from eggs).

That both "come first" should not be taken to mean that each does not exist as a distinct entity. Dialectical thinking does not tend to collapse the subject into the object, but to maintain that they exist together in a holistic relationship that is continually transforming. Totality is intended as a vehicle for understanding the whole. Thus, concepts of both "Ideas" and "materiality" are inherent in the term, as are dualisms such as "theory and practice," "individual and community," "human and world," and so on. As the analogy of "chicken and egg" illustrates, theory does not cause practice, ideas do not cause materiality, production does not cause consumption; each is always implied in the other.

If we were to take the example further, we could see that arguments about cloning and so on do not negate its usefulness as an example, but merely allow us to illustrate another aspect of dialectics. The nature of chickens changes as the conditions under which chickens exist change. Leaving the barnyard and returning to Marx, technological innovations (object) transform humanity (subject). Simultaneously, it is the nature of human beings to create technologies; that is, to create both objects and themselves.

We can now turn to a more complicated example from the introduction to Marx's *Grundrisse*. Marx takes pains to show that production and consumption are two moments in the same process. He writes that "consumption is twofold, subjective and objective."[10] In producing, one must also consume (e.g., in industrial production one is consuming natural resources). In consuming, one produces (e.g., in nourishing one's body, one produces the body). Further, "consumption posits the object of production ideally, as an inner image, as a need, as an impetus, and as a purpose. It creates the object of production in a form which is still subjective."[11] In this example, production and consumption, subjects and objects, shift position, each being the cause of the other, sometimes being an object, and sometimes a subject. At the same time, the entire relationship is transformed according to history (a term which, for Marx, includes geographical location); the object of consumption "is not an object generally but a specific object which must be consumed in a specific way, a way (to be) mediated again by production itself. Hunger is hunger, but hunger which is satisfied with cooked meat eaten with a knife and fork is a hunger different from that which devours raw meat with the help of hand, nail and tooth."[12] In this way, Marx argues that the interrelationship between subject and object exists across time. "A Negro is a Negro. He only becomes a slave in certain relations." We might add that we now know he is only a "Negro" under certain conditions as well. Marx continues, "A cotton-spinning jenny is a machine for spinning cotton. It becomes capital only in certain relations. Torn from these relationships it is no more capital than gold in itself is money or sugar the price of sugar."[13]

Totality denotes the contingency of historical and geographical location, and is meant to imply that dualisms do not stand hypostatized in opposition to one another, but are part of the same whole. The terms of dualisms are invoked, therefore, to prove that they do not exist *as such*. Critical Theorists referred to this complex and contingent relationship as "totality" and not simply "reality" in order to stress the relational aspects of it. Thus, the term is an anti-positivist one. Furthermore, it resists the notion that either half of the whole constitutes the sum total of the real. They resist the term "reality" since it is their claim that what is called the real is, in fact, no more than the trump used to stifle critique, by hierarchalizing the above speculations about what could be. Totality is meant to encompass both "what is" and the latent possibilities for "what could be." Reality, in contrast, is merely the dead ideas of a past generation which we are now doomed to reproduce because we can no longer conceptualize an alternative.

If totality was central to Critical Theory, dialectics ("the method") was even more so. Georg Lukács can be credited with elaborating on the importance of the method and totality, and for initiating the Marxist cultural turn. He wrote that *authentic* orthodox Marxism "does not imply the uncritical acceptance of the results of Marx's investigations. It is not the 'belief' in this or that thesis, nor the exegesis of a 'sacred' book. On the contrary, orthodoxy refers exclusively to *method*."[14] For Lukács, the very purpose of theory was to criticize the existing totality in an effort to aid the political effort at transformation. Theory in and of itself was, as Marx had charged repeatedly, mere metaphysics, and, as such, worthless. As theory was tied to action, so thought was tied to practice. Therefore, the notion of a "truth" that existed apart from material reality became either absurdity or ideology. This did not mean that truth did not exist. Rather, truth was contingent upon its ability to become real. As Bertolt Brecht was fond of saying, "The proof of the pudding is in the eating." Hegel put it more esoterically in a phrase often recalled by Critical Theorists: "the real is rational and the rational is real."

The question of truth becomes crucial in Marxism insofar as Marx (like other thinkers from the Enlightenment) tied it to universality. For them, truth must, by definition, be true for all. But since truth is not merely an abstract idea, it is also tied to the point of view of the universal subject who can concretize it. Marx argued that the proletariat was just such a universal subject. The proletariat could only rid itself of its dismal condition by also ridding everyone else of his or hers. In this way, the proletarian perspective that appears to be particularistic (i.e., that appears to belong to members of the proletariat class alone) is universal. It is universal in that its point of view, if acted upon, would solve universal problems related to "necessity" and would enable the concretization of universal "freedom" for the first time in history. The problem was that the proletariat had to be constituted as a class "for itself." That is, it had to know itself to be a class and act on its own interests, as opposed to internalizing the point of view of that formerly revolutionary class, the bourgeoisie. That the proletariat did not (for the most part) do this explains why a huge proportion of Marxist theory is devoted to the problem of "false consciousness."

For Lukács and others, the political problem became, how can one act politically on behalf of the proletariat when it is not yet constituted as a self-conscious revolutionary agent? Could one aid the proletariat in so defining itself? For Lukács, the answer was to take the point of view that one believed the proletariat would take *if* it were constituted as a class. Lukács wrote that "it becomes possible to infer the thoughts and feelings which men would have in a particular situation if they were *able* to assess both it and the interests arising from it. . . . Now class consciousness consists in fact of the appropriate and rational reactions 'imputed' [zugerechnet] to a particular typical position in the process of production."[15]

Culture, specifically art, would be crucial in helping the proletariat to see its place in the totality. For Lukács, it was the form of epic realism that would enable the proletariat to recognize its class position and objective circumstances. Lukács's notion rested on the largely Hegelian premise that one could not always perceive one's situation authentically. Or, to put the matter in Hegelian terminology, one could not perceive one's situation "immediately." One needed "mediation." There had to be (and was) a mediation between subject and object that would enable the subject (in this case, the proletariat) to reflect rationally on its situation as against merely "being" in it. For Lukács, culture provided such a mediation.

The centrality of "totality" in Lukács's work was self-consciously understood both by him and by others as an alternative to the base/superstructure model of dialectical materialism associated with Lenin and Leninism.[16] Thus in 1924, the Soviets condemned Lukács's *History and Class Consciousness*, ultimately leading Lukács to recant his own ideas from that work.[17] It is in this perverse form that we can see the beginnings of the split in Marxism between political economy (as reflected in Leninists) and cultural studies (as written about by Lukács). The political economists of the period stressed the role of objective circumstances, while Lukács, as the major representative of a nascent Left cultural studies, stressed the role of consciousness, subjectivity, and philosophy. Stalin's dismissal of Lukácsian-style dialectics can be traced to his admiration of Lenin. On an epistemological level, Lenin substituted the vanguard, the Communist party, for what Lukács had called the "standpoint" of the proletariat. This radically undercut the democratic possibilities of the Soviet revolution and foreshadowed the authoritarianism of Stalin: If the vanguard could "stand in" for the proletariat, Stalin could stand in for the vanguard.

Where Lukács's early work had stressed the mutual interaction and constitution of subjects and objects, Lenin and his followers took the view most firmly espoused by Engels, that the objective circumstances (economics) determined the subject (consciousness). As Engels wrote, "From this point of view the final causes of all social changes and political revolutions are to be sought, not in men's brains, not in man's better insight into eternal truth and justice, but in changes in the modes of production and exchange. They are to be sought, not in the *philosophy*, but in the *economics* of each particular epoch."[18]

Some communists reasoned that if the objective circumstance determined consciousness, it could be concluded that changing them, no matter what one's method, would create socialist consciousness. It was conceivable that the period of socialism, the dictatorship of the proletariat, wherein humankind was to learn how to govern itself democratically, and from whose form the state would wither away, could be forcibly introduced. Moreover, since the proletariat was not yet constituted in Russia as a class "for itself," the vanguard could step in and, as per Lukács's own analysis, act in its stead by imputing class consciousness. Lenin wrote that "the dictatorship of the proletariat"—that is, the organization of the vanguard of the oppressed as the ruling class for the purpose of crushing the oppressors—"cannot produce merely an expression of democracy. . . . [It] produces a series of restrictions of liberty in the case of the oppressors, the exploiters, the capitalists."[19] The proletariat still needed the state, Lenin argued, to crush capitalism, after which the state would wither away as Marx had predicted. However, in light of Stalin, Lenin's famous dictum—"While the state exists there is no freedom. When there is freedom, there will be no state"—takes on a wildly different meaning.[20]

Lenin's claims about the nature of imperialism proved useful in legitimating Stalin's regime. Where Marx had argued that the socialist revolution had to be worldwide, and that in some countries the revolution might be nonviolent, Stalin countered that the advent of imperialism made both violence and "socialism in one country" necessities. Capitalism had to be attacked, as Lenin had argued, at the weakest link in the chain. This explained how a relatively less developed country might have a socialist revolution before a relatively more developed one. Moreover, the dictatorship of the proletariat now accomplished through the vanguard's and Stalin's alleged abilities to impute class consciousness and act on that basis would simply go on indefinitely. "Does this mean," Stalin wrote, "that all that is required is to assume power, to seize it[?] . . . The whole point is to retain power, to consolidate it, to make it invincible."[21]

On an epistemological level, the Lenin/Stalin strategy emphasized the "objective" elements of consciousness. In short, both stage theory and the base/superstructure model suggested to them that if the historical conditions changed, so would the people. Even apart from the more idealistic Critical Theorists, that view did not prevail among the entire international Communist movement. Rosa Luxemburg and others lamented the choice the Bolsheviks had made to forsake democracy in favor of party rule. She argued that the "dictatorship of the proletariat" was not properly understood as a mere instrument of terror against the bourgeoisie. She reminded them that the socialist state also had the important function of teaching public spiritedness and self-governance to the workers. For Luxemburg, Bolshevik-style socialism was the antithesis of socialist democracy. "The public life of countries with limited freedom is so poverty-stricken, so miserable, so rigid, so unfruitful, precisely because, through the exclusion of democracy, it cuts off the living sources of all spiritual riches and progress." In a true socialist democracy, "the whole mass of people must take part in it. Otherwise," she declared prophetically, "socialism will be decreed from behind a few official desks by a dozen intellectuals."[22] Against the notion that vanguardism was what Marx meant by the dictatorship of the proletariat, she pleaded, "Exercise a dictatorship, but a dictatorship of the class, not of the party. . . . That means in the broadest public form on the basis of the most active, unlimited participation of the mass of the people, of unlimited democracy."[23]

As Stalinism gathered momentum in the USSR, the Nazis began the trek to power in Germany. Though Germany was no stranger to the Right, the development of capitalism and the potential for democracy in the Weimar republic must have seemed hopeful signs to Communists of the period that Germany was indeed progressing toward socialism. This was especially true given modernist theories about progress and teleology. Indeed, the onset of totalitarianism was shocking to those on the Left who had convinced themselves that socialism naturally followed from capitalism and bourgeois democracy. To their dismay, the Nazi case showed that capitalism could go retrograde and slip into the abyss of moral relativism and state terror. This, combined with technocracy and imperialism in the United States, and the disaster of the so-called worker's state to the east, correctly raised serious questions about the role of objective circumstances in the creation of radical consciousness.

Critical Theory, Consciousness, and Culture

Although Critical Theory is represented by a diverse set of theoretical perspectives, several things can be said about it across the board. First, it represents a deepening of the Lukácsian tendency to turn away from political economy and toward culture. As such, it is also a turn away from the "scientific" Marxist ideas of Lenin and Stalin. In asserting that consciousness does not spring up whole from the world, and in rejecting a base/superstructure model, critical theorists returned to the dialectical *method* as outlined by Lukács. They did so without adhering to his conclusions about imputing class consciousness. Second, insofar as they did not adopt a deterministic view of human consciousness and action, Critical Theory is about politics in a way that deterministic Leninism cannot be, since if one's consciousness and actions are preordained, politics as such becomes a meaningless notion.

Lukács's views, coupled with those of the young Hegel and the early Marx, lead them to begin from the premise that the world and human subjectivity are mutually constitutive. The turn to culture in Marxism is, thus, a by-product of the Critical Theorists' desire to comprehend the formations of subjectivity and knowledge according to this view. They conceptualized this, not as an abstract philosophical exercise, but as one that was crucially political. For them, what we now call "cultural studies" was directly related to the most heinous atrocities and failures of Europe and America in the mid-twentieth century. That is, socialism had not emerged from the Weimar Republic; Nazism had. Progress from capitalism to socialism was not inevitable. Socialist consciousness did not spring deterministically from objective conditions. The world was not moving in a one-way direction toward more justice and more democracy, as thinkers of the high Enlightenment seemed to assume. Though the Nazis were defeated, Critical Theorists believed that totalitarian consciousness lingered in the endless and grotesque reproduction of a reality devoid of imagination or radical change.

Consciousness was bounded by its own historical circumstances, but it was not determined by them. While it could, if acted upon, reproduce the world unchanged, it could also transform it. The political problem, then, was how to combat colonized consciousness to the extent that it had ceased to be speculative and transformative. Further, how did one analyze and combat oppressive ideologies when consciousness itself was saturated with them?

Critical Theorists now came to hold that totality encompassed different levels of the development of consciousness. As Adorno wrote,

> After the catastrophes that have happened, and in view of the catastrophes to come, it would be cynical to say that a plan for a better world is manifested in history and unites it. Not to be denied for that reason, however, is the unity that cements the discontinuous, chaotically splintered moments and phases of history . . . the unity of the control of nature, progressing to rule over men, and finally to that over men's inner nature. *No universal history leads from savagery to humanitarianism, but there is at least one that leads from the slingshot to the megaton bomb.*[24]

There was chaos in history, but nonetheless it remained united by a totality in the broadest sense of the term. "Totality" was now understood by Adorno almost as a heuristic device. In such a totality, "subject" was not identical to "object." In short, consciousness was not the deterministic outcome of history. In this way, Critical Theory returned to the position of the early Marx, who wrote in the third thesis on Feuerbach: "The materialist doctrine that men are products of circumstances and upbringing, and that, therefore, changed men are products of other circumstances and changed upbringing, forgets that it is men who change circumstances and that it is essential to educate the educator himself."[25]

If totality was not monolithic, as Lukács had contended, there could be no "true" way to represent it artistically. There was no single subjectivity. Rather, there were many subjectivities constituted within any given totality. While all are constituted under the oppressive conditions of modernity, some reproduce it, others challenge it from the point of view of the past, and a few challenge it from the point of view of the future. The future itself is indeterminate, however, and so even those who pose an alternative do not pose the same alternative. Thus, culture reflected both the world as it was, and the world as it could be, and it did so complete with all the various subjectivities that existed within a given totality. The danger in this is that "the absorbent power of society depletes the artistic dimension by assimilating its antagonistic contents. In the realm of culture, the new totalitarianism manifests itself precisely in a harmonizing pluralism, where the most contradictory works and truths peacefully coexist in indifference."[26]

Culture could be both a site of "non-identity" or of "identity." Culture that did not reflect the world as it was had the potential to show the world as it was not. In so displaying "negativity," it could instruct the world-weary subject in the art of the possible. "Art's utopia," Adorno wrote, "the counterfactual yet-to-come, is draped in black. It goes on being a recollection of the possible with a critical edge against the real; it is a kind of imaginary restitution of that catastrophe which is world history; it is freedom which did not come to pass under the spell of necessity and which may well not come to pass ever at all. . . . Art is the promise of happiness, a promise that is constantly being broken."[27] A more hopeful Marcuse wrote that "art contains the rationality of negation. In its advanced positions, it is the Great Refusal . . . the protest against that which is."[28]

Marxist cultural studies, as manifested in German Critical Theory, centered around the overall possibility of radical transformation through culture. Culture was the repository of the imaginary that had yet to be realized. In culture, there was hope. Since they were interested in consciousness, Critical Theorists were of necessity concerned with the role of the audience (or reader) in the cultural experience. Likewise they wondered about the effect of the commodity form on the very concept of art. Was culture the sole remaining space for alterity and speculation, as many of them came to believe? Or, was culture colonized by the commodity form and doomed to reproduce the steady "thump, thump" of the factory, as Adorno so often seemed to contend?

Walter Benjamin held down a position somewhere between these two extremes. For Benjamin, the commodity form had permanently transformed cultural expression, but that transformation had an indeterminate outcome. In what is probably his most famous essay, "The Work of Art in the Age of Mechanical Reproduction," Benjamin argued that technological reproducibility had a dual effect. By destroying its uniqueness in time and space, technology destroyed art's "aura," and thus the ability of art to reach beyond itself to the universal and to truth. But the very reproducibility of cultural artifacts made them democratically accessible. In effect, the entire concept of art was itself transfigured. He writes, "Earlier, much futile thought had been devoted to the question of whether photography is an art. The primary question whether the very invention of photography had not transformed the entire nature of art . . . was not raised."[29]

The capacity of technologically reproduced art to be truly critical, however, is always mediated by its status as a commodity. Marcuse agreed with Benjamin, writing much later, "It is good that almost everyone can have the fine arts at his fingertips by just turning a knob on the set, or by just stepping into a drugstore. In this diffusion, however, they become cogs in a culture-machine which remakes their content."[30] Benjamin was led to take a dim view of the possibilities for a radical cinema. "So long as the movie maker's capital sets the fashion," Benjamin wrote, "no other revolutionary merit can be accredited to today's film than the promotion of a revolutionary criticism of traditional concepts of art."[31] That is, capitalist ownership of the film industry created radical film critics, but very few radical films. On the plus side, Benjamin argued, technological reproduction does have the potential to transform the popular audience into critics and experts. That anyone can lay claim to being filmed or being a critic further democratizes the form, he contended. While the form mitigates against radical messages, it does not render such messages impossible.

Benjamin's essay illustrates the attention to which Marxist cultural critics paid to the impact of capitalism and its technologies on art itself. Even Adorno's well-known distinction between high and low art is only offered as evidence of this point. The argument is not, as is so often said, that Adorno privileged high art over low. His argument is that the distinction between high and low art becomes meaningless once the culture industry becomes hegemonic. Art itself is transformed as the culture industry commodifies even so-called high art. Adorno is more comfortable fixing the blame with capitalism rather than the more ambiguous and muddy "technology" to which Benjamin refers.

It is important to remember, though, that in both cases, art was being studied only insofar as it could further one's understanding of the impact of capitalist forms of modernity on consciousness and politics. The deepening commodification of the artistic realm had serious implications for its ability to function as the kind of mediation necessary to aid one in transformatively interpreting one's own experiences under conditions of capitalist alienation. Moreover, the possibility that culture retained some autonomy from the controlling influence of capitalism suggested it as a crucial site of resistance.

That the reader, the audience, or the watcher could be shocked out of their normal state of complacency and transformed into critics by technologically reproduced art made Benjamin optimistic. Adorno forcefully stated an opposing position, admonishing Benjamin, "The laughter of the audience at a cinema . . . I discussed this with Max [Horkheimer], and he has probably told you about it already . . . is anything but good and revolutionary; instead it is full of the worst bourgeois sadism." He concluded in a huff, "I very much doubt the expertise of the newspaper boys who discuss sports."[32] Why not take a look at what I am writing about jazz, he asked in conclusion. "I believe that I have succeeded in really decoding jazz and defining its social function," by "revealing its 'progressive elements' . . . as facades of something that is in truth quite reactionary. . . . Max was quite taken with [it], and I could well imagine that you will be too."[33]

Critical theorists continued to hold deeply to the belief that capitalism (and its more ambiguous sibling, modernity) was in large part responsible for the mutilation of the human spirit and the stultification of critical consciousness. Though Marx's critique of capitalism lurks behind all Marxist cultural theory, there was precious little discussion of the kinds of topics found in Marxist political economy. Class, labor, markets, and so on were not commonly discussed by the Critical Theorists, who confined themselves largely to studying what scientific Marxists would have called the "superstructure."[34]

Still, Benjamin in particular did experiment with employing the categories of Marxian economics (as opposed to Marxian dialectics) in analyzing culture. In "The Author as Producer," Benjamin suggests that the important question for political aesthetics is not a given work's attitude about its time, but rather its position in the relations of production.[35] Thus he sought to mimic the political economic notion that one's class position is determined vis-à-vis the means of production. Like class, art and the artist are determined by their places in the production process. To be in line with the goals of socialism, one ought to alienate the productive apparatus of art he argued, "from the ruling class by improving it in ways serving the interests of socialism."[36]

This, he believed, was being done in the theater by Bertolt Brecht. Through interruptions of the plot, Brecht sought the creation of a critical distance between the audience and the art form necessary to create didactic theater. His techniques of "estrangement" and his concept of "epic theater" responded to the ways in which capitalist modes of technology had transformed art. Employing methods developed primarily in film and photography (such as "montage"), Brecht attempted to radicalize the theater. In Benjamin's view, Brecht's theater constituted a move away from plot-centered works and toward forms that would call attention to the production of art—and production overall.

Adorno, by contrast, thought that Brecht was an economistic, unsophisticated thinker who misunderstood both Marxism and aesthetic theory. Taking the view that one had to assume a "bad reader," Adorno argued that Brecht's epic theater preached only to the converted. "Whatever is educational in Brecht's plays can be taught more convincingly by theory—if it needs teaching at all. His audiences were not exactly unfamiliar with insights like these: that the rich are better off than the poor; that the world is full of injustice; that repression continues amid formal equality, that private goodness turns into its opposite in a public context of objective evil."[37] Brecht's uniqueness lay not in his political commitment, but in the fact that the bombastic nature of his plays illustrated the disintegration of art. Art that was so didactic and preachy could not perform the very function that art had to perform if it were to be a counter-hegemonic force. It could not be a force for free thinking.[38]

Benjamin's work on the "aura" notwithstanding, Richard Wolin makes much of Walter Benjamin's and pre-Marxist early work, on the *Trauerspiel*. Wolin writes that the "profane" character of these German counter-reformation melodramas allowed Benjamin to show "the illusion of the Enlightenment vision of cumulative historical progress and its concomitant myth of the infinite perfectability of man."[39] This would have been of obvious importance to Critical Theory given that part of the project was to critique the notion of the inevitability of progress while retaining the idea of possibility. Benjamin's work on *Trauerspiel* did both. It showed how it was possible to read against the grain of a work of culture in order to reveal its message of transcendence and hope. Indeed, Adorno himself praised Benjamin's work in this regard.[40] The *Trauerspiel*'s tales of mankind's utter irrelevance and anguish could be read as exhortations about the absolute necessity of transcending one's circumstances into what the *Trauerspiel* was not. Employing the Marxist tool of immanent critique, Benjamin argued that works of art contained the seeds of their own criticism and existed entirely apart from the intent of the author.[41]

Adorno was less sure than Benjamin that a radical popular culture—or even art—was really possible at all under conditions of oppression. In any case, works of art should not be judged to be radical simply because of the political commitment of those who produced them. Writing to Benjamin about a different one of Benjamin's essays, Adorno said, "I feel that our disagreement is not really a discord between us . . . but rather that it is my task to hold your arm steady until the sun of Brecht has once more sunk into exotic waters."[42]

Conclusion

In the end, Adorno himself was left with a paradox. Art was the site of negativity, and thus the site of the conceptualization of all possible futures. Yet it itself depended upon interpretation by a consciousness that was colonized by a totally administered world. Further, the popular culture most accessible to the masses was the most commodified of all and, therefore, the most ideologically loaded. It did not reach beyond itself into the negative, but was merely a site of identity; that is, it reflected what is. Likewise, reason was a double-edged sword not necessarily tied to justice. Its opposite, irrationality, Adorno continued to believe was linked to various nihilistic slips into the abyss of which National Socialism was only the best and most recent example.

The riddle for Adorno lay in the fact that art, which was a major (if not the only) site for what Gramsci would have called "counter-hegemonic" thought, was itself a product of that hegemonic society. Moreover, culture's "message," if you will, remained dependent upon a consciousness that could interpret and act upon the vision of its negativity in a progressive way. Yet the only consciousness able to do this was itself being reproduced under conditions of unfreedom. These conditions made the development of the kind of critical consciousness necessary to understand art's utopian character dubious. In general, it rendered the critical consciousness of utopia *per se* equally remote. In terms of culture, Fredric Jameson writes that Adorno had no choice but to exhort us to "denounce culture (as an idea but also as a phenomenon) all the time we continue to perpetrate it, and perpetrate it while continuing tirelessly to denounce it. It is with culture as with philosophy, which famously 'lived on because the moment to realize it was missed.' "[43]

It would be completely inaccurate to conclude that Adorno's work overall represented the views of most Critical Theorists. Still, the debates they had with him and among themselves did not digress from several common points. They all agreed that cultural studies was a political project, and that both culture and theory played important roles in the possibility of critical thinking overall. As Adorno and the others stressed repeatedly, the work of Critical Theorists on culture was not merely *kulturkritik*. It was not engaged in the analysis of culture for the sake of the cleverness or elegance of the rhetoric. Rather, it made sense only as *ideology* critique; that is, as cultural criticism from the point of view of a critique of capitalism. The possibility raised by Critical Theory is that totalitarianism lingers on insofar as alternative modes of social organization become inconceivable. Cultural studies is the study of human possibility and political inaction, but at the level of consciousness.

action or distraction? cultural studies in the united states

PAUL APOSTOLIDIS

Primary Thoughts

The novel and film *Primary Colors* treat their audiences to a soap opera–like maze of betrayals, emotional crises, and scandalous plot-twists. They borrow from the real-life saga of personal calamities and trials that embroidered the 1992 Clinton campaign. Ultimately, the story confronts the viewer with a specifically political question: does politics in the United States matter anymore? And if it matters, how?

Primary Colors enters a political-cultural terrain where a twenty-year accretion of policy shifts in both parties has made the prospect of ideological investment in politics seem increasingly self-delusory for many citizens, even as alternative, culturally prescribed paths of political commitment have proliferated. The Reagan deficits, George Bush's retreat from the pledge of "no new taxes," Bill Clinton's health-care reform debacle and signing of the 1996 welfare reform act, and Bob Dole's refusal to bear the standard of the Christian right in 1996 stand out as only the most flagrant incidents in a pattern of actions by which Reaganite Republicans and the "new" Democrats alike have shown themselves to lack solid ideological moorings. Nonetheless, *Primary Colors* registers a historically distinctive sense that there is still reason to care about politics today, despite the evanescence of ideological commitment among leaders. Specifically, the story both reflects and reinforces the experience widely shared among Americans in the 1990s that politics is in fact a significant and durable element of everyday life, although it is embedded in everyday experience to a far greater extent through cultural mechanisms than through participation in political institutions.

Primary Colors reproduces this experience of the culturalization of politics in two ways. First, in formal terms, the plot converts scandals involving a sitting president's election campaign into the narrative material for a Hollywood blockbuster in an unprecedentedly frank and thorough manner, taking to an extreme the reformulation of political discourse as melodrama, a process pursued to lesser degrees by "serious" news sources and "soft" media alike.[1] Second, with regard to its content, *Primary Colors* explicitly insists that an emotional investment in mainstream politics is genuinely possible. It does this in a way, however, that defines political fulfillment less in the prospect of acting upon a substantive concern for the public good than in the satisfaction and security of (1) reaffirming racial, gender, and sexual differences, and (2) joining the cynical majority in accepting given political processes as they are rather than trying to change them. In short, *Primary Colors* confirms the historical sensibility that politics indeed has a vital presence in the everyday lives of Americans today—but *as culture*, above all as a source of commercial entertainment, a means for the stabilization of identities, and a mode of developing a diffuse and disillusioned acceptance of the *status quo*.

The recent growth of cultural studies as an intellectual movement in the United States likewise responds to this historical moment when politics has become a thoroughly cultural sensibility. As a genre, cultural studies makes this sensibility self-reflective in part by uncovering the dynamics of power that structure cultural phenomena, and thereby discovering political dispositions intrinsic in or suggested by these objects. By amplifying anti-feminist dynamics in an oedipal-patriarchal movie plot or transposing hip-hop sound textures into a figure for social activism, for example, cultural studies jars the refrains of American popular culture into a strange and more acutely political register.[2] Some work in cultural studies draws the political consequences of culture even more vigorously, however. It does this by forging connections between a given cultural object and a historically elaborated domain that transcends the boundaries of the object itself. When cultural studies critically analyzes the mobilization(s) of cultural objects within historical fields of political and economic struggle, it illuminates with particular intensity the high political stakes of cultural production and criticism.

The writings by bell hooks, Lawrence Grossberg, and Andrew Ross discussed below exemplify the capacity of cultural studies to take this additional, politically sharpening step. They provide insight into not only how power works within spheres of culture, but also how political action attuned to cultural modes of power might involve practices that subvert the culturalization of politics. Thus, while countless contributions to film studies criticize the class, gender, sexual, and racial dynamics of movies, hooks amends this endeavor by problematizing the relationship between text/image and political practice.[3] Similarly, Grossberg not only unveils the expressions of a postmodern consciousness within contemporary pop/rock but further explores the complicity of this music-culture with the hegemonic project of the new right. Ross, finally, undertakes a careful scrutiny of the class- and sexual-liberationist elements within Popular Front writings and pornography, and then joins this account with a critical interpretation of political intellectuals' responses to these phenomena.

Nevertheless, it is possible to ratchet up the political intensity of cultural studies beyond the level achieved even by these particularly influential, theoretically sophisticated, and politically oriented writings. *Primary Colors* obsessively reduces politics to the personal traumas of individual leaders. Cultural studies, in turn, persistently sidesteps basic issues regarding the purposes, methods, and justifications of political leadership. Cultural studies' reticence when it comes to theorizing political leadership and *Primary Colors*'s enthrallment with the persona of the political leader are thus two sides of the same coin, historically speaking, for neither imagines political practices in specifically political terms. That is to say, neither asks the question: what tasks are of primary importance for political leaders who take the politics of culture seriously, and why? Neither asks: what can cultural criticism suggest about the processes by which the responsibilities of political leadership should be distributed, and by which ordinary people may distinguish legitimate from illegitimate leadership? And neither asks: what criteria define successful political leadership, in the face of culturalized politics?

Cultural studies' reluctance to confront these questions originates in part in the failure of interdisciplinarism to achieve its potential—in the persistent and invidious segregation of the social sciences and the humanities. But it also stems from more profound social forces than those structuring the academy. The political silences of cultural studies reflect a "political-cultural contradiction of late capitalism," to adapt Fredric Jameson's phrase. That is, cultural studies' avoidance of fundamental problems of political leadership reflects the everyday experiences of post-Fordist capitalism of major segments of American society, for whom the latest stage of capitalist development has meant not an expansion but rather a diminution of economic and political agency. More precisely: just as postmodern culture in general witnesses to the quandary of attaining critical distance in relation to the totality of global capitalist society, so likewise does cultural studies in particular exhibit the political disorientation that this system generates, as the reconstitution of capital and the swarming of cultural forms transforms citizenship, social structures, and movement identities to block previous roads to a radical reconfiguration of political power.

Nevertheless, as Grossberg, hooks, and Ross illustrate and anticipate, it is still possible for cultural studies to chart the political bearings of culture with tenacity and specificity, and to break free from the formidable compulsion of the times safely to sequester radical politics within the realm of culture. Their theories help us to see the politics of *Primary Colors* from a diversity of critical angles, foregrounding the story's gestures to the new conservatism, its sexism and its racism—as well as its sexual liberationism.

They also provoke us to ask more pointed questions, however, concerning the precise contribution that cultural criticism can make to progressive, anti-racist, feminist, and sexual-liberationist political activism.

A final introductory note: any attempt to evaluate cultural studies in this country today must confront the thorny problem of defining what counts as "cultural studies." This is a problem, above all, because on this side of the Atlantic there is no institution comparable to the Birmingham Center in England, with which an association could serve as a convenient and accurate marker of writing in the field. Those who produce cultural studies in the United States are an interdisciplinary bunch scattered throughout a great number of unaffiliated institutions in widely varying geographic, sociological, and professional contexts.[4] Moreover, the field of authors who self-consciously describe themselves as participants in cultural studies, explicitly linking their endeavors to the paths charted by Stuart Hall and others in the United Kingdom, is too narrowly circumscribed to provide a sufficient sense of the various ways in which theorists in the United States today are probing the politics of culture.

In this essay, I concentrate on American theory that addresses the politics of commercial popular culture. Culture of this sort is a distinctly American contribution to the international culture of modernity and has served as a primary agent in the Americanization of the emergent, postmodern, global culture. Critically understanding its politics thus helps us to theorize the meaning and methods of radical struggle in the contemporary historical situation.

Grossberg and Politics That Matter

Theorizing the political significance of popular culture in a historically "contextualist and interventionist" manner is axiomatic for Lawrence Grossberg, whose monograph *We Gotta Get Out of This Place: Popular Conservatism and Postmodern Culture* (1992) stands as the most fully worked out and sophisticated critique of contemporary American popular music. Acknowledging his intellectual debt to British cultural studies, Grossberg elaborates his critical practice as follows:

> Cultural studies is not a theory of the specificity of culture; it does not assume that anything, especially culture, can be explained in purely cultural terms. It does not attempt to explain everything from a cultural point of view. Instead, it locates cultural practices in complex relations with other practices which determine, enable, and constrain the possibilities and effects of culture, even as they are determined, enabled, and constrained by culture. Hence, cultural studies argues that much of what one requires to study culture is not cultural.[5]

For Grossberg, the politics of culture thus hinges most crucially on the articulation of cultural experiences to extra-cultural phenomena.[6] More specifically, popular culture is political inasmuch as the "sensibilities" or "affective investments" that are derived from the experience of popular culture are discursively and practically joined to historically-specific ideologies and events. Ultimately, according to Grossberg, Americans do not simply consume popular culture or otherwise enjoy it in a purely instrumental way. Rather, they "live in popular culture," in the sense that popular culture is a vital component of a more general network of processes by which identities are constituted. It follows for Grossberg that the appropriate object of cultural studies is not simply popular music or any other cultural form *per se* but rather, additionally, the entire "cultural formation" in which affective investments, ideological discourses, and nondiscursive events are vectorally interconnected to produce a historically distinctive "accumulation or organization of practices," feelings, and ideas. Grossberg further insists that any cultural formation is the product of historical struggles rather than the necessary result of inevitable historical tendencies. By making these contestations transparent through the schematization of the contingent connections among popular culture and metacultural aspects of society, cultural studies discloses the spaces in which alternative articulations could be constructed.

We Gotta traces the mutations from the 1950s to the 1980s of what Grossberg names the "rock formation" in American popular culture. If the crisis-laden sensibility to which fifties rock answered was the impossibility of earnest devotion to the specific values of the postwar "liberal consensus," then by contrast the rock formation by the 1980s responded to the more dire sense that forming affective attachments to any ideological projects at all was no longer tenable. As Grossberg puts it, in its more recently reconstituted state the rock formation became centrally articulated to the "postmodern" sensibility. For Grossberg, the signal characteristics of this new sensibility were a generalized fear of commitment, a reflexive grasping for ironic distance, and the disposition to deny that distinguishing between reality and its images, or between authenticity and superficiality, matters. Through the simultaneous "proliferation of authenticities" in diverse styles (such as those of Bruce Springsteen, Sting, and Tracy Chapman) and celebration of "images of inauthenticity" (epitomized in an ironic mode by Madonna), the new rock formation's unapologetic incoherence mapped out a way of living in the postmodern moment. It provided "a site of investment in the face of the irrationality of any act of investment" and a motivation "to act in the face of the assumption that actions cannot make a difference."[7]

The paradoxes of the eighties rock formation, however—its ambivalent relationship to the postmodern sensibility, now embracing it, now taking flight from it—rendered this cultural system vulnerable to attack and cooptation by what Grossberg calls the new conservatism. For Grossberg, the new conservatism has sought hegemony by designating the postmodern sensibility as a "frontier" and then establishing sites along that frontier, above all the family, as the only places within the terrain of the social in which "caring" is possible. With regard to politics, in turn, the new conservatism lays less emphasis on the content of what it claims matters than on the simple fact of caring as such—for only the family is substantively worthy of affective investment. The new right thus has asked Americans "to make a commitment to commitment"; it "does not replace a lost source of optimism, but rather speaks directly to a desire for optimism in the face of the postmodern frontier."[8] Meanwhile, "living in" the new rock formation has helped to make this curious stance toward politics—a commitment that is at once excessively abstract and intimately felt—intelligible and workable in an everyday, practical sense.

Grossberg's analysis thus moves beyond an interpretation of the political dynamics inherent in rock culture by drawing links between the new rock formation's immanent features and the historical-political field where new-rock culture has been situated. When cultural studies does this, the political purchase of culture and cultural theory crystallizes with particular clarity. Indeed, Grossberg unwraps the ligaments joining popular culture to metacultural domains even further when he suggests the strategic function of the new conservatism in blocking the politicization of capital's global reorganization in the post-Fordist era. (For Grossberg, the new conservatism's bid to establish culture as *the* realm of political struggle strategically "creates a temporal and spatial demilitarized zone in which the political, social, and cultural energy of the U.S. is contained, enabling capitalism to confront its own crisis.")[9] Finally, Grossberg explicitly poses the problem of the migration of politics into spheres of culture, analyzing it as the result of the new conservatives' successful incorporation of the postmodern sensibility within their hegemonic project and observing the new rock formation's facilitation of this transformation.

But what exactly are the political imperatives that derive from Grossberg's interpretation of the new-rock cultural formation? How can experiencing and/or being aware of the political character of new-rock culture decisively influence efforts to resist the new conservatism? Sounding a theme typical of much writing in cultural studies, Grossberg insists that the political possibilities of popular culture are multiple, may well be counterintuitive, and are not determined in advance by the methods and technologies according to which commercial cultural products are designed, produced, and distributed. The new-rock formation, in other words, is not logically or necessarily bound to service the new conservatism. Yet when it comes to naming the transformative political commitments that might accompany an affective investment in the new rock formation, Grossberg's thinking becomes stubbornly vague. For example, at the climax of Grossberg's interpretation of the eighties rock formation, we read the following:

> Rock empowers people to act in the face of the assumption that actions cannot make a difference, even though it itself may no longer inscribe its own difference. Without a center, rock can only produce an endless mobility, spaces without any places, a paradoxical strategy by which people live an impossible relation to their own everyday lives. Rock will, by placing you within its own spaces, free you from the moment, but it will not promise any alternative spaces. It remains forever ensconced in its own reproduction of the very conditions of everyday life it once sought to transcend. But it still promises, however briefly and weakly, that there is something beyond everyday life.[10]

Here, Grossberg's wistful and melancholic musings leave opaque the alternative political valences of rock's mysterious "promise." Under what circumstances could rock "empower" groups that are systematically deprived of social power more than those representing white, male, affluent and/or heterosexual Americans? Under what conditions, and for whom, could the resolve to "make a difference" mean a commitment to transforming social and political power relations? It may well be *possible* for new-rock experience to stimulate a politics of resistance to the new conservatism. But precisely what should political leaders do to channel everyday experience in the new-rock formation into affective commitments to political action that effectively challenges the new right? How can leaders simultaneously convey a recognition of the very real postmodern crisis of affect—indeed, taking this crisis as a point of departure for political action—without merely mimicking the new conservatism in telescoping the political into the cultural?

Persuasive answers to these questions could probably be found, given a sustained effort to analyze a selection of specific phenomena within new-rock culture, including an account of their particular affinities to concrete political initiatives. Grossberg's work has motivated other scholars to carry out just this sort of critique in relation to new-right cultural forms, as illustrated by Linda Kintz's insightful discussion of the relocation of affective investment "directly and intensively into the sacred site of the family" by Christian right popular culture.[11] Kintz moves an important step beyond Grossberg by considering particular books, videos, and other paraphernalia of evangelical conservative pop culture at some length, and pointing out the specific contiguities linking such cultural phenomena as "Christian" sex manuals and Promise Keepers rallies to political initiatives by the Christian Coalition and the U.S. Taxpayers Party. Nevertheless, while Kintz thus provides a more vivid account than does Grossberg of how the new conservatism operates, and while her desire for America to "get out of this place" in which the new right holds sway is quite apparent, like Grossberg she does not clarify how a left-liberal politics of "passion" could be mounted without playing into the hands of its foes. Still, her project suggests that one promising way to work out this dilemma would be to engage individual elements of the new-rock formation and chart their connections to political projects with a similar *precision* to that with which she handles Christian right culture. Doing this might show just how "empowering" the rock formation is today or might become—and in what ways, and for whom.

hooks and Political Pedagogy

bell hooks's film criticism offers another model of careful, microscopic engagement with specific cultural phenomena, but in her case (as opposed to Kintz) the analysis is directed toward cultural forms that can more readily be seen as possible elements within a radical counter-hegemonic project. hooks's primary objective in her recent collection of essays, *Reel to Real: Race, Sex, and Class at the Movies* (1996), is to examine the political tendencies animating the aesthetic and textual characteristics of various films. hooks uncovers the critical edge in movies that many critics have dismissed as sexist and/or racist, such as Spike Lee's *Girl 6* and Mike Figgis's *Leaving Las Vegas.* She contends that in *Girl 6,* a film about the unfulfilled longings of a phone sex provider for an acting career and a committed love relationship, Lee successfully depicts the battle of women, especially black women, to "create a space" where their "sexuality and . . . sexual voices can speak freely."[12] For hooks, the character of Girl 6 eludes the stereotypes of victim and dominatrix (which, she argues, hobble Lee's earlier venture *She's Gotta Have It*), emerging instead in all her complexity and contradictoriness. Likewise, *Leaving Las Vegas* features a leading female character who asserts an "agency in relation to her body" that flies in the face of common stereotypes, and whose "refusal to be a victim, or an object without choices," constitutes a liberatory plot dynamic.[13] In contrast to Lee, however, Figgis ultimately stumbles into sexist banality in his movie: for hooks, this film acquires "a conventional, predictable patriarchal pornographic slant" when Sera is raped, for here Figgis "succumbs to the usual stereotypes and has the 'bad' girl punished."[14] Still, hooks contends, this retreat from the film's more daring forays does not entirely mute the movie's politically and spiritually transcending message that a woman's "surrender" to love can be "conscious," "an act of choice," and "a gesture of agency and power."[15]

It is crucial to note that for hooks the politics of film is more than simply a matter of aesthetics—that is, more than a question of the formulaic or innovative composition of characters and plots. Like Kintz and Grossberg, that is, hooks does not confine her critique to the interior features of cultural forms but situates the politics of these forms within a metacultural terrain. She thus insists that films have a "pedagogical" function that can only be realized in the interactions of viewers after the house lights come back on, and perhaps in a distinctly political sphere. hooks explains this notion as follows: "Movies not only provide a narrative for specific discourses of race, sex and class, they provide a shared experience, a common starting point from which diverse audiences can dialogue about these charged issues."[16] This is a promising start toward clarifying the practical implications of affirming that "changing how we see images is clearly one way to change the world."[17] Still, it is only a start, and ultimately hooks has far more, of a much more specific nature, to say about the films themselves than about their mobilization in transformative pedagogical contexts. Again, key questions regarding political leadership in a context informed by cultural criticism remain unaddressed. How would one (or many) set in motion a pedagogy of popular culture that would be both critical and political? What modes of organization would such a project entail? How should responsibilities for motivating "dialogue" and carrying out the political endeavors which would presumably be the fruits of such conversation be distributed? A political theory of popular culture would benefit from asking these questions, knitting the meticulous criticism of narrative and text to a more robust conceptualization of political leadership as pedagogy.[18]

Ross and the Political Intellectual

Andrew Ross's essays in *No Respect: Intellectuals & Popular Culture* (1989) move into especially fertile territory for analyzing the politics of pop. Ross hones in on the problem that hooks and Grossberg tentatively acknowledge but sidestep: leadership, or the task of forging alliances between political intellectuals and groups of ordinary people. In *No Respect*, Ross examines a number of missed opportunities to exercise such leadership. One of these missed opportunities involved liberal intellectuals' contemptuous reception of the published correspondence between Ethel and Julius Rosenberg while the two were imprisoned. For Ross, the "dialogue between culture and politics" that the Rosenbergs carried on in their letters manifested a genuine "ideology of the people's culture," the organic and critical consciousness of the "lower middle class constituency of the Popular Front."[19] But while the letters "helped to mobilize thousands of readers" who recognized in them their own passions and modes of address, their potential political force was lost upon "Cold War liberals." Ross argues that by dismissing the Rosenberg communiqués as "cultural Stalinism," these intellectuals let pass a moment when a new, radical historic bloc could have been formed. Why did liberal leaders like Irving Howe fail to perceive this opening for transformative action? According to Ross, liberals misrecognized the political import of the Rosenberg letters, and of their enthusiastic reception by a large readership, because doing otherwise would have meant "taking popular culture seriously . . . as a terrain on which political meanings could be won or lost."[20] For Ross, political-intellectual leadership therefore requires an openness to forms of cultural expression that may not fit into conventional genres, and an effort to listen carefully for currents of resistance that others—especially those who are not elites—have already set in motion.

Ross sees a recapitulation of postwar liberals' posture of disrespect in more recent feminist sallies against pornography. For Ross, anti-porn intellectuals mistakenly assume that the response of the porn consumer is "simply determined in advance by what he is offered in the way of images."[21] Above all, Ross argues, writers such as Susan Sontag, Gloria Steinem, and Catherine MacKinnon fail to see that experiences of pornography are mediated in complex ways by the different contexts constructed by varying "markets of consumption." For example, the market in videos generates the context of home-viewing, where technical controls like fast-forwarding allow for diverse and individualized enjoyments of pornography. In a Foucauldian vein, Ross stresses that complex and multivalent effects of power are set in motion by the contested constitution of pornographic pleasures, and that pigeon-holing pornography as just another subsidiary of a repressive culture industry overlooks more local and less puppet-like exercises of power. The commodification of sex may therefore have "liberatory" potential for "sexual minorities."[22] Through reflecting upon these and other frequently overlooked uses of pornography, as well as listening to the proliferating organizations fighting for the political rights of sex workers, Ross contends, intellectuals can avoid "perpetuating the weary circuit of victimization and redemption" of ordinary people who are presumed to be incapable of speaking for themselves, and add their labors to genuinely transformative causes.[23]

Unlike the other theorists, then, Ross focuses on particular responses to popular culture by leaders who have had opportunities to turn the enjoyment of popular culture into a catalyst for political action. The trouble begins when one attempts to sort out and at least minimally harmonize the varying visions of political action that Ross appears to hold. Following Gramsci, Ross deliberately takes an expansive view of what it means to be an "intellectual," drawing explicitly though loosely upon Gramsci's concept of the "organic" intellectual and including under the category of intellectuals figures ranging from Lenny Bruce to Amiri Baraka to Andrea Dworkin. In his eagerness to rid his critique of all "vanguardist" traces, however, Ross creates no minor confusion as to the kinds of political practice that he expects from intellectuals.[24] Sometimes, it is a matter of writing for a public in its "own" language, while at the same time participating in political party activity, as in the case of Ethel Rosenberg. At other times, however, as with Bruce, being an intellectual can mean engaging in art/performance that crystallizes certain political polemics and attitudes, defending one's "right" to do so in legal courtrooms, and becoming the focus of a cult following without, however, doing anything to make that following into an organized and goal-directed collectivity. Finally, Ross elsewhere depicts the work of intellectuals as essentially academic, for instance when he stresses the need for an expanded "inquiry" into the multifarious "forms and discourses of popular pleasure," including "a properly audience-oriented study of pornography as a traditional 'men's genre.' "[25]

When Ross stretches the limits of what it might mean to be an intellectual, the emphatically political sense of that term thus gets lost. In its place we find a mélange of Gramscian, Foucauldian, and liberal resonances—that is, politics as the organized struggle for hegemony, exemplified by the creative alliance between the free jazz and Black Power movements; politics as the unplanned and transgressive experimentation with various uses of pornographic pleasure; and politics as the defense of individual and minority rights, attained through legal and legislative petition. But these do not add up to a political theory of culture. Such a theory might reasonably ask: which of these strategies should take precedence for leadership that is both attuned to the political dynamics of culture and committed to achieving concrete objectives?

Post-Fordism and Political Obscurity

How are the evasions of core political problems by American cultural studies to be explained? The most obvious solution to this puzzle would be to argue that cultural studies theorists have allowed their thinking to be boxed in by the disciplinary division of labor in the American academy. In the United States, cultural studies emanates from English, media studies, women's studies, and film studies departments, but rarely from departments of political science.[26] The questions posed above regarding the "who" and "how" of political action are not central to the mundane business of these scholars in their teaching and professional interactions, and are consequently less likely to find their way into cultural studies texts. The same dynamic of market-propelled specialization helps to explain, in turn, why so few conventionally trained political theorists have contributed to cultural studies in the United States. Most American political theorists focus on liberalism. Moreover, the most common hermeneutical approach to the history of political theory involves liberal assumptions regarding subjectivity, agency, and the role of philosophy in society. Thus, political theorists tend not to problematize the relationship between politics and culture, and they thereby sidestep the central interest of cultural studies.

Perhaps, however, the reason for the reticence of cultural studies on political matters also lies with social conditions that are less immediately felt (by academics) than the academic division of labor. Cultural studies is at root a species of postmodernism. Thus, insofar as postmodernist aesthetics and cultural criticism in general can be grounded within a historically specific constellation of social circumstances, a similar relationship pertains to cultural studies. Jameson has analyzed postmodernism as an expression of recent, systemic developments in capitalism: multinationalism; the elimination of "enclaves of precapitalist organization" in what has been known as the "Third World"; and the overshadowing of machine technologies of production by technologies of reproduction as the dominant technological forms within the mode of production.[27] Particularly as a result of this last transformation, in turn, the "new global space" of late capitalism is characterized by not only the geographically worldwide penetration of multinational capital but also the saturation of everyday life with cultural representations. As Jameson puts it, post-Fordist capitalism has witnessed the "prodigious expansion of culture throughout the social realm, to the point at which everything in our social life—from economic value and state power to practices and to the very structure of the psyche itself—can be said to have become 'cultural.' "[28] In turn, the "moment of truth" in postmodernism consists in its figuration of this transformed, global totality.[29] For example, the ebbing of individual affect and fragmentation of subjectivity characteristic of postmodern culture reflect the evaporation of intellectual vantage points offering critical distance on society, given the world system's unprecedented complexity and the superabundance of cultural signification.

The political silences of cultural studies likewise express the contemporary confusion of (embodied) consciousness in a rapidly reorganizing and not-quite-cognizable global economy, "a network of power and control" that is exceedingly "difficult for our minds and imaginations to grasp."[30] When cultural studies stops short of fully realizing the political potential of cultural criticism, it registers the disintegration of borders and differences by multinational capital and the explosion of the cultural throughout the social. Under these historical circumstances, political activists lose their bearings: their sense of who their "organic" constituencies are, where the most obdurate barriers to political transformation reside, and how political organization may most successfully proceed. In such a predicament, cultural criticism and cultural struggle recommend themselves as the paths of least resistance for those who embrace the general cause of resistance. But these historical incentives do not in themselves preclude the possibility of clearing a way through the current political obscurity, rather than tip-toeing around it, by thinking through the hard questions of hegemonic (or pedagogical) leadership in a way that strategically accounts for the culturalization of politics without accepting it at face value.

This said, it does not follow that cultural studies in the United States ultimately does nothing more than ape the gestures of power. To the degree that cultural studies has yet to confront core issues of political leadership, cultural studies and *Primary Colors*—which fetishizes the leader as an object of personal, sexual attraction—are obverse aspects of a single historical situation. Yet the theories of Grossberg, hooks, and Ross can also help us to reflect critically on the politics of *Primary Colors* and to show how it both feeds and contests the new conservatism. Seeing how this works thus offers a vivid sense of just what is at stake in the bending of cultural studies in this country toward a new preoccupation with leadership in politics.

Reading and Resisting the Politics of *Primary Colors*

Primary Colors (the movie) adapts to the screen the novel by "Anonymous" (later revealed to be journalist Joe Klein), providing a fictional account of Bill Clinton's 1992 presidential campaign.[31] The story is told from the point of view of Governor Jack Stanton's campaign manager, Henry Burton. Burton, a *wunderkind* professional who still retains more than a trace of moral idealism, is patterned after George Stephanopoulos, except that Burton is black. Through Burton's eyes, the audience watches the candidate withstand the buffetings of a series of scandals: revelations of an extramarital affair with his wife's hairdresser, charges of evading the draft for service in Vietnam, and, most sensationally, accusations of having fathered the unborn child carried by the daughter of Fat Willie, a black barbecue chef from Stanton's home state. The candidate's—and Burton's—climactic character test comes toward the end of the film, when Burton and Libby Holden, the campaign's covert intelligence operative, obtain evidence that Stanton's only remaining rival for the nomination, the apparently squeaky-clean Freddy Picker, has a secret past involving a cocaine addiction and sexual trysts with male dealers. Burton declares his resignation from the campaign following his utter disillusionment when Stanton shows neither compunction nor hesitation in his intent to use the damaging information to his fullest advantage. Nonetheless, Burton appears to have reconciled with his boss at the film's close, after Stanton has had a slight change of heart and given the evidence of scandal to Picker rather than the press, thereby ensuring Picker's voluntary withdrawal from the race and his own successful conquest of the nomination.

Grossberg's theory of postmodern popular culture as a response to the contemporary crisis of affect in everyday life offers a convenient and fitting framework for understanding the politics of *Primary Colors*. On the most immediate level, the film is about whether it is still possible to care about politics, or, more precisely, to become emotionally and cognitively invested in the electoral quests of major party candidates. Initially wary of becoming involved in the Stanton campaign, Burton's commitment is sparked when he sees the governor shed what appears to be an authentic tear after listening to an ordinary man's story of the humiliation he has suffered because he is illiterate. Burton's choice to join the team requires him to sacrifice a love relationship with a female activist who refuses to accept his plea that Stanton might really be the one—that is, the candidate who will genuinely "make a difference," the leader for whom people of goodwill have been longing ever since the murders of King and the Kennedys. Libby Holden's sacrifice is more fearsome: she commits suicide after Stanton and his wife reveal their true colors upon receiving the damning information about Picker and furnishing apparently irrefutable proof that the Stanton cause has at last run dry of (sixties) idealism. The hope for transcending the venality of political combat is represented not only by Holden but also by Picker, who shocks his opponents by refusing to run an ad campaign; instead, he crafts his message simply as a plea for the restoration of calm and reason in the electoral process. All three of these characters thus illustrate the desire for an authentic, personal investment in political life. Yet each in other ways confirms Grossberg's thesis that affective commitment in the postmodern condition is structurally impossible. For Picker and Holden there are ultimately no transcendences but only tragic exits. Burton's apparent reconciliation with Stanton, in turn, seems based on a resolve simply "to go on," as Grossberg puts it, despite the shattering of his ideals. Thus, like the new rock formation, *Primary Colors* allows the hope for transcendence to resonate fleetingly, while insisting that this wish be abandoned in favor of the resigned determination "to act in the face of the assumption that actions cannot make a difference."

Grossberg's theory not only facilitates these insights into the film's entwinement with the postmodern sensibility but also prompts us to see this dynamic as empowering, in the sense of enabling the viewer to salvage some capacity to feel that politics matters. But this is the limit of the theory's usefulness. For it begs the question of why political commitment should be valued at all, once we are forced to admit that there is nothing *substantive* left in politics that is worth caring about. In fact, *Primary Colors* empowers not so much ordinary citizens themselves as the institutions that depend upon citizens' depoliticization and disillusionment. Above all, it legitimates an electoral system that functions largely as an organizational consortium of corporate, party-bureaucratic, and professional interests and an ideological apparatus that encourages purely affective attractions to leaders. What might be genuinely empowering for viewers are hints that options exist besides simply adjusting to this apparently immutable reality. After all, proposals for electoral reform do exist that could make it more reasonable to grant or to withhold support for office seekers because of their substantive policy commitments, such as the removal of legal barriers to the successful competition of minor parties and the public funding of campaigns. Grossberg thus beckons cultural studies to seek further insight into how the affective investment in *status quo* politics that *Primary Colors* fetes could be rechanneled into political initiatives to democratize the electoral process.

If Grossberg's work enables us to interpret the politics of *Primary Colors* as an effort to stimulate emotional involvement in politics at a time when joining affect to ideology has become impossible, hooks prompts us to investigate how dynamics of race, gender, and sexuality in the film accentuate its legitimationist pull. For example, what representations of black women does *Primary Colors* provide? The most prominent black female character is Burton's initial lover. This character, an activist for a nondescript but apparently left-progressive black media organization, comes across as simultaneously dogmatic and cynical in her persistent ridicule of Burton's idealistic hope that Stanton might stand for real change. Her role is completely one-dimensional: unlike Burton, she is never shown to wrestle with the moral complexities of political involvement. Thus, when the film ultimately vindicates Burton's decision to let himself become attached to Stanton and coaxes the audience to imitate his example, this act of conformity has been predefined as an alignment that positions black women as political-cultural outsiders. In case one has any doubts, *Primary Colors* drives the point home by having Burton sleep with a white woman staffer after he joins the campaign and is rejected by his former partner. Immediately and gratuitously sexualized at the film's beginning, when she appears naked in bed with Burton, this black woman character is later ironically revealed as the ice queen who will not be seduced by the hope that Stanton signifies, and who blindly and coldly refuses the imperative to "care."[32] Dispensing with all subtlety, finally, this character is further villainized by being cast as a scandal-mongering journalist: it is she who first breaks the story of Stanton's affair with the hairdresser. In sum, in *Primary Colors*, empowering viewers to become invested in politics is inextricably linked to a positionality that holds black women in contempt.[33]

Such critical musings would seem to be appropriate elements of an effort to use *Primary Colors* as a pedagogical resource in the manner that hooks proposes. (In addition, the pedagogical refunctioning of the film could find additional and highly provocative material in the representations of white women, black men, working-class individuals, and sexual minorities here.) What sorts of organizations, however, formal or informal, are best equipped to turn pedagogy into political action capable of transforming the pervasive ideological and material other-ing of black women in American society? In what institutional contexts is critical dialogue about these matters by viewers of *Primary Colors* likely to be most fruitful—unions, universities, the Democratic Party, African-American churches, black women's cinema groups, or all of the above—and why? That we lack direction in answering these questions points to the political shortcomings of hooks's theory. That we arrive at the questions in the first place, however, testifies to the vital contribution that hooks's brand of cultural analysis makes.

Finally, Ross bids us to be on the lookout for missed opportunities to deploy a critical awareness of the film's subversive dynamics in the context of political leadership. *Primary Colors* frequently highlights sexual relations that contradict the norm of straight sex in each of its racial, heterosexual, and marital algorithms. Jack Stanton's liaisons with Fat Willie's daughter are mirrored by his wife's sexual betrayal with Burton (a transgression alluded to in the movie but treated more vividly in the book); as already noted, Burton's regular lover for most of the movie is a white woman on Stanton's staff. Another young female campaign aide winds up in a relationship with Libby Holden, after the former blithely ridicules a male strategist who exposes himself to her. Ross would have us inspect not only the film itself but also its cultural context. Here, the film's unconventional representations of sex and sexuality resonate with the unprecedented level of frankness in everyday conversations about sex, especially the traditionally taboo act of oral sex, that characterized public responses to the investigation of President Clinton's affair with Monica Lewinsky. True, much of the talk took the form of jokes and thereby evinced an abiding discomfort with the subject. And to be sure, *Primary Colors* does not hesitate to remind us that lesbian and gay love must never be thought of apart from death, addiction, and crime, through the downfalls of Holden and Picker. Nevertheless, the reimagining of lesbian, interracial, and oral sex as normal pleasures is an irrepressible element of the culture of scandal generated in combination by *Primary Colors* and the Lewinsky affair.

Ross's theory does not provide much guidance, however, for any effort to understand how this moment of liberation might comprise or be related to political change. Is it enough to see the political payoff of the scandal culture as the deployment of a new matrix of discourse and physicality, effective on the micrological level of individual bodies and precisely thereby realizing a significant transformation? Alternatively, do the politics of the popular culture of scandal take on a progressive hue when sexual minorities bring claims into the courtroom, their confidence in asserting their sexual rights bolstered by the thawing of public opinion about sexualities traditionally condemned as transgressive? Or is the point rather that somehow the sexual-cultural constellation involving *Primary Colors* and the Lewinsky scandal has the potential to nourish movements to increase public acceptance of lesbian, interracial, and oral sex, if political intellectuals are alert to the subversive dimensions of the popular? As Lauren Berlant argues, sex-radical politics needs a strategic vision that avoids the pitfall of unintentionally advancing the opposition's aims. Simply taking a stand in support of diverse sexual expression, for instance, underscores the current construction of citizenship around sexual practices and identities by the state and other social agencies and collaborates with the new right's withdrawal of a sense of public, responsible engagement from citizenship.[34]

Cultural studies today faces highly consequential choices in political strategy and therefore in political theory. It is tempting to try to elude this quandary by believing that theorists can reasonably draw unapologetically eclectic and multiple political lessons from each of the approaches to cultural studies considered above. But the problem with repeatedly deferring the task of thinking systematically about the political theory of culture that makes the most sense in light of historical circumstances is that it too easily legitimates a buffet-style political activism that is abruptly rendered powerless by the exceedingly well-coordinated and well-funded new right. This is not to say that the new right lacks for strategic diversity. Its constituents can weep at Promise Keepers rallies, join combat-shooting schools, tune in to James Dobson's *Focus on the Family* radio show, picket (or bomb) women's health clinics, work their neighborhoods and churches for the Christian Coalition, and/or petition legislators on behalf of "tax-paying families." But the new conservatism has also patched these pieces together into a movement that smoothes the way for ordinary people to catch a spirit of political activism and develop a desire to lead while they ponder the pros and cons of spanking toddlers, hone their riflery skills, and watch videos on how "cool" sexual abstinence is with their teenagers. It has linked enthusiasms of popular culture to organizational power centers in private corporations, voluntary networks, direct action groups, media projects, Republican Party committees, state legislatures, ballot initiative campaigns, and the national defense establishment. And it has done this largely by cultivating effective modes of political leadership—not the only possible kinds of leadership, to be sure, but highly serviceable and carefully fashioned ones nonetheless.[35]

Cultural studies in the United States falls short of its critical potential—and veers toward the apologetic position of *Primary Colors*—insofar as it evinces a celebration of politics that ultimately distracts efforts to theorize political leadership. This distraction cannot be overcome simply on the basis of will, for it has deep roots in global economic forces, the mark of which is born by postmodern culture in all its varied permutations. Nevertheless, theory that attends to the political lacunae in cultural studies' engagement of American popular culture gains the power to think what is forbidden by the neo-conservative historical bloc. That is the power to conceive of political action that rejects both the disillusioned embrace of politics as they are and the disjointed casting about for alternatives in favor of a genuinely hopeful, scandalously coherent, liberatory response to popular culture.

III. Generating Politics

democracy and national fantasy: reflections on the statue of liberty

LINDA ZERILLI

In the course of my work on the Statue of Liberty, I came across the following description of the Chinese "Goddess of Democracy":[1]

> For five days, between May 30 and June 4, 1989, visitors to Tiananmen Square in the center of Beijing witnessed an unusual sight. Standing close to one of the gates that opened onto the square was a statue of Styrofoam plastic and plaster, approximately ten meters tall, a chalk-white female figure draped in a robe, with her two arms thrust above her head holding a torch. . . . The Beijing statue was created by students who had organized a pro-democracy demonstration against the Chinese government, demanding political reforms and personal liberties. The statue symbolized the yearning for freedom among ordinary Chinese people; its resemblance to the Statue of Liberty was intentional, not accidental.[2]

The author of this account is Neil Kottler, program officer of the Smithsonian Institution, that hallowed guardian of America's cultural heritage. I found his mimetic conception of democratic symbolism in a book he coedited, entitled *Making a Universal Symbol: The Statue of Liberty Revisited*, published, appropriately enough, under the imprimatur of the Smithsonian.

In the 1989 U.S. context, Kottler's certainty of vision was hardly unique. Virtually every political commentator remarked on the astonishing resemblance of the female colossi, a likeness that gestured toward a common language of liberal democracy.[3] The universalization of this language had already been proclaimed in the very same year by the self-described neo-Hegelian Francis Fukuyama, and embraced by Americans eager to justify their way of life, as "the end of history." Read as part of that history, the Goddess of Democracy's resemblance to the Statue of Liberty was said to be so uncanny that she even had "Caucasian features and a large Western nose." Would it not "have been more appropriate for her to have Chinese features?" asked one reporter for the *New York Times*, only to conclude that "nobody seemed too concerned about such particulars."[4]

We can better appreciate the extent to which American accounts of the "Goddess with a Caucasian face" entail an interpretive act that affirms

Student activists work on the *Goddess of Democracy* at a campus near Tiananmen Square as the pro-democracy demonstrations continue. Reuters/Ed Nachtrieb/Archive Photos.

America's idea of itself as the model democracy destined for replication on a global scale if we consider the following, rather different, description of the Chinese colossus (a description, I should add, which can be found in the very same book that was co-edited by Neil). It was written by the Chinese art historian Tsao Hsingyan, who, in contrast to Kottler and other American commentators, witnessed the making of the statue. She describes how the students at the Central Academy of Fine Arts came to produce a large-scale sculpture for the planned demonstration on May 30. The student federation, which was coordinating the democracy movement, had "suggested that the sculpture be a replica of the Statue of Liberty in New York," writes Hsingyan.

> But the sculpture students rejected that idea because it might be viewed as too openly pro-American and because the copying of an existing work was contrary to their principles as creative artists. . . . They decided to save time by adapting for their purpose a studio practice work that one of them had already made—a half-meter-high clay sculpture of a man, grasping a pole with two raised hands and leaning his weight on it. . . . The students cut off the lower part of the [man's] pole and added a torch at the top. . . . They changed the man's face on the original model into a woman's also adding breasts and long hair. . . . This is how a half-meter-high statue of a man became transformed into a ten-meter-high statue of a goddess.[5]

Let us bracket, for the time being, the question of the fabrication of sexual difference in the democratic symbolic. Contrasting Kottler's and Hsingyan's very different descriptions of the origins of the goddess, I want first to distance myself from a reading that would settle the question of meaning with an appeal to either the authenticity of an "eyewitness account" or the authorial intent of the art students. The question I want to pose is not: Is the Goddess of Democracy a copy of the Statue of Liberty? Rather, the question is: What is at stake for certain configurations of American national identity in seeing it as a copy? To rephrase this question slightly: What is at stake for those of us who go under the sign of Americans in locating the origins of the Goddess of Democracy in our own democratic symbolic, in our own myths of origin? Why do we see the Statue of Liberty when we look at the Goddess of Democracy—or for that matter, at any female figure holding a torch? What political anxieties are assuaged by the certainty of our cultural vision?

I want to suggest that this certainty of vision—the Goddess of Democracy is nothing but a replica of that all-American icon, Lady Liberty—betrays the political problem of legitimation which haunts (American) democracy. Because democratic power is taken rather than granted, justification of the radical act of founding is always *post hoc* in democracies.[6] As Hannah Arendt has argued with regard to the American founding, "It is in the very nature of a beginning to carry with itself a measure of complete arbitrariness. Not only is it not bound into a reliable chain of cause and effect, a chain in which each effect immediately turns into the cause for future developments, the beginning has, as it were, nothing whatsoever to hold onto; it is as though it came out of nowhere in either time or space."

This interruption of the temporal order by the introduction of something new—a democratic revolution—defines the problem of origins and incites the search for an absolute that could both account for the break in "the continuous sequence of historical time" and justify the act of democratic founding. The absolute can take the form of a False higher law "that bestows validity on all man-made laws";[7] alternatively, it may take the form of a "concept of [historical] process" which "alone makes meaningful whatever it happens to carry along."[8]

The appeal to an absolute, then, marks the enormous difficulty that democracies have in accounting for and justifying their origins in a radical act of beginning. Although Arendt holds that democratic founding has no other authorization than the act of founding itself, American democracy has rarely been able to do without external and metaphysical reassurance. Following Arendt, we might speculate that the rush to find the referent of the Statue of Liberty in the Goddess of Democracy is just another instance of *post hoc* justification for the radical act of political founding. When Americans reduce the one colossus to a mere copy of the other, they deny not only their own nation's radical act of beginning but also that of the Chinese democracy movement. Both beginnings are submerged in an engulfing historical narrative of democratization that begins in the West and ends in East. We may be inclined to interpret this narrative strictly in terms of the triumph of capitalism—particularly after President Jiang Zemin's 1997 visit to the United States in which the democratic moment symbolized by the Goddess of Liberty was obliterated by Wall Street's trade euphoria—but the Goddess of Democracy, as it is scripted in the American democratic symbolic, is not reducible to economic explanations of market forces.

At stake in American appropriations of the Goddess of Democracy is precisely the problem of what authorizes American democracy. To interpret the Chinese colossus as little more than the reiteration of what has already been (the American Revolution), however, does not answer to another, equally important aspect of democratic founding: namely, what Thomas Paine called each generation's power to "begin the world over again." Paine recognized that a democracy that denied this power would soon lose its legitimacy. But the spirit of starting something new, as Arendt observes, stands in an uneasy relationship to the attempt to establish something enduring.[9] What is more, laments Arendt, the Founders never succeeded in resolving this tension, and, in fact, were primarily concerned with the durability of political institutions, with the consequence that the revolutionary spirit in American democracy has been virtually lost.[10]

Following and departing from Arendt's account of democratic founding, I argue that American appropriations of the Chinese Goddess of Democracy exhibit not only an attempt to anchor the otherwise arbitrary act of beginning in a teleological conception of world history but also a fantasized relation to what she calls the "lost treasure" of the American Revolution—the revolutionary spirit. If it is the case that America looks to China "for its own lost origins, its own lost original experience of democratic invention," as Slavoj Žižek has written more generally of the West's relationship to Eastern Europe since 1989, what are the consequences for democratic agency?[11] Does viewing the (attempted) enactment of democratic founding in 1989 China as a reenactment of democratic founding in 1776 America invigorate or foreclose democratic action?

These questions are especially relevant for considering claims about the mimetic relationship of the Goddess of Democracy to the Statue of Liberty. Even if we grant that the one colossus is a replica of the other, a question remains as to what exactly is being replicated: the revolutionary spirit or the concern with durability; the unprecedented act of beginning or the necessary process of world history; the practices of human freedom or the guarantees of transcendent law? Contrary to commentators who assume that the Statue of Liberty does indeed carry a unitary meaning, which in turn makes it available for export and import, we shall find that the Statue of Liberty has been the site of vigorous political contest over the meaning of the American founding and over what it means to be an American. Perhaps more than any other political symbol or national monument, the statue is at the center of the creation stories that Americans tell themselves about the beginnings of their democracy, stories that are at once stabilizing and destabilizing in the ways suggested by Arendt's account of democratic founding. Far from settling the meaning of China's democracy movement, the act of finding the original of the Statue of Liberty in the Goddess of Democracy merely raises anew the very problem of democratic founding that I have been discussing. With this in mind, I turn to the history of the "original."

The Gift No One Wanted

La Liberté clairant le Monde (Liberty Enlightening the World), as the statue was originally called, was proposed in 1865 by the French jurist Eduoard de Laboulaye as a gesture of Franco-American republican friendship. It was designed and built by Frédéric-Auguste Bartholdi, and formally accepted as a gift from the French-American Union in France by the U.S. Congress in 1877. It took close to a decade before the Statue of Liberty was installed on Bedloe Island and unveiled to the American public—or rather, to a restricted subset of that public, since women were not invited to the unveiling ceremonies. The suffragettes, who crashed the party in New York harbor and hired their own boat, issued a statement declaring: "In erecting A Statue of Liberty embodied as a woman in a land where no woman has political liberty, men have shown a delightful lack of consistency which excites the wonder and admiration of the opposite sex."[12] Indeed, why should the iconic body of woman be used to figure the universal language of republicanism when actual women occupied a tenuous relationship to the public sphere?

Pondering this question, Marina Warner suggests the answer lies in the intrinsic emptiness of the female form itself, a form which, in contrast to that of the male, is divested of any particular content and thus lends itself to the symbolization of abstract and universal concepts. But Warner's answer simply begs the question.[13] We might well ask, "*Why* is the female form so well suited to such symbolization?" Rather than answer with another generalized statement about the intrinsic nature of the female form, I shall argue that the imbrication of the female form and an abstract concept (like liberty) entails culturally specific practices of public fantasy and is thus crucially dependent on political context. We need therefore to attend to the historical conditions in which the female embodiment of liberty came to bear public meaning, starting with the complex story of the less than enthusiastic American reception of the French gift.

Far from being warmly welcomed by the American public, Lady Liberty was something of a *persona non grata.* Apart from the French who created and financed her construction, and a group of New York–based enthusiasts, no one wanted her. Indeed, raising funds for Liberty's pedestal proved extremely arduous. Added to the fact that America had yet to establish the tradition of funding public sculpture through popular subscriptions was a series of deeply embedded social antagonisms that derailed the fund-raising effort. The clergy claimed that the French gift was a pagan goddess and a Masonic plot; the poor suspected that the statue was an excuse for the rich to throw expensive dinner parties; many of the rich feared that the celebration of liberty might be an invitation to anarchy; New Yorkers were accused of trying to get the country to pay for their monumental fantasy. Above all, the statue simply lacked a definitive national identity. "The idea of a gigantic personification of an abstract concept," as June Hardgrove writes, "might be intriguing, even appealing, but hardly compelling enough to prompt a Midwestern farmer or a confederate veteran to dig into his pocket."[14]

In some respects, the obstacles faced by the fund-raising committee can be explained in terms of nineteenth-century America's muted enthusiasm for public sculpture. Relatively bereft of monuments before 1840, America was a country in which the natural landscape functioned as a source of public character and as a substitute for the usual rallying points of civic identification (such as a royal family or a national church). To experience the uplifting sensation of the sublime, Americans went to a natural wonder such as Niagara Falls or a public work such as the Erie Canal. In the 1840s and

1850s there was an increase in monument building (the Washington Monument, 1848–86; Bunker Hill Monument, 1825–43; the restoration of Mount Vernon in the 1850s) that reflected what John Higham has characterized as a widely felt "malaise," the "disturbing sense of remoteness from the heroic age of the Revolution."[15] It was hoped that monuments would "commemorate and revitalize the nation's republican ideals" and, as one monument enthusiast put it in 1846, "bring before us in our daily walks the idea of the country in a visible shape."[16] The primary goal, however, was not to incite the revolutionary spirit, as Robert Byer observes, but to "make present again a convincingly unified vision of the nation."[17] By the 1870s, this task took on renewed urgency as America struggled with the divisive legacy of the Civil War, slavery, a heightened conflict between classes, and what many saw as an increase in selfish materialism.

Although this interest in monuments gripped the well-to-do members of the American committee, it was not widespread enough to rally the general public around what one critic called "Bartholdi's folly," a statue that "had nothing but its colossal exaggerations of size to recommend it." Indeed Lady Liberty was doomed to remain in 214 crates until the Hungarian immigrant Joseph Pulitzer mobilized a mass fund-raising campaign in his newspaper, the *World*, to construct her pedestal. Pulitzer mobilized the sentiments of his working-class and immigrant readers, reminding them that Lady Liberty was "not a gift from the millionaires of France to the millionaires of America but a gift of the whole people of France to the whole people of America." The *World*'s campaign, as Lauren Berlant observes, provided an opportunity for the masses "to take ownership of the symbolic material of national fantasy."[18] The gift no one wanted, Liberty went on to become the first monument that was financed completely by public contributions, the first that was owned and generated by the people themselves.

What made Pulitzer's campaign unique was its strong articulation of a political relationship among the working people of America as well as between them and the working people of France: "We must raise the money! The WORLD is the people's paper, and now it appeals to the people to come forward. . . . The statue . . . was paid [for] by the working men, the tradesmen, the shop girls, the artisans [of France]. Let us respond in like manner. Let us not wait for the millionaires to give this money."[19] As a rallying point that brought together otherwise diverse and, in many cases, mutually hostile groups of immigrants and workers, the Statue of Liberty became the cause of the people, a democratic people bound not by some transcendent principle but by mutual promises. Whereas other fund-raising vehicles called on the people to memorialize the founding as the act of canonized forefathers—thereby emphasizing the importance of the monument for symbolizing the stability and durability of political institutions—the *World* called on its readers to reenact the performative political moment of popular sovereignty—but it did so in sentimental terms. The *World* printed the names of contributors, followed by touching letters from widows, pensioners, immigrants, and children.[20] Whether these letters were contrived—and many probably were—is irrelevant. They were small but important exercises in the practices of re-founding which provided immigrants with a vehicle for political action. The immigrant and working-class energies that finally rescued the statue from oblivion were inspired by the revolutionary spirit that the Founders cherished but deeply feared.

The emphasis on popular sovereignty—not to mention the barely veiled class antagonism—in the *World*'s fund-raising appeals initiated the process whereby the statue would serve as a site in the democratic symbolic for contests over the meaning of the American Revolution. This first stage in the transformation of a white elephant into a site of intense mass-affect, "Bartholdi's folly" into "our Lady Liberty," indicates that we are concerned here not with a stable content that inheres in the monument and gets communicated to the spectator—as the monument enthusiasts would have it—but with a meaning that is fully contingent on the spectator's subjectivity and the particular conjuncture of political forces. Indeed the question of referential meaning, the "what" of signification, cannot account for the broadest historical shifts in the statue's meaning: from a symbol of transnational republicanism to a symbol of immigration; from a symbol of immigration to a symbol of the American nation-state threatened by the wrong kind of immigrant; and from a symbol of America's national heritage to a universal symbol of democracy in a post–cold war political context. The Statue of Liberty was in no way destined to become the symbol it became (whatever that may be at any given historical juncture), nor is its history a story of the unfolding of any inherent meaning—as almost every popular narrative of the statue would have us believe.

In the Beginning Was the Copy

Those popular narratives, in which the Statue of Liberty is read teleologically as the symbolic expression of a national destiny and consensus, unity and continuity, proliferated in the context of the 1986 centennial campaign to refurbish the monument. Then President Ronald Reagan, seeing the opportunity for a media event, turned the responsibility for the campaign from the National Park Service over to the American people, calling on it to renew its debt to the Founders and to reassert the principle of popular sovereignty. Within the larger framework of Reaganomics, however, the call to popular action was hardly an incitement to insurrection or mass participation in public affairs. Rather, it was already limited to the assault on "big government" (including departments like the Park Service) and the dismantling of the welfare state. From coffee-table books to the press, as Berlant argues, a crisis of national proportions was produced around what Reagan called the Lady's dire need for a "face-lift."

The national anxiety occasioned by the statue's immanent dismemberment—in Reagan's version, decaying femininity—raises the question of the statue as the symbolic placeholder for the stability and durability of American democracy. The anxiety was hardly new. As Philippe Roger observes, "Americans from the beginning fantasized the statue as being fragile, threatened."[21] To comprehend the statue as the locus for a fantasy of national disintegration, we might consider that it was in precisely this fragmented form that Lady Liberty found her way into the American democratic symbolic. Liberty was an image before she existed as an object; she was first known to the American public as a collection of parts. For years her body was literally in pieces; the hand that held the torch was on display at the Philadelphia Centennial in 1876 and in New York's Madison Square in 1877. Her head was viewed at the Paris exhibition of 1878. Numerous photographs, miniatures, and trade cards of the statue-in-process, not unlike those that are for sale today, were circulated for purchase in both France and America to raise funds for its construction. The Statue of Liberty—which has been used to sell everything from war bonds to Coca-Cola to Sure Deodorant to the Modern Language Association—was, right from the start, a commodity. The artist Marta Minujin highlights this aspect of our most beloved national monument with her 1979 work, "The Statue of Liberty Lying Down." "The Statue of Liberty," she writes, "is one of the great symbols of the world. The consuming of a subject that important made me think of creating a replica stretched out on the ground that one would eat, to attempt to break down a collective mythology." And so this metallic structure was designed "to be covered with hamburgers and sprinkled with ketchup to be consumed by the public."[22]

Rather than thinking about the Statue of Liberty as a national monument whose origins get corrupted by being commodified, then, we do better to think of it as a commodity at origin—one that mediates the citizen-subject's relation to the nation and its moment of political founding. Apart from the souvenirs that were sold to finance the construction of the statue (not to mention the lawn movers, tonics, and sewing machines that bore its trademark), the world's fairs in which Lady Liberty was exhibited in all her fragmented, fetishistic glory are testament to the imbrication of commodity culture and liberal nationalism. At those fairs, as Anne McClintock writes, "a crucial political principle took shape: the idea of democracy as the voyeuristic consumption of commodity spectacle."[23]

Head by Frédéric-Auguste Bartholdi. The Paris Exposition of 1878. Musée Bartholdi, Colmar, reprod. C. Kempf.

Lady Liberty, Mother of Exiles, was herself a child of American consumerism, love of gigantism, and the late-nineteenth-century fascination with technology. She was truly "the work of art in the age of mechanical reproduction," in Walter Benjamin's famous phrase; in place of the aura was a plurality of copies. Liberty is an "original" whose originary status as the one and only, the genuine article, was paradoxically constituted through processes of mass reproduction—a point that could not be lost on the American master of the subject, Andy Warhol, in his poster for the 1964 New York World's Fair. I don't know how many Americans have actually seen the monument that stands in New York harbor. It doesn't really matter. The symbolic power of the Statue of Liberty rests now, as it did a century ago, on the availability of the image for public fantasy: for mass consumption and circulation in national narratives of origin and immigration.

The National Thing

But immigration, which is a dominant meaning of the statue today, and which Ronald Reagan celebrated in his centennial speech, was not part of the official meaning of the statue in 1886, and was strongly resisted by a variety of forces through the late 1930s.[24] By the early 1880s, there was already "considerable alarm about the huddled masses pouring through the golden door," in John Higham's words, as immigration reached its highest point in the nineteenth century. The "new immigration" of this period, stemming principally from southern and eastern Europe and from Asia, consisted of peoples of vastly different cultural backgrounds, who, it was feared, could not be readily assimilated into American society. As Higham observes, it was only after the restrictive Immigration Act of 1924, "after immigrant ships no longer passed under the New Colossus in significant numbers," that the statue was declared a national monument and came to enshrine "the immigrant experience as a transcendental national memory. Because few Americans were immigrants, all could think of themselves as having been immigrants."[25]

I would like to suggest another explanation of why the Statue of Liberty became a symbol of immigration. If we remember that America has acquired its diverse population partly through immigration and partly through the violence of conquest, invasion, and enslavement, it is not difficult to imagine why the immigrant came to be the national icon of choice (that is, once the masses of actual immigrants had been denied entry). The fabrication of the Immigrant as a collective symbol of the imaginary community of the nation, the symbol of America's unique social contract, recalls Freud's concept of the totem: a symbol whose idealization conceals the violence at the origin of the social bond. As Bonnie Honig argues in a forthcoming book, the symbolic Immigrant functions to secure America's dominant myth of origin in freedom and contract.[26] As the official symbol of America's immigrant heritage, the Statue of Liberty conceals a rather different history of national origins, the history that was symbolized in Pezzicar's "The Emancipation of Slaves," which was exhibited at the Philadelphia centennial where Liberty's hand and torch were displayed.[27]

The other face of the beloved Immigrant who confirms a pleasing myth of origins is the stranger who would steal our enjoyment and ruin our way of life. In the 1880s and 1890s, to say nothing of the 1980s and 1990s, we find a wide range of images depicting the Statue of Liberty as menaced by newly arrived immigrants and American subversives. In the wake of the Haymarket Riot, foreigners became synonymous with radicals and subversives, as the first Red Scare gripped the nation. In an image that appeared in an 1892 issue of the *Evening Telegram*, the purity of American Liberty is threatened by the dregs of Europe and the garbage they bring with them, including every manner of political radicalism. Liberty holds a bottle of carbolic acid (used to treat venereal disease) in her hand and lifts her skirts to avoid contamination. In another image from 1890, Liberty tells Treasury Secretary William Windom: "If you are going to turn this island into a garbage dump, I'm going back to France."[28] In these images, the Statue of Liberty safeguards the foundations and institutions of the American Revolution against the threat of the revolutionary spirit embodied by immigrants.

Images such as these suggest that the question of national identification—what holds people together in an imaginary community—entails more than a conscious commitment to a set of shared values. As Žižek observes, "The element that holds together a given community cannot be reduced to the point of symbolic identification: the bond linking its members always implies a shared relationship toward a Thing, toward Enjoyment incarnated. This relationship towards the Thing, structured by means of fantasies, is what is at stake when we speak of the menace to our 'way of life' presented by the Other." The Thing "appears to us as 'our Thing' . . . , as something accessible only to us, as something 'they,' the others, cannot grasp, but which is nonetheless constantly menaced by 'them.' " "We always impute to the 'other' an excessive enjoyment; he wants to steal our enjoyment (by ruining our way of life) and/or has access to some secret, perverse enjoyment" (which is costing taxpayers a lot of money).[29]

In his own way, it was Tocqueville who first understood the dimension of fantasy that obtains in the realm of democratic national monuments. He spoke of the individual's sense of insignificance, a crisis of singularity as the price for equality. What is always already being snatched away by the other, in Tocqueville's account of democracy, is just this sense of individual uniqueness. The fear of becoming lost in the mass, says Tocqueville, drives

THE EVENING TEL

284. NEW YORK, SATURDAY, SEPTEMBER 10, 1892—EIGHT PAG

port that has already furnished scores of victims of the pestilence.

Eleven hundred people left Hamburg in the vessel, of which number thirty-two have already suc-

Brooklyn City, from Swansea; the St. Pa... from London, and the Alene, from Port Lemon.

It is expected that there will be cholera ... the four vessels from Hamburg, and their arrival is dreaded by the health officials.

known of quarantine regulations that were enforced at New York.

The body of the dead woman was admitted to the county Morgue and placed in a separate room. The clothing was fumigated and ...

The Dregs of Europe." *The Evening Telegram*, 10 September 1892. Bibliothèque du CNAM-Paris.

the passion for the gigantic in public sculpture. In America, the love of gigantism is linked to the smallness of the citizens' lives. "Individuals in democracies are very weak, but the state, which represents them all and holds them in the palm of its hand, is very strong. Nowhere else do the citizens seem smaller than in a democratic nation, and nowhere else does the nation seem greater, so that it is easily conceived as a vast picture. Imagination shrinks at the thought of themselves as individuals and expands beyond all limits at the thought of the state. Hence people living cramped lives in tiny houses often conceive their monuments on a gigantic scale."[30] Monuments are the medium of national identification that lifts the citizen out of the ordinary and inserts him into a fantasy space governed by what Tocqueville calls "the Idea of Infinite Perfectibility" and the pretension "to represent the destiny of the whole human race." This space is, not coincidentally, marked by the very notion of a historical process that Arendt found to be typical of attempts to resolve the complex problem of democratic founding.

Tocqueville's remarks capture the fantasy of sheer size that governed the republican Bartholdi's entire conceptualization of "Liberty Enlightening the World." Putting the statue in a historical continuum of which it is itself to be the culmination, Bartholdi wrote: "This statue will rise to an extraordinary height; on its twenty-five-meter pedestal it will stand thirty-four meters tall from head to foot, or forty-four meters counting the upraised arm and its torch." Bartholdi compared it to other famous colossi, concluding that "it will be equal in stature to the famed Colossus of Rhodes, which was intended to remain forever unsurpassed."[31] With that fantasy of size, however, came a risk: "On a small scale it was easy to make use of a specifically female figure to convey a lofty idea, even an aspiration toward the ideal, but, once enlarged above life-size [to forty-four meters], it was flirting with the grotesque."[32]

Our Lady Liberty

The risk of the grotesque in public sculpture is not limited to female figures, but perhaps female figures present a special risk of the grotesque. Indeed, when it comes to "monuments and maidens," to use Warner's phrase, the grotesque poses a quite specific risk: namely, the risk of the female body set loose in the public sphere—a risk that haunted nineteenth-century American and Western European cultures. The problem of transforming the female body from the site of unruly excess into the bearer of the Law was not lost on Bartholdi. Not only did Bartholdi come over the course of the 1870s to downplay or eliminate those symbolic elements that had been crucial to the presentation of liberty in the French context (like the broken

Le 28 juillet 1830: La Liberté guidant le peuple. Eugène Delacroix (1798–1863). Louvre. Photo RMN—Hervé Lewandowski.

chains and the Phrygian cap, the Roman mark of the freed slave), he also radically refigured Eugène Delacroix's radical republican image of liberty as a woman whose public sexuality symbolized the revolutionary power of the people.

If we compare Delacroix's "Liberty Leading the People to the Barricades" to Bartholdi's "Liberty Enlightening the World," we can appreciate the extent to which the presentation of femininity was central to the representation of the difference between the French and the American revolutions. Kaja Silverman argues that Bartholdi buries the female form beneath mounds of copper drapery. "What Bartholdi's statue held out to his compatriots was the promise of a liberty uncontaminated by passion, a republic without republicanism, and a political arena from which the female body would be discreetly barred."[33] Edouarde de Laboulaye had already said as much in 1876: "This will not be liberty in a red cap, striding across corpses with her pike at the port. This will be the American Liberty whose torch is held high not to inflame but to enlighten."[34] This will not be the liberty of the barricades but liberty under and assured by law. Holding the female body in its proper place, says Silverman, is Gustave Eiffel's metal trusswork, which might be said to be the law that inhabits Laboulaye's vision of Liberty and that protects her from succumbing to either sexual or republican passion.[35]

It would appear, then, that whereas Delacroix's "Liberty" embodies the revolutionary spirit, Bartholdi's embodies the stability and durability of political institutions, and both moments of democratic founding are articulated through competing versions of femininity. With a mosaic tablet bearing the inscription July 4, 1776, in her left hand, the modestly attired "Liberty Enlightening the World" gives solid form to the revolutionary moment, turning it into the rule of law and thereby warning against any subsequent reenactments. The statue thus celebrates the moment of an original taking—as democratic origin stories inevitably must—while simultaneously closing the space of civic energies that would put that original taking itself into question.[36] Delacroix's "Liberty Guiding the People," in contrast, appears to embody a revolutionary passion, an eternally recurring moment of an original taking that knows and respects no limits.

We need to modify the interpretation just offered—which locates meaning in the objective quality of the work of art—to account for the cultural narratives that map meaning onto the work, giving sexual difference its specific significance in the representation of democratic founding. Consider, for example, the reception of Bartholdi's Liberty by British and French commentators, who are so often stunned at the discrepancy between what Margarete Iverson sees as the statue's downright phallic attributes and the sappy American tributes to *our Lady* Liberty, which sound like so many mother's day cards. As Kathleen Chevalier put it: "Is she really a woman? She seems so abstract and frigid . . . an armed non-woman with whom men certainly would prefer not to mess."[37] This discrepancy in reception and meaning, which defines the history of the proliferation of the statue's image, cannot be settled by appealing to the supposedly objective qualities of the monument. Whatever objective quality is ascribed to the statue is already an act of interpretation structured by narrative. Whether one sees the statue's visage as loving and maternal or as stern and unforgiving, to take just two competing versions of the monument, concerns the power of those narratives to shape the very act of seeing.

What interests me, then, is less the question of why liberty is figured as a woman (which is posed by the tradition of art history) and more the question of how a central principle of democratic founding itself is represented through specific representations of femininity, which, in turn, cannot be accessed or "seen" apart from the structuring practices of cultural narratives about sexual difference. Consider in this context the centennial celebration book by Richard Schneider which bears the sentimental title *Freedom's Holy Light* and which boasts a foreword by Ronald Reagan and a preface by Lee

Iacocca (the chairman of Chrysler who headed the Statue of Liberty-Ellis Island Centennial Commission). The book begins with what Schneider calls the "measurements of America's One-Woman Welcoming Committee":

- Her height from head to heel: 111 feet, 1 inch. About the height of an 11 story building
- Her right hand measures 16 feet, 5 inches in length
- Her index finger extends 8 feet, almost two feet longer than the average bed
- A fingernail covers almost one square foot
- Her waist measurement is 35 feet

Describing the Lady in a familiar gender narrative of female proportions, Schneider goes on to reassure his readers that America's One-Woman-Welcoming Committee is not so big after all. Recounting the return of his battalion to New York Harbor at the end of World War II, Schneider writes:

> As the Statue moved before us with the passage of our ship, I was surprised by her size. . . . [She] seemed so small. . . . For a moment I wondered if the original had been temporarily replaced with a smaller model because of war hazards. . . . Later I learned that her creator had intended that she appear just as she was to arriving travelers. "I do not want her to dominate the harbor," he said. And so, like the gracious hostess that she is, she greets her guests and family without overpowering them.[38]

We could not be further from Chevalier's armed non-woman.

Schneider's narrative account, which turns the symbolic public woman into the domesticated hostess and mother, builds on a structuring principle of American democracy, namely a naturalized conception of sexual difference that authorizes the gendered public/private distinction. Following Tocqueville's remarks on the subject, the domestication of women preserves the difference between the sexes and thereby counters the democratic passion for equality from turning into the nightmare of the common mass. In contrast to their European counterparts, he argues, American women do not make the same claim to participation in the public sphere and thus do not carry the leveling force of equality into the difference between the sexes. What Tocqueville shows is that women's difference from men, which is the mark of their sameness as women, allows difference among men as equal citizens to exist. To disturb the order of the sexes, he suggests, is to disturb the foundations of the American Republic: sexual difference is the stable, prepolitical ground that anchors the far more volatile (because political) institutions of democratic equality.

The danger for American democracy, as Tocqueville had seen in his native France, was that women, swept up by the revolutionary spirit that in-

Suffragist Margaret Wycherly striking the pose of the Statue of Liberty. Library of Congress, LC-B2-3541-12.

habits democracy as a permanent threat to its stability, would carry the principle of equality into the relations between the sexes, thus uprooting democracy from its anchoring in nature, the putatively pre-political ground of sexual difference. When the suffragettes asked why liberty should be embodied as a woman in a land where no woman has political liberty, they were asking what it means for sexual difference to serve as the naturalized ground of a democracy. They called the question on sexual difference and exposed, in their own way, not only the hypocrisy of simultaneously elevating and excluding women, but also sexual difference as the wish for what Arendt called an absolute, that is, for a pre-political foundation that guarantees in advance the legitimacy of particular political arrangements.

Following Arendt's claim that democracy cannot be legitimated through the appeal to an absolute and her comments on the paradox of democratic founding, we can appreciate the place of feminist appropriations of the Statue of Liberty as reenactments of an original taking, a taking that, as we have seen, is at the heart of every democratic origin story. In a 1915 image of the suffragette, Margaret Wycherly posing as the Statue of Liberty, we witness just this moment of wresting power from the privileged (men) and thus are invited into the revolutionary moment of founding.[39] A similar (and more startling) moment is visible in the 1972 image of Angela Davis as the Statue of Liberty by the French artist Jean Lagarrigue. Like Wycherly, Davis is positioned as taking power and enacting the moment of beginning.[40] The force of the image speaks to the disruptive place of racial difference in the American founding. Like sexual difference, the difference between the races has served as an absolute that authorizes in advance political arrangements.

The Imperative of Translation

The images of Wycherly and Davis as the Statue of Liberty challenge the idealized story of America's political origins, but they are also necessary to that story in as much as it is narrated around an original taking of power, the revolutionary spirit. One way of thinking about the place of the statue in America's ambivalent relationship to the continual re-performance of its foundational social contract is to consider Arendt's point that democratic authority depends for its very life on the augmentation of its terms of common association. Inasmuch as democratic founding has no other authority than the act of founding itself, she suggests, there is an incompleteness at origin which, not withstanding all attempts to fill it with an absolute (e.g., God, natural law, racial or sexual difference), calls out for amendment and augmentation—in a word, translation.

As Jacques Derrida (following Benjamin) argues, translations are augmentations that give new life to the original text. Indeed the original depends on the translation for its very afterlife: "What sounded fresh once may sound hackneyed later; what was once current may some day sound quaint," writes Benjamin. The relationship of the original to the translation in not "representative or reproductive," as Derrida glosses Benjamin. Translation "is neither an image nor a copy." It is more on the order of the supplement—an amendment or augmentation. "And if the original calls for a complement, it is because at the origin it was not there without fault, full, complete, identical to itself."[41]

If American democracy is kept alive by translation, augmentation, refoundings—in a word, by the copy that is not One—we can now better appreciate the place of the Goddess of Democracy in the American democratic symbolic. To treat the Goddess as a copy of the Statue of Liberty (as Kottler does) neglects the generative process of translation that, precisely because it is not merely reproductive (as Tsao Hsingyan shows), is productive of unexpected political meanings. The history of the proliferation of the statue's image in the service of competing causes—feminism, civil rights, commercialism, imperialism, nativism—shows how difficult it is to restrict the meaning of America's most potent political symbol. And yet this semiological plasticity, as we also have seen, carries with it fantasized threats to the statue and by extension American national identity. It is as if the very availability of the statue for translation into other contexts (whether at home or abroad) makes it intrinsically vulnerable to what inevitably appears to some groups as an inappropriate appropriation, an illicit copy that betrays what the original stands for.

Returning in this way to the question of the fraught relationship between the "original" (the Statue of Liberty) and the "copy" (the Goddess of Democracy) with which I began this essay, I conclude with the *New York Times* story of Ovidiu Colea, an immigrant who fled Romania in 1978 and who now has the official contract to make 50,000 to 70,000 replicas of the statue in a corner of Queens, New York, called Blissville. Although Colea hires only immigrants because, as he says, they work hard, as artisans charged with producing accurate and consistent copies, they have their shortcomings. The Chinese sculptor whom Colea hired to make the original statuette mold "got Miss Liberty's body just right," but "her face presented difficulties." Instead of the stern gaze of the statue, says Colea, the sculptor made the eyes "too Chinese." Holding a statuette whose eyes popped out of their sockets, Colea adds that, on his second try, the Chinese sculptor made the eyes too round. Pointing to another statuette, Colea sighs at her thin upper lip, the round cheekbones, small chin, and non-existent forehead: "It's more like an Armenian face, because the sculptor is Armenian. The sculptor has never been able to fashion a non-Armenian face.

I routinely decapitate his models, sculpting new faces with my own hands."[42]

Let us not underestimate the difficulty of sustaining the integrity of the American original in what Hillel Schwartz calls "the culture of the copy." Apart from the problem of producing an accurate copy in the first place, copies tend to self-replicate, and it can become quite difficult to tell the difference between the original copy and all the other copies. Holding two models that he says were stolen from his molds, Colea sneers at how every line and fold of the imposter's gowns matches the ones of his replicas. He has spent $50,000 suing a former distributor whom he says stole his molds to manufacture reproductions in Taiwan and sell them at cut-rate prices in the United States. One wonders whether the Taiwanese will produce statuettes with a Taiwanese face. The problem of the illegitimate copy, the copy that is not an original copy, is hardly new: it dates back to the 1870s, when Bartholdi himself began making tiny replicas of the statue to help pay for the real one. New York was flooded with cheap, illegal knockoffs of the official replicas. The present owner of the gift shop on Liberty Island assures us that the copies we buy are indeed originals: he does not carry knock-offs from Americans, whose favorite manufacturing site is not Taiwan but China. "To make the Statue of Liberty where there is no Statue of Liberty or no liberty," protests Colea, "that's nonsense. That's supposed to be made here." But of course, one wants to add: it is, after all, our (national) Thing.

And so, with this prohibition on replication—from a man whose own living consists in making 70,000 copies per annuum of an original whose originary status is a question—I want to return to what is at stake for those Americans who saw in the Goddess of Democracy a copy of the Statue of Liberty, namely, what Žižek calls the West's "own Ego-Ideal: the point from which it sees itself in a likeable, idealized form, worthy of love. The real object of fascination for the West is thus the gaze, the supposedly naive gaze with which Eastern Europe [or China] stares back at the West, fascinated by its own democracy. It is as if the Eastern gaze is still able to perceive in Western societies its own agalma, the treasure that causes democratic enthusiasm [what Arendt called the lost treasure of the revolutionary spirit] and the West has long ago lost the taste of."[43] The Eastern gaze gives back to the West its ideal image of itself, confirming the status and value of the original by showing it worthy of replication. To put it simply: "America is copied; ergo America is good."

In the case of the Goddess of Democracy, however, the copy that is not quite an exact replica always threatens to reveal the gaps in the original, and thus shatter the fantasy of self-identity; this bad copy, however, whose difference haunts identity, is also a godsend of sorts. It marks the singularity of the original, the particular absolute that resists universalization: in other words, the Thing. The national Thing is haunted by the copy, by the very process of replication that is also necessary to America's ideal image of itself. *E Pluribus Unum*—Out of the Many, One—is haunted by its opposite—Out of the One, Many. The 70,000 statuettes produced yearly in Blissville and the interdiction on producing them elsewhere simply point to the strange global economy of national identity in which mimesis is at once demanded and forbidden. Copy me, don't copy me! Call it the American version of that curiously contradictory Oedipal command which structures the paradoxes of identification and the masculine subject's relation to the paternal law: Be like me, don't be like me!

Not unlike the decapitated statuettes produced in Colea's Blissville factory, the Chinese colossus had its origins in nothing less than a dismemberment. Recall the manner in which a half-meter-high statue of a man leaning on a pole was transformed into a ten-meter-high statue of a goddess. Before this manly figure was decked out with the female attributes of breasts and long hair, he sustained the sex-change operation of having the lower part of his pole cut off. Assuming that there are indeed moments when a pole is not just a pole, the fabrication of female sexual difference in the democratic symbolic entails a castration that must be effaced just as it effaces sexual difference. That lack in the national body, which cannot be seen even from the safety of American shores, must be covered over with the blind certainty of vision that secures the twin fantasies of the Woman and the replica in the culture of the copy.

imagined immunities

PRISCILLA WALD

A monkey, smuggled in against government regulations, bites the owner of a pet store. A car comes speeding down a hill and crashes into a gas pump; a man staggers out of the burning vehicle, face pock-marked and pained, screaming for the crowd to help his wife and child, both already dead of a mysterious illness inside the car. A lab technician sticks her finger with a needle. A young girl loses her virginity to a persuasive adolescent who assures her that unprotected sex is better.[1] These have become stock scenes in popular culture. They mark the site of transmission of bacterial or viral infection, signature events in fictional and nonfictional stories that take as their central conceit the spread of contagious disease and the efforts of the state and medical establishments to control it. I call these stories "carrier narratives." They are not new ones. While I will be concerned in this essay primarily with their appearance in the United States in the past decade, they have resurfaced throughout history, especially at times of important cultural contact, such as the European discovery of the New World. According to one legend, for example, Columbus imported venereal disease into Europe in the person of a monk named Boil.[2] Evident in their remarkable contemporary proliferation—in journalism, film, and even museum exhibitions—is a widespread fascination that is the subject of this essay.

The idea of healthy human carriers of disease long preceded the bacteriological discoveries of the late nineteenth century that enabled scientists to document their existence. But those discoveries gave the stories a new urgency and a new status, a visibility that complements—or compensates for—the invisible spread of disease that the healthy human carrier embodies. With the transformation of Irish immigrant Mary Mallon into the notorious "Typhoid Mary" in 1908, public health officials first alerted the U.S. public to the existence of such people; the apparently healthy stranger or friend beside you, they cautioned a frightened populace, could make you sick. Thus the stories brought the lessons of bacteriology to the public, but healthy carriers were not their only featured protagonists. Equally important were social engineers like George Soper, who identified Mallon as the source of a series of typhoid outbreaks in families where she was employed as a cook, and who exemplified the expert, trained to identify and control the spread of disease.[3]

Bacteriological discoveries demonstrate the danger healthy carriers proved to the households or extended communities in which they lived by documenting the aetiology of contagious diseases and the routes and consequences of their transmission. The stories that accompanied them, by contrast, crystallized nebulous concerns about cultural contact, the increased interaction among strangers promoted by urbanization, immigration, and imperialism. Anxieties about strangers and contacts, of course, did not begin with the ability to document healthy carriers. Those anxieties were already in place and already described through metaphors of contagion. But the stories harnessed those anxieties as they helped to (re)imagine a national community against the backdrop of the changing demographics of the United States at the turn of the twentieth century. As I shall suggest, the resurgence of these stories signal similar reimaginings at moments of profound demographic change (such as the globalization of our current moment).[4]

With my title's play on Benedict Anderson's much-discussed *Imagined Communities*, I mean to suggest the central role of disease in the articulation of a national community. I summon Anderson because I believe both that his analysis of the "imagined community" helps to explain the complexity of the fascination with contagion and carriers, at the turn of the century and at present, and that the *imagined* in his imagined communities merits further consideration, which the study of these stories facilitates.[5] The nation is imagined, argues Anderson, because most of its members will remain strangers, "yet in the minds of each lives the image of their communion."[6] The expression *imagined community* has subsequently been stretched beyond recognition, at least in part because scholars across disciplines (especially in the humanities) have recognized the importance of bringing the imagination more directly into politics. Most commonly, the term *imagined*, despite Anderson's distinction, becomes synonymous with *fictional* or *fabricated*, and the specificity of Anderson's discussion of the nation form gets lost. For him, "all communities larger than primordial villages of face-to-face contact (and perhaps even these) are imagined. Communities are to be distinguished, not by their falsity/genuineness, but by the style in which they are imagined."[7] The Enlightenment legacy of this idea for him yields a political entity "imagined as *sovereign*" and "as a *community* . . . always conceived as a deep, horizontal comradeship."[8] Anderson's ideas have held particular appeal for students of literary criticism, since he underscores the resonance between the kinds of imaginings represented and reproduced in the cultural forms of novels and newspapers and those necessary to the nation, at once recognizing the importance of literary forms to the articulation of nation and enabling a literary critical approach to its study.

The centrality of narrative to the articulation of a national culture has brought political and literary theorists into dialogue, and it has offered a vocabulary in which to understand how the imagined community structures the experience of personhood as well as peoplehood. "*Every social community reproduced by the functioning of institutions is imaginary*," notes the political theorist Etienne Balibar, by which he means that "it is based on the projection of individual existence into the weft of a collective narrative, on the recognition of a common name and on traditions lived as the trace of an immemorial past."[9] The historically specific imaginary of the national formation is marked by "a people" that finds its reflection in the state. The "fundamental problem" for him "is to make the people produce itself continually as national community."[10] But how, he asks, can this "fictive ethnicity," as he terms it, "be produced in such a way that it does not appear as fiction, but as the most natural of origins?"[11] I have rehearsed this familiar discussion here because it has been the basis for much of the critical thinking about nation in literary and political theory in recent years, and I think it is important now to consider the stress that is implicitly placed on *community* rather than *imagined*, as in Balibar's assumption that the community's imaginary basis must be obscured.

To the extent that the stories of carriers and contagion that I discuss here imagine the literal threat of dissolution posed by epidemics and their consequences, they do not trouble this claim; a national emergency typically calls forth patriotism, with anarchy as the everpresent threat that compels it. But the precariousness of the imagined community also emerges in these stories as they depict global connections that implicitly underscore the constructedness—and the arbitrariness—of national borders. The conspicuously *imagined* community is certainly in danger of dissolution, but from its fragility—its tenuousness—it also derives power, reminding its participants that the community, and all of the benefits they derive from it, is contingent upon their acts of imagining.[12] In what follows, I will use these stories of carriers and contagion to explore the imaginings that I see at the center of the strategy of community.

Stranger Anxiety and "Medicalized Nativism"

The publicity surrounding discoveries of bacteriology made scientific evidence available for representing fears about demographic changes, with immigrants, migrants, and the urban poor disproportionately embodying the threat. Historian Alan Kraut has coined the term "medicalized nativism" to mark the stigmatizing specifically of an immigrant group through its association with a contagious disease.[13] Long before the sources or routes of transmission could be identified, of course, contagious diseases were blamed on foreigners, strangers, and travelers as well as other internally marginalized groups. Yet the discovery—or, as Bruno Latour argues, the *invention*—of microbes made it possible to document the routes of transmission and the existence of healthy human vectors of disease.[14]

That invention coincided with the rise of sociology in the United States, which in part took shape around the study of social control: the attempt to understand how groups form, cohere, and establish unwritten laws that minimize collision and to make sense of the extralegal—the affective—relationship of the state and the individual. For prominent sociologist E. A. Ross, a Progressive and outspoken nativist, that relationship was rooted in the individual's perception that the state safeguarded his interests: "The more the state helps the citizen when he cannot help himself," he explained, "protecting him from disease, foes, criminals, rivals abroad and monopolists at home, the more he will look to it for guidance."[15] The healthy human vector of disease posed precisely that threat, as it established the need for and role of social engineers. If, that is, healthy carriers posed an invisible and pervasive threat to individuals and to the community, there were people (representing the state) who were trained to detect and control them. They were the visible agents, in effect, of social control.

Not surprisingly, the spaces where immigrants lived, already tainted by the metaphors and dogged by the experience of disease, came under increased scrutiny by Progressive sociologists and journalists as well as public health officials at the turn of the century. Journalist Jacob Riis dubbed the Jewish East Side of New York "the typhus ward," where filth diseases "sprout naturally among the hordes that bring the germs with them from across the sea."[16] Jews were certainly not the only victims of scapegoating; every immigrant group of the period shared that experience. To take in—assimilate, digest—strangers, especially in any kind of numbers, was a risky proposition for any body politic. And the United States at the turn of the century, with the violent struggle over national self-definition still fresh in its collective memory, was no exception. The language of contagion offered a vivid analogue for a less easily defined and justified anxiety about immigrants—that "they" will make "us" somehow unfamiliar, unrecognizable, to ourselves. Cultural observer Barrett Wendell sums up a prevailing sentiment when he complains about the influx of immigrants to his former student, the well-known theorist of cultural pluralism Horace Kallen: "We are submerged beneath a conquest so complete that the very name of us means something not ourselves. . . . I feel as I should think an Indian might feel, in the face of ourselves that were."[17] In his complicated remark, the conservative Harvard English professor, also an outspoken nativist, offers a "we" (native-born white Americans) who are clearly threatened by the influx of immigrants, just as the Indians were overrun by the settlers. The immigrants, who, as the analogy also makes clear, remind Wendell that "we" were once immigrants as well, trouble him because they make "the very name of us mean something not ourselves." The intangible fear of annihilation through a kind of defamiliarization (expressed as unrecognizability) to which Wendell gives voice underlies the widespread and more easily named dread of infection brought into the country by immigrants.

A connection between immigrants and microbes is not surprising, since travelers certainly do introduce new microbes into a community, which can wreak particular havoc in a group of people that has not developed immunity to them. Within a historical memory that might even have informed Wendell's analogy, European colonizers of the Americas had spread numerous diseases, most notably smallpox, to indigenous populations that lacked immunity, and therefore resistance, to the disease, resulting in the conquest and subjugation of these populations. The colonizers' accounts of these events seek to justify (as God's will or intrinsic biological superiority) the European conquest of the Americas. For a microbiologist, they attest to a biological dimension of community: a group of individuals in sufficient contact to adjust to each other's germs.

But not all diseases that affected communities were contagious, and the carriers of contagious diseases were not the only carriers restrictionists sought to exclude. The eugenic implications even of Wendell's nonmedical words are evident. The movement had caught significant public attention by the time he penned them, and inherent degeneracy was imputed both generally to marginalized groups and specifically to communities that had significantly intermarried. Chicago sociologist Louis Wirth, in his influential 1928 study entitled *The Ghetto*, cites an essay from the *Jewish Review* that attempts to counteract eugenic anti-Semitism and exclusion of Jews by attributing "the frequency of insanity among Jews" to "social considerations. . . . An ordinary population is spared the degenerating effects of many generations of town life, because any incipient decadence is neutralized and compensated for by the infusion of fresh country blood, as the stream of life is constantly flowing toward the large cities. A Jewish population, on the other hand, has not this reserve of vitality, and thus the evils generated by city life are so liable to remain impressed upon future generations."[18] While the writer's point was clearly that the high incidence of insanity among Jews was environmental (a result of inbreeding) rather than intrinsic and inevitably biological, such reasoning still fueled nativism, since it was what the immigrants carried in their blood or genes and not how they came to carry it that concerned their antagonists. Inadvertently, however, he captures a paradox: strangers are at once dangerous and necessary to the health of the communiy.

The implied relationship between disease and community is striking here. On one hand, the absence of epidemics of contagious disease suggests a stable community—implicitly configured by an immunological balance to which a stranger poses a threat.[19] On the other hand, too closed a community, which leads to inbreeding, constitutes another kind of threat. The community articulated through disease is balanced precariously between its fear and exclusion of strangers and its need for them, poised anxiously between desired stasis and necessary flux.

Contagion, Metaphor, and the Body Politic

The relationship among conquest, contagion, and community is, for historian William H. McNeill, a grievously underwritten chapter of history. With trade routes, military campaigns, migrations, and immigrations came infections that blazed through populations often with devastating effects. But gradually these diseases burned out. Communities, like individuals, adjust to disease. As McNeill explains, "When a given disease returned at intervals of a decade or so, only those who had survived exposure to that particular infection could have children. This quickly created human populations with heightened resistances": plagues sweeping through populations etched communal affiliations in the genetic resistances of their survivors.[20] Through such adjustments, communities form that can effectively be defined by their shared immunities. These diseases, in other words, mark civilization, and their spread constitutes communities.

While communities did not need specific scientific knowledge of the immune system to configure the idea of their own stability through their members' relative lack of susceptibility to each other's illnesses, the lessons of bacteriology made such concepts more available. Bacteriology was a required class not only for medical students and immigrants, but also for students of Home Economics from its foundation as a course of study at the beginning of the twentieth century, and medical researchers and public health officials routinely wrote for newspapers and magazines as well as specialized journals.[21]

The metaphors of two members of the literati, for example, bear witness to the availability of the concept of populations constituted through disease to the nonmedical public in the early decades of the twentieth century. Ezra Pound, in his correspondence with fellow poet William Carlos Williams, a physician, ironically asks his friend "what the h—l" he, "a blooming foreigner," knows about America. "Your *pere* only penetrated the edge," he chides, "and you've never been west of Upper Darby, or the Maunchunk switchback. . . . You have the naive credulity of a Co. Claire emigrant. But I (der grosse Ich) have the virus, the bacillus of the land in my blood, for nearly three bleating centuries."[22] Of course, Williams knew that his expatriated friend was critical throughout his career of the provincialism of his native land. But the use of disease to configure cultural affiliation is telling; culture itself is an infection in this metaphor, as Pound playfully naturalizes and nationalizes community through the trope of illness. Suggestively, his metaphor offers the infection of culture as an environmental and genetic inheritance passed through the blood over time ("three bleating centuries").

A former student of Barrett Wendell, writing in memory of his mentor, uses a similar analogy to describe Wendell's conviction that literature both expresses and shapes a tradition and the community to which it bears witness. Daniel Sargent summons the survival of great literature in spite of its near debasement in certain popular trends thus: "Pseudo-mysticism and so-called romance, leaving their refuge in poetry, spread through the minds of the nineteenth century with the thoroughness of a plague through people who have acquired no immunity."[23] The popularity of debased forms, in other words, is a result of a population that has not been exposed to their more benign manifestations through the beneficial effects of a serious literary education. Wendell's Harvard students, by contrast, are presumably the survivors who are now immune to such debasement and thus constitute a stable community.

Contagious diseases may have shaped populations, but their ravages are inseparable from their myths in that process. Accounts like McNeill's do not sufficiently attend to the precariousness of community or to the role of the imagination in its articulation. The meaning of shared immunity is invariably an act of interpretation. Harold Lauder (Corin Nemec), the lovesick poet of the television movie version of Stephen King's *The Stand*, tries to make shared immunity a basis for his own sense of community. To the object of his unrequited love, Frannie Goldsmith (Molly Ringwald), the only other survivor of a deadly superflu in their small Maine town, Harold gushes, "For two people from the same town—two people who know each other—to both be immune to something this big—it's like winning the megabucks lottery. It has to mean something." To Frannie it does mean a common bond, but she protests that there must be others, as indeed there are, and a new and improved community constellates around them, as the noble-hearted among them are drawn in their dreams to the brave new world founded by Mother Abagail (Ruby Dee) in the name of God.

The idea of a biological or physiological basis for community need not in itself lead to any particular ideology or meaning (as Harold Lauder hopes it might), but its articulation is also never neutral. Disease and conquest are sufficiently intertwined historically to make it easy to imagine why the concerns about the immigrant threat such as Barrett Wendell articulated might find expression in medicalized nativism and the immigrants' own concerns about the unhealthy culture in which they found themselves. Fear of disease conjoins a concrete anxiety about damage to the body with a less tangible one about social relations, enabling a connection between bodies and the body politic that turns a metaphorical connection (between contagion and cultural change) into the possibility of a metaphysical one. Fear of germs, argues historian Nancy Tomes, emerged from "a growing sense of interdependence and interconnectedness among people, objects, and events far separated in space and time."[24] With her phrase "the gospel of germs," she marks a culture that is not just afraid, but, in a more complicated way, preoccupied. As the demographic changes of migrating populations, increased markets and tourism, and imperial expansion changed the disease map, stories of carriers and contagion reflected the need to imagine—or imaginatively rearticulate—communities.

The production of a particular kind of story in popular culture is certainly evidence of a cultural preoccupation; if it is not an imaginary, it surely helps to shape what individuals within that culture imagine or perceive. One need not argue for the hegemony of that imaginary to identify a concept with a fairly broad appeal. Nonfiction bestsellers like Richard Preston's *The Hot Zone* (1994) and Laurie Garrett's *The Coming Plague* (1994) and movies like *Outbreak* (Wolfgang Petersen, 1995) and *The Stand* (Mike Garris, 1994) signal a contemporary topical concern. It is to that concern and its relation to the idea of an imagined community of the (U.S.) nation that I now turn.

Mapping a Cultural Imaginary

In what remains of this essay, I will show how contemporary carrier narratives offer contagion as a way of (re)imagining the bonds of community and interdependence and how the state remains at the center of such imagining in spite of the pressures exerted on it by the relations of globalization. I will also posit the individual's active engagement in the imagining of community. Stories of carriers and contagion are multifaceted and complicated, reflecting the very ambiguities and uncertainties of nationalism in the contemporary United States. The aspect of these various accounts and stories that concerns me is centered in the role of the epidemiologist—or of the medical detective who is serving in that capacity—in containing an epidemic, a major part of which involves tracking down the host, or carrier, of the disease. These mappings are emblematized by literal maps, which make frequent appearances in the backdrops of movie sets and the pages of carrier narratives. In the film *Outbreak*, for example, geographic maps and charts form the visual thread of strategic planning from hospital labs to military bases. Sam Daniels (Dustin Hoffman), a colonel working for the United States Army Medical Research Institute of Infectious Diseases (USAMRIID), must track down the host of a hemorrhagic virus from Zaire that has ravaged a small northern California town. Working with a team that includes his ex-wife, Robby Keough (Rene Russo), an epidemiologist from the Centers for Disease Control (CDC), Sam monitors the progress of the disease on genealogic tables that chronicle its spread. Brigadier Sutami, in Patrick Lynch's 1995 novel, *Carriers*, keeps a record of new outbreaks of the epidemic spreading through Sutami by placing small black pins on the map laid out in the center of the room each time a new case is reported. In a two-week period, Sumatri charts the dramatic progress of the disease, as the pins move from "a line, shadowing a fifty-mile section of the Hari River," to a network reaching "out in every direction: north and south to villages on the Trans-Sumatran Highway, west toward the Minang Highlands and now east as far as Jambi."[25]

Epidemiological maps help the epidemiologists solve the puzzle of the disease.[26] They are frightening, as the outbreaks appear in dots or lines that signal a spreading infection, often following the routes of trains, planes, buses, cars, and trucks as they transport carriers rapidly around the globe. But these maps can also be reassuring. In most stories, the audience sees evidence of experts on the case, a materialization of the epidemiological work that generally gets the threat under control (*The Stand* is an exception here). Such maps are familiar to aficionados of war movies; the epidemiologist is the general directing the campaign against the germ. After all, as the opening credits of *Outbreak* announce, Nobel Laureate Joshua Lederberg, a geneticist, has pronounced the virus "the single biggest threat to man's continued dominance on the planet."

If epidemiological maps visibly chart the path of microbes, the progress of a communicable disease, they also illustrate, as they materialize, the contacts of imagined communities, global as well as national or local. Consider what makes the diseases communicable: generally human contact, often among strangers, frequently (typically) unnoticed. As the microbe makes its way down truck routes and across airways, it chronicles the contact among people (and other hosts) who carry it from one to another. Obviously, the way in which a disease is transmitted will change the meaning of these contacts; airborne diseases show a different type of contact from diseases that are passed more directly. But all of them illustrate the networks of globalization. "A hot virus in the rain forest lives within a twenty-four-hour plane flight from every city on earth," writes Preston in *The Hot Zone*. "All of the earth's cities are connected by a web of airline routes. The web is a network. Once a virus hits the net, it can shoot anywhere in a day—Paris, Tokyo, NY,

LA, wherever planes fly." Preston makes this point in order to dramatize the potential spread of infection when Charles Monet, the index case of an outbreak of the hemorrhagic fever Marburg, "and the life form inside him had entered the net."[27] The expatriated Frenchman, a loner, contracted the disease while living and traveling in the Kenyan rain forest. Monet travels out of the jungle, across the country, and eventually into a major urban emergency room, the virus spilling into the environment with his leaking bodily fluids—evidence, as Preston describes it, of the struggle between virus and host that produces "a great deal of liquefying flesh mixed with virus, a kind of biological accident."[28]

Stephen King devotes a full chapter of *The Stand* to detailing the casual contacts and ready transmission of the lethal superflu that ends the world as we know it. An insurance salesman, Harry Trent, contracts the virus from a highway patrolman who stops him for speeding. "Harry, a gregarious man who liked his job, passed the sickness to more than forty people during that day and the next. How many those forty passed it to is impossible to say—you might as well ask how many angels can dance on the head of a pin."[29] These catalogues attest to communities linked by more than our imaginations—linked rather by the experience of being human in and moving bodily through the same shrinking world.[30] We may sit with our morning coffee, reading our newspapers and imagining (implicitly) our connections with the strangers engaged in the same acts, as Anderson suggests, but those connections become much more palpable on the epidemiologist's map.

Even more than bacterial infections (which antibiotics, at least until recently, made less threatening), viruses assume an almost mystical quality in many of these accounts, a strange, symbiotic life of their own. "The strain of virus that had once lived in Nurse Mayinga's blood," writes Preston of an Ebola vector, "now lived in small glass vials kept in superfreezers at the Institute."[31] At times almost spiritual in tone, Preston's language suggests a kind of communion: Nurse Mayinga living on through the sacrament of the virus. Carrier narratives, always with us, proliferate in periods of major demographic shifts and increased social contact—the rise of the cities (and their attendant migrations and immigrations) at the turn of the century, the rise of the global village today. But their mappings do more than register the related anxieties of contagion and assimilation. Rather, they address even as they express those anxieties, materializing the lines of communication that are, in the end, the theology of the imagined community. They are at the same time stories of tragedy and triumph, horror and salvation. That struggle is most explicit (and religious) in *The Stand*, where survivors really do divide into saints and sinners and struggle for control of what is left of the world. But even in the secular versions of science writers, the state emerges as the (at least temporarily) victorious guardian of those who dwell (legally) within its borders. While Nurse Mayinga dies a terrible death, her blood, like her story, has followed the circuit of a scientific community from Africa to Maryland. In both lies the promise of a cure, the triumph of (U.S.) medical science. In her way, she has entered into the sacred space of the imagined community of the United States, and she is invoked throughout *The Hot Zone* and referred to in fiction and nonfiction alike, a kind of patron saint of the virus who died somehow for our sins and ultimately for our salvation.

There is a tension in these stories, at both the beginning and end of the twentieth century, between the contact with strangers enabled and compelled by immigration and other manifestations of globalization and the imagined community of strangers that constitutes the nation. "A human population usually needs at least a century or so to stabilize in response to an unfamiliar infection," according to science writer Arno Karlen. And he calls increased infections in the Old World "the biological price of urbanization, trade, travel and war."[32] Patrick Lynch gets at the heart of the tensions in *Carriers* with the description of a group of dead imported monkeys in a Maryland laboratory:

> When you moved an animal from one part of the world to another, you inevitably exposed it to new microbiological environments to which its immune system was not adapted. When Europeans and Native Americans first started coming into contact with each other, epidemics were often the result; a bacterium or virus that gave a Mayan laryngitis could kill a Spaniard, and vice versa. That was what ecosystems were all about. Yet there was something about . . . the way all eight monkeys had fallen sick at the same time, within hours of each other, and just the look of the dead animal, that felt—it wasn't easy to find a word for it—unnatural.[33]

Here again immunity marks a stable community; strangers bring the threat of new microbes that can introduce a destabilizing element, manifested as a disease outbreak.

Lynch's move from the premise of an ecosystem to a historical example is jarring, however, because of its inaccuracy. The contagion did not typically work in both directions between the Mayans, or any of the indigenous populations, and the Spaniards. "The inhabitants of the New World," notes McNeill, "were bearers of no serious new infection transferable to the European and African populations that intruded upon their territory—unless, as some still think, syphilis was of Amerindian origin—whereas the abrupt confrontation with the long array of infections that European and African populations had encountered piecemeal across some four thousand years of civilized history provoked massive demographic disaster among Amerindians."[34] The historical inaccuracy shows how readily contact is cast in the language of contagion. Invoking the concept of an ecosystem, Lynch naturalizes an equation that is only half accurate. Moreover, it is an easy step from the concept of an ecosystem to the naturalization of a community of people through the trope of disease. That slip is evident in Lynch's faulty move from contemporary primatology to human history. A naturalized, and potentially racialized, basis for the understanding of community is evidently a danger not only of the science of eugenics but also of a community imagined through its shared immunities.

Reports of a recent scientific theory similarly brings the epidemiological genealogy of community into focus. In May, 1989, the *New York Times* reported a hypothesis that grew out of the discovery of a strikingly high percentage of certain populations that have an HIV-resistance gene, suggesting that "it conferred a breathtaking selective advantage."[35] Since the HIV virus is presumably too recent a disease to have already generated such a high incidence of a genetic mutation, scientists speculated about other possible selective advantages of the genetic mutation. Using DNA analysis to date the emergence back to the fourteenth century, they noted a remarkable correspondence between maps of the frequency of the HIV-resistance gene in ethnic populations and of the routes of the bubonic plague epidemic, from which they hypothesized a connection between a genetic mutation that protects against bubonic plague and the HIV-resistance gene. According to this theory, the disease indirectly caused the genetic mutation in a classic illustration of selective advantage. People with the mutation were much more likely to survive and reproduce, thus passing along the mutation. As a result of the contagious disease, people became carriers of a genetic mutation that now can mark them both by kinship (the passing on of the mutation) and by community (the survivors of a plague-ravaged area). Geography and biology come together here as people's genes can offer biological evidence of their peoplehood, immunity once again marking community.[36]

Journalistic accounts of this hypothesis verge on conformity to the racial politics of (predominantly white) accounts of HIV and its African origins. In place, for example, of support communities that have formed by and around AIDS sufferers, journalists describe (with some inaccuracy) a theory that reads the genetics of people of mainly European and Turkish ancestry as evidence of a biological (or naturalized) community formed by partial if not total resistors of another catastrophic pandemic. Implicitly, this hypothesis reconstitutes the ancestry of another *white* community threatened by a new *Black* Death (the Black Death is never once referred to as bubonic plague in the *New York Times* account that I am citing), this one, as so many of these stories go, having come from Africa.

The imagined community of the nation, argues Anderson, should be treated "as if it belonged with 'kinship' and 'religion,' rather than with 'liberalism' or 'fascism,' " more as a belief system than an institution.[37] In the studies and narratives I have been considering, immunity replaces kinship, offering a bodily connection through which to imagine a distinction between the communion of connected strangers and the threat of invasive or undesirable ones. As I have noted, kinship, conceived as a closed system, marks the other potential threat to a group, and a community must mediate between the threat of too many strangers (disease carriers) and the threat of inbreeding (genetic carriers). The balance of the stable community, marked by immunity, is always precarious, with the requisite number of strangers—those required to ensure a healthy and diverse gene pool—weighing constantly against the threat of too many strangers (hence social breakdown or anarchy in politics and germs).

"We're All Related"

In suggesting that epidemiological investigations in carrier narratives chart the quotidian contact of strangers, thus potentially mapping the relations of the imagined community, I do not mean to minimize the anxiety they summon. In fact, it is the combination of anxiety and reassurance that makes them so effective in the depictions of those relations. The imagined community is precarious, with the continuing infusions of the foreign necessary to the ideology of the community but nevertheless experienced as a threat. Patrick Lynch uses the word *unnatural* to describe the unsettling feeling of the eight monkeys' simultaneous deaths. The death of some monkeys in such circumstances is presumably natural, showing a community in balance—implicitly one, moreover, in which the danger is to the newcomer and not the host population. The deaths become unnatural when there are too many of them, the result of a more virulent and potentially uncontrollable disease, and that threat is always impending.

The "third world" village decimated by such a disease is a staple of many medical histories, journalistic or fieldwork accounts, as well as fictional depictions. It is an ambiguous symbol in U.S. literature and film, showing both that it cannot and that it actually might happen "here." *Outbreak* opens with a shot of a decimated military camp in Zaire and the image of dying American mercenaries. They perfectly embody the ambiguity, since in their capacity as mercenaries they are and are not Americans. The decision of General Donald McClintock (Donald Sutherland) to treat the citizens of a northern California town no differently from mercenaries in Zaire—to order its annihilation just as he had ordered the bombing of the camp—

constitutes the dramatic denouement (and the horror) of the film: the unsettling feeling of (mis)recognition captured in the shocked refrain, "but these people are Americans, sir." Outbreaks are frequently the unwitting or intentional result of greed—personal, corporate, or governmental—caused by anything from exploitation of resources to cover-ups and illicit experimentation or even deliberate biological terrorism. Even the minions of Satan's henchman, Randall Flagg, protest the "un-American" behavior of their leader in the movie version of *The Stand*, and General McClintock's *perceived* anti-American decisions result in mutiny. True Americanism, as manifested by the maverick Sam Daniels, entails the reassertion of borders and ideals—in this case, saving the nation through science (a medical cure rather than a military solution).

The means of transmission and the virulence of a disease, as well as the site of its outbreak, certainly affect the kind of representation for which it is available. A disease that is too virulent, one to which immunities do not readily develop, threatens total annihilation (although most such diseases eventually burn themselves out). But it is precisely the intensity of the moment when the deadly disease is spreading and its progress is uncertain that makes it most available for the representational purposes that I have identified. Most obviously, it summons a crisis, a state of emergency such as I referred to at the beginning of the essay. But the language of crisis is hard to sustain; soon it loses its efficacy to disbelief or psychic numbing. The more subtle and complex power of these works lies less in their sustaining the language of crisis than in their invoking the precariousness of the imagined community.

The impending catastrophic epidemic is a dramatic way of representing the half-truth of the community as a balanced ecosystem. One need not dispute the epidemiological histories of McNeill and others to note that demographic movement and disease mutation, among other factors, certainly complicate the idea of a community configured through shared immunities. The epidemiological maps demonstrate the porousness of borders and the impossibility of total regulation. The sites of regulation—the censuses, maps, museums, and, more broadly, national narratives that Anderson calls the "institutions of power"—promote national self-definition, as Anderson claims, but they attest equally to an ongoing metamorphosis, to the struggle as well as the strategy to contain.[38] The ever-present health threat, in other words, signals at once the (presumed) need for the power of the state to regulate its borders and protect its citizens and the limits of that power. Stories of carriers and contagion use precisely that precariousness to empower the individual and elicit what I see as a consensual act of imagining. What, after all, keeps citizens believing in the authority of Anderson's "institutions of power" even when they have recognized them as the source and products of their own imagining? Knowing that the community is tenuous and vulnerable, it seems, puts the burden of upholding it—through actions or through acts of the imagination—on the ordinary citizen. The community needs its imaginers.

Especially in the fictional narratives, this act of will (or of imagination) is what constitutes the imagined community—individuals' awareness, however tenuous, that they participate in the act of imagining community, that they must commit themselves to its articulation. Carriers embody that precariousness, the threat of contagion materializing the threat of the stranger among us. No matter if the carrier is other or brother, the disease makes the very name of them mean something not themselves, turning us all (back) into strangers in the process. But common susceptibility, even more than immunity, at the same time itself reaffirms relatedness.

In Robin Cook's *Invasion*, a strange virus erupts, killing only those with genetic defects and leaving others feeling better than ever but barely recognizable to their closest friends and relatives. The increasingly small number who manage to avoid infection gradually learn that the virus has been activated by aliens who had planted it in the primordial DNA out of which human life eventually sprang. It is, in other words, in all of us, and the reminder that we are all made from the same materials reinforces a sense of relatedness. In the words of Cassy Winthrope, one of the book's uninfected heroes and the fiancé of the index case, "knowing it is happening and that all humans are at risk, I feel connected in a way I've never felt before. I mean, we're all related. I've never felt like all humans are a big family until now. And to think of what we have done to each other."[39] Vulnerability to the virus confirms her sense of humanity and connection, but if all human beings are a "family," then the term signals a change in an understanding of relatedness. Hers is a global vision, one that, moreover, recognizes both the precariousness of community and the need to take action to preserve it.

On the surface, the aliens seem to offer the imagined community *par excellence*. The infected individuals experience a profound sense of their connections with strangers. "It's like they're different people," complains one uninfected teenage girl about her parents. "A few days ago they had like zero friends. Now all the sudden they're having people over . . . at all hours of the day and night to talk about the rain forests and pollution and things like that. People I swear they've never even met before who wander around the house. I've got to lock my bedroom door."[40] The infected abandon their cars, preferring to walk, and Cassy is horrified when, on a furtive trip into town from the cabin where she is hiding out, she notices that "a lot of people were gardening. Everyone was smiling, and there was little conversation."[41] Cassy's fiancé, Beau, speaks for the aliens when he casts an approving eye over a sylvan scene. "It's awe-inspiring," he explains. "It shows what concern for the environment can do, and it provides a ray of hope. It's such an unbelievable tragedy for an intelligent species like human beings to have done the damage they have to this gorgeous planet. Pollution, political strife, racial divisiveness, overpopulation, mismanagement of the gene pool. . . ."[42] The aliens stand for cooperation and community; they have no need for the Internet, explains one of the uninfected, because they have their own kind of net. They live as a colony, with Beau as their head. But the eugenic dimension of the virus complicates the utopian vision, casting the other social ills in a remarkably different light: rabid environmentalists and peaceniks emerge, by implication, as social control freaks, with eugenics as their logical extension and individuals as irrelevant.

Cassy and her co-survivalists, on the other hand, emerge as spokespersons for humanity, which is synonymous with individualism and which looks remarkably American in its articulation. (Is it coincidence that her last name, Winthrope, summons the first governor of Massachusetts, John Winthrop?) The virus steals people's identities, quite literally making the very name of them mean something not themselves. It takes away their imaginations and the possibility (and will) for individual action. As Beau explains to Cassy, "The alien consciousness increases with every person changed. The alien consciousness is a composite of all the infected humans just like a human brain is a composite of its individual cells."[43] The imagined community, by contrast, requires the act of imagination—the strangers who must constitute the community by imagining, not just accepting, their connections.

Not surprisingly, the aliens are anti-emotion. "Primacy of the emotions," Beau tells Cassy, "translates to an exaggerated importance of the individual, which is contrary to the collective good." Speaking in the language of conversion, Beau proselytizes for the alien way: "From my dual perspective it is amazing humans have accomplished as much as they have. In a species in which each individual is striving to maximize his circumstance above and beyond basic needs, war and strife are inevitable. Peace becomes the aberration."[44] Like a good American Cold Warrior, Cassy is appropriately horrified, more so when she learns that Beau cannot draw upon the collective information available to him to learn where his home planet was or what his original physical form was. He is the ultimate colonizer. In response to Cassy's query about whether it ever occurs "to the virus that it is somehow wrong to take over an organism that already has a consciousness," Beau quickly replies, "Not when we are offering something far better."[45] But while colonizers work to replace the narratives of the colonized with their own, the aliens lack any narrative of identity, any sense of home or even original form. They live entirely in the present and parasitically. The alien community is, in effect, too assimilative; strangers become absorbed too fully and literally lose their identities. And this assimilation is extended past the experience of the individual to the group; the aliens have arrived to assimilate the earth into a larger cosmic community. Cassy is speechless when Beau explains that earth's isolation is over; he is building a transportation mechanism that will bring earth out of its isolation and into the galaxy, a cosmic analogue of globalization, but with the U.S./earth as colonized space.

The central conceit and working out of this plot is, of course, little more than *Invasion of the Body Snatchers* done through metaphors of contagion, with anxieties of Soviet expansion bleeding into concerns about globalization. But the resolution brings back the focus that concerns me. The not-so-buried political subtext breaks through to the surface when the renegades find a maverick scientist who is working in an underground laboratory in Arizona that was originally designed against possible Russian germ warfare. One of the group finds it "ironic" that a facility "built to help thwart a germ-warfare attack by the Russians . . . instead is to be used to do the same thing for aliens."[46] But most interesting is the solution they develop to solve the problem. Working together, the renegades gradually figure out that another virus can bring the alien virus into the open and destroy it. From among the variety of viruses stored in the facility, they choose an artificial rhinovirus (a cold) to which no one will have immunity and which will spread easily and relatively harmlessly—without, that is, killing its hosts (shades here of *War of the Worlds*). Since the rhinovirus exclusively kills the alien virus, only those who have been sufficiently taken over by the alien virus die from the cold. If, as I have been suggesting, the spread of disease charts the contacts with strangers that materialize the relations of the imagined community, the spread of this disease actually recognizes (as it defines and salvages) what is human about human beings. It separates them out, and then it puts them back in contact.

Significantly, the aliens are ultimately defeated in part because Beau cannot relinquish his love for Cassy. "Our kind," he muses, "has never come up against a species with such interpersonal bonds. There is no precedent to guide me."[47] Those bonds mark what it means to be human, and they become the basis for the affective ties of community in *Invasion* and generally in carrier narratives. But they also imply a separation and the space for acts of the will and imagination. The act of imagination is what the virus prohibits in *Invasion*; it is a community without imagination and without, therefore, the possibility of negotiation between the individual and the community that, as I have suggested, lies at the heart of these imaginings. The imagined community of the United States works by engaging an individual posited in just the terms *Invasion* lays forth—in the language of individual freedom and consent, of liberal Americanism.

While *Invasion* implicitly defines humanity in those terms, Patrick Lynch is much more explicitly nativist in *Carriers*, a work that reads almost as a paean to isolationism. Here the problem starts with the aptly named Jonathan Rhodes, a botanist who is living in the rain forest of Sumatra pursuing his research, which consists mainly in "mapping out the huge variety of plant species in environments perpetually under threat of destruction by settlers, ranchers, or logging companies."[48] An environmentalist and general do-gooder, Rhodes also flirts with eugenicism, which is, not surprisingly, where the trouble begins. The epidemiological disaster starts in his compound, where his twin daughters have come to spend their summer vacation and where their mother, Holly Becker, and her boyfriend, are expected to join them. The compound becomes a ground zero both for the epidemic and for the plot, as a USAMRIID team and Holly collide in the jungle searching, respectively, for the hosts of the disease and Holly's twins, who turn out to be one (or two) and the same.

The hemorrhagic virus that begins on Dr. Rhodes's compound resembles Marburg and Ebola, and the early chapters of *Carriers* reads like a fictionalized version of *The Hot Zone*. However, the virus turns out to have emerged not from the jungle, but from ethically questionable top secret scientific research conducted on human embryos in an underground laboratory in New Mexico that has its counterparts in both *The Hot Zone* and *Invasion*. The problem begins when research conducted on a rare genetic defect called the Methuselah syndrome turns to gene therapy; when scientists remove the defective gene, they simultaneously remove the mechanism for suppressing a virus that is embedded in the DNA. This alteration results in the expression of the virus, and it kills all of the scientists in the laboratory. Not, however, before they had implanted genetically altered ova in a carrier of the Methuselah syndrome. As Holly explains to Lieutenant Colonel Carmen Travis, Jonathan Rhodes had used his scientific connections to arrange the procedure. "Unless Jonathan had been there, pushing me," she recalls, "I don't think. . . . It was too, I don't know, *experimental*. But Jonathan was convinced it was the right thing to do. He was really . . . convinced. Enthusiastic. And when I hesitated, because I just didn't know very much about it, about the risks, he started talking about our responsibility to the child, to give it the best possible chance."[49] Jonathan's eugenicist leanings result in the creation of a carrier of the deadly virus, since the genetic alteration leaves the virus open to unchecked expression when the carrier comes into contact with a triggering agent.

Holly speaks more aptly than she knows with her desperate outburst, "We don't belong here. . . . We're the disease here. We're the virus. The forest knows that. And it wants to destroy us."[50] One of her twins is, in fact, the carrier, and only Holly and the other twin seem to be immune to the disease. But where Holly's "we" meant westerners, the nativism of *Carriers* emerges more allegorically, and forcefully, in the description of the creation of the carrier. Although the unholy marriage of western science and capitalism (the corporation doing the research has a profit rather than a primarily humanitarian motive) gives birth to the carrier, it is her foray into the jungle that results in her exposure to a presumably foreign triggering agent. Speculating before the fact (before, that is, he has knowledge that an altered egg has been implanted), the scientist who has discovered a presumed link between the disease and genetic experimentation imagines the possibility of such an event: "The kid wouldn't necessarily know anything was wrong. In fact, things would be great—no hereditary defect. The child might be short a few million of this protein kinase that has no particular function in the normal run of things. Maybe he'd suffer some obscure side effect. A small deformation of the cuticles, who knows? Or nothing. Then along comes the antigen. Florists in Chicago start stocking a new South American cactus, whatever. It flowers once a year. Kid walks by the florist, catches up, and half the population of Chicago dies of a viral hemmorhagic [*sic*] fever."[51] The significant detail is the importation of the cactus. The carrier is inadvertently exposed because of a global economy; the epidemic represents its unchecked dangers (as well as those of scientific experimentation). And globalization produces a conflict that bears at least a psychological resemblance to the ambivalence about assimilation at the turn of the century.

"Like science," writes Richard M. Krause of the National Institutes of Health, "emerging viruses know no country. There are no barriers to prevent their migration across international boundaries or around 24 time zones."[52] Yet those borders reassert themselves in the monitoring and treatment of epidemics. General McClintock, as I have noted, can authorize the incineration of a mercenary camp that includes Americans in Zaire, but he cannot bring that strategy home. When he asks the president to authorize the annihilation of the infected California community, a horrified General Billy Ford (Morgan Freeman) reminds him that "these people are American." McClintock's chilly response, "These people are casualties of war," gives a defiant Sam Daniels the unambiguous moral edge not only for the audience but also for those in the film who are otherwise caught up in the army's chain of command. The nation's job is to safeguard its citizens, reclaiming its own as it reestablishes the stability of the community.

It is certainly true that the diseases mapped in most contemporary carrier narratives know no national boundaries. Carmen Travis justifies her efforts to repatriate Holly Becker and her twins by assuring the Indonesian general, "If there's one thing this outbreak has taught us, it's that Muaratebo [the virus] does not respect national boundaries. Neither should science, or medicine for that matter." But Carmen is also an officer in the military. As the narrator ominously remarks, "The fact that they [the U.S.

government and the military] would never share" their information about Holly's twins "with the Indonesians was something Iskandar [the general] could not suspect."[53] If epidemiologists map the imagined community of the global village, charting diseases as they cross national borders. If epidemiologists map the imagined community of the global village, charting diseases as they cross national borders, the depiction, as much as the management, of those diseases reinforces the boundaries. The use of disease to imagine as well as regulate communities powerfully enacts the most anxious dimensions of national relatedness. The inextricability of disease and national belonging shapes the experiences of both; disease assumes a political significance, while national belonging becomes nothing less than a matter of health. With their powerfully defining ambivalences, those terms mandate the dangerous necessity of the stranger and the technologies by which that stranger is brought into the community. As a cleansed Oedipus blesses the Athenian democracy, a contaminated but contained Nurse Mayinga blesses the land that stores her blood. For her story, like so many others, at once implies U.S. medical (and military) supremacy and inspires the imaginings at the heart of the community.

race and the romance of american nationalism in martin luther king, norman mailer, and james baldwin

GEORGE SHULMAN

This essay tries to think through the consequences of the fact that American nationhood (or national identity) has been wed to democratic idealism, on the one hand, and white supremacy, on the other. This fact produces the following dilemma: to resist racial domination by refusing the language of nationhood is to be cut off from the vast majority of citizens, but to invoke national identity is to repeat racial domination or reiterate its racial symbolism. I address this dilemma by exploring how Martin Luther King, Norman Mailer, and James Baldwin conceive nationhood and position themselves toward it in their efforts to oppose white supremacy and foster democratic politics.

While I was writing this essay in May 1998, the simultaneous appearance of Richard Rorty's *Achieving America* and Warren Beatty's *Bulworth* crystallized these issues. Rorty criticizes the "cultural" and "academic" left for ignoring class inequality and spurning a language of nationhood in a way that rejects the concerns of most Americans. To promote broad social reform, he claims, thinkers and actors on the left must draw from and thus renew American "civil religion." For Rorty, this civil religion is rooted in the idea of personal and national "self-creation" voiced first by Emerson and Whitman and then adopted by Dewey to address social justice in the industrial age. Rorty acknowledges that nationalism has justified domination, but "love of country," he claims, is still the strongest motive for social reform, which is ignited and sustained by loyalty to ideal images of the nation, on behalf of which people criticize actuality and toward which they aspire and thus organize. He approvingly cites Herbert Croly: "The faith of Americans in their own country is religious . . . in its almost absolute and universal authority."[1]

Left politics therefore needs, he claims, not the disenchanting "theory" of academics and its focus on culture and stigma, but inspiring poetic visions of a broadly national focus. By wedding democracy (and social justice) to the idea of America as a special site of possibility, democratic idealism again could fuel, but also redeem, American nationalism. Accordingly, Rorty takes the title *Achieving America* from the last line of James Baldwin's *The Fire Next Time*. Baldwin would not "forgive" his country for its crimes, but remained committed to "achieving" it.[2]

Rorty's politically minded defense of nationhood as imagined community receives unintended commentary from Beatty's movie. Criticizing American politics for serving corporate power, *Bulworth* voices a populism like Rorty's renewed left, but also shows why white supremacy deprives this politics of mass support. As well, it demonstrates why Rorty is wrong to align the left with class rather than culture: Senator Bulworth (played by Beatty) is enabled to speak leftist truth only by becoming what Norman Mailer once called a "white negro," which is to say, the movie participates in the racial symbolism that sustains the domination it means to oppose.

This classic American story of rebirth begins with a corrupt politician, deadened and suicidal because he lives only by mass images. But he is regenerated and redeemed by identifying with the position, and by appropriating the style, dress, and voice of the racial other he fantasizes, a rapper in hiphop costume. This white man who takes on blackface then bears the hope of regenerating the nation's political body.

In part, the movie shows the extraordinarily creative energy in sections of the black community called nihilist by Jesse Jackson and Cornel West; indeed, this "underclass" energizes national culture, which lives by exploiting it. Thus, the movie bespeaks a democratic idealism opposing class domination and white supremacy, but by voicing its racialized imaginary, the attribution and appropriation of potency in all senses. The universalism of democratic idealism seems impossible to advance without enacting the racialized script that always mocks it.

Rorty celebrates civil religion by making race only the violation of equality. He fails to address how it is also the cultural script through which, as Beatty demonstrates, self and nation repeatedly are joined and renewed. Like so many reformers, including King, Rorty would abstract a universalist promise from its tainted racial ground. *Bulworth*'s tangled messages return Rorty's imagined community to that ground. Standing there, I would complicate rather than dismiss Rorty's concerns, exploring alternative ways to rethink and engage the vexed bonds relating nationhood, white supremacy, and democratic idealism.

King, Mailer, and Baldwin are my examples because they negotiate these morally complex and politically torturous bonds. Each links the fate of democracy to the issue of race, and these to the meaning of America. For each, race determines the fates of democracy and the nation. But each also uses a language of nationhood to engage racial domination, for each justifies and fosters a broad attack on white supremacy in part by invoking an ideal nation and narrating its fate. How? They revise rather than reject inherited myths of rebirth that have been crucial to the culture and deeply implicated in white supremacy. They retell stories of rebirth to narrate what it means, collectively and personally, to confront a continuing history of racial domination and its legacies. Caught in the racial imaginary that shadows languages of nationhood and myths of rebirth, their examples help us rethink the relationship of myth and political life.

Their limitations could warrant refusing any language of national identity and common destiny, which seem impossible to recuperate in a way that overcomes a history of domination. Besides, theorists must be marginal: they should analyze but not enact the pressures of belonging and legitimacy that signal the power of imagined community; they should disenchant, not restore, images of national community and related myths of rebirth. Such theoretical asceticism may be warranted but still seem a dishonest and politically ineffective position: dishonest because it disowns its own idealism, and so cannot account for its anger at domination, its desire for change, and its claim to authority; ineffective since changing the American racial regime requires a hope or commitment, and a broad scope, fostered by tropes of rebirth and ideal(ized) community, however problematic.

Through King, Mailer, and Baldwin I suggest the value in efforts to use and thereby work through images of nationhood and stories of rebirth. I also show how their difficulties must be respected because they are hard to avoid. There is no single right way to negotiate the relationship of race and nation or narrate change; all the alternatives are problematic. I would theorize rather than simplify the dilemmas these figures face, to take on rather than defer responsibility for being similarly entangled.

Defining the Problem

By democratic idealism I mean the promise of equality and full inclusion, of personal and political self-government, within a community overcoming all inherited hierarchies and ascribed identities. How is this idealism joined to American nationalism? The rhetoric of democracy locates a specifically American promise in the Declaration of Independence proclaiming equal rights, but also in the cultural declarations creating American identity by separating a New World and chosen identity from an Old World and fixed identity. The declarations thus promise self-determination, both self-making and power exercised in concert. A democratic nation, then, appears to be a voluntary community constituted through consent to a transcending principle of equal rights, which binds self-making individuals together by making possibility and plenitude available to each.[3]

Marx calls these declarations of political and cultural self-determination a "Beautiful revolution" that defines liberal nationalism; Tocqueville calls them "poetry," which he defines as "the delineation of the ideal."[4] For both theorists, idealizations of nationhood and individuality abstract from and flee history, groups, and politics. (In the myth of "America" these signify old world corruption.) In Europe, class drives such poetry, even while exposing declarations of personal sovereignty and national unity as wishes, not promises. And in America?

Differently situated actors repeatedly have symbolized the nation by differentiating new and old worlds; here is the promise that people are liberated by destroying tradition. But for Tocqueville and his mass society heirs, this promise creates a monstrous twin. As individualism destroys older forms of authority and community, including bonds of class, atomized people are organized as a mass by a new kind of authority in public opinion, consumer culture, and nationalism. By a second line of argument, however, this problem is internal to a liberal society sustained by materially dominating and culturally exploiting people marked as uncivilized racial others.[5]

The peculiarities of American liberal society thus arise from the conjunction of mass society and white supremacy, each troubling the poetry of the open and changeable, and the romance of "America" as a special site of possibility. Claims about the fluidity of American society then seem a wish, a way to deny or evade stubborn forms of domination, and very much in the American grain. But fluidity is related to fixity: fixing racial others has been the material condition of fluidity for colonists and immigrants, who also endow their self-making with racialized meanings. So the idea of rebirth, central to civil religion and consumer culture, imagined community and ideal selfhood, has been entwined with racial hierarchy and its meanings.

As Michael Rogin argues: "The society that developed materially from establishing rigid boundaries between white and dark developed culturally from transgressing" them. Myths of the frontier, wilderness hero, and regenerative violence shaped "the first distinctive meaning of America," while blackface minstrelsy also emerged "as the first and most pervasive form of American mass culture." Each fixed racial others in social and symbolic space and thus "exploited identification, for the Indianization or blacking up of the white was the crucial step in leaving . . . an Old World identity and making a new." American identity thus was formed by "racial aversion" and "destructive racial desire."[6]

For Rogin, national identity is formed by the related myths of regeneration through violence and blackface, each enacting a story of rebirth, of making anew the self and the community. While Rogin folds that story into his account of race, mass society, and nationhood, I invert his argument, exploring how King, Mailer, and Baldwin retell myths of rebirth precisely to confront this regime. While he tightly binds stories of rebirth to domination, I ask: How do their stories represent and produce regeneration? On whom and what does it depend? How, and with what consequences, does each take up the burden of redeeming the twinned promise of democracy and America?

Martin Luther King

Martin Luther King spoke directly within the democratic idealism recurrently wed to American nationalism. By invoking the Declaration of Independence and Christian gospel as constituent elements of what Gunnar Myrdal called the "American creed," King authorizes resistance to legalized American apartheid and appeals to whites on the ground of their own idealized image; he thus demonstrates a literal Protestant religiosity and its tie to the religiosity of American nationalism, enacting Tocqueville's claim that theistic faith, Christian morality, personal conscience, and liberal rights form a civil religion that enables resistance to public opinion and state power.

Invoking ideals at the core of what Tocqueville named a "dogmatic" faith and "consensus," King insists that no one should be denied rights on the basis of ascribed (racial) identity, so that everyone can develop a God-given potential by exercising God-given rights. By narrating a providential history—in which Judeo-Christian morality and liberal democracy produce ideals of equality, self-development, and political self-rule—King puts the liberal tradition in prophetic terms: protesting the gap between inherited ideals and daily practice, he calls a special people to make good its founding promise. In his Puritan view, those divided by sin can be reborn by access to God's grace; this enables fulfillment of God's law, a beloved community of mutuality, and, consequently, a "new" nation.

Insisting that "injustice anywhere is a threat to justice everywhere" because "we are caught in an inescapable network of mutuality tied in a single garment of destiny," King declares that "now is the time to make real the promise of democracy," and thus to fulfill "the goal of America," which is "freedom." To African Americans, he therefore says: "Abused and scorned though we may be, our destiny is tied up with the destiny of America" because "the sacred heritage of our nation and the eternal will of God are embodied in our echoing demands." Indeed:

> One day the South will know that when these disinherited children of God sat down at lunch counters they were in reality standing up for the best in the American dream and the most sacred values in our Judaeo-Christian heritage, and thus carrying our whole nation back to the great wells of democracy, which were dug deep by the founding fathers in the formulation of the Constitution and Declaration of Independence.[7]

As King links God's law, democratic idealism, and American nationalism in a providential history, he binds the fates of whites and blacks, while making African Americans the special redemptive protagonist by virtue of their historical exclusion and continuing faith.

By King's prudential political logic, black emancipation depends on liberating whites from racism; by his Christian practice, this means generating their guilt and repentance to reanimate their founding faith. In part, King believes chosen suffering in nonviolent resistance will "purify" and regenerate African Americans by channeling their hatred at injustice. By "using our very bodies as a means," they will bring "to the surface the [racial] tension that is already alive" and "lay our case before the conscience of the local and national community." Thus would he elicit guilt at gross violation of the national creed in a way that reveals whites' own capacity to redeem racial hatred with love. As purified African Americans regenerate whites to free themselves, they redeem the twinned promises of America and democracy.

In defending the "creative tension" in his form of politics, King claims to "stand in the middle of two opposing forces" in the African-American community. On one side are those "Negroes who . . . have adjusted to segregation." On the other are those "who have lost faith in America, who have absolutely repudiated Christianity, and who have concluded that the white man is an incurable 'devil.' " King warns whites: if "channeling discontent through the creative outlet of nonviolent direct action" fails, "millions of Negroes, out of frustration and despair, will seek solace and security in black nationalist ideologies," which "will lead inevitably to a frightening racial nightmare."

King lives and thus demonstrates a myth of rebirth in Christian and national terms. By making a racial apocalypse the alternative to a reborn (unified) community, however, he suggests the political and racial questions we need to pursue. King lives by the faith that a harmonious community of mutual recognition is possible, and without violence. This faith, condensed in the phrase "more perfect union," is still enormously powerful, partly because it carries two wishes, one to transcend politics and the other to transcend race. This faith and these wishes are the myth King lives out, the condition of his strategic and political action on behalf of African Americans and American democracy, but also a profound limitation shaping on thought and action.

King invokes a dream of escaping politics: universally beneficial principles, internalized by all, harmonize individuals by removing systemic inequality and group conflict. In the absence of loyalty to these transcendent ideals, black bitterness and white recalcitrance will fuel irreconcilable and violent racial conflict. Enacting his faith in these principles, and in the power of words and love, he opens spaces for dialogue and action in the fathers' house; King forges a politics that gains formal equality in all senses. The horizon of his action, though, is the dream that a providentially sanctioned actor will redeem his adversaries by recalling them to principles whose self-evidence render politics superfluous. In part, his moralized prophetic language cannot engage the impersonal structuring of racial domination and poverty. In part, King would never conceive politics as a practice compelled by a lack of self-evidence in truth or justice, and thus by struggle (and dialogue) among adversaries with different interests and perspectives.[8]

These limitations relate to the second wish in the dream of rebirth to perfect union, the wish to escape white supremacy and racial consciousness. That is why, though treated as an outcast, he identifies *with* the disinherited but never *as* an outcast: by claiming that African Americans are true heirs of the covenant whites betray, he would gain rights and power, but also subvert the racial symbolic in which black means, as Toni Morrison says, "insanity, illicit sexuality, and chaos." Through his need to be an Isaac and escape the identity of Ishmael, King gained an uncanny ability to voice, but could not risk deeply questioning, the ideals he attributed to his god and nation.[9]

King has complex motives for embracing the identity of the good son, and nonviolence in particular. Partly, he recognizes the political necessity that a minority needs allies to persuade a ruling majority. Partly, he denies that violence ever can be regenerative. Partly, he insists that democracy and black emancipation require dialogue. Partly, he would free African Americans from the racialism linking them to sex and violence, or sin. By scripting a drama of national sin and redemption, however, King does not escape the racial symbolic. As the good son, he reiterates the other symbolic meaning of black, the unconditional—sacrificial—love that regenerates whites.

The good son's faith in the redemptive power of love and words is sorely tested by evil, the refusal to recognize. By suffering without retaliation King means to redeem this evil, and the anger it causes. But oppression and suffering replenish his anger, jeopardizing his persona as a redeemer as well as the authority of the God endowing him with legitimacy. Rather than break God's law by striking at whites, or condemn God for allowing suffering, King follows the logic of the good son. His anger appears as renewed willingness to suffer and thus as moral superiority. Unable to turn against the authority that justifies him, he chooses (self) sacrifice to redeem it. Unable to violate the dialogic terms of his democratic faith, the others' refusal of recognition drives him toward self-sacrifice.

In contrast, King's black power critics refused the romance of liberal nationalism, claiming that transcendent principles masked white power, and openly sought power as and for a group. To kill off the good son who, by internalizing a Christian and liberal identity, lived (and died) for whites, they took on the identity of Ishmael, asserting cultural difference and embracing willful self-assertion. By refusing appeals to formal equality or conscience, and by refusing appeals to redeem whites or America, they exposed domination and conflicting group interests in a racialized regime. Despite openly claiming interest and power, though, they turned internally to a cultural politics that denied the needs of a minority to build coalitions or fashion broad appeals across racial lines.[10]

Moreover, by the posture of their identity politics they were enmeshed in the other image of "black." While assertions of will terrified whites, who project violence behind the mask of love, threatened violence also became a chosen mask for young men reclaiming what they called their manhood. Rejecting a redemptive meaning to "America" and the role of redeemer, but using white myths of regenerative violence, they were placed in and yet took up the role of "Bigger." Cast by Richard Wright as the true "native son" and "monster" haunting a white republic, Bigger is read by Baldwin into the white psychodrama that creates only two self-destroying roles for blacks, either unconditional, sacrificial love or unbounded instinct. This split makes African Americans invisible, forbids individuality, and demonizes assertions of power or interest.[11]

How to address this legacy of racial domination is one issue raised by the conflict between King and his critics. A second is whether white supremacy can be opposed politically without appeal to ideals of American nationhood. A third is how to conceive and whether to relate two sides of politics: the forging of group identity and action in conflict with others and the fashioning of a common stage and destiny. These issues are at play in the stories of rebirth by which Mailer and Baldwin relate race, nationhood, and democratic idealism.

From King to Mailer

King and Mailer both would redeem a nation defaulting on its historic promise. For King, that means invoking the political Declaration of Independence, by renewing its roots, not in slavery, but in Protestant faith and conscience. For Mailer (and Baldwin) liberalism and Protestantism create what William Carlos Williams calls the "spiritually withering" plague of worldly asceticism. In response, male American writers repeatedly seek rebirth not by God's grace, but in nature and by reclaiming what liberal and Christian culture has projected onto racial others. Thus do they imagine a "new" and truly "American" identity.[12]

Whereas King stands within Christian and liberal traditions, to refuse the identity of Ishmael imposed by white supremacy, Mailer voices a tradition that refuses the identity of a liberal or Christianized Isaac, whether given or imposed. King appears as the good son of God and founding fathers, defining the true America through Tocqueville's civil religion. Mailer, however, uses American literature to define the true America in terms of heroic individuality, the frontier experience of the forbidden, regenerative violence, and racial miscegenation. Standing on different grounds, both authorize themselves by invoking a true America linked to the promise of democracy. Both decry a political life cut off from the most important and troubling issues in the society. Both find renewal in efforts that "bring to the surface" disavowed realities. And each claims that this renewal requires faith, King's in (providential) truth and Mailer's in existentialist myth, but for both tied to faith in an ideal America. As both invoke a meaningful purpose in politics to regenerate a deadened social body, each seeks a protagonist whose minority action embodies such poetry and thus the meaning of America.

Like King, Mailer narrates the "double life" of a nation that has not lived its ideals; Mailer, however, shifts their meaning:

> Since the First World War Americans have been leading a double life, and our history has moved on two rivers, one visible the other underground; there has been the history of politics, which is concrete, factual, practical, and unbelievably dull if not for the consequences . . . and there is a subterranean river of untapped, ferocious, lonely, and romantic desires, that concentration of ecstasy and violence which is the dream life of the nation.[13]

What is this dream life? "America is the country in which the dynamic myth of the Renaissance—that every man was potentially extraordinary—knew its most passionate persistence." But the end of the frontier and bureaucratization drove that dynamism out of daily life and politics. Desire and fantasy, cut off from history and politics, were concentrated in a "superheated dream life," and experienced only privately and vicariously in films and advertising. In the Second World War the "life of the nation" again was "intense, of the present, electric" as dream life surfaced into history and collective action. But that very electricity generated anti-communism, "a terror of the national self: free-loving, lust-looting, atheistic, implacable."[14] In his story of a nation fearful of the morally problematic ideal self portrayed in its myths, Mailer still concludes:

> This myth, that each of us was born to be free, to wander, to have adventure, and to grow on the waves of the violent, the perfumed, and the unexpected, had a force which could not be tamed no matter how the nation's regulators—politicians, medicos, policemen, professors, priests, rabbis, ideologues, psy-

> choanalysts, builders, executives, and endless communicators—would brick in modern life with hygiene upon sanity and middle-brow homily over platitude: the myth would not die.[15]

But neither are Americans willing to live it: regimented by corporate life, they are ruled by fear and haunted by fantasy, disowned desire, and self-loathing. Mailer warns:

> As cultures die, they are stricken with the mute implacable rage of that humanity strangled within them. So long as it grows, a civilization depends upon the elaboration of meaning . . . as it dies, a civilization opens itself to the fury of those betrayed by its meaning, precisely because that meaning was finally not sufficiently true to offer a life adequately large. The aesthetic act shifts from the creation of meaning to its destruction.[16]

Like Nietzsche, Mailer makes the authority of myth an explicitly political question: when "sufficiently true" about society and nature, myths generate cultural forms that sustain human loyalty because they enable people to enlarge and deepen their capacities and experience. Thus, he insists that the key postwar issue in America is "the fate of its myth." Convinced that every nation needs to project "an ideal image" and devoted to his "love affair with the secret potentialities of America," he rearticulates inherited ideals of imagined community.[17]

That effort is initiated by his notorious 1957 essay, "The White Negro," his first inverted retelling of the Puritan story. In it self and society cut off from the source of life are regenerated by access to grace, albeit by descending below safely contractual liberal surfaces to desires, fantasies, and ways to live that authority casts as delinquent, deviant, and pathological. Insisting that we move "forward into growth or backward into death," Mailer links growth to adventure and mortal risk, to encounters with the unknown and forbidden, and thus to that moral risk and change which comprise the true meaning of the American myth he renews. The alternative is living death as "a square cell in the totalitarian tissues of American society."[18]

To dramatize this "choice" and confront ambivalence about it, he celebrates the bohemians, psychopaths, and delinquents who live on moral "frontiers" to contact "ecstasy and violence." In his effort to internalize frontiers, he relates these figures to "the Negro," in whom he lodges the sexuality, moral complexity, and cultural inventiveness he would infuse into the square life he implicitly codes white. Indeed, the true subterranean America is embodied by "the Negro," a fantasy Mailer invokes, apparently without irony, as fact:

> Any Negro who wishes to live must live with danger from his first day. . . . The cameos of security for the average white: mother and home, job and the

> family, are not even a mockery to millions of Negroes; they are impossible. The Negro has the simplest of alternatives: live a life of constant humility or ever-threatening danger. In such a pass . . . the Negro had stayed alive and begun to grow by following the need of his body where he could. Knowing in the cells of his existence that life was . . . nothing but war, the Negro (all exceptions permitted) could rarely afford the sophisticated inhibitions of civilization, and so he kept for his survival the art of the primitive, he lived in the enormous present . . . relinquishing the pleasures of the mind for the more obligatory pleasures of the body, and in his music he gave voice to the character and quality of his existence. . . . Hated from the outside, and therefore hating himself, the Negro was forced into the position of exploring all those moral wildernesses of civilized life that the Square automatically condemns as delinquent or evil or immature or morbid or self-destructive or corrupt [but in which] the Negro discovered and elaborated . . . an ethical differentiation between the good and bad in every human activity.[19]

What does Mailer achieve by inverting a pathologized caricature to create a romanticized other? He symbolizes racially what he calls an "existential" way of living. By identificatory desire for the "primitive" passion and mortal risk, and thus for the moral complexity and creativity he finds in the racial other he fantasizes, he narrates personal rebirth as a regression that enables "growing up a second time." Thus does he kill off his given self as "a nice Jewish boy" and renew himself as a writer.[20]

But he also means to engage American culture: he laments the assimilation of Jews and Blacks into mass society, whereby they efface "the minority within" the self and "bleach" worldly differences in culture. Finding cultural renewal in the assertion of difference against homogeneity, he imagines a "wedding" of disaffected youth, artists, and "the Negro," who "brings the cultural dowry." But any "counter-culture," and the broader renewal it could foster, depends on whether "the Negro emerges as a dominating force in American life." Mailer thus defends the "dominance" of African Americans, but by fixing in "the Negro" the sensibility that will regenerate whites.[21]

In a prosaic and less racialized way, he imagines that the struggle over civil rights could regenerate American politics. "Conventional politics," he argues in 1963, has "so little to do with the real subterranean life of America" that "the real—which is to say the potential—historic nature of America" is unknown. How "the mass of Americans" would "react to radically new sense" is unknown as well. In both regards, reality cannot be known as long as the terrain of politics is a "No Man's Land" on which "opposing armies never meet." However:

> any army which would dare to enter it in force might not only determine a few new political formations, but indeed could create more politics itself, just as . . . an existential political act, the drive by Southern Negroes led by Mar-

> tin Luther King . . . an act which is existential precisely because its end is unknown, has succeeded en route in discovering more of the American reality.[22]

Politically, then, Mailer praises the civil rights movement in the name of justice, but also because "armies" (Tocquevillean associations) foster "more politics," thereby disclosing and creating "reality." Indeed, an "existential politics" could replenish the "life of myth" and invigorate the culture. So for Mailer, the "fate of the myth" and democratic politics depend in part on bringing the subterranean to the surface, to face the meaning of race in our culture and history. He supports this cultural politics by recasting mythic ideals of frontiers, individuality, and risking the unknown. A movement King fosters by invoking law and conscience, Mailer folds into an existential story about the struggles through which a nation faces real frontiers and determines the fate of its myth.

Mailer's value compared to King is this more critical and dynamic view of culture and politics, one gained by standing outside and against the creed King remains within. By invoking an ideal America linked to action into the unknown, Mailer revises a myth that may be sufficiently true to offer a life adequately large. True enough because racial domination and mass society, but also divided selves and political conflict, appear as facts denied at great cost. A life large enough because purposes and practices are opened to question, such experiments change actors and the world in unpredictable ways, such changes risk what they know and assume, and, such risks can ennoble their bearers. But as Mailer embodies this existential myth in "the Negro," he repeats the racial coding and myth of regenerative violence at the core of the culture he claims to resist. His call to appropriate what he projects onto African Americans is linked to their emancipation, not subordination, and to what he credits as cultural achievement, not nature. Still, Mailer fixes African Americans in symbolic place as he puts on blackface; he uses African-American culture to serve white renewal.

Mailer celebrates minority doubleness as a fruitful tension lost in assimilation, but he refuses an overtly Jewish identification; he turns to "the Negro" because he links "the Jew" to the ethical spirit, not the libidinal body. Seeing Jews as what Philip Roth calls "the super-ego's man in Manhattan," Mailer repudiates them to own his sexuality and aggression. He might not have needed "the white Negro" if he had conceived "the Jew" as Roth did, but Mailer therefore created a broader and political exploration of American society. Indeed, his texts are revelatory to the degree that he enters with some awareness the fantasies and fears he shares with a dominant culture. But "woman" and "homosexuality" are thus also charged markers in his texts, as in the myths he revises. Mailer assumes an adversarial stance toward his culture, but his obsessions and mythic retellings always betray (and illuminate) his privileged position within it.[23]

From Mailer to Baldwin

In the late fifties, Baldwin and Mailer were friends. They also shared a broadly comparable view of American life. Both oppose white supremacy, but not by invoking providential history, moral law, and liberal rights. Standing against the creed King defends, each reaches below contractual surfaces and moral laws to contact what Mailer calls the subterranean and Baldwin "the depths." For both, renewal of culture and politics unfolds only as those calling themselves white confront racial domination. As both thus theorize renewal of a life-denying culture, each situates and credits but also surpasses King's politics.

But their difference in positioning and in their views of change and nationhood appear in Mailer's essay and Baldwin's response. Personally, Baldwin is horrified for his friend, whose blatant fantasies of rebirth are so self-exposing and adolescent. Because of his own social positioning as a racial other, Baldwin also rejects Mailer's celebration of "the Negro," which reduces complex individuals and communities to merely symbolic status by trading on rather than working through racial images. Unmasking Mailer's "myths" of individuality and heroism, Baldwin also refuses Mailer's jeremiad. Instead of redeeming a true America by existentializing a frontier ethos, Baldwin shows a nightmarish racial past imprisoning everyone in barren repetition. To say too simply what I will explain: unlike King and Mailer, he does not appeal to an idealized nation, and he makes freedom depend not on rebirth but on digesting the constitutive power of the past.[24]

Baldwin argues that American history originates in the twinned facts of democracy and slavery and thus entwines white supremacy and democratic idealism. Still, both are European ideas: founding "democracy on the American continent was scarcely as radical a break with the past as was the necessity, which Americans faced, of broadening this concept to include black men." Though "America of all the Western world," could best "prove the uselessness and obsolescence of the concept of color . . . it has not dared to accept this opportunity or even to conceive of it as an opportunity" because Americans see Europe and civilization as "synonyms" and refuse "other standards and sources of vitality, especially those produced in America itself." Baldwin writes:

> If we, who can scarcely be considered a white nation, persist in thinking of ourselves as one, we condemn ourselves . . . to sterility and decay, whereas, if

> we could accept ourselves as we are, we might bring new life to Western achievements and transform them. The price of this transformation is the unconditional freedom of the Negro. . . . He is *the* key figure in his country.[25]

As Baldwin's locution shifts from an "America" that excludes Blacks to a "we" of membership, he enacts his ambivalent view of nationhood and his purposely doubled positioning toward it. He also links change to "accept[ing] ourselves as we are," even as that "we" is whites and blacks separately, and as Americans.[26]

In both regards, Baldwin differs significantly from King and Mailer, but in ways that become clear by first asking why "we persist" in imagining a white nation:

> The racial tensions that menace Americans today have little to do with real antipathy—on the contrary, indeed—and are involved only symbolically with color. These tensions are rooted in the very same depths from which love springs, or murder. The white man's unadmitted—and apparently, to him, unspeakable—fears and longings are projected onto the Negro.[27]

Racial thinking involves self-denial and projection: "we" persist in white supremacy, dominating and symbolically using specific people, to control aspects of the self and of life in fact beyond our control, but for that very reason especially threatening to members of a culture invested in sovereignty and anxious about order. Baldwin repeatedly mentions death and "the dark forces in life," as well as love and bodily impulse, which can make anyone helpless, but also suffering, change, and moral ambiguity, which defeat efforts to control or rationally order experience. The fears driving white supremacy create a white (or "American") culture cut off from life because it denies death.

Unable to "accept" what is in themselves and life, and thus haunted by fear and envy of specters bearing what they disavow, whites also refuse to "accept" the centrality of white supremacy in their history, or how it has tainted their professed beliefs, destroyed millions of lives, but also formed them in every sense. In Baldwin's words:

> The American vision of the world—which allows so little reality, generally speaking, for any of the darker forces in human life, which tends to paint moral issues in glaring black and white—owes a great deal to the battle waged by Americans to maintain between themselves and black men a human separation that could not be bridged.[28]

By irony, he suggests how whites in fact are blinded and trapped by the order that privileges them racially. Of the legacy of this history for blacks,

Baldwin says: "no American Negro exists who does not have his private Bigger Thomas living in his skull."[29]

But Baldwin narrates this legacy in terms of freedom. The black man *must* "accept the fact that this dark and dangerous and unloved stranger is part of himself forever" because "only this recognition sets him in any wise free and it is this necessary ability to contain and even, in the most honorable sense of the word, to *exploit* the 'nigger' which lends to Negro life its high element of the ironic."[30] Herein lies Baldwin's conception and narration of change, which profoundly differs from languages of rebirth in King and Mailer. There is no "growing up a second time" as in Mailer, no purifying and rebirth as in King, no starting again as in liberal self-making; there is no escaping what has been taken inside the self, or purifying what a self or people have become through history. There is rather "accepting ourselves as we are," which precisely sets us free, free *from* resentment, thus free *to* "exploit" what we cannot change, and change what we can.

To a people committed to Christian ideas of rebirth, or to the romance of self-making, the poetry of an acquisitive society, Baldwin is emphatic about the power of history:

> White man, hear me! History . . . does not refer merely or even or principally to the past. On the contrary, the great force of history comes from the fact that we carry it within us, are unconsciously controlled by it in many ways, so history is literally *present* in all that we do. It could scarcely be otherwise since it is to history that we owe our frames of reference, our identities, and our aspirations. And it is with great pain and terror that one begins to realize this . . . because, therefore, one enters into battle with that historical creation, Oneself, and attempts to recreate one-self according to a principle more humane and liberating; one begins the attempt to achieve a personal maturity and freedom which robs history of its tyrannical power and also changes history. But obviously, I speak as a historical creation which has had to bitterly contest its history, to wrestle with it, and finally accept it in order to bring myself out of it.[31]

Americans using a language of rebirth seek the unprecedented to escape history, but thus generate repetition. One alternative is an idea of renewal in and through history: principles, practices, bonds, or commitments become alien and imposed, but are renewed by a reinterpreting that refounds or chooses them anew. We enact freedom by remaking—not passively repeating—the origins or principles from which we derive ourselves. But this Machiavellian or jeremiadic view of legacy and renewal, to a degree voiced by King (and Rorty) when invoking civil religion, is refused by Baldwin.

Humans are constituted by history, but their freedom, their aliveness or newness, arises not by renewing origins conceived as resources, but in the paradox of acceptance and wrestling that is dictated by conceiving origins as a problem. This language grants gravity and friction to human agency: we are capable of a kind of re-creation but paradoxically, only by recognizing our historical constitution. Nietzsche uses the metaphor of "digestion" and the idea of *amor fati* similarly: to "accept" the past does not preclude change, but shifts its motive and meaning. To recognize history is to rob it of the power denial gives it, thus to be less ruled by fantasy and resentment, hence to act more than react, and therefore to attempt a "re-creation" that is neither denial nor repetition.[32]

As wrestling involves "contesting" the past, it also means grappling, not only with the question of identity, but thus with deciding what can(not) or should (not) be changed. Such wrestling is always personal, but the word denotes an agon with others and also suggests that these issues are political. And by insisting that wrestling is a condition of life, Baldwin presents "re-creation" not as redemptive but as an ongoing struggle at the core of selfhood and collective life. Baldwin's politics, then, also appears in his claims about what "we" must accept.

"We need" to recognize, first, that our society always has been multiracial: "like it or not . . . we are bound together forever" in bonds of rivalry and conflict he calls "a wedding":

> Indeed, the relationship of black to white is not simply the relationship of master to slave, oppressor to oppressed, nor is it motivated merely by hatred; it is also, literally and morally, a *blood* relationship, perhaps the most profound reality of the American experience, and we cannot unlock it until we accept how very much it contains of the force and anguish and terror of love.[33]

To "accept" this is to begin to work through the meaning of racial categories and how they divide and yet entwine us. Their power can be drained, paradoxically, only by recognizing their continuing impact, and the projections that constitute them.[34]

But Baldwin advances a second fundamental fact to accept:

> The one thing all Americans have in common is that they have no other identity apart from the identity being achieved on this continent. This is not an English necessity, or Chinese necessity, or French necessity, but . . . the necessity of Americans to achieve an identity is a historical and a present personal fact and this is the connection between you and me.[35]

But by stipulating these two facts as "the connection between you and me," has he fashioned a way to talk about nationhood and change that includes rather than escapes politics?

Early in *The Fire Next Time*, Baldwin proclaims: "We, with love, shall force our brothers to see themselves as they are, to cease fleeing reality, and begin to change it. . . . We can make America what America must become." Then: "In short, we, the black and the white, deeply need each other if we are really to become a nation . . . to create one nation has proved to be a hideously difficult task: there is certainly no need now to create two." Rather, "relatively conscious" whites and blacks "must, like lovers, insist on or create the consciousness of the others." Only then might we "end the racial nightmare and achieve our country and change the history of the world."[36]

Baldwin attributes not an essence to a character, but a history to a relationship; he derives culture from a history of conflict. Unlike King, he does not say, "The goal of America is freedom." Unlike Mailer, he voices no "love affair" with its "secret potentiality." Rather, "our nation" is our life together, as "we" are those who have inhabited "this continent," "built this country," and been shaped by the encounter with each other and this place. To some degree, then, Baldwin means by "nation" something like our relationship and life together: to "create one nation" has been "hideously difficult" because some disown others, but there remains a "bond" characterized by all the registers of "love." "America" thus appears not as a transcendent ideal, even one incarnated in time, but as a mutually constitutive history and relationship. It is who and what we have become, contingently, a result of conflicts and dependence, but perhaps also our creation, partly independent of our wills, a reality of its own and hard to change.[37]

But if the injunction to "accept ourselves" means accepting that our history is both white supremacy and a "wedding," what is the sense in then saying: we can "achieve our country" or "must make America what America must become"? What is to be achieved? What "must" the nation, this relationship, become? Here, Baldwin may participate in the romance of America: if our history shows an unprecedented wedding of white and black, then the achievement Baldwin invokes is surely the unprecedented overcoming of white supremacy, hence a full embrace of ourselves as multiracial, and thus a first try at democratic life.

Partly, we make conscious, celebrate, and use rather than deny what we are already; partly we thus become "one" nation in a real and not illusory way. To "achieve" this nation is to "exploit" the facts of our history as an "opportunity" to prove "the uselessness and obsolescence of color." But partly, we "must" achieve *this* or we "condemn ourselves to sterility" and "abdicate all hope of freedom." So Baldwin does create a poetry of aspiration for shaping the constitutive relationship behind the signifier "America." His "nation" is not abstracted from life but anchored in a racial history, so the "we" implies not unity or sharing as communion or sameness, but wrestling or "struggle" with each other and the history that joins and divides us.

Still, Baldwin's language of acceptance is also a problem. For him, the issue is white self-denial of self-evident truths and realities, which makes their crime willful innocence. In a prophetic mode of address he says: face the truth, not only the fact of slavery but that it means white supremacy, and that this is the truth of our history. As an *interpretation* of history and attribution of meaning is presented as self-evident truth, it is drained of politics, but so is history, in which truth is "faced" or denied, not contested by differing interpretations or stories. The "fate" of a nation is governed by politics conceived as a prophetic struggle against blindness, not as conflict among interpretations linked to different groups, standards of evidence, and ranking of values.[38]

Baldwin's ethos of acceptance elides politics in another sense. King's language risks the dangers of false transcendence, but is anchored in political organizations and black churches. Mailer's "romance" with "America" and "existential politics" is enacted by what he calls "armies," organized forces articulating divergent positions, and by "heroes," leaders who personify institutions and movements. Baldwin maps cultural meaning, but without reference to institutions and organized politics. His nation is a bond of love and struggle, not a bureaucratic regime or terrain of interest groups. But he is a poet framing an ethos to guide action:

> To speak in my own person, as a member of the nation's most oppressed minority, I want to suggest . . . we cannot discuss the state of minorities until we first have some sense of what we are, who we are, what our goals are, and what we take life to be.[39]

By speaking this ambiguous "we," Baldwin accomplishes another purpose besides performatively creating an intersubjective space. He enacts responsibility for a common destiny by posing questions of identity, desire, and purpose, which in turn frame whether and how race is (to be) addressed. But Baldwin presses intensely on more specific questions: What fosters acceptance of the past? Does black freedom require white renewal? Does taking up this redemptive burden mean or risk repeating the racial symbolic? Does refusing it doom us all? By posing the problem of moving beyond a history of repetition, Baldwin, in all ambivalence, engages the fate of democracy and the meaning of America.

Conclusion

Mailer and Baldwin suggest, *contra* Rorty, that a "left" politics requires a cultural dimension, indeed, that his "social democratic" politics will fail because of white supremacy, whose roots and meaning it cannot address precisely because it devalues cultural politics. But Baldwin and Mailer also echo Rorty's claim that political reform requires the articulation of vision. So the issue is how they narrate change and figure forth imagined community.

Their examples suggest the value in practices of citizenship that defeat idealization but not aspiration, as idealization flees actuality while aspiration finds in it gifts to exploit. By making race the core of actuality, Mailer and Baldwin open to politics the vexed and charged issue, played out in *Bulworth*, of what counts as a gift and "honorably" exploiting it. Aspiration also takes form by asking what adversaries would become, or wish to make of themselves, since they will be remade and entwined by their engagement. The question of becoming is always answered by action's haunting legacy, but is not often asked or articulated as an aspiration we bring to and test by action. To pose becoming not as a problem to solve once and for all, but as a question of actuality and aspiration to continually ask and answer, may be poetry's gift to politics. Perhaps that is why Baldwin quotes from Proverbs: where there is no vision the people perish.

making of the unwanted colonies: (un)imagining desire

AIDA A. HOZIC

In early February 1994, just days before the massacre that killed sixty-six people in a market in Sarajevo, Universal Pictures announced that it had bought the rights to the war diary of a twelve-year-old girl, Zlata Filipovic, better known as "Sarajevo's Anne Frank." *Daily Variety* reported that the rights were sold for a seven-figure sum. "[The film] begins with Zlata's daily life in peacetime Sarajevo," explained Phil Alden Robinson, the writer/director assigned to the project. "She watches *Murphy Brown* on TV, she loves Ninja Turtles, she is a very Western urban kid. At a certain point, this charming young woman's observations turn into front-row seats on a nightmare."[1] The article proceeded to explain that Mr. Robinson's attachment to the project and his previous visit to Sarajevo ("It's the most haunting place I'd been") persuaded Zlata and her parents to "go with Universal," although a number of other directors, producers, and studios had fought for the project.[2]

The announcement was disturbing on several accounts. Was the fact that little Zlata used to watch *Murphy Brown* and knew by heart the names of all the Ninja Turtles really an indication that she was a "very Western urban kid"? Would her account be less credible or less interesting if she were not? Could the comparison with Anne Frank be insulting to the victims and survivors of the Holocaust? Most of all, could the transaction, by now routine, of buying and selling the rights to one's own life story be anything but obscene in light of the ongoing war? No one in Hollywood, wrapped up in posters of *Schindler's List* in preparation for the forthcoming Oscars, seemed to care. Re-born Anne Frank was selling the rights to her made-for-publication diary while people in the ghetto were still being killed, and Sarajevo—with all its horrors—was turning into the entertainment capital of the world.[3]

Cut to Rwanda, where no Hollywood movies (as yet? ever?) have been shot and where mass reproduced images of violence have never reached the level of individuation that characterized Zlata's story. In the summer of 1998, *National Geographic* published a ten-page story on central Africa's "cycle of violence."[4] Amidst the story of "hatred, flight, death," there was also a drawing of the slaughter by a Rwandan child, a surviving eyewitness to a murder. The drawing had three segments. In the first segment, a man with a machete was cutting the face of a much smaller figure, possibly a boy, and the blood was streaming out of his face. In the second segment, a man was setting a house on fire. In the third segment, a different male figure was cutting the throat of yet another boy, and blood—again—was pouring out of his tiny body. The accompanying text explained that "the recent genocide in Rwanda wasn't about ancient tribal hatreds but about power"; and that the name of the child who "drew horrific memories in therapy" had been obscured in order to protect his identity. The text, however, failed to note that the perpetrators in the child's drawing were *white*, Rambo-like figures, and that even the muscular bodies of their victims appeared to be *white* with little resemblance to the slender dark figures of children in central Africa. Even if we allow for the possibility that the drawing may not have been that of a Rwandan child (with so much violence around the world, the *National Geographic* editor could have easily made a mistake), the sketch is still a stunning testimony to the power of mass-mediated imagery: in an age in which oppression has been turned into entertainment, even a child's memory of personally experienced violence cannot but take the form of a bad Hollywood movie.

Sarajevo's Hollywood-style narratives, which have thus far inspired more than forty fictional or documentary films, and the memories of a Rwandan child, which cannot find their own representation, constitute the boundaries of an imaginary space whose political significance has dramatically increased over the past decade. As Martin Shaw argues, media representation of "distant violence" has now become a necessary ingredient in political production of global crises: the attention and media space given to war-torn areas seem directly proportional to the propensity of the international community to intervene in their troubles.[5] Journalists and politicians alike are disturbed by the growing political independence and economic power of media conglomerates. The fear that CNN may be dictating U.S. foreign policy and forcing events to happen is matched only by the fear that the Pentagon will indefinitely continue to monitor and orchestrate any media coverage of any American military intervention.[6] Thus, both Baudrillard's ironic contention that the Gulf War never took place (that it was nothing but a well-staged media event and its victims just "sacrificed extras")[7] and the popular contention that a live broadcast of Secretary of State Madeleine Albright's protest-filled town meeting at Ohio State University in February 1998 (where she attempted to explain administration policy in Iraq) prevented the Gulf War's reenactment rest on a similar assumption: that the political now matters only if visually represented, if mediated, if broadcast as simulacra.

Yet such media-wrapping of the political does not address the question of what kind of political is actually being produced by these mediated images of "distant violence." Nor does it address the critical issue raised by this volume—how is the political produced in the age of virtual money, virtual warfare, virtual news, and much too real violence? Who is constituting whom in these imaginary relations, what accounts for their political potency, and what are their consequences?

The imaginary space produced by media representation of ethnic violence disturbs, in my view, some of the premises upon which debates about the relationship between the West and its *other* have been built over the past few decades. A no-one's land, cleansed and swept over in the name of culture and identity and structured, fractured, and reconstructed through global media, zone of ethnic violence haunts the cosmopolitan center as a repugnant specter, an unpleasant reminder of its own violent past and present, a drawback in the age of digitality, transnationalism, and hybridity. Yet, at the same time, consumed as an image but rejected as a territory, the ethnic war zone emerges as a new kind of colony—*unwanted, undesired, uncalled for*—and, thus, as a playground for a new type of capitalism. Complicating the assumed synchronicity between *power, desire*, and *gaze*, the unwanted colonies pose a challenge to postcolonial "economies of desire" while securing for themselves a place in the world economy much better than abandonment and much worse than indignity.

Media as a Colonizer, Colonized as a Medium

The success of *Little Zlata* in Hollywood and the elevation of Sarajevo into the symbol of contemporary martyrdom were products of the complex confluence of factors of which the war, the siege, and the tragedy of its citizens were not necessarily the most important. Unlike many other places in Bosnia and unlike Somalia, Rwanda, or Chechnya, Sarajevo was well equipped to host a surging number of foreign journalists in the wake of the war. The portrayal of Sarajevo's multicultural ethos stood in sharp contrast with the images (or, better, with the absolute lack thereof) of the ethnic hatred that was flaring throughout Bosnia. Ethnic violence, as cameramen quickly discovered, was not particularly conducive to visual representation, and the inability to racialize the conflict perplexed representatives of the U.S. media.[8] In their early reports from Bosnia, journalists often expressed surprise at the absence of visible physical differences between Serbs and Croats and Muslims; similarly, two years later, in Rwanda, much would be made out of differences between Tutsis and Hutus, which were, in reality, negligible and could not be visually demonstrated.[9] The visual chasm between the two worlds created a certain degree of "Bosnia envy" among those who held that other tragedies, in the former Yugoslavia and elsewhere, were equally worthy of the world's attention.[10] Perhaps more importantly, Sarajevo served as an example of what media can and cannot display, and made it apparent to what extent the very survival of localities and individuals had become dependent on media representation of their fate. The war in Bosnia and Herzegovina, writes Tom Keenan, was a quintessentially "postmodern" one, "fought over culture and identity, with civilians and television cameras,"[11] while Sarajevo itself, "in its own cataclysmic turn [became] a kind of museum, or rather a kind of strange test site where wit and fatigue cross in the adaptation that seeks less to preserve than to transform."[12] The showcased destruction constituted the city as an exhibit of ironic survival and of transformation.

The tale of Sarajevo's inclusion into the global media industry—vis-à-vis its own history and vis-à-vis the places where outbreaks of violence and humanitarian disasters have gone unreported and under-reported—reveals an intricate link between representation and its object in the contemporary international system. "Whatever logic is applied by the rest of the world to the lunacy of Bosnia," said ABC's Ted Koppel, in a *Nightline* special several years ago, "let it not be said that we did not know. People like Jeremy Bowen [a BBC journalist] have deprived us of that excuse."[13] Koppel's statement, which deserves a more detailed analysis than this essay can afford (from the assumption that "logic" is the property of the "world" as opposed to the "lunacy" of Bosnia, to yet another allusion to the Holocaust when the world supposedly "did not know" and therefore did not act, to an implicit belief in the messianic role of a Western journalist), brings to light what is presumed to be the main task of media coverage of international conflicts and crisis: to enlighten the observers who "don't want to watch" about injustice being done elsewhere and to provoke them to act against it. Once again, leaving aside the problematic assumptions that knowledge equals action and that the media are morally superior to their audiences, it is obvious that the critical question of media coverage and political action then becomes—how can the world stand by and watch when a tragedy has already been brought into its own living room? Yet without any desire to be cynical or dismissive about the presumed lack of compassion (or interest) on the part of the audiences, I would like to suggest that a much more fruitful starting point to an analysis of media representation of "distant violence"—and, yes, of contemporary capitalism—would be the question, "Why is the world watching?" Namely, not just the question of "Why Bosnia and not Rwanda?" or "Why Rwanda and not Burundi?"—although they are also, as we shall see, quite revelatory—but "Why Bosnia, Rwanda, Burundi at all?"

A closer look into the extensive coverage of Sarajevo's siege offers a partial answer to these questions. The attention bestowed upon Sarajevo during the war was an inadvertent consequence of the city's earlier attempt to become a part of the global image industry—the 1984 Winter Olympics—and of the changes that the Western, but particularly U.S., media industries have undergone since that time. The Olympics endowed Sarajevo with an infrastructure and skills to deal with reporters even under duress; the transformation of the world's largest media companies created a demand for the continuous news coverage and real-life stories that Sarajevo—and other places of disaster—could provide in abundance. Combined, they have achieved what Sarajevo and its local politicians had long yearned for: the recognition of Sarajevo as a place worthy of the world's attention, the constitution of itself as a colony in the world's imagination.

Of course, there is irony in this survival and this transformation. Envisioned as a stepping stone for the development of a local tourist industry, the Sarajevo Olympics were a great financial and organizational success but they could not alter the image of the city as the capital of a backwater country in the middle of the Balkans. Almost in their entirety paid for by ABC Sports, the Sarajevo Olympics were the first "made for TV" games and a landmark in the future commercialization of the Olympic spirit. Consciously courted by the local government, the American network all but colonized the city in 1983 and 1984. As the largest single sponsor of the games, ABC executives were given royal treatment in their dealings with the local Olympic committee and the Bosnian government. The network employed over a thousand people, mostly overqualified yet unemployed local youth, and accounted for one quarter of press accreditation at the Olympics;[14] it had its own direct multilateral satellite line from Sarajevo, exceptional access to the best spots on the sites of the events, privileged rights to close-ups during the medal ceremonies, and, in the course of several months surrounding the Olympics, even its own cafeteria in Sarajevo's television center. The food—including burgers, coleslaw, and cheesecake—was shipped daily from New York to prevent unnecessary exposure of ABC's employees to the local cuisine.

Nonetheless, the games—and all sixty-three and a half hours of their prime-time coverage—turned out to be a disaster for ABC Sports. The ratings were the lowest in the history of televised Olympics, and the network was forced to give away a significant number of commercials to make up for the poor showing. In addition, the low Olympic ratings ruined the prospects of ABC to win the February sweeps—one of the four times during the year when ratings are used to set advertising rates for the network-affiliated stations. Among numerous reasons for this failure—few medals for U.S. athletes, few bankable stars, competition from ESPN and CNN—the most important was probably, as the *Christian Science Monitor* put it succinctly, that "Sarajevo Games were much like the town itself: earnest and eager to please, but just short of the grandeur that spoiled aficionados have come to expect of these quadrennial sports spectaculars."[15] Namely, despite all its efforts and unprecedented media presence, Sarajevo was still featured as a "socialist working class" city located in the "primitive central Yugoslav republic of Bosnia and Herzegovina," which lacked the "sophisticated charm" of places such as Chamonix, St. Moritz, or even Lake Placid.[16] Even the city's cultural diversity gathered little praise. "Bosnians of whatever origin—Croat, Serb, or Moslem—feel inferior," wrote the *Economist*. They are "looked down on by other Yugoslavs as people lacking polish and sophistication." The Olympic games, "which should have been held in a much more Westernized and developed northern Republic of Slovenia," are "an attempt to show the rest of the world just what these Bosnian backwoodsmen are capable of."[17] The *New York Times* offered a similar Orientalist assessment of the city. "Before a recent multimillion-dollar environmental cleanup program went into place," wrote the paper, "the air in Sarajevo was mostly thick gray soot, and the rippled Miljacka River that cascades through it was virtually an open sewer."[18] According to the same article, Sarajevo was a "city of nearly 450,000 citizens, including Serbs, Croats and *indigenous* Bosnians [emphasis added], and the mosques and minarets of its sizable Islamic Community gave it the flair of the Arabian crescent."[19]

Not surprisingly, Sarajevo saw few lasting positive effects of the games. The sale of television rights and corporate sponsorship allowed the games to be produced under budget, but the Olympics never led to the development of winter tourism or to the creation of more than 4,000 jobs as had been planned. Although the government continued to court representatives of the world media in an effort to sustain their attention on Sarajevo, the city and the Bosnian economy in general remained dependent on the Yugoslav military-industrial complex in a country strangled by foreign debt and rising unemployment.[20] Instead of a badly needed inflow of foreign capital, Sarajevo was left with an Olympic Museum, a canary-yellow Holiday Inn, a versatile bobsled/luge run on Mount Trebevic, and a gigantic TV and broadcast center as mementos of a bygone era. Mostly under-utilized in the late 1980s, many of the Olympic objects—aside from becoming the prime target for the Serb forces that encircled the city—regained a *raison d'être* only with the advent of the war in 1992. At the same time, the know-how and media savvy acquired during the Olympics allowed all sides in the conflict to "manage media coverage so as to shape international opinion and local sympathies."[21] The existing infrastructure—from the television center to satellite links (CNN installed its own dish behind the television center several months before the beginning of the war), interpreters, and hotel services—was superior to whatever war correspondents had seen in other crisis areas. Consequently, many foreign journalists never ventured out of Sarajevo and eagerly adopted interpretations of the war offered by locally based representatives of the international community and the English-speaking representatives of the Serb, Muslim, and Croat leadership. In addition, Sarajevo also provided them with a number of ready-made narratives—from the beauty pageant in the building of the National Theater and street performances of the cellist Vedran Smajlovic to the heroics of a rapist-turned-savior immortalized in a photograph by Annie Leibowitz—and readily posed as a picture-perfect war-torn landscape in films and MTV videos. Judged against the background of Third World countries, where similar "savagery" was to be expected, and no longer compared to the glamorous ski centers in the West, Sarajevo set a visual—and perhaps political—standard for the New World Order and its limitations: a failed experiment in social tolerance, a multicultural project gone astray, a battle of rural against the urban, a jeopardized model of cosmopolitanism.

But a change in the functioning of global media industries also contributed to the acceptance of Sarajevo as a palatable source of news. Unknown to its citizens and independent of (indifferent to?) their fate, the conglomerization of the media and the increased concentration of power in the hands of distributors created the need for a constant flow of news and visual products. Starting in 1987, when Rupert Murdoch bought 20th Century Fox, NBC produced the first three episodes of *Missing* (a precursor of *Unsolved Mysteries*), and CNN started experimenting with its *Headline News*, American television witnessed an evolution of a new genre: Reality TV. The phenomenon had a variety of manifestations—from "law and order" programs such as *Cops* and *America's Most Wanted* and talk shows such as *Oprah*, *Donahue*, *Sally Jesse Raphael*, and *Geraldo* to the so-called "tabloid TV"–magazine-type news programs like *Current Affairs* and *Hard Copy*. All have signaled an important shift in media programming—from fictional stories, once assumed to be more controllable and easier to produce—to real-life stories whose erratic occurrences could now be managed thanks to the low-cost of satellite connections, a number of globally dispersed freelancers willing to risk their lives in order to record a story, and a public eager to supply its private life to the media. The direct transmission of the Gulf War brought about a 28 percent increase in advertising revenue for CNN, and led many to believe that coverage of wars and humanitarian disasters could be both morally right and profitable as well. As it could be expected, both CNN and the networks lost their interest in Sarajevo and Bosnia as soon as the low ratings signaled that audiences had reached a saturation point and indicated a possible decline in revenue. Unlike their predecessors from before the Dayton peace accords, films and documentaries made after Dayton had difficulties in finding distributors regardless of their quality.

Friction(s)/Representation(s)

The ups and downs of Sarajevo's relations with world media demand us to forge a new link between political, cultural, and economic aspects of imaginary relations between the West and its *other(s)*. No longer a matter of binary categories such as colonized and colonizer, center and periphery, Sarajevo's complex story allows for a variety of possible interpretations of what representation is and may be. Representation, obviously, can be a mirror image of its object, an unfettered replica of the *other;* alternately, it can be a projection of the subject's own desires, a self-centered conversation with oneself for which the *other* is only a convenient excuse—a process, as Joan Copjec would say, through which the subject is "produced as the master of the image";[22] finally, representation can also be a reflection of that Lacanian *Other* to which both the imagining subject and the imagined object are subsumed, possibly a structure such as capitalism, patriarchy or imperialism.

As we have seen above, at various points over the past fifteen years, representations of Sarajevo have flirted with each and all of these possibilities. Much like Somali khat-chewing drug-dependent gangs that represented a transparent projection of America's inner-city problems onto African politics, Sarajevo's multiculturalism—a term that before the war had little meaning in the Bosnian context since it presumed the preexistence of separate cultures—was an obvious projection of America's own fears of and hopes for diversity. Similarly, the inability of Sarajevo to control its own image despite the media eloquence of its elite during the war seems to indicate that representations of Sarajevo were mostly determined by an overall economic structure in which both Sarajevo's government and media industries had to operate. Finally, although the least likely of explanations, we could speculate that, at certain moments, the graphic images of the warfare were little but just that—an equally brutal, violent, and gruesome reflection of the war itself.

Or, were they? What is missing from all these interpretations is the element of friction between the apparent colonial imagery and Sarajevo's past and current economic and political status. The extant analyses of colonial and post-colonial discourse have been reluctant to explore the link between cultural texts and contemporary capitalism; in the words of Stuart Hall, the omission has been "remarkable."[23] Similarly, political economists have either avoided or severely criticized post-*Orientalism* debates about the role of imagination in the maintenance and perpetuation of political and economic order; they found such discussions either irrelevant or self-indulgent, or both.[24] Paradoxically, however, while the link remained neglected and under-theorized, it was taken for granted that it existed, and that imagination, political power, and economic activity were all governed by a confluence of interests that required no further theoretical elaboration. Hence, despite significant disagreements within the post-colonial literature, there appears to be a consensus that economic interests, territorial conquest, and cultural construction of the *other* always go hand in hand; or, in other words, that colonialism, by definition, rests on a synchronicity of *power*, *desire* and *gaze*.

The gaze of the foreigner—a foreign correspondent, a returning expatriate, a humanitarian worker, an adventurous traveler—that features prominently in all fictional and documentary accounts of contemporary ethnic conflicts seemingly confirms this view: it visually institutionalizes power inequalities between the West and the zones of military intervention; it fetishizes the object of its curiosity like the male gaze fetishizes women;[25] and it forces us to ponder whether ethnic hatred—or even ethnicity in itself—may be a phenomenon that exists only in the eye of the beholder.

But by focusing on the gaze only, without exploring its context, we miss important elements of difference from the colonial past. The assumed confluence of interests has become problematic, demanding a theoretical reexamination of the relationship between politics, economics, and culture. The purely economic explanations of colonial relationships assume that military and political occupation accompanies investments with "high asset specificity,"[26] yet most places of military intervention in recent years have had none. The purely cultural interpretations of colonial discourse assume that discursive construction of the colonized "as a population of degenerate types on the basis of their racial origin" serves as the precondition of conquest and a justification for the establishment of administrative control,[27] yet, in most cases where such discursive construction has recently taken place, it was used as a justification for non-intervention and restraint from administrative control. To put it simply, guns are now going to places where there is no investment, money is going to the areas where guns are not necessary, and the *other* is located within national boundaries as much as in mysterious Orient. The emerging friction between colonial might, greed, and fantasy is then, possibly, the friction between *power*, *desire*, and *gaze*. It is not that the representation of the *other* or its status has been dramatically changed; it is just that the *other* has become *unwanted* in any other form except as an image of itself.

Unwanted Colonies: From "Desiring Machine" to "Voyeuristic Capitalism"

If countries, much like lovers, first need to be imagined to be conquered or abandoned, then how do we imagine *unwanted* countries and *unwanted* lovers? Perhaps, one could argue, media representation of ethnic violence produces a new category of *otherness* and a new type of colonies, fundamentally different from either Said's and Bhabha's or even Spivak's accounts of colonial imagery.[28] Namely, unlike traditional colonies, the places struck by ethnic violence and demanding international intervention appear to be *un-desired.* The insistence on ganglike violence in Somalia or on "the myth of ethnic conflict" in Bosnia or Rwanda[29] has helped construe them as unconquerable, ungovernable, even repulsive: all three places have been characterized as strategically unimportant lands featuring hostile peoples and hostile terrain with no or little possibility for lasting order or positive change. The portrayal of these troubled spots as potential quagmires has justified the need for their containment and a military presence in their regions but has fallen short of providing either serious guidance in institution building or any equivalent of administrative control. In addition, it has obscured the systemic causes of the self-destructive violence and the fact that the latter is often the only hope for inclusion in this post-colonial post–Cold War world. *Desire*, if it enters the picture at all, this time seems to be located entirely on the side of the once desired object, disturbing the premises of that "economy of desire" often associated with Deleuze and appropriated by postcolonial theorists.[30]

"Colonialism," writes Robert J. C. Young, "was always locked into the machine of desire."[31] Following Deleuze's and Guattari's notion of capitalism as a "desiring machine,"[32] Young describes colonialism as a libidinal process in which territorial expansion and sexual conquest went hand in hand. "For it is clear," writes Young, "that the forms of sexual exchange brought about by colonialism were themselves both mirrors and consequences of the modes of economic exchange that constituted the basis of colonial relations; the extended exchange of property which began with small trading-posts and the visiting slave ships originated, indeed, as much in exchange of bodies as of goods, or rather of bodies as goods: as in that paradigm of respectability, marriage, economic and sexual exchange were intimately bound up, coupled with each other."[33] The psychoanalytic interpretation of colonial desire (and its repression) coincides with economic interpretations which concede that the relationship between colonizer and colonized was ruled by some (uncanny?) combination of power and greed. In both Marxist and transaction cost analysis, colonialism is seen as the most extreme manifestation of capitalist expansion and control: its natural consequence ("imperialism as the highest stage of capitalism") or the most efficient way to protect valuable yet distant investments. For both, it was the way to secure something that the colonizer seemed to be lacking: the way to fulfill and control his desire. For Deleuze and Guattari, on the other hand, the relationship has been characterized by the exact opposite: "Desire does not lack anything; it does not lack its object. It is, rather, the subject that is missing in desire."[34]

In their view, capitalism is a "desiring machine": it does not only produce the objects of its desire but desire itself. Yet desire—for progress, for profit, for markets, desire for desire—is corporeal only insofar as it is territorial; and if capitalism is not necessarily territorial (indeed, argue Deleuze and Guattari, it is constituted through a sequence of territorialization, de-territorialization and re-territorialization), colonialism cannot be but territorial, acquisitive, forceful, controlling, appropriatory. Hence, concludes Young, "It is this link between capitalism, colonialism and spatiality that is so effectively articulated by Deleuze and Guattari [which reminds us] that colonialism above all involves the physical appropriation of land, its capture for the cultivation of another culture."[35]

But what happens in this era of pulverized space, of the new global economy of culture that rattles the link between capital, identities, and location or place?[36] Compare Young's "colonial desire" with this statement of a *Washington Post* reporter who followed the war in Bosnia, and subsequently wrote a best-selling book about his experience: "The Holiday Inn became a grandstand from which you could watch the snipers at work. A journalist could convince himself on a slow afternoon that he was doing his job by peering through a window at people running for their lives. Watching them was work, not voyeurism. Just ask any of the photographers who found safe spots near a sniper zone and waited for someone to be shot."[37] Is the account of this journalist any less colonial because it does not involve "physical appropriation of land"? Is his gaze any less arresting or violent because it does not request anything in return? Is his work any less exploitative because it consists of watching and watching only? Is his voyeurism redeemed because it is reflexively examined in a Knopf bestseller?

If Arjun Appadurai is correct in suggesting that media, migration, and imagination constitute the key components of the new global order,[38] then it is plausible to argue the capitalist "desiring machine," though entirely based on commerce, no longer demands territorial appropriation. Instead, the critical power of "capital controllers" rests precisely in their mobility, in their lack of attachment to any particular place. The power to withdraw and relocate investment resources is so overwhelmingly on the side of the financiers—and, I would add, merchants in general—that Jeffrey Winters may be correct when he defines it as "structural."[39] But even such structural power depends on agents' perceptions and observations. Watching, "peering through a window at people running for their lives," is the constitutive force not only of media industries but of the world economy as such. Much like media, commerce is increasingly organized as a trade in images: authors of a recent OECD study on aid to developing countries suggest that regions such as sub-Saharan Africa should work on developing local markets, which are always attractive to investors, and—more importantly—on projecting a *positive image* about themselves. For "once investors are convinced that growth prospects and economic governance have entered a new positive phase, there is every reason to look forward to a rising flow of investment which will help to create the image of a region on the move."[40] Should we then be surprised that "information gathering," "transparency," and "surveillance" are key words in orthodox economic vocabulary, and deconstruction of the financial Panopticon the principal objective of residual radicals?[41]

Yet let us not be fooled by the absence of force and territorial conquest in the economic world: the shift from capitalism as a "desiring machine" to "voyeuristic capitalism" is not a peaceful process. The relationship between those who are watching and those who are being watched offers no possibility of reconciliation and is, therefore, always on the verge of becoming violent. There is nothing that those who are watched can do to please those who are watching, for the pleasure of the latter is not derived from acts of the *other* but from the watching itself. Conversely, there is nothing that those who are watching can ever do to adequately reward those who are being watched, for the latter will never admit to the indecency of their own position. The tragedy—and the violence—of their relationship is embedded in the absurdity of this situation.

An Afterthought

Back to images. In April 1999, more than 40,000 Albanian refugees squatted in no-one's land between Macedonia and Kosovo. With no food or water, stuck in a valley of mud, in cold rain and in subhumanly unsanitary conditions, they patiently waited for Macedonians to let them into their country. On the morning of April 7, the refugees, whose pictures had been flashed all over the world as the example of a tragic exodus, unseen in Europe since World War II, mysteriously vanished. What was left behind were piles of litter and excrement, carefully examined for clues by Western journalists and just as carefully depicted in morning papers.

"Where did everyone go?" asked the headlines. The void opened by the overnight disappearance of 40,000 people, who had been captives of cameras just as much as of the Macedonian border patrol, was staring back at photographers. And while the no-one's people from no-one's land were allegedly bused around from camp to camp and from Macedonia to Albania without anyone's notice, the fascination with the void and the traumatic loss experienced by relief workers and journalists apparently prevented them from actually going after the lost refugees. The void was telling, too.

Like *Little Zlata* and the drawing of the Rwandan child, the disapperance of the Albanian refugees suggests that media representation of "distant violence" is more than a sociological phenomenon; it is possibly the example of the political and of the economic of our time. Media does not, as it is feared, produce violence or otherwise intervene in the reality (presuming that there is one, different from representation) of the *other*. It does not desire the *other* or find any pleasure in his or her destruction. It simply watches, and by transforming its gaze into the most precious commodity, a vehicle for other commodities, it is coming closer and closer to mistaking the *other* for a no-one's land.

IV. Haunting Affiliations

real american dreams (can be nightmares)

KATHLEEN STEWART

Things are complicated and they're not going well. Suddenly it looks as if we're in a zero-sum game and everyone is either a winner or a loser. Under the guise of "the good economy" and the now almost total facelift of the country in strip malls, chain stores, and master-planned communities, U.S. public culture in the 1990s finds itself both singing the cheerful ditty of a resurgent American Dream and haunted by the nightmares of trauma, monstrosity, and abjection. The winners anxiously shore up the walls of increasingly privatized zones of safety, while the losers end up on the street or get their pictures broadcast all over the airwaves in the all-day din of talk shows and prime-time reality television shows such as *COPS* and *America's Most Wanted*. The winners have dreams to dream and futures to protect; the spectacle of "losers" encodes the disaffections and injuries of those for whom the American Dream is only a distant memory or a taunting voice that whispers in their ear in a refrain of "failure, failure, failure."

Here I will track some of the twists and turns of American dreams and nightmares as a particular kind of entrance into the American political imaginary. To track dreams and nightmares is to tweak the nerve of a nervous system[1] fueled by tensions, oppositions, and contradictions. It is also to look with a kind of double vision at two sides of the same coin; the dreams and nightmares that make up the American political and cultural imaginary are intimately and inescapably joined in a relation of opposition and negation.[2] They face in opposite directions but mirror each other; each side is everything that the other side is not and what it both fears and secretly desires. But one is filled with visions of progress and carefully laid plans; the other one spends its time in crisis mode and ducking for cover. One enacts the cultural politics of the dominant, the central, and the self-possessed while the other bears the stigma of the marginal, the subaltern, and the illegitimate. One is by definition "on track" and the other is constantly living out its derailment and setting up camp in a space somewhere "beyond the pale."

All systems of inequality and exploitation produce "centers" and "margins" that mark particular, often opposed, cultural-political strategies or ways of life. In this case, the plain and brutal language of "winners" and "losers" marks a moment of intensification and increased polarization between those at the "top" and those at the "bottom" of the economy. The lean and mean transition to a post-Fordist phase of capital accumulation has produced deepening immiserization on the bottom of the economic scale and an unprecedented amassing of wealth on the top.[3] It has also intensified class cultural polarization and the isolation of the marginal[4] to the point where class[5] has begun to look more like caste. Class differences can be immediately read out of body styles, clothes, hair, food, expressive forms, states of health, the style of public spaces such as restaurants and bars, tastes in movies, and the kinds of newspapers and magazines and books that people read. But these meanings have taken on an added weight in the context of a social order in which "winners" must protect and defend their secured zone against the threat of risk, crime, and all those "others" "out there." With the now intense emphasis on an underclass of outcasts figured as the homeless, the addicted, the diseased, and the criminal living in marginalized and stigmatized spaces "beyond the pale" such as "the inner city," "the streets" and pockets of abject poverty, danger, and wildness all over the American countryside, coded class differences can take on the nightmarish valence of absolutely demarcated ways of life that are separate, mutually contaminating, and charged with the finality of winning or losing. The polarization of insiders and outsiders has produced for "losers" an intense disorientation and disillusionment and for "winners" an anxious, rigid, and naive reinvestment in the American Dream, citizens' rights and "victim's" rights—an order of sheer "values" and "ideals."[6]

The new economy has been accompanied by a conservative reformation of the state, the realigning and dismantling of public agencies and their functions, and transformations in the role and form of the public sphere and public culture. We have seen not only the evisceration of relatively coherent and systematic programs to alleviate poverty and the shifting of funds for the poor to policing and the prison system but a virtual criminalization of poverty, difference, and the "hard living" that often accompanies these in a dog-eat-dog U.S. public world. "Politics" has become more narrowly defined as the politics proper of the state and the official public sphere.

Meanwhile, in the real world of cultural politics, there has been a massive proliferation of fragmented "publics" based on narrow and hierarchically coded interests, identities, and "life styles" including class, ethnicity, race, gender, sexuality, age, religion, fitness level, forms of disease, trauma and disaster, forms of pleasure, and precise interests in entertainment, education and consumption. Partial publics have proliferated in industrial-commercial venues; these, following Miriam Hansen, are "publics" of a sort that remain more or less hidden from public view from anyone who is not directly paying for, or participating in them.[7] This has greatly exacerbated the polarization of difference and enabled the fashioning of nearly complete separate worlds. Increasingly, a cosmopolitan and transnational professional-managerial class lives a private public life shielded by partial public memberships and clubs that give it a life of its own and enable it to move between spaces of luxury, safety, and uniformity without ever making contact with the "others." The habitus of enclosed separated publics makes otherness itself monstrous and unimaginable. Meanwhile, the "others" have also proliferated myriad partial publics and counterpublics[8] of their own, many of which posit an identity politics based on injury, oppression, and political struggle.[9] "Othered" identities, too, can become deeply separated identites through a complex combination of "choice" and forms of force. There are even distinct physical spaces for the others "beyond the pale"; spaces like "the inner city," "the street," new ethnic enclaves of all kinds in urban, suburban, and rural places, and chronically poor rural enclaves such as Native American reservations, Appalachian hollers, migrant labor camps, rural African-American communities in the south, and "white trash" pockets in the countryside of virtually every state in the country become symbols of danger, degradation, isolation, excess, opposition, and a kind of freedom. They also become the place holders of silenced yet nagging questions in the U.S. public sphere: What happens when the very claim to a normative public sphere hunkers down like a claustrophobic glass ceiling on the submerged pains and possibilities of an everyday life beaten down into the cracks? Where do the wild leaps of fancy and bitter faiths go when the American Dream sags under the weight of disemployment? What happens in places beyond the pale where the optimistic wallpaper of progress has been rubbed raw by aching limbs and where the ideology of hopes and plans lies barely rustling under an avalanche of wasted possibilities?

I suggest here that contemporary cultural politics in the United States is a set of practices and technologies structured both by polarizations in inequality and difference, and the crises and tensions these produce, and by emerging forces of privatization and new forms of publicness. This is a cultural politics that is invisible to models of the official public sphere which assume that politics is a thing structured by, and transparently evident in, the simple self-evident "realities" of ideals, rationalities, and the universal subject as citizen.[10] I suggest, rather, that politics has to be tracked through the twisted machinations of everyday experience and meanings buried in habits of life, interpretive practices, and forms of sociality. It takes on force as a cultural politics precisely when it is beyond a narrowly demarcated politics proper and so carries the charge of a latent force that threatens to erupt. The "politics" I am interested in following here is one that emerges on the charged border between official politics and everything marked as "other," between instrumental politics and the politics of the imagination, between "public" and "private" politics, between the politics of the state and the politics of daydreams and desires. When politics is viewed as movements, eruptions, and negotiations along such borders, it becomes critical to track how political voices and effects emerge into the public and what incites the very desire for publicness itself.[11] It is also critical to note, as others have,[12] that in contemporary U.S. public culture the very notion of "the public," and the construction of a collective identity we call "the public," is often activated or invented in moments of spectacle, accident, trauma, and wound—moments when the American Dream meets its nightmare.

Here, I am interested, for instance, in all those odd moments of the everyday when the Muzak of the American Dream hits a bad chord. Like when you're driving by a homeless man on the side of the road and out of the corner of your eye you half-notice the sign he's holding that tells a story, begs for help, and blesses you and God. Then the dream needs a jump start to go on and it becomes a little tainted, a little resentful of interruptions, and a little scared of wake-up calls. It is only with the prophylactic work of the constant jump start that the leaner and meaner economy gathers itself into an order of business as usual, the normative public sphere sings a too-cheerful tune haunted by half-submerged furies, and the "winners" claim a protected center stage that is more fragile than it looks. Always haunted by nightmares, and propelled forward by fear and the need for distraction, the American Dream picks up a harmony with the eerie new lullabies of "community" and "politics": the gated community walled in on itself, the master-planned community where the blank slate (everything new and clean and starting over) meets the mirage of the instant city on the hill (total, complete, self-sufficient, without contingency), and the politics of the normative public sphere where it is as if ideals (or, in the conservative discourse, "values") could (or should) be magically writ large on the world through reasoned debate and universal rules of order.

In its mix of naivete and cynicism, the resurgent American Dream of the 1990s is continuously interrupted by odd moments when reasoned debate seems suddenly infused with the specters of conspiracy, corruption, and confusion or when the rules of community order reach a point of frenzied self-parody (garage doors must be kept shut at all times, drapes in neutral colors only, no digging in the yard without permission). There are moments of trauma when everything seems to stop; ears prick up and eyes scan the cultural horizon. Somewhere a lurking latent possibility suddenly erupts as a horror show: a bomb goes off; disgruntled workers and disappointed lovers and kids with guns appear in public and open fire; paranoid loners go after the government; quiet, orderly single men who keep too much to themselves turn out to be serial killers burying bodies in their backyards; wild men kill scientists or cops and then disappear into the woods and deserts for months. For "winners" anxiously planning their futures in safe enclaves, news of horrors and unassimilated forces from beyond the pale comes as a shock; the normal and the expected are suddenly fractured to reveal a dark and inexplicable underside to things. For "losers," life is an endless series of shocks and a thing as inescapable as the air they breathe or the water they drink.

The American Dream is a world of anesthesia and shock.[13] The newly resurgent modernisms of professionalization, self-discipline, master-planned communities, and therapeutic-spectacle culture play side by side with a public culture filled with images of trauma, conspiracy, and the uncanny. People grow fascinated by accidents on the side of the road, unsolved mysteries, and figures of desperation or sudden, spectacular wealth. Some people start remembering satanic ritual abuse or get abducted by a UFO; more people just look for a "healthy lifestyle" and the self-help industry booms in a chorus of new hopes ritualized into therapeutic routines that sustain us for a week or a month or a year before there is a new distraction and a new hope. It is best to keep busy. The hum of the American Dream keeps its decibel levels up and its feet moving. But somewhere beyond the pale, monsters and outcasts hold up a mirror to the American Dream, reflecting its own worst nightmare and its abject limit. Not so much outsiders as "others within," like wild men wailing at the gates, they stand as a living reminder of an unthinkable Real that in moments of trauma and other eruption can pop the bubble of the dream world of sheer ideals. The dream begins to show its contradictions and "the center" is confronted with the limits of its own self-possession and reminded of the force of unassimilated fault lines.[14] Things get more tense and more effort is put into the resurgence of the dream. Meanwhile, in life beyond the pale, the American Dream drifts by like a hot-air balloon overhead.

The metaphoric phrase "beyond the pale" carries the cultural weight of a British colonialist dread and fascination with those parts of its colonies, particularly its early colonies in Ireland and Scotland, that remained somehow "beyond" its "civilizing" jurisdiction and rule. The term has carried well into other such instances where dominating forces find themselves surrounded by an otherness that is never quite assimilated or domesticated. The space beyond the pale demarcates an excess at a border and gives that border a charge. It posits a fearful negation that produces both the fixed certainty of a "center" by dramatizing its boundaries, and an uncaptured excess that remains a latent threat and an emergent force. The space "beyond the pale" takes on the valences of things half-realized and yet enduring and prolific; like the charge of the imagination itself, it indexes forces of generativity; it stands like a sign pointing to a "something more" beyond the enclosures of self-discipline and "centered" ways of life.

For those living within the pale, the space "beyond" is a monstrosity waiting to erupt. There are monsters and wild men out there who are capable of anything; by definition they live outside the law. The monstrous, like the space beyond the pale from which it emerges, carries the doubled and haunted meanings of things unspeakable and yet fascinating. The term monstrous hearkens back to the Latin terms *monere*, to warn, and *monstrare*, to demonstrate.[15] It is a deviation or malformation; something extraordinary or unnatural. It is also a sign, a divine portent or warning that announces something from beyond. It is alarming and so demands interpretation or explanation and yet it is also unreadable. Like a rude wake up call from one dream world to another, it embodies the effects of power and condenses them into a nightmare image that demands response.

Everyday Life beyond the Pale

The Appalachian hollers of southern West Virginia[16] are one such space beyond the pale for the modernist American imaginary. Try to enter them as a tourist passing through and the physical plant of banal national culture will fail you. Master-planned communities, convenience stores, and strip malls give way to the butts of rifles perched precariously on wood piles, tarpaper entrepreneurial shacks advertising the vices on rough cut signs—"BEER, CIGARETTES, POP"—and handmade Christian billboards propped up in yards in heated debate over the signs of the END TIMES. People gathered to talk at the post offices, gas stations, and "stands" (stores selling "commodities" with long shelf-lives such as instant coffee, canned evaporated milk, soda pop, Twinkies, and cans of weenies) will stare back at you, interrupted in mid-sentence. In dark, cinder-block bars without names, hard drinking men fold into themselves over a beer and a song or stick each other with knives in the vain hope of momentary relief from God knows what. Hell and damnation preaching comes over the radio. Or a disk jockey who is not kidding makes a not very funny joke about K. D. Lang being a dyke *on the air* and you wonder and you feel as if you have suddenly dropped off the edge of the national public world. It comes as a shock to suddenly and unexpectedly find yourself inside a virtual hillbilly reservation with all its signs of otherness.

In the imaginary of a bourgeois public sphere focused on the rationalities and ideals of an abstracted citizen-subject and abstracted space of "the nation," "the country" is either the picture-perfect image of the pastoral landscape or the Wild West vista laid out in the distance of vast open space or a strange "outside" land that threatens to capture those who meant only to pass through; it is too local, too out of the way, too much a separate place with laws of its own. The very term "the country" carries meanings of otherness and wildness; derived from the Latin *contre* or *contrada* meaning opposite, against, that which lies opposite, and from *encontrada* meaning that encountered or met with. Its modern pejorative meaning, as a backward backwater in the theater of progress, dates to the seventeenth century and it has made "the country" a figure of romance and horror ever since—two sides of a coin.

Southern West Virginia is a living symbol of the "dark side" of "the country." An out-of-the-way place that was settled and colonized by an industry, subject to a century of cultural destabilizations and diasporic migrations with the booms and busts of coal, and finally abandoned to ruin in the mid-1980s, it is now feeling the marginal effects of the new economy of the 1990s and beyond. With the highway finally finished into Beckley, there are corporations coming in to exploit hard times and negligible taxes, and there are jobs in fast-food chains if people can figure out a way to get to town and make enough to cover gas money. In the camps everyone is talking about the new Wal-Mart in town and the all-you-can-eat buffet at the Golden Corral—"it has everything."

But it is not, as the American Dream would have it, that the new highway has brought "the light of day" or a simple assimilation into a mainstream America. It is not as if sheer proximity to "the center" effects the erasure of difference; on the contrary, proximity engages difference. So it becomes more notable, for instance, that there are no fire departments here and houses routinely burn to the ground while people can do no more than stand and watch and try to figure out who did it. It seems stranger that there is no regular police presence in the coal camps,[17] only the occasional roadblock set up at the narrow mouth of a holler to stop everyone coming in and out in search of stolen goods and people driving without insurance or an "operators" (a license). With no middle-class presence in the hollers to set the standard, the order of things feels not so much like a civilizing presence enacted in well-tended lawns, balanced check books, disciplined bodies, educated reason, and routinized careers but more like a distant conspiratorial threat. Power's radical oscillation between cruelty and a friendly face embeds itself in the diffuse daily rhythms of life's ups and downs. People's places are not where they "live" but where they "stay at," as if the staying has to be marked, like a temporary respite requiring constant vigilance against permanent displacement and threat. The schools stigmatize the kids from the camps as dirty and ignorant. People complain about mean teachers and social service workers and the rationalized discipline of the schools, the agencies, and the courts. Local sociality is a tense and intimate performance of encounters and eruptions. They say people should visit; one quick knock on the door and someone will just walk right in, sit down, and wait for someone from the house to come and join them when they get around to it. Yet an unannounced stranger who appears on the edge of a property will be met with a challenging stare, gun close to hand. People who fail to "speak" to others are "no account." Those who "hole up" "get squirrelly"; they "turn in on theirself" and grow "backward"; or they "show theirself" and "get into it" with the others. People watch out for each other with a hypervigilance fueled as much by co-dependency as by old-time ways; they notice black eyes and lights on in the middle of the night. They know who has been saved and who is in the middle of a backslide.

The everyday becomes a continuous stream of those odd moments when the American Dream is interrupted by a haunting suspicion of things uncanny, traumatic, or "other."[18] People have apparitions; they see Jesus at their window or hear the devil's voice coming out of the bottom of a bottle. The visits and phone calls of every day are filled with stories that cull seemingly ordinary moments into a sensibility attuned to extraordinary threats and possibilities. The line between fantasy and the real grows both vague and charged. Lodged in the cramped, intimate circulations of life beyond the pale, these stories mark both a vital protection from the world outside and a claustrophobic disaffection looking for moments to erupt. They conjure a profound excess latent in the everyday[19] and then lodge haunted sensibilities in bodies and the objects of everyday life.

In the place of the fears and fantasies still available to "insiders" of the American dream of progress, mobility, and privately cordoned freedoms, life in the camps in-fills with a fascination for the traces of things left out, hidden from sight, or buried in the seemingly familiar. Things are not what they seem. Things fall apart and in the process ghostly effects come to the surface—a chafing. Where the American Dream dreams of an everyday life in synch with business as usual, the underbelly nightmare life it produces as its real failures and symbolic negation gives us instead an everyday life whose heartbeat is a hypervigilant watching for odd moments when things erupt.

Odd Moments

In the jingle-jangle world of the American Dream, dream world and nightmare come together in a nervous system of fits and starts. The political finds itself twisted in the machinations of everyday experience and daydream. It plays a game of hide and seek with prolific imaginaries and half-audible reminders of things excluded from public voice.[20] Counterpublics and partial publics circulate, picking up density as they travel, and threatening to erupt into the normative public sphere. Cultural sensibilities adopt a politics of style.[21] The political and the cultural cling to each other, holding each other up, like the desperate dance partners in the movie *They Shoot Horses, Don't They?* The dance itself becomes a fascinating spectacle as we watch for signs of collapse, or resistance, or an unassimilated moment—a chafing that brings something forgotten or unimagined half to mind.

Imagine "resistance" not as a thing of clear consciousness and purposive, instrumental agency but as something more diffuse and pervasive and fundamental. Picture it as that pregnant and potentially portentous moment of chafing. It registers a haunting; it approaches what Lacan calls the Real, or that which resists assimilation to the symbolic order[22] (such as the American Dream). It interrupts the dream or erupts from an unassimilated otherness within. It may disappear literally "before you know it" but remain an affecting presence left in traces and symptoms. Like a blot on the lens of a camera, it may become an irritant that lodges itself in the matter of things.[23] In the nervous dance of cultural politics the Real embeds itself in forms of pleasure and pain; it leaves structures of feeling in its wake—at once palpable and elusive. Maybe the dancers can feel the Real as the fear of failure latent in swollen feet and exhausted faces. Maybe with this half-felt sense of things half-hidden and unthought, their perspective will shift, taking a kind of sidestep that allows them to see the uncanny, alien presence in things.[24] Maybe they will be haunted by a structure of feeling left as a trace—a feeling that things are not quite what they seem. They might grow vigilant, scanning for signs of eruption.

What they notice might look like just a tiny detail but it might feel like a tell-tale sign. Like the time in West Virginia when some of the women in Amigo (the camp where I was living) grew suspicious of all the official news talk of low-fat, low-salt diets. They began to scan the surface of things for tell-tale signs and traces. A neighbor went to the supermarket in town to check things out.

> You know they say there's all this *salt* in things? Well I went and looked on the cans and its doesn't even *say salt*, it says "*sodium*" and if you didn't know to *look for it* you'd never *know*.
>
> So why do they put "*sodium*" on the can?

Or there was the time that they put in the new mailboxes with combination locks at the Amigo post office and no one could get their box open. Someone said, "Well, they're not 'new,' I don't know where they came from." And this led to speculations that there are actually two completely different versions of the newspaper out of Beckley—one for the city people and one for the camps people. They said this had come to light in Amigo because the town straddled two counties. Two neighbors could be reading two completely different newspapers. Some said they thought they had noticed something funny.

In the camps, no one ever knew anything for sure (that would be considered "bragging") but any fool could see that things were not what they seemed. When "things happened" people would get a feeling, like the time Patty Walker's brakes went out coming down Hinton Mountain and just before they did she got a feeling that something was about to happen. There was a pervasive sense that "something funny" was going on and people were always poised to "make something OF it."

The nervous dance of the political and the cultural can be seen in the strangest places, *especially* in the strangest places. Lodged in structures of feeling and collective forms of expression, it can be seen in moments of hypervigilance or suspicion, in conspiracy thinking and in the love of spectacle, in forms of intimacy and recognition, in daydreams of release, and in partial public and counterpublic spaces, politics, and identities.

One night in West Virginia a group of striking miners sat waiting to see the doctor in a poor people's health clinic. They talked intimately in a slow rhythm of story and ruminative pause. It was at the end of a long, hundred-day contract strike that had failed and everyone was saying that the union was dead, that the mines were closing down for good this time, that the miners were being reduced to "company sucks." You could feel the mantra of stunned defeat come to settle down on the room as heavy talk gave way to even weightier pauses filled only with the shallow breathing of men slowly suffocating to death from black lung disease.

Then Bobby Cadle "started in" on an elaborate fantasy of scaling the big brick walls of Governor Rockefeller's mansion to loot it for all it was worth, and the others drew their focus to it in a moment of intimate publicity. In the story, power grew graphic to become high brick walls that could be breached by a collective working-class masculinity lurching into view in an act of instant redistribution. The daily pains, depressions, and disabilities of class gave way to a dream world of sheer, potent agency. In the sudden upsurge of a riotous dreamscape, the lines between private home, private wealth, privately held power, and public circulation were suddenly erased and power itself appeared as a thing broken up, made tactile,[25] and dispersed like loot.

The eruption of the story itself marked the haunting presence of a local world fallen between the cracks of the "normal" and a dream world that can only emerge at odd moments of condensation and free association. Given under the sign of fantasy and daydream, the story points to itself as the momentary repository of excess and remainder. Here, agency is born as an eruption out of a world "got down"; it posits a turn of events in which the possible is instantiated in the actual and the emergent arises out of the immanent. The story is "political" not only, or primarily, because it throws up an image of unthinkable, rebellious, collective political action but, more fundamentally, because it performs a subaltern, counterpublic imaginary that circulates along its own intimate routes and emerges at odd moments. Here, fantasy leads to the eruption of the Real. It is a moment like the one that Walter Benjamin theorized as a "profane illumination"—a moment when shock opens the dream world to the sharp, bodily impact of politically charged images and reveals "aspects of visual worlds which dwell in the smallest things, meaningful yet covert enough to find a hiding place in waking dreams."[26]

When people scan for signs of power, trying to literally "figure it out," they find that even (or especially) the most ordinary things can carry the inflection of the Real—the unspeakable and unimaginable "something" beyond the limits of figuration itself. The nervous speculation this produces buzzes around the American Dream like a fly in the ointment.

One day in Amigo, Sissy's husband, Bud, came home saying that there was something he wanted to tell me. He had talked to a friend from Virginia who was an electrical engineer in a nuclear plant.

> Real smart, really got the intelligence. He may be wrong but he really knows what he's talking about. He told me that the economy is going to bust.

Sissy paused on her way out of the room, interested—"You mean good bust or bad bust?" Bud said:

> In one and a half or two years. He didn't have time to talk long enough to really understand it. I'll have to go over it in my mind to get it straight. But he says the price of gold will go way up—like ten to one—and something about how they'll have to change the standard.

Then there was a long talk, which I was completely unable to follow, about what the gold standard is. "And they'll print up a whole different kind of money—red money." Bud thought that meant that the color of the money would be red but Sissy and I didn't take it that way—we thought the real smart guy from Virginia was talking about communist money somehow, though we didn't know how. Bud said the guy said they had already printed up the red money so they are planning it—our money won't be worth anything—and he says that it's a revolution. What revolution? Sissy says, "us because we're fed up." Bud says he guesses it's a revolution of the government—they're gonna start a whole new system to start over again—wipe out the debt and start the money cycle all over again. Sissy said, "Who cares? My money ain't worth anything anyway." We talked about how the value of gold is all imaginary anyway—and diamonds, too—people say they're the best investment but they saw a thing on *60 Minutes* where they went around to all these jewelers and they can't tell the difference between zirconium and diamonds—everybody got mad at each other. Sissy says, "Just our luck—I always thought I could bank on my wedding rings. They're high now but that's only because one man owns all the mines but now there's others gettin' into it and they'll break that—have too many and pretty soon they won't be worth nothin'." This moved on to talk of how the stock market can be doing well if the economy isn't—it don't figure. Sissy said it's just rich people, she don't see no recovery. Although they say its fine over in North C'raliny.

Nightmares in Public

In the lived yet unassimilated "Reals" of permanent disemployment, disability, eruptions of action, and abject, waste-sifting daydream, the everyday gathers itself to news of the tragic, monstrous, and weird like the pull of addictive desire. The McKinneys claim that there is something "in" the Graham blood that's "off." The Christians say the sinners are going straight to hell and the sinners say the Christians give them the heebie-jeebies. Old man Guerrant keeps his windows blacked and sits at night in the back corner of his house in the "colored" part of the camp listening, in fear of a sudden irrational moment of racist attack. Disfigured figures with severed limbs and broken backs from working in the mines, or from running the roads to break up endless unemployed days in a reckless dance with death, stare out from porches or restlessly drift by in wheelchairs. Poverty diseases take a monstrous toll as well. A young couple who are not "all there" live in a car with their new baby and the back seat is stuffed to the ceiling with dirty diapers and pizza boxes; people track their progress over the hills as they are spotted from time to time parked in one deserted spot or another. Half-seen cars shoot at people on the road at night and then disappear without a trace. The guy next door holes up, drinking himself to death for a week or a month or a year while the others count the days until he erupts in a fit of rage, tearing down the pieced-together walls of his house in a frenzy.

The monstrosity that hunkers over the look of the place in the eyes of the tourist passing through takes a different turn when you hang out at the stands and the gas stations and the kitchens of the place long enough to overhear the stories people tell. When they "run their mouths" the stories that come out are like a conjuring that initiates,[27] or a search for something more or something other.

Bits of information of news of the weird become objects of fascination in which people look for "proof positive" that strange and inexplicable things are buried beneath the surface of business as usual, waiting to erupt. In the process of conjuring, figures that mirror their own "otherness" are given embodied form and take on the secret meaningfulness of things ordinarily ignored, hidden from view, or silenced from public voice. Like the day I was over visiting Harvey Thaxton—an elderly African-American man—and the subject turned to strange things. He and his wife told me about a woman who had sores all over her legs and the hoodoo doctor came in from North Carolina to see her. He gave her a salve and told her to put it on and throw the tube over her shoulder into the river without looking back. Then worms came out all over her legs and she was cured. Mr Thaxton got up to look for a "book" that had "proof positive" of the existence of a "devil child" while his wife Martha rolled her eyes at me. After a long ten minutes of searching while Martha claimed there was no such "book," he came back with a copy of the *National Enquirer* and showed me a picture on the cover of a young African girl born with two horns.

Stories circulate indiscriminately from intimate experience and from the talk shows and tabloids. In them, fantasy and materiality coincide in an extreme literalism that "refuses the pacifying lures of specular idealization to insist on the gross palpability of the flesh and heightened emotion."[28] They voice a warning or an announcement, in which those most vulnerable track the latent horrors of class exploitation, racism, and sexism half-buried beneath the surface of the floating dream world. As they say in the camps, "things happen" and "there's no tellin' *what* people might do." Marginalized places become filled with the sense that something is about to happen or that something may be going on next door or down the street or "out there" somewhere.

The cultural politics of haunted knowledge and vigilant scanning become true structures of feeling, as Raymond Williams described them. They are forces that are emergent not only because they are embryonic and not fully articulated in the bourgeois public sphere but precisely because they exist in states of opposition and negation—in the space of the Real or that which cannot be articulated. Structures of feeling evoke "just those experiences to which the fixed forms do not speak at all, which . . . they do not recognize."[29] They posit the return of what has been reduced to nonsense or explained away by the dominant categories of reason and meaning.[30]

To the American Dream—a world of sheer ideals—such structures of feeling become the "other within" precisely to the extent that they embody lived and felt domains of experience. They index not the ideal, prefab "community" of the master-planned community and the official public sphere but a different order of community conjured or initiated in the interruption, or rupture, of the mythic space, or sheer abstract ideal, of communion. As Jean-Luc Nancy has argued, we encounter community at moments of being driven outside ourselves, being beside ourselves. It marks the break or caesura, the noncoincidence of ideals and reality.[31]

As I write, Sally Jesse Raphael is staging today's talk show performance through the figure of an old man in from West Virginia. He sits in a wheelchair and the tears run down his face as he tells the nightmare story of one day in 1976. His old lady had left him and he was raising his two-year-old daughter alone. When he got up to go to the bathroom his daughter, playing on the porch, went over and drank from a can of kerosene that a neighbor had left for him that morning. The old man's story launches into the graphic details: he had a broken down car in the driveway, with no plates on it, and at the time his driver's license had been revoked for drunk driving; but it was an emergency and rather than call for help he just put the baby in the car and took off flying. When he got to town there was all kinds of traffic and people wouldn't let him through the red light. He was screaming: "I got a *baby* in here and she's drunk *kerosene*! I gotta git her to the *hospital*!" But they wouldn't let him through so he ran the red light and someone hit him hard and broke his neck (that's the reason he's in a wheelchair today). When the police got there they took the baby to the hospital because he was screaming and carrying *on* about it, but they wouldn't let him go with her! They took him off to the jail for driving without an operator's! Finally, when they got the little girl to the hospital they saw that she had scrapes on her knees (where she had been playing on the cement porch) and they decided to take her away from him. The last time he saw her was on July 6 in the welfare office by the elevators and she was crying and he told her, "Don't cry, poodle doggie, daddy's gonna come back and git you some day." And that was the last day he ever saw her. He's been looking for her ever since.

Sally, of course, reunited them for the spectacle and they hugged and kissed until Sally pulled them apart. Then he looked at his daughter, his mouth trembling and the tears pouring down his face, and said, "I *wanted* you, poodle dog, I wanted to *keep* you, I *always* wanted *you*, honey!"

Here trauma TV draws the negation of the American Dream into public view as a pathetic spectacle and performs a drama of redemption that attempts to recuperate nightmare back into dream. But in that very process of conjuring the unspeakable it also displays an irrecuperable remainder in the form of shock and embodied disaster.[32] Nightmares in public walk a line between the anesthetized shell-shock of anxious, mind-numbing distraction and another kind of shock that gives pause and throws up a warning. They mark the space of a double wish—the hegemonic wish to fold nightmares back into the dream of ideals and the counter-wish to remake publicity itself into a force that can drag hidden effects up in its wake and give voice to difference and desire. Both wishes draw their force from the haunted sense of half-known things, but one secures a safety zone and shores up the walls with a resurgent dream; the other walks the line out there beyond the pale looking for odd moments of eruption.

wild things

THOMAS L. DUMM

> I caught a glimpse of a woodchuck stealing across my path, and felt a strange thrill of savage delight, and I was strongly tempted to seize and devour him raw; not that I was hungry then, except for that wildness which he represented. . . . I love the wild not less than the good.
>
> HENRY DAVID THOREAU, *Walden*

A Song Is Being Sung

In the spring of 1989 Jean Baudrillard attended a conference at the University of Montana in Missoula that was devoted to a wide-ranging exploration of his work and its cultural implications. After delivering the keynote lecture for the conference, he listened to a response by an American L-A-N-G-U-A-G-E poet and then-editor of the *Socialist Review*, Ron Silliman. Silliman allegorized Baudrillard as "the drag queen of theory."[1] Misunderstanding Silliman's comments, or taking the compliment as too little, too late, or deciphering a deep insult that some of us missed, or suffering from an uncharacteristic failure of imagination, for some reason Baudrillard took offense. So on the last night of the conference he snubbed Silliman by arriving late to a coffeehouse where the poet was giving a reading (the reading consisted of one long poem about a day in San Francisco: I remember a description of a dumpster and some riders on a bus).

Silliman's reading was the warm-up act for a performance by a fairly obscure but highly esteemed guitarist/performance artist named Eugene Chadbourne. Chadbourne had at one time been a member of a 1980s pseudo–New Wave, post-punk band called Camper Van Beethoven, whose best known song was "Take the Pinheads Bowling." After Silliman finished, but before Chadbourne began, Baudrillard sat down at a table where several participants in the conference were gathered with students and faculty from the Missoula community, drinking beer and enjoying ourselves. Baudrillard watched with the rest of us as Chadbourne began to play. He sat, placid, bored perhaps. The entertainment unfolded.

Chadbourne's performance was an example of post-punk picturesque at its finest. Overwrought, frenzied, humorous, playful, loud, and silly, he inhabited the role of clown with gusto, moving from old Spike Jones songs with updated lyrics about Barbara Bush and urban conflagration to homages/parodies of rock and roll classics. In keeping with the high silly aesthetic of the performance, toward the end of the set Chadbourne unveiled an unusual instrument—a rusty old garden rake, strung with guitar strings and with pick-ups attached to it, what he called his "electric rake." He began producing noise, feedback, strange chords, odd static. In his seat Baudrillard smiled slightly. After several minutes in which he produced a whole lot of noise, Chadbourne, a heavy-set man who at this point of the evening was sweating profusely, leaped off the stage, which was composed of low risers cobbled together in the tradition of temporary stages in modernist cafeteria utility spaces of student union buildings everywhere, and crawled under it. He barely fit and could not be seen by most of the audience, but some of the listeners were able to infer somehow that he was somehow connecting the rake to the stage, that he was starting to play the stage itself. As this realization spread through the audience, the cheers and applause began and then intensified. There was more noise coming from that audience than there was from Chadbourne's amplifier; almost everyone was up, cheering, whistling, stomping feet, laughing, craning to get a better view, trying to figure out what would happen next. Baudrillard continued to sit.

Then, suddenly, a familiar melody emerged from the speakers, simple, primitive, inevitable, based on the most common three-chord progression in rock and roll. Chadbourne was playing the one, four, five chord progression for either "Wild Thing" or "Louie, Louie" (which, until the lyrics are sung, are for most discernible purposes identical; the words "wild thing" but two beats, versus the double time of the words, "Lou-ie, Lou-ie," set a singer on slightly different paths). As if with one voice the audience began to sing: "Wild Thing, you make my heart sing, you make everything groovy, Wild Thing." At this moment of audience participatory bliss, a look of uncomprehending panic crossed Baudrillard's face. The theorist (in)famous for his implacable stoicism in the face of the collapse of reality, the person who only two nights before had been urging an audience of Montana ranchers, hippie farmers, black-garbed graduate students, and avant-garde literary theorists to "drive (slowly) to a delirious point of view" in response to what he claimed to believe to be the fact of a world driving us to a delirious state of things, appeared to be resisting the trip to delirium.[2]

It seemed to me then, and it seems to me now, that this look of incomprehension betrayed Baudrillard's studied indifference, that the event somehow overcame his faith in a stoicism that he had imagined could match the depthless nihilism he had prophesied. In observing the enthusiastic response of these (alleged) postmodern intellectuals, by an audience composed primarily of his assembled admirers, Baudrillard could not discern an answer—a really good answer—to questions he himself had been posing for years concerning the paths that mutual recognition and attempted acknowledgment of others might take in an era when signals have come to be as important as, if not more important than, signs. These people seemed to be possessed of a knowledge, they seemed to know, with an irresistible intuition, that what was being played was one song instead of another. They anticipated the lyric that was emerging from under that stage—and they sang.

Why do I dwell on this moment? Baudrillard's reputation is not what it was then, and my worries concerning his influence on an impressionable mind—namely mine—have abated. His work does not inform the arguments I care about the most these days. So there must be other reasons I return to this moment, and this essay is an attempt to think about those reasons one more time, undoubtedly not the last time.

I am confident about this need to return to this particular thought, because it is implicated in the project of resistance I increasingly identify with the ordinary. In explorations of the ordinary the question of method always engages the return of thinking to places where we can work through who and how we are in the world. The questions that are raised at such places (junctures of skepticism) are uncomfortable, or unhandsome. How does one separate oneself from the field of the ordinary that is inevitably a part of one's self? How does one reckon oneself as a self against claims of identity, on the one hand, and the void, or the nothingness that awaits us all, on the other? Underwriting all of our concerns about justice, fairness, and freedom, political theorists tend to whistle by the graveyard of meaninglessness and the questions that it raises. With a sense of resignation many become Rawlsians or Habermassians, submitting to Church, law, or other powers, hoping that this Kantian bid for a freedom achieved through surrender will at least assuage the nightmare of nihilism. But when we return to the ordinary we find that all of our pretense has not dispelled the question: why exist?

Each and every day we return to this question. It is in keeping with the aspirations of the ordinary to do so. And to do so we have a practice of theorizing available to us. It is not a practice that has been followed by Baudrillard, though he has kept this important question visible. There is no doubt I have had trouble with Baudrillard's thought in the past: I have thought his provocations to be shallow, unserious in a dead-end kind of way, superficial, but most importantly for me, uninspirational, not helping me breathe, in fact, suffocating to my aspirations to think about what it means to lead a democratic life. The role of theory is to inspire, to help us breathe, to inspirit us as we turn to the task of thinking and as we turn away from it. But Baudrillard's simulated indifference, as far as I can tell, has in the long run not helped the project of inspiration and has done something instead to steer people toward a strange indifference over the very fate of breathing. Worse, his identification as an avatar of postmodernism has made it easier for conservatives of left and right, who are invested in the contests of the present hegemony shared by each other, to dismiss what some of the rest of us find vitally important in popular culture and its expression of ordinary aspirations. So I have had it in for Baudrillard for some time.

But I have a problem. Some of my friends have always thought highly of Baudrillard, in a way that is familiar to me, and that makes me admire them, if not him. Once I come to know a contemporary thinker well enough I try to be steadfast in my regard for that thinker, through the predictable cycles of their reputational rise and fall and reconsideration. Indeed, ill-considered attacks on some of them have often made them more worthy in my mind. My affinities with others are usually strengthened if I can note that they exercise this sort of loyalty, not through blind submission to mastery, but through a cheerful insistence on the worth of a thought carried by someone. Baudrillard has been a lucky thinker in that regard because he has had William Chaloupka as a cheerful defender. My friendship with Bill was partly why I was in Missoula in the first place. He was hosting this conference, and it seemed that this was one way I was going to get to visit him, then a new friend (and still a friend, not so new).

In retrospect I can see more clearly the condition of our friendship then. At the time the maneuvering between the passions of friendship and a sense of responsibility versus my too often mean insistence on criticizing and demystifying arguments that seemed deeply wrong to me, especially by deflating what I would judge to be the pretentious claims of those who had become complacent in their thought (in their despair), worked to create some very unhappy scenes, and required great tolerance on Bill's part. I knew I sometimes acted like a jerk, so I was in an odd position that evening. I wanted to think about the failings of Baudrillard in a way that would not do the sort of damage to such friendships that I imagined my usual jerkiness might do. Some people might call this a lesson in growing up. But I am not sure what is learned in that kind of growing, especially since it seems to involve a growth into silence.

Do such issues of manners, or what might be called the substantive etiquette of friendship, matter in this larger scheme of intellectual struggle? One might ask more pointedly: Is the truth of things immune from reflections on friendship and performance that might be deflected or muted, or heightened and amplified, depending upon the passions one carries with one? Political theory is performed by political theorists, after all. We teach each other, we learn from each other, and we hurt each other, even in the strange empire of imagination. Ten years later, I still wonder what is right and what is wrong in this regard.

But I would still make a claim, against my friend Bill, against Diane Rubenstein (who had been trying to warn me against my jerkiness by praising it), against other friends gathered that spring evening in the mountains, that I think that Baudrillard failed to be a wild thing that night. Others did not. I want to think about why that might be the case, and why it might be important to approach an understanding of what happened that night in Missoula, to speculate about that unbidden yet determined moment of singing, the expression of a common sense in the face of a collapse of meaning that was supposed to have occurred sometime around 1989.

Mediated Uncanniness, Elective Affinities

My claim from memory is that the audience knew that the song was "Wild Thing" that they started singing that song, that the cues given to sing were ambiguous, that they were instead embedded in a complicated set of collective memories that variously informed individual members of the audience as they participated in the comedy staged by Chadbourne. Would it make a difference in my claim if I misremembered, that is, if there were cues directly given to that audience by the performer, that is, if Chadbourne himself had started the singing? Only that I would then refer the question to him, to his own intuition, to what he thought he might know or infer about the audience, to his acknowledgment of their part in his performance, to his role as entertainer, to what he did not know about what he said and sang. Chadbourne would not be standing in for the collective sense of the room, but pursuing his historically contingent, loosely situated position as singer. His performance is what led us to that moment of song, and if we were following him, we were following his spontaneity, as he was by then following us in our spontaneity, like Walt Whitman and America. The relationship of the performer to audience plays out this way in improvisation, and Chadbourne was improvising that night.

Why did we sing "Wild Thing," instead of singing "Louie, Louie?" Why does it matter at all? That one song might have been sung instead of the other and that it could have been "Louie, Louie" as easily as it was "Wild Thing" might be the case. But the fact is that "Wild Thing" was the song that was sung. Was there a conspiracy operating here, was there a Pynchonian logic to the singing of that song, was something systemic going down that night? How did we, Chadbourne and the rest of us, come to sing this song, and not that one?

The explanations are alternative, multiple, and non-exclusive. Here is one. A popular logic of association, a kind of paralogy, was doing its work that evening. Chadbourne began his set with an adaptation of an old Spike Jones song, "Fhhhpp in der Führer's Face," for which he dressed in drag as Barbara Bush. His earlier performance established an associational clue that prepared the audience to sing "Wild Thing" instead of "Louie, Louie." For while "Louie, Louie" never inspired a popular political parody, in the winter of 1967–68 a satirical cover of the Troggs hit song "Wild Thing" swept the AM airwaves of the United States, with a comedic imitator of Senator Robert (Bobby) Kennedy performing a stuttering reading of the song in a Kennedy accent, speaking the lyrics over the music. The embedded memory of this earlier song could have triggered associations for at least a couple of people in that audience, and once they began to sing, the rest might have gone along in a happy recognition of the appropriateness of the song as a fitting finish to the evening.

I enter the record into the record. The song "Wild Thing" was written by Chip Taylor and originally recorded by Jordan Christopher and the Wild Ones. In 1966 it was covered by the Troggs, and became a major hit, spawning the parody, "Wilder Thing (with Senator Bobby)," recorded by The Hardly-Worthit Players, who produced an entire album of such covers, called *Boston Soul* (Philadelphia: Tames-Parkway Records, 1967). "Wild Thing" was also covered later that year at the Monterey Pop Festival, by a then (relatively) unknown American guitarist and singer living in England named Jimi Hendrix, who, upon being recommended to the organizers of the Monterey Pop Festival by Paul McCartney, returned from exile to give a performance of the song that is now a legendary moment in rock and roll history, and is often considered to be the definitive performance of the song.[3] This song, then, may have had deep associations for some members of the audience, who under the influence of beer, nostalgia, and the slightly sweet smell of something, either recalled or didn't, but nonetheless responded to a provocation, and when faced with the music, when faced with a past, when faced with a scene of happy silliness and a crescendo of joyful noise, offered up the lyric of "Wild Thing," a positive response to music, past, silliness, and noise.

There is yet another, more local reason for the singing of this song. When compared to "Louie, Louie," itself one of the most covered songs in the history of rock and roll music, "Wild Thing" would have a greater appeal to an audience composed of English Ph.D. candidates, political theorists, and cultural studies mavens. Why? Because the ranks of the humanities professoriate are generally composed of people who as students have shunned or have been shunned by the dominant campus cultures of fraternity life. "Louie, Louie" has been legendarily connected through the most obvious of film iconography to fraternity life in America. The popular comedy of 1978, *National Lampoon's Animal House*, in which a drunken, toga-clad slob, played to perfection by John Belushi, leads his fellow slobs in choruses of the song, is exemplary of a kind of drunken excess that this audience might not have viewed as being as resonant with their own (now hidden) utopian aspirations. Indeed, at a base level, the beery associations of "Louie, Louie" with a transcultural politics of misogynistic violence, the cult and culture of the brownshirts,[4] would have been anathema to the deeper aspirations of this crowd of men and women in black. In the contest of Eros versus Thanatos, "Wild Thing" stands for sex, and "Louie, Louie" for beer.

Here is a second explanation. The lyrics of "Wild Thing" inspired the audience to respond to Baudrillard's injunction to drive slowly to a delirious point of view. Each verse intensifies the feelings the narrator of the song has for his wild thing. He wants, he needs, he loves, in each successive verse, in a slowly building crescendo of desire. Perhaps it was a spontaneous acknowledgment by his disciples and admirers of Baudrillard's better self, the sensibility that guided him some years later to perform a nightclub act in a casino in Nevada. What Baudrillard's sympathetic interlocutors might have hoped he wanted could go by the name of Wild Thing. In the most generous reading of intent, Baudrillard's Wild Thing could be connected, at the only American university with a mountain on its campus, with the democratic experience of confronting nature.

Here Henry David Thoreau might be offered into conversation. His deeply *serious* resignation from the unnecessary presents at very least an anticipation and an overcoming of a sensibility of Baudrillardian nihilism.[5] Thoreau insisted that the tropes through which we are invested in ourselves also allow us to return to society, to lead new lives, born again after crises of meaninglessness, making our mark in response to but slightly beyond the skepticism that is engendered by the losses we incur every day. Thoreau's nature, as Jane Bennett has illuminated it, presents the conditions of uncertainty necessary for the development of an art of self appropriate to democratic politics.[6] Thoreau knew wildness well enough to love it, to recognize its depthless indifference to the fate of any one of its representatives, including us and errant woodchucks. He knew this indifference as an essential element of human being. Thoreau would not scorn Wild Thing, but sing it in his own way. We might ask, in retrospect of the event and inspired by Thoreau, how we are to (con)front nature when we are in the Rocky Mountains, only to discover that Nature here is as it is everywhere else, a figment of the imagination that continually has the most profound effects on us because of its unknowable character. We gathered in Missoula—"Baudrillard in the Mountains" was the advertisement, the call for papers, the conference title—to hear a lecture on the death of nature, among other things. Baudrillard delivered, and then, on the final night of the conference, it may be said that Baudrillard took it back, refused to play, refused this unbidden gift. The point of turning had been reached, and Baudrillard turned away.

At very least, the hearty unpredictability, the historically contingent accidents of association that make up the democratic aesthetics of such an event, were on display that night in Missoula, and it may have frightened Baudrillard. Maybe, when faced with such a display of free association, to paraphrase Jack Nicholson in one of his more delightfully cheesy film roles, he couldn't *handle* the truth.[7] If this were so, his next step was prescribed by his own thinking: seek the comfort of a blank emptiness, evade and avoid the lively and frightening unpredictability of the dance. As millennium passes, Baudrillard himself seems a distant memory to many, firmly a part of a decade of speculative theory at its seemingly worst, a charlatan who failed to live up to his own public image in the end and disappear. Baudrillard recently performed wearing a gold lamé jacket in a Nevada casino.[8] In the face of his terror he still seeks the secret of America (which is yet another example of a wanton courage). But by turning away from the signs of life that are right in front of him, he cannot hear the singing that surrounds him. This deafness is not a result of "foreignness," though foreignness can be the excuse for it. It is not overcome simply by turning up the volume (like an American yelling at a Japanese tourist, believing that by speaking more loudly he will be better understood). Instead, to hear the singing we are required to listen more closely, with a greater care and attention to the nuances of each message that comes to us, the overlay, the implicit tones, the careless play of puns and associations that inform the music of the ordinary.

It could have happened that way, that night in Missoula, and the truth is that we do not know what the final truth is. Can we handle that? "Wild Thing" was sung, not "Louie, Louie." We might call this phenomenon mediated uncanniness. It is hardly the concatenation of coincidence, but it is a category of event that is becoming subject to intensive explorations in cultural studies, with sometimes powerfully disturbing results.[9] What are we to name the combination of recalled cultural effluvia and reflexive response to unexpected situations, the forums for the staging of events, that inform these moments of public life? How are they more than mechanical responses prefigured in the affirmative culture of commodification that seems in retrospection to have been the postmodern moment? How do such responses inspire more than mechanical reactions to the style of the moment?

These are questions that might be asked in a politics of the ordinary. The varying explanations for the reception to the song "Wild Thing" I present above suggest that the habitations of language that we construct and that bear us both enable us to negotiate between the ordinary and the event and to reflect upon their interplay. Of course it can do no more than that, but the direction of its suggestion is toward the wildness of language itself, its strangeness in its familiarity. This wildness, this contingency, this inclination toward what Emerson might have called an intuitive reception, is a part of the play of the ordinary. It is a rededication to the ordinary, akin to what Stanley Cavell refers to as a resistance to the dictation of others, giving it the form of Emersonian self-reliance,[10] and it requires a particular valorization of ordinary experiences, an attempt to emphasize the powers of experience while avoiding the temptation to make experience into a force for normalizing the ordinary.

Democratic Sentences, Democratic Songs

Why shouldn't the representation of everyday life hold our interest as intensely as Thoreau may have wanted to hold that woodchuck in his teeth? What does it mean for the study of politics that so much of what is written about it in scholarly journals is basically unreadable, and hence unread? What is unreadability, though? Is it a question of difficulty? No, what is problematic is the lack of difficulty to be found in most of what is written and thought. For instance: "Policies that provide alternative opportunities for those caught in dysfunctional networks are as important as those that stimulate and encourage positive networks."[11] This sentence seems to mean: "Getting people out of bad situations is as important as putting them in good ones." What stops the author from making this simple observation is not what is usually, and accusatorily, called jargon. Every word ever written is jargon to somebody else. What stops her is instead the need to hide the obvious so as to obscure the difficult, namely, that the obvious is not so obvious after all. The relentless positivity of the style of science demands that everything be knowable. To insure that everything is knowable the science of politics never leaves the firm ground of what is always already known. This is the old problem of behavioralism, and it is revisited in the rational choice theory of the present, which demands of its practitioners only that they not leave the ground of the knowable and the known. What is already known, however, is dead. In this sense, Baudrillard's observation, "For ethnology to live, its object must die," is apt.[12] The critique of objectivity in the social sciences, which for at least a fragment of the last generation of scholars won for its champions a space in which to explore the qualitative substance of arguments, has been largely forgotten by a new generation of thinkers who have lost (or squandered) that space once won for lack of sensing better what to do with it. To paraphrase Emerson, we have instead succumbed to the temptation to submit to the more prosaic slavery to books.

But, as Emerson reminds us, "Books are for the scholar's idle times."[13] But there is a trick in this question, for when is the scholar idle? What are the conditions of our idleness? They are precisely when we are not thinking, when we are not singing, when we are not writing books for the next generation to read, when our work is so concerned with knowledge that we fail to acknowledge the limits of what we can say to each other. Can we afford to waste the opportunity that may once again open up for us? Are we ever even to try to realize ourselves philosophically, and hence politically, as democrats? Or must we count our meaningful sentences on the fingers of a single grasping hand, and turn away in quiet desperation?

* * *

Who in the world of letters is writing the books for the next generation to read? Who is marking the experience of the present? I do not think to look to those who insist upon deriving the rules of morality from timeless principles, nor to those who fight endlessly and exhaustively over small differences in the meanings of words, sentences, and paragraphs. Too many scholars are not equipped to do better than regurgitate a partial and illusory past or to repeat an endless present. But there are others who try to write criticism that lights fires, who attempt to conjure specters, who seek out the contest of tears, who show us how to make trouble, celebrate minority, and pluralize differences.[14] These scholars, among others, provide us with guides for looking at the present and seeing it, not as dead reckonings but as mobile armies of metaphors, mysterious and powerful forces that must be acknowledged. They, among others, suggest that the rigors of vision must not slip into rigidity, but that we must instead be prepared to be surprised by what we see. All of them, in ways direct and obscure, help prepare us for an engagement with a politics of the ordinary. In their own ways, these thinkers, who struggle on the boundary line between what is experienced and what is known, can sense that the ordinary does not come cheap, that the claims we make concerning it must be approached with extraordinary delicacy and care, and that the overwhelming sense of loss that could swamp us when we approach its unknowable vastness must be converted to a cheerful engagement and resolution to amend our selves and hence our fortunes. In the face of events, on the one side, and the normalization of vast tracts of life, on the other, the repository of the unknowable and indefinitely open ordinary is an imaginary site where we might dream democratically.[15]

This list of concerns and names is amendable, expandable, and contestable. Like any list it marks certain kinds of engagements as inspirations for thinking, and in these cases the thinking prepares us for singing. Such engagements, such thinking that prepares us for singing, might in turn guide us toward yet another way of writing, inscribing our experiences with the aim of opening some possibilities for an imaginative rethinking of what, for lack of a better term, we still might call the human condition. Rising above and sinking below the threshold of method, this writing would turn, always incompletely, blessedly incompletely, toward the possibility of re-connecting currents of poetry and philosophy, making better the love that we might have for both.

We return to the nocturnal by way of the diurnal, and greet the sun by being fully awake before it rises. Good morning and good night. Wild thing, you make my heart sing.

the politics of the "family"

MICHAEL J. SHAPIRO

Prelude: Nosebleeds in Salt Lake City

Shortly after the turn of the century, my paternal grandfather, Benjamin Shapiro, a man of humble origin and limited means, sought to move up in the world. After emigrating with his extended family from Czarist-held Vilna on the Russian pale at age ten, he had gone to work almost immediately upon his arrival in the United States in the factories of the Connecticut River valley. He never attended school but was a self-taught reader. By the time I knew him, he read the newspaper with his eyes following his forefinger across the page, and his spoken English was in an unpolished idiom not unlike the itinerant laborers in Dos Passos and Steinbeck novels.

After a brief time as a corporal in the U.S. Army—he was stationed in the Philippines during the Spanish-American War—he was reluctant to resume working as a machinist in the dark factories in which he had been intermittently employed before enlisting. Reading a Yiddish language newspaper one day, he chanced upon an item placed by a (self-described) "Wealthy Jewish family in Salt Lake City." They were looking for a young Jewish suitor for their daughter, who was recovering from her injuries sustained in a house fire.

As an old man Ben—having married my grandmother, Anna, also an emigre from Vilna and a Connecticut resident, introduced to him by a marriage broker—liked to tell the story. Perhaps he was wistful, for his marriage was not a happy one. By the time they were elderly, Ben and Anna lived apart most of the time; I don't recall having ever seen them together. Ben was in and out of a veterans home and Anna was in and out of a mental institution.

Ben's story always began with a very brief account of his journey westward. First there was a long train ride, taking a number of days. Then there was his body's uneasy accommodation to the altitude of Salt Lake City; he told about getting nosebleeds in his sleep and discovering blood on his pillow in the morning. My brother and I would become impatient with the travel narrative and beg for details about the western venue and especially about the courtship: "The girl, gramp! What about the girl?" The story always ended with the same cryptic line. "Dem hands; if dey coulda only done sumpthin about dem hands."

For years I have imagined Ben's western adventure, mentally filling in details. His version of the story was more or less biblical, in the sense in which Erich Auerbach characterizes Abraham's journey to fulfill Jehovah's command that he sacrifice Isaac. The Genesis story has a chronology but is bereft of descriptive detail: "The journey is like a silent progress through the indeterminate and the contingent, a holding of the breath, a process which has no present, which is inserted like a blank duration, between what has passed and what lies ahead, and which is yet to be measured: three days!"[1] Auerbach explains that the absence of detail makes sense when one recognizes that the Hebrew Bible is a genre designed for a particular kind of reader. The text is meant not to dazzle and entertain with descriptive imagery but to summon continuous interpretation: "Since the reader knows that God is a hidden God, his effort to interpret it constantly finds something new to feed upon."[2] The explanation of my grandfather's sparse treatment of detail is also genre-related. An old man was engaging in self-indulgent reminiscing; the story was about him, about a decisive moment in his life. It was not meant to enrich our understanding of the West, of wealthy Jewish families at the turn of the century, or even about "how the other half lives."[3]

Nevertheless, I have been continually engaged by my recollections of Ben's story, in part because of my imaginative additions to it. And because I keep the story of Ben's western experience alive in my imagination, fantasies about Ben's trip were evinced again when I saw Jim Jarmusch's film *Dead Man*. Filmed in black and white, the story opens with a young man, William Blake (Johnny Depp), on a train, dressed in a plaid suit and bowler hat. The passage of days is indicated with fade-outs, and the monotony of the journey is maintained with a montage of shots that cycle and recycle images of Blake's bored expression, other dull-looking passengers, the movement of changing landscape from the train windows, and the moving train, shot from various angles outside of it.

Although the repetition of camera shots and the black-and-white medium with which it is filmed lend Blake's journey a quality akin to the "blank duration" to which Auerbach refers in his treatment of Abraham's journey, the changing landscape and changing clothing styles of the passengers provide a directional cue; it is clear that Blake is headed west. Like Ben, Blake is an unattached young man, headed west in search of a new life—in this case an accountant's job in a steel mill in the far West. But Blake is moving away from a failed marriage prospect rather than toward one. When, upon his arrival, the job is no longer available, and a series of violent events makes him a (gravely wounded) fugitive, pursued by both bounty hunters and badge-wearing lawmen, he is picked up by a Native American, "Nobody" (Gary Farmer)—also unattached—who, after dressing his wound, leads him through a wilderness and toward the place where he will die.

The film has a variety of powerful themes, among which is Nobody's passionate interest in the poetry of William Blake's famous namesake. For him, this William Blake is a renewed version of the old but is already a "dead man" ("Some are born to sweet delight/Some are born to endless night," he quotes from *Auguries of Innocence*). But it is one of the film's minor episodes that has captured my attention. Blake almost becomes part of a "family." When he and Nobody spot trappers by a camp fire, Nobody orders him to join them, under the apparent assumption that being "white men," they will make compatible living companions. As the camera zooms in, the three men (Iggy Pop, Jared Harris, and Billy Bob Thornton) turn out to be a family unit with elements of traditional gender differentiation. One of the men (Iggy Pop) is wearing a dress and bonnet and is doing the cooking. Blake's arrival interrupts a domestic quarrel.

One trapper (Harris) is disparaging the evening meal; the transvestite cook (Pop) is responding with a lament about how hard he tries, and the third (Thornton) is intervening to contradict the complaint and praise the food. As Blake approaches, the culinary issue is rapidly displaced by a sexual one. Blake's appearance constitutes a reconfiguration of the "libidinal economy" of the family. With a new object of desire, the prior structure of investments is disrupted.[4] As the group fondles Blake, paying particular attention to the fine texture of his hair ("your hair is soft like a girl's"), an argument starts over who his sex partner is to be: "You had the last one; this one's mine." After the argument turns violent, with Harris shooting Thornton in the foot, Nobody, seeing that Blake's new living situation will not work out, rushes in and kills Thornton by cutting his throat, and he and Blake kill the other two in a shoot-out. Even as he is struggling to load his gun, Iggy Pop is muttering, "I cooked, I cleaned. . . ."

What can one make of this group of trappers, whom Jarmusch likens to "a trace element of a family unit"? Jarmusch supplies a brief discursive answer: "Because these guys live out in the fuckin' nowhere."[5] But Jarmusch's cinematic answer is more elaborate and compelling; it helps situate the relationship between my Grandfather Ben's aborted family story and the ones developed in *Dead Man*. At a thematic level, *Dead Man* exceeds a simple biographical genre. While at one level the film is about William Blake's death, at another, it—like my grandfather Ben's story—is about *the radical contingency of the family*. And, as a film, it achieves the contingency thematic with its composition and temporal spacing of camera shots. It shows how a variety of forces and events, well outside "natural" inclinations and forces of attraction, create and dissolve familial structures. In the filmic narrative, the ties that bind are more the result of contingent circumstances than they are initiating forces.

Family Values

Jarmusch's expression, "fuckin' nowhere," has special resonance in reference to his filmic story. None of the sex depicted is confined within the traditional nuclear family or the home. When Blake alights from the train in the town of Machine, where he expects to find his job waiting, one of the first things he sees as he heads up the main street is a cowboy, getting a "blow job" in an alley. When Blake stops and stares, the man points his gun at him. Blake also interrupts another extra-familial episode of sexual intercourse—one on the ground in the forest between "Nobody" and a Native American woman (she is fucking Nobody "fuckin' nowhere!"). And, perhaps most telling as regards the diremption between families and fucking, is a story about the bounty hunter, Cole, told by one of his companions, pursuing Blake through the wilderness. When out of earshot of Cole, he tells the third companion, apropos of Cole being dangerous, that Cole had "fucked his parents" and, moreover, had proceeded to kill them, cut them up, and eat them.

In various other ways, the far West encountered by William Blake is anarchic. By the time Blake's train is in the West, the passengers are mostly buffalo hunters in buffalo skin robes, armed with long rifles. At one point, they leap up to shoot at buffalo from the train windows. Blake's letter with a job offer at the Dickinson Steel Mill turns out to have no value. Indeed, he is forewarned in a conversation on the train with the train's (illiterate) stoker, who says, "I wouldn't trust no words written down on no piece of paper written by Dickinson out in Machine." The West, as it turns out, is "wild" in the sense that words do not work conventionally.

Apart from the letter's empty promise, verbal intercourse turns out to be as vexed as sexual intercourse. While hiring the bounty hunters, for example, Mr. Dickinson (Robert Mitchum) addresses many of his remarks to a stuffed bear in his office. And Nobody's speech is aphoristic, full of poetic and biblical references, and in various Native American languages as well as in English. At one point Blake says that he has not understood a single word Nobody has uttered. Even Nobody's most frequent, seemingly coherent utterance, which he directs to Blake—"Do you have any tobacco?"—makes no sense to Blake, who had told him early on that he didn't smoke. Blake fails to understand the semiotic significance of exchanges of tobacco in an other America, long effaced in Cleveland but still very much a part of the far West.

Bullets, like words, have unstable structures of articulation in Jarmusch's wild West. They are also either wildly aimed, or fired with little provocation: "Every time someone fires a gun at someone else in this film, the gesture is awkward, unheroic, pathetic; it's an act that leaves a mess and is deprived of any pretense at existential purity."[6] Blake's wound results from a bullet aimed at someone else. Cole shoots one of the other bounty hunters simply because the man had said, "Fuck you." Nobody shoots one of the trappers without aiming at him, and Blake acquires deadly aim only after the world is a blur because Nobody has taken his glasses and traded them. Moreover, there are no clear fiduciary responsibilities for the use of deadly force. Dickinson is an unprosecuted captain of the local industry despite being a homicidal maniac with several killings to his credit. And he sends off "lawmen" and bounty hunters ("the finest killers of men and Indians in this half of the world") alike in pursuit of Blake.

One concept, expressed by the young woman whom Blake meets in Machine, knits the episodes of anarchic violence—of both representational structures and deadly projectiles—into a single text. When Blake asks her why she has a gun, which he finds under a pillow on her bed, she answers: "Because this is America!" Jarmusch's film is not complicit with the mythic story of America's West as the venue in which a people has fulfilled its prescripted destiny. Instead, it offers a series of disjointed individual stories that intersect as a result of arbitrary encounters among their protagonists.

As this incoherent "America" emerges in *Dead Man*, the film's cinematic structure resists a single biographical perspective. Benjamin Shapiro's story of his trip to Salt Lake City, which clung closely to his experiences, (such as his nosebleeds) was not cinematic; he offered no verbal montage of shifting scenes and alternative viewpoints or voices. The autobiographical genre of his story owed most of its character to his unwavering first-person narrative. Films approximate biography if the camera follows, quite strictly, the actions of an individual. In contrast, as Gilles Deleuze has shown, cinema's use of the "time image" constitutes a way of interpreting events that is more critical than mere perception.[7]

As long as the camera merely followed action, the image of time was indirect, presented as a consequence of motion. The new "camera consciousness" is no longer defined by the movements it is able to follow. Now, "even when it is mobile, the camera is no longer content to follow the character's movement."[8] The thinking articulated through a film whose shots shift among a variety of scenes and alter their depth of focus generates meaning not on the basis of the experiences of individual characters but on the basis of the way an ensemble of shots are connected. These practices of filmic composition resist the simple chronologies that were the basis of "organic film narration," a story line produced when the camera adheres to a linear action sequence.[9] In contrast, in "crystalline film narration," like that which structures *Dead Man*, the filmic description creates its objects. Chronological time, that which is imposed by following the actors, is displaced by "non-chronological time."[10] Instead of composing movement images to treat the tensions explicitly acknowledged by William Blake, which would have restricted *Dead Man* to a fictional biography, Jarmusch's camera shots create an ensemble of time images that constitute a parody of "America's" heroic history in which, among other things, it expanded westward thanks to the actions of frontier heroes.[11]

The film also challenges the political mythology in which the nuclear family is the stable moral foundation that gives rise, contractually or otherwise, to the nation-state. Its cinematic narrative substitutes arbitrary events for this mythic narrative, representing collective groupings, familial and others, as consequences of encounters rather than as foundational causes. Similarly, at the level of discourse, the film stages encounters among different vernacular idioms and—through montage—allows a hybrid cultural world with various normative disjunctures to appear.

The film displays the centrifugal forces constituting "America" at the level of the image as well. It explores spaces, which are as normatively vexed and non-institutionalized as is the cacophony of languages, idioms, and syntactic styles constituting western speech. More generally, in his cinematic mapping of "fuckin' nowhere," a space in which a gender-differentiated family, composed of three male trappers could emerge, Jarmusch produces the West as a place where violence is spontaneous rather than institutionalized. Compared with densely "striated spaces," in which governmental states have imposed a pattern of normativity, such as Cleveland, William Blake's place of birth, Jarmusch's West is "smooth."

As Deleuze and Guattari have suggested, "striated spaces" are heavily coded with normative boundaries. Movement within them produces a tightly controlled ascription of identity to those who enter and traverse them. Striating space, they assert, is one of the fundamental tasks of the state, a function aimed at preventing nomadism.[12] This function operates both physically and symbolically. When they say that the state "does not dissociate itself from a process of capture of flows of all kinds, populations, commodities or commerce, money or capital, etc.," they are not simply referring to border patrols, toll booths, and revenue collection; they also mean the function of coding. The state is in effect a "town surveyor" and it responds against everyone who tries to escape its coding operations by striating space.[13]

In contrast, smooth spaces, such as Jarmusch's West, are places of contingency that the coding apparatuses of the state have yet to domesticate. Unlike striated spaces with sedentary routes that "*parcel out a closed space to people*, assigning each person a share and regulating the communication between shares," smooth spaces contain nomadic trajectories that "*distribute people (or animals) in an open space*, one that is indefinite and non-communicating."[14] In such spaces, people invent relationships rather than succumbing to the preexisting codes that constrain individual and collective identities.

In addition to its treatment of the arbitrariness of connections—the eventualities through which solidarities and separations occur—Jarmusch's *Dead Man* is itself an important event. It constitutes a disruption at two levels of political mythology. At a larger level of collective organization, it produces an America that emerged from anarchic and violent encounters; for example, the camera pans scenes of burned out Native American villages during Blake's canoe trip toward his last stop with Nobody, which points to the more genocidal episodes that accompany the individual ones occupying the film's main story line. At a lower level of collective organization, it challenges two kinds of discourse on the family: the universalizing political discourse that valorizes the traditional family as a foundational and ethical condition of possibility for national political coherence, and the episodic eruption of "family value" discourses, which seek to restore a model of family structure that has been altered. To appreciate the significance of the film's disruption of the myth of the natural family, it is necessary to characterize more fully the foundational discourses on the family.

Hegel's Ethical Family

G. W. F. Hegel is doubtless the most influential thinker among those in the history of political thought who have seen the traditional nuclear family as the primary unit within the social domain and as the ethical foundation of the state. Like John Locke, Hegel distinguishes between the state and "civil society," roughly that domain of association and structure of allegiances existing outside of the purview of the state. For Locke, civil society precedes the state. It is a naturally constituted, prepolitical community which retains prerogatives that each individual exercises in the form of rights. Seeing the state as a contractual extension of the society, Locke views each individual's allegiance to it as an implicit agreement to forego a degree of autonomy in exchange for certain protections.

Hegel departs from the Lockean model because of his steadfast rejection of contingency. Although in Hegel's legendary narrative the state is an extension of both the family and community, that extension is not a contractual one. Neither the family nor the state could be contractual because that would imply that associative connections were "the transient and utterly chaotic accidents of contingent agreement."[15] For Hegel, the family possesses a "natural unity" that is threatened when civil society "tears the individual from his family ties" and "estranges the members of the family from one another, and recognizes them as self-subsistent persons."[16] And, worse, civil society replaces that natural unity with contingency: "For the paternal soil and the external inorganic resources of nature from which the individual formerly derived his livelihood, it substitutes its own soil and subjects the permanent existence of even the entire family to dependence on itself and to contingency."[17]

Ultimately, however, the state, as the historical evolution of the Idea, constitutes the realization of the ethical life that begins in the family. Hegel's family is the first "ethical root of the state"; it contains an "objective universality in a substantial unity."[18] Hegel's story of how the state emerges from the family and civil society is teleological rather than contractual. Because universally emerging mind governs all levels, the state, as the ultimate level of organization, is "the end immanent within them" (the family and civil society).[19] At the same time, however, the state creates the condition of possibility for the ethical life of the family. Hegel's teleological narrative therefore resists chronological time. The state is the beginning as well as the end; it is, in Hegel's terms, "not so much the result as the beginning" of the natural ethical life: "It is within the state that the family is first developed into civil society, and it is the Idea of the state itself which disrupts itself into these two moments."[20]

What can we make of Hegel's story of the family and state? At a minimum, it is a piece of fiction in which "nature" plays a paradoxical role. First, it is left behind (as civil society substitutes contingency for the organic solidarity of the family) and then nature returns (as the state restores the ethical life that is dissipated in civil society). Hegel's resolution of the paradox is to substitute immanence for chronology; he locates the state both at the "beginning," where it creates the conditions of possibility for the moral family, and at the end, where it embodies the enlargement of an ethical life begun within the family.

Hegel's family/state story is an exemplar of what Etienne Balibar has called a "fictitious universality."[21] Contending with earlier, religious constructions of personhood, Hegel's philosophical project was an attempt to replace a religious universality with a political one. But the stories are homologous; while religious and political modes of hegemony differ in terms of what they ascribe as being "essential to human personality," both aspire to a universal community of meaning that unites the status of each unit within a common understanding.[22] More specifically, the political universality, which Hegel saw as a common historical destiny for all peoples (although some, he thought, still resided in earlier temporal stages), was ultimately a historically inevitable world of state citizens, whose national allegiances would be enlarged versions of those that structure the natural (and therefore ethical) solidarity of the family.

An antidote to Hegel's fictitious universality is achieved with a more finite treatment of history. "Finite history" is Jean-Luc Nancy's expression for an anti-Hegelian approach to characterizing "our time" in a way that ascribes to it neither a definitive past nor an expected future. History, in the finite sense, is a series of events in which people share a time without natural boundaries and share relationships without definite warrants such as "nature" or "reason." Finite historical events cannot "take place" because there is no prearranged space for them to occupy. They are happenings that make their place in time.[23]

In effect, Nancy's "finite history" accords well with a cinematic representation of events. Cinematic time images resist Hegelian and other modes of spatializing temporality, which universalize the emergence of the state and expunge the contingencies associated with other ways of being-in-time.

Yet Hegelian, fictitious universality continues to haunt contemporary discourses on the family, which attempt to moralize the nuclear family, valorize traditional parental authority, and locate traditional familial structures as foundational elements in the emergence of a democratic society and state. If we resist legendary narratives, however, and focus instead on the finitude of "our time," we can substitute a genealogical apprehension of familial structures, one which recognizes the character of families, at any historical moment, as events. This allows us to restore the contingency that the Hegelian story is aimed at expunging and, at the same time, provide a critique of aspects of contemporary "political reason."[24]

The Emergence of the Modern Family

Jacques Donzelot's analysis of the production of the modern family, based on historical inquiry rather than moralistic fantasy, provides a counter story to Hegel's fictitious universality. Like Hegel, Donzelot recognizes that the family occupies a paradoxical position vis-à-vis the state. The family, he notes, is "both queen and prisoner."[25] But this paradox is not a result of a model that gives the family two incompatible places in a narrative. Donzelot's family is both "the strategic resultant of . . . diverse forces" and a mythical unity on which moralistic reactions to its transformations are based. It is, in effect, manipulated by nationalistic reasons of state and then moralized as being in crisis by nationalists.[26]

What are the forces that have shaped the modern family? Donzelot's inquiry takes us back to the late seventeenth century to map the emerging forces that were operating both within and outside of the family. Perhaps most significant were the changing structures of occupational recruitment. As work became increasingly supplied outside of extended family structures, families continued to regulate marriages, but whereas before the purpose, beyond maintaining the family's reputation, was to preserve the family order as a working unit, by the nineteenth century, the family became increasingly concerned with preparing children for a marriage that would facilitate achieving the credentials necessary for fitting into orders outside the family.

At the same time, states were intervening to transform families. With the development of nationally regulated economies, they sought to regulate the way the family helped to produce a work force and to control the effects on families of fluctuations in the economy. This required increasing degrees of intervention in the health, education, and fiscal conditions of family members.

As a consequence of changes in economic structures and the related development of a state-manipulated social order, "a tactical collusion" developed between states and families: "What troubled families was adulterine children, rebellious adolescents, women of ill-repute—everything that might be prejudicial to their honor, reputation, or standing. By contrast, what worried the state was the squandering of vital forces, the unused or useless individuals."[27] Ever since the altered conditions of an emerging modernity have imposed new pressures on familial structures and tactics, from within and without, there have been elements of collusion as well as degrees of opposition in the pattern of state-family relations. Moreover, the patterns of complicity versus resistance in these relations have differed for different classes, in part because they have had to cope with different kinds of intervening agencies (e.g., social workers for the poorer classes and psychoanalysts for the wealthier ones). And, in general, various intermediaries—for example, doctors and therapists—have played different roles in the process of either reinforcing or challenging parental authority.

Whatever levels of pressure and blame various intervening agencies have leveled at the family, it has been in a context, encouraged by the state, of seeing the modern family as an institution whose responsibility is to qualify children to function outside of the family's boundaries—within the state-managed, social milieu.[28] Donzelot points out the bind of the contemporary family subject to such expectations. On the one hand, its ability to exercise its authority in relation to other institutions has been diminished; its "margin of autonomy" has been reduced. But, on the other hand, "its internal life is in demand"; it is ordered to strengthen its bonds, to maintain an affective hold over its members, which may have the paradoxical effect of lessening members' ability to function outside its boundaries.[29]

Yet the ability of a young person to function within the social milieu—to find steady work, to maintain the bonds of affection with a partner, to manage a parental role effectively, and to qualify children ultimately to do the same—is increasingly determined by exogenous forces.

Moralizing discourses on the family are insensitive to the forces constructing the contemporary family's bind. They seek instead to bind the family-state nexus by evoking the mythic normative family that emerged in Hegel's discourse. The high levels of surveillance of sexuality, to which Foucault referred in his analyses of modern governmentalities,[30] are aided and abetted in the activities of contemporary culture conservatives, who insist that high levels of surveillance of sexual and other practices are necessary for the maintenance of "decency." The nation's public sphere is a place where "decent" or "civilized" behavior must be maintained to ensure its respect in the world of states.

Indeed, throughout its modern history, nationalism and codes of decency have been significantly connected.[31] Their more recent inter-articulations have been evident in campaigns of those associated with saving "American civilization" against sexually explicit media. In a recent op-ed piece in the *New York Times*, for example, William Bennett and C. DeLoris Tucker praised the Wal-Mart store chain for refusing to stock "compact disks with lyrics and cover art that it finds objectionable."[32] They make an appeal for "simple decency," which they claim has the support of "concerned parents and politicians of both parties."[33] The evocation of "decency" has been articulated during the past decade with a more general family-values right-wing political initiative, aimed at essentializing the conventional family and locating it in a mythic story in which the dissolution of traditional family structures is a threat to a previously vital national character.

Apart from the ways in which this story conjures away the impacts of changing economic circumstances on family structures—telling a mythic values story instead of a money story[34]—its crisis mode is belied by a history of nationalism's appropriation of issues of sexuality and codes of decency, which intensified throughout the nineteenth century as states increasingly used the idea of a unified national culture as part of their legitimation of their territorial sovereignty claims.[35]

The idea of decency, which has been part of nationalism's construction of a normative sexuality, has a historical trajectory that challenges a crisis model, which sees the present as a qualitative change in the evolution of morals. The idea of decency is a legacy of the concept of civilité that was employed in Europe as a guide to behavior during the period of state formation. In the "age of absolutism," it was associated with the processes through which western societies imposed domestic pacification. While the behaviors were being shaped, there developed a concurrent concept of civilization that was to become part of European self-appreciation, although in different states, that civilizational discourse took on different qualities and was variously connected to antagonisms between different classes.[36]

Most significantly, the norms prescribing constraints and codes of decency, that initially related primarily to within-society class dynamics as well as to state-sponsored aspects of pacification, eventually acquired a collective, ontological significance; they became part of a cluster of ideas about national distinctiveness. As George Mosse put it, the norms comprising civilité needed a broader warrant; they "had to be informed by an ideal if they were to be effective. . . . In most timely fashion, nationalism came to the rescue."[37]

Although the idea of decency no longer has the official warrant it enjoyed at one time—it is a quaint anachronism when it appears in policy discourses—it has been central to the arguments of various factions in the right wing's continuing war on the arts and entertainment industry. While much of war has been waged in academic publications and opinion journals, one of the more exemplary counterattacks has appeared in the form of a feature film, written and directed by Paul Thomas Anderson. His *Boogie Nights*, a film about the pornography industry in the disco days of the 1970s and its move from theaters to videos in the eighties, features a pornography production company organized as a family. The film is, among other things, an ironic reversal of the relationship between decency and family values; a part of an industry that produces "indecency" turns out to be a more effective "family" than the other, traditional nuclear families that are shown in the film.

Boogie Nights opens with shots of theater marquees, emphasizing part of the entertainment structure of Los Angeles in the seventies. Porn film stars were marquee names, and drugs and discos were voguish parts of urban life. Jack Horner (Burt Reynolds), who plays the role of a surrogate father in his porn production company, adds young Eddie (Marky Mark), who soon adopts the name Dirk Digler, to his "family." Upon meeting Eddie, who is a busboy in a night club, he exclaims, "I've got a feeling there's something wonderful in those jeans waiting to come out." Once Eddie becomes Dirk Digler and is acting in Horner's films, it comes out often and to much effect; Digler becomes a star with strong name recognition. Apparently seventies porn star Johnny Wadd, known for his large sex organ, is the Digler prototype (Digler's qualifying attribute is also reminiscent of the sole qualification of Madame de Saint-Ange's gardener in the Marquis de Sade's *Philosophy in the Bedroom*, with which I compare *Boogie Nights* below).

But *Boogie Nights* is not itself a porn film. The sex scenes are few and are focused more on production than sex. Anderson's camera emphasizes the political economy of porn production—the recruitment and organization of the crew, the management of their relationships, and the actual work involved in setting and filming scenes. As Jack Horner tells Eddie/Dirk Digler: "You got your camera. You got your film. . . . You got your lights. You got your synching. You got your editing. You got your lab. Before you turn around you've spent maybe twenty-five or thirty thousand dollars."

Horner's remark reflects a pervasive filmic strategy in *Boogie Nights*. Anderson's primary focus on the work of producing and staging pornography disrupts the usual spatiality of pornographic cinema. If we recognize two kinds of filmic space, "that included within the frame and that outside the frame,"[38] we can appreciate this disruption. It is accomplished by bringing in the social organization of the pornography production ensemble into the same space as the action. The violation of this spatial separation reorients the film's thematic. It is more about families than about sex.

From the outset, shortly after Horner discovers that Eddie may be the talent he is seeking, it is evident that Horner is a surrogate father figure and his main female attraction, Amber Waves (Julianne Moore), is a surrogate mother. Thematically, then, *Boogie Nights* is a story of a surrogate family formed around the production company and located primarily in Jack Horner's home. The story opposes the family values stories emerging in a variety of genres with varying degrees of cultural authority,[39] for the heteronormal families depicted throughout the film are seriously impaired and/or fractured structures. Although they are aiming to qualify their children for survival on the outside, their disturbed interactions have the opposite effect (at least in the cases of Eddie and "Roller Girl," one of the younger porn actresses).

In this context, Jack Horner's family is a throwback. Unlike the modern family, whose major effort is to qualify its children to function outside of its boundaries, Horner's is a pre-modern family from the point of view of the locus of work. Moreover, with the coming of the video age, which threatens the film star aspirations of Horner's children/actors, Horner acts to protect his family from the vagaries of economic change, prompted by technological change. And he does his best to protect his "children" from problematic consumers of porn as well as from outside forces. For example, even the drug use in his household is less excessive among his crew than among visitors at his parties.

Two external contexts bear especially on implications of the familial solidarity that Horner tries to maintain. First, the seventies disco era is a time of various challenges to social coherence. Not only are families being increasingly broken, but also the perceptual field as a whole is disintegrating into a pluralizing set of signs, all offering different styles of personhood. In the face of these changes, various moralizing responses are underway—efforts at symbolically binding relationships that are being sundered—which ultimately impact on the fates of the various characters in Anderson's story.

Second, the situation for women is being altered, for the seventies marks the beginning of the process Nancy Fraser has referred to as "the crumbling of the old gender order," an order centered on the "family wage."[40] Among the consequences of this alteration is a situation in which "needy women" have been increasingly subject to an "exploitable dependency."[41]

The women and men in Jack Horner's film company are all ill-suited to the changing outside order. His film company and home operate as a temporary refuge from forces that are radically compromising the viability of traditional family structures. But more importantly, Jack Horner's substitute family is not a traditional patriarchy. Horner does not function as "the law"; indeed, he is more of a Sadean than a Freudian father. The sex scenes he directs are mostly boring and repetitious, and although the sexuality practiced within his films and household is all extra-familial, only one member of the film crew, "Little Bill," holds onto a traditional family model of sexuality. Upset at his wife's repeated adultery, he finally shoots her, a lover, and himself. Little Bill retains his Horner family connection, however; one of the film's last scenes, a panning of the walls of Jack Horner's home, shows a photo portrait of Little Bill on a wall. Even his dramatic deviance fails to disconnect him from his surrogate family.

Like Sade's boudoirs, Jack Horner's home is less about sex than about singularity. He shows no personal interest in sex, and as a director—in his films and in his home—is nondirective; his characters choose their styles. Roller Girl never removes her skates, even while nude for sex scenes. Dirk Digler, having invented his own name, is also allowed to invent plots and is permitted to select his moments of climax, even when they violate the script. Other members of the crew display diverse and even anachronistic styles (e.g., Buck Swope, a black former stereo salesman dresses in an outmoded cowboy style and is continually in search of an effective "look"). Horner shows himself to be completely nonjudgmental with respect to all the choices of individual style.

In contrast, when the various members of Horner's family try to survive economically and socially outside the family—seeking bank loans, music careers, or visitation rights with children—various social forces, from the informal censoriousness of a society intolerant of pornography workers and alterative sexualities to the more institutionalized agencies of banks and judges—resist or batter them.

Horner is a Sadean father, therefore, in the sense that his management of space is aimed precisely at protecting the singularities of people who cannot operate comfortably within the normative climate of the outside life world.[42] Like Sade, he rejects the naturalness of the traditional family. He sharply distinguishes the family and sexuality and sponsors a pluralistic idea of attachments. Although, unlike Sade, he encourages a familial style for his collective, he remains Sadean in the sense that familial structures for him are contingent and sexual acts are transient and insignificant with respect to the establishment of social or affectual bonds. Ultimately, however, Anderson's film neither valorizes nor disparages Horner's model of bonding. Its juxtapositions map a significant change in the forces that create the conditions of possibility for attachment and encourage critical thought about bonds, while recognizing the problematic claim any model of family structure has for political allegiance.

Conclusion: Binding Community

If we regard the family as a contingent after-effect of various forces rather than as a stable (natural or moral) basis for sociality and political commitment, what are our political options when it comes to seeking exemplars for the bonds of community? To approach the question, I want to focus attention on the concept of binding, treating it as it is used by Jonathan Crary in his analysis of a Manet painting, *In the Conservatory*.[43] Among the aspects of the two figures in the center of the painting that attract Crary's attention—a woman seated on a bench and a cigar-smoking man, leaning on the bench from behind it—are each of their hands. Both are wearing wedding bands but seem to be an adulterous couple.

In his analysis of what he calls "the binding energy of the work," Crary argues that Manet's work was set against two aspects of fragmentation afflicting perceptual and social coherence in the late nineteenth century: the painting works to reconsolidate both a perceptual field being sundered by a breakdown in normative attentiveness, and a breakdown in the marriage bond reflected in adulterous relationships.

In contrast with Manet's emphasis on binding, *Boogie Nights* explores a complex dynamic of binding and unbinding. This exploration is aided by the capacity of film, with its cuts, juxtapositions, and other spatio-temporal modalities, to enact a social bond without a normative fixity. Anderson's filmic story valorizes singularities while at the same time exploring alternative structures of being-in-common in ways that respect those singularities.

Anderson's film recognizes—without resolving—the tensions between singularities and affectual ties. As a result, his *Boogie Nights* aligns itself with Jean-Luc Nancy's suggestion that there are ways to be in common without foundational guarantees. Nancy's model of being in common eschews ontological grounding because it rejects a "truth of a common subject" or a general model of sense, outside of the "numerous singularity of each of the 'subjects of sense.' "[44] Collective identities have no coherent horizon behind them and no essence to be attained.[45] The social bond, for Nancy, is an unending process of tying and untying. Insofar as identity is involved in the process, it is provisional and contingent on the ties that are formed. And, insofar as there is a politics of the family one can endorse within such a contingency-affirming perspective, it is a politics that embraces and protects singularity while encouraging a plurality of ties that bind (familial and otherwise).

declarations of independence

JODI DEAN

Suspect Terrains

Although Hillary Rodham Clinton openly supported her husband through the sex scandals that characterized his years in national office, linking these scandals to a conservative plot to bring him down seemed excessive even for her. Yet on NBC's *Today* on January 27, 1998, she did exactly that: "For anybody willing to find it, and write about it, and explain it, is this vast right-wing conspiracy that has been conspiring against my husband since the day he announced for president. A few journalists have kind of caught onto it and explained it, but it has not yet been fully revealed to the American public. And actually, you know, in a bizarre sort of way, this [the Lewinsky scandal] may do it."[1]

Hillary Clinton's sweeping indictment fits with the broader politics of her husband's presidency. It evokes a politics of excess that reveled in Bill Clinton's transgressions and desires, in the big hair, lips, and stories of the women with whom he has been linked, and in the endless array of scandals around a special prosecutor, White House, and media out of control. But were her declaration simply another instance of these public excesses, it would not seem so audacious, so paranoid, so potentially crazy. For even as conspiracy is in the air, even as the *New York Times Magazine* could feature a cover story on those Clinton haters who weave conspiracy theories about Vincent Foster's suicide, obscure episodes in Arkansas politics, and schemes to make money and abuse power, the First Lady's embrace of conspiracy as an explanation for political events violated the rarely acknowledged norms of debate within what is presented as the national public sphere.[2] She dared to take conspiracy seriously. She dared to omit from her statement the all-to-common disavowal, "I'm not a conspiracy theorist, but. . . ." In so doing, Hillary Clinton crossed the border separating normalized political discussion from the "extremist" and "radical." And she entered a suspect terrain.

As if the risks of this terrain were not clear, as if the audaciousness of Hillary Clinton's words were not obvious, internet writers spelled it out, filling in the missing parts of her interview: "You know what I mean. Ken

Starr is part of the New World Order that's implanting chips in everybody and keeping the UFOs hidden at Area 51 and giving everybody cancer. I've seen him flying a black UN helicopter."[3] In a similar though less amusing vein, William F. Buckley used the First Lady's words to remind his readers that she had exited from normal political debate. Conspiracy theory isn't *real* politics; it's kooky. Buckley associates "right-wing kookism" with the John Birch Society. He racializes "the kooky left" as those who claim that "AIDS was an invention of the CIA to arrest the growth of the black population." Those on the left who Buckley thinks actually were conspiratorial aren't kooky; they're "mischievous," Buckley's odd, dismissive term for "American communists and their fellow travelers, who did everything from infiltrating government to stealing the secrets of the atomic bomb."[4] The *Washington Post*, also anxious to restore the order and space of public political discourse, provided assurances that whereas the *American Spectator*, British tabloids, conspiracy theorists, and Jerry Falwell have indeed persistently attacked and denounced the Clintons, the Lewinsky matter is significantly different. "The news that Starr is investigating allegations that Clinton had a sexual relationship with the former White House intern and lied under oath about it was broken by mainstream news organizations—the *Washington Post*, ABC, *Los Angeles Times*, and *Newsweek*—not by the conservative press."[5]

These responses to Hillary Clinton's declaration establish the contours of the national public. They produce the arena within which politics takes place, that space where words and actions are to be engaged carefully and thoughtfully, where debate and disagreement are safe exchanges between adversaries rather than life and death struggles between enemies. By establishing and policing the borders of the political, these responses secure a predictable, normal, public sphere.

Beyond this normal public sphere is a chaotic miasma of kooks and crazies whose irrationality makes them politically unworthy. They can't be taken seriously. Buckley and company chastised the First Lady for evoking conspiracy because in breaking the political rules, she violated the very borders that make politics possible. She left the terrain of the normal public, of official politics. She—and those like her—must be stopped.

Public Secrets

A number of politicians, pundits, and political theorists find themselves duty bound to ensure that the rest of us know the difference between responsible political thinking and crazed conspiracy theory, especially now amidst the heady uncertainties of technoglobal entertainment culture.[6] Often, their worries about conspiracy theory latch onto bodies. Some want to immunize the body politic from infection by conspiracy theories. Others want to protect innocent citizens from the tricks and seductions of the paranoid. The dark underside of reason, its private parts or parts of shame, conspiracy thinking stimulates not the mind, but the body. We must avoid titillation as well as infection. For example, Daniel Pipes likens conspiracy theory to pornography; each is ripe with suggestive fantasies. He doesn't say why conspiracy seduces, but he invites readers to join him in his struggle against it.[7]

Given the advice of pundits and the risks of infection, why would Hillary Rodham Clinton venture into the suspect terrain of conspiracy? Why might she violate the norms of safe politics in a rational public sphere? Perhaps because they are already in disarray, functioning haphazardly if at all. The scandal around Monica Lewinsky can hardly be understood in terms of a public exchange of reason. Perhaps Hillary Clinton ventured into a dangerous political space because legitimate politics, or those politics that claim themselves as legitimate, are too confining. She may have been too constrained by the usual political norms, finding that they prevented her from acting. Perhaps her's was a declaration of independence.

For a moment, at least, her conspiracy theory did create some breathing room. Scrutiny immediately shifted from Bill Clinton to his critics, prosecutors, and enemies. The secret was no longer what happened between the president and a White House aide. It was now the possibility of a conspiracy. Following Hillary Clinton's charge that not one person but "an entire operation" was behind the assault on her husband, mainstream news media such as the *New York Times*, the *Washington Post*, *Time*, and *Newsweek* provided detailed accounts of links connecting key figures in the Lewinsky case.

Finding the public of official political discourse too confining, the First Lady may well have been attempting to use conspiracy theory to go behind it. That is to say, she may have been engaging in the long practiced performance of "going directly to the people." After all, conspiracy thinking is deeply embedded in American history and particularly resonant in the national present. It is clearly part of American politics, regardless of the admonitions and dismissals of elite experts. At least some people respond to it. These are the people and this is the politics Hillary Clinton was trying to access. Her effort to change what was understood as the secret did not hail television viewers as rational subjects in an officially sanctioned public sphere. She was inviting her audience to occupy subject positions in a different discourse, one characterized not by norms of rational exchange but by suspicion, doubt. Her words interpellated—called into being—as supporters those who might share her frustration with what functions as official politics, with partisanship, corruption, and media excess.[8] The First

Lady used television to produce a people beyond the authorized public, a people who would join her in rejecting the terms, dimensions, and enactments of the national public sphere.

The Paradox of the Public

Hillary Rodham Clinton's use of conspiracy theory suggests the paradox of the public, that is, the deep connection between conspiracy thinking and norms of publicity. Both depend on what is secret, hidden.[9] The very concept of the public requires a contrast with the private and unseen. To produce an audience of those who might be counted on as the public, who might be evoked in the justification of a principle or a policy, practices of publicity seek to uncover the secret, to bring it to light. Like conspiracy theories, they endeavor to bring "to public attention" an object that the public can know, discuss, and judge. Rather than linked to incommensurable ways of thinking, then, conspiracy and publicity are part of the same political rationality.

Although the possibility of a secret seems to generate the public, publicity itself is generative. Publicity produces the secret and the hidden through its investigations and judgments. Questions become allegations. Are you having an affair? Did you declare everything on your income taxes? If one answers no, to most anything, it can be construed as a denial: no, I am not having sex with her. But the public has a right to know. Ironically, the more information that is brought into the light of the public, the more that is disclosed for public consumption, the more that the people, the masses, seem to displace the public. At least that's what critics imply when they deride the vehicles of publicity as well as its audience for their irrationality, prurience, bad taste, and fall from the norms and standards of the public sphere. An effect of the paradox of the public, then, is that the concept of publicity creates the excesses that must be disavowed in the very name of the public. It produces conspiracy theory.

Hillary Clinton's declaration of independence from the official public sphere points to several components of the American present that make it a friendly environment for conspiracy thinking. Each of these components is linked to the paradox of the public and the drive to uncover the secret.

Her comment first evokes technocultural anxieties regarding knowledge production in the information age. We live in a world of networked communication. On the one hand, this exacerbates the drive for content, for the scoop, for information, as various media compete for audience. There must be some secret out there that has not yet been revealed. On the other hand, with the abundance of information available on the internet, cable television, and radio come more personal concerns about the disintegration of privacy.[10] Many of us are monitored in our day-to-day activities. Hidden cameras observe nannies. Tape recorders track telemarketers, "to enable them to serve you better." We are accustomed to seeing video clips from ATMs and 7–11s on the evening news, especially when they feature black faces. Anywhere at any time anyone of us may be tracked, traced, observed. Websites can deposit a "cookie" or trace code onto my hard drive, making me readable, usable, tradable.[11] We are all potential information. Hillary Clinton's outrage over the monitoring of her husband's activities, then, may well resonate with the frustration of some employees over their experience in the workplace. Not even the office of the President is safe from prying eyes. Inquiring minds want to know.

Second, the First Lady's comment taps into our compulsion to reveal and disclose. As if commanded by an alien implant, we seem driven to rid ourselves of secrets, to tell them to anyone and everyone who will listen. Michel Foucault associates this compulsion to reveal with contemporary discourses of truth. His well-known account of sex as that which has to be confessed points to the place of the secret that impels its own discovery, that operates as an incitement to speech even as it is exploited as "*the* secret."[12] Similarly, his analysis of the disciplinary mechanisms that produce the modern subject attends to processes of observing, knowing, and rendering visible. For Foucault, these are the procedures by which truth is established and bodies are made docile.[13] For us, the politics of sexual confession manifests itself in tabloid television, in therapeutic injunctions to speak one's pain, and in the pressures of outing.[14] Observation, as Thomas Dumm shows, has morphed from surveillance to monitoring, from "the correction of individuals to the control of populations."[15]

The compulsion to reveal is the most important link between the notion of the public and conspiracy theory. Each endeavors to bring to light what has remained hidden. In his account of the public sphere, Jürgen Habermas emphasizes not only the place of revelation in classic conceptions of the public ("Only in light of the public did that which existed become revealed, did everything become visible to all"), but also, and perhaps more surprisingly, the public's deep connection with conspiracy.[16] Describing the secret societies popular in Europe in the early eighteenth century, he draws out their intent to promulgate enlightenment and cultivate reason. Habermas writes:

> The coming together of private people into a public was therefore anticipated in secret, as a public sphere still existing largely behind closed doors. . . . As long as publicity had its seat in the secret chanceries of the prince, reason could not reveal itself directly. Its sphere of publicity had still to rely on secrecy; its public, even as a public, remained internal. . . . This recalls Lessing's

famous statement about Freemasonry, which at that time was a broader European phenomenon: it was just as old as bourgeois society—"if indeed bourgeois society is not merely the offspring of Freemasonry."[17]

What Habermas conceptualizes as the bourgeois public sphere has early roots in secret societies; indeed, he allows that publicity itself, as a norm of reason, might require secrecy. Paradoxically, those adepts, who like the Freemasons and Illuminati, understood secret societies as organizations for the cultivation of reason, would better represent Habermas's public sphere than associations that did not cloak themselves in secrecy but stuck to custom and tradition. For the illuminated, secrecy was a condition for the publicity of reason. In the historical context of monarchical rule, the norms of reason thought to underlie an expansion of rights and liberties of the people had to be protected from prying eyes. They depended on remaining hidden.

Under different political conditions, say those of late capitalist societies with claims to democracy, publicity still depends on secrecy in order to produce a public. Today, however, neither the norms of reason nor those trying to cultivate them are hidden. Instead, the very idea that the public has a right to know, that public rule depends on access to information, on full disclosure, puts the secret at the heart of the public. Without a secret to discover, something hidden that can be exposed, that we can talk about, there is no public. Indeed, in the contemporary politics of public confession and conspiracy theory, disclosure is everything. The focus of politics is exposure, outing.[18] Doing something about what has been exposed, formulating a policy, or suggesting alternatives seems somehow less significant. It is certainly less exciting than discovering, knowing, and telling a secret.

The Lewinsky affair climaxed with the spilling of the Starr report on the Web. In the initial hours, or even days, there may have been something like a public—nearly all of "us" responded to the disclosure, reading, hearing, talking about little else. Did you see note number 138? But after "it"—the secret—was all out there, what was there left to do? The drive to impeachment pursued by some Republicans seemed misplaced, inappropriate. Few of the rest of us could make sense of it. The Republicans did not quite understand that the political moment had passed and the public had withered away. With no more questions, no more secrets, there was no more "we."

To be sure, it is rare for everything to be revealed all at once. Publicity tends to defer revelation even as it compels it. How something is disclosed, the rules and procedures that have been adopted, the context in which a revelation is made and the company it keeps, affect its connection with truth and reason. Not just any secret can hail a public. It has to be a secret uncovered by those who are authorized, in the name of the public, to delve into the hidden, to get their hands dirty. Hence, because of the political effects of disclosure, because disclosure is imbricated with the power to call a public into being, who can uncover a secret is a volatile issue.[19] For the sake of clear political boundaries, a safe public terrain, the unworthy must be excluded. So, serious media like the *New York Times* are in. The *National Enquirer* is out. Cornell physics professors like Carl Sagan are in. Ufologists like Budd Hopkins are out.[20] Independent prosecutors like Kenneth Starr are in, though this is debatable. Independent investigators such as those who post their theories and judgments on usenet groups are generally out. But it can be hard to say for sure. Because of the power of disclosure it seems that we need to be able to tell the difference between real knowledge and crazy conjecture. We need to know who is a conspiracy theorist. Fortunately, pundits and political theorists are here to tell us.

Finally, Hillary Clinton's evocation of conspiracy draws on American history. Not just a sideline to a mainstream politics of reasonable discussion and rational exchange, conspiracy thinking has long occupied a central place in American politics. America is, in fact, embedded in it. From the anti-Freemasonry and anti-Catholicism of colonial America, to the recurrent nativism of the nineteenth century, to the McCarthyism and Cold War nuclearism of the twentieth century, major political movements in the United States have been informed by fears of conspiracy as well as by the actual need to engage in conspiracies to combat threats to national sovereignty.[21] Indeed, one might say that conspiracy thinking produces America as a nation; it provides narratives that tell Americans who "we" are.

Arguing that conspiracy thinking (or, in his words, a "countersubversive tradition") is at the core of American politics, Michael Rogin documents the patterns of demonization in American national identity.[22] "The alien preserves American identity against fear of boundary collapse," Rogin writes. "Taken inside, the subversive would obliterate the American; driven outside, the subversive becomes an alien who serves as a repository for the disowned, negative American self."[23] These aliens have been the Freemasons and Illuminati thought to have brought about the French Revolution and to have threatened the stability of the new America with atheism and radical democracy. They have been the Catholics seen as conspiring against Americans' religious freedom by bringing popery to bear against the nation. They have been the abolitionists and Communists accused of plotting against Americans' right to property. They have been the blacks seducing white women, immigrants taking American jobs, dissenters casting doubt on the dream through their un-American activities. The "inside" and "outside" that Rogin invokes, then, rather than aspects of an American identity, are themselves drawn through the evocation of conspiracy. "We" are the ones at risk of being subverted; "they" are those who threaten us. And "we" may not be able to know for sure who "they" are, which is why "we" must be vigilant in bringing "them" out of their hiding places and uncovering their secrets. The secret at the heart of the public, then, is a secret generated by an uncertainty, an inability to know who "we" are. That secret must be concealed and repudiated through ever more vigilant efforts to reveal the aliens and secure the borders of the nation.

The America that conspiracy theory produces is not meant to satisfy the identity needs of the weak and dispossessed; it is not merely compensation for the sufferings of those with some sort of status deficit disorder. Conspiracy theory is central to the story of American pluralism. It plays an integral role in producing the reliable center, the public, the "we" recognized and accepted by mainstream American political science.[24]

American liberal pluralism sees politics as a balanced search for coalition and compromise. Within the safely sanitized sphere of the political, actions are predictable, rational. Diverse groups push their interests while nonetheless working to keep conflict to a minimum. They calmly introduce their claims, make their arguments. Although competitive, these interest groups do not aim for total victory. They are content with practical solutions capable of accommodating a variety of needs and demands.

Although pluralists premise politics on diversity, they do not include an endless variety of political positions. Pluralism is not about multiple networks of political struggle and multiple forms of political engagement. As William Connolly explains, "Outside the warm, protected spaces of the normal individual and the territorial state, conventional pluralists project a lot of abnormality, anarchy, and cruelty in need of exclusion or regulation. . . . Stark definitions of the outside contain the range and reach of diversity on the inside, and vice versa."[25] Pluralism seems a strong account of a fair and legitimate process of political bargaining precisely because anything that can threaten it is blocked from the terrain of politics.

Consequently, extreme positions are disallowed. The very constitution of the political requires that what is radical or extreme be excluded in advance, before politics can get underway. For example, Seymour Martin Lipset and Earl Raab view "pluralism" and "extremism" as mutually defining terms: "Extremism basically describes that impulse which is inimical to a pluralism of interests and groups, inimical to a system of many nonsubmissive centers of power and areas of privacy. Extremism *is* antipluralism or—to use an only slightly less awkward term—monism."[26] Politics depends on discerning extremism and setting up barriers against it. There are limits to what the public can tolerate, limits to what can count as reasonable. Eliminating conspiracy thinking, thinking that might challenge the very terms of politics, is necessary if there is to be a politics at all.

Lipset and Raab view American history as a struggle between pluralism and extremism or monism. They characterize monism as moralistic, simplistic (searching for historical explanations that rely on binary oppositions), and rooted in conspiracy theory. (In his recent study of conspiracy thinking, Daniel Pipes takes an opposing position. He claims that "common sense accepts simple explanations; in contrast, conspiracy theories add complicating elements."[27]) As Lipset and Raab acknowledge the prominence of moralism in "mainstream" politics and point out the complexities of the various conspiracies alleged to have threatened American democracy, however, the way they determine exactly what counts as a monist position becomes unclear. Are they those movements that Lipset and Raab simply don't like? Rogin writes, "Claiming to cover right-wing extremism as a whole, the authors actually attack movements of which they disapprove that were neither right-wing nor extremist, and they cover up a countersubversive tradition that cannot be reduced to religious prejudice, ethnic conflict, and status anxiety."[28]

In conventional accounts of pluralism, contesting the basic structure of American political proceduralism—the terms of inclusion and participation—is not allowed.[29] In the Lipset and Raab version, moreover, pluralism itself rests on a single "conceptual heart" and "article of faith," namely, the "properties of human reason."[30] Faith guarantees that there is a singular human reason that forms the basis of pluralism (although this faith is rational whereas other kinds of faith may not be). The possibility of a variety of forms of reason, of what Connolly calls the pluralization of pluralism, is excluded in advance, in fact by the use of conspiracy thinking to demarcate the limits of inclusion within an American national political "we."

Conspiracy theories produce America as they interpellate those who might believe them, or even those who might simply consider the possibilities conspiracy theories unfold, as the American "we" that must be awakened to the truth, informed, protected. They call into being another America, one outside the restrictive boundaries of the usual politics. Although this might indicate a kind of rejection of politics in favor of other-worldly remedies, American conspiracy theories are for the most part resolutely activist in their search for other means of engaging the powers and systems structuring politics. They are also far from radical in their assumption that the truth is out there and can be revealed according to norms of publicity.[31] JFK assassination theories hail us as those who need to resist the secretive machinations of a government-Mafia-CIA-Cuban-military-industrial complex (take your pick). "We" are the uncorrupted who lost our leader. Alien abduction and UFO cover-up theories hail us as those who, despite the claims of governmental, scientific, and media elites, remain insecure. "We" are the Americans who do not trust our government to tell us the truth, to let us know what is going on. In her efforts to create a space outside the usual politics, Hillary Clinton draws on this tradition. She invokes an America beyond the official public sphere. She calls into being a "we" that thinks politics is not about her husband's sex life, but about the conspiratorial machinations of the political right.

In short, conspiracy theory evinces a skepticism toward the credulous audience posing as the pluralists' public. Challenging those claims, rules, and revelations that produce this rather pious "we," conspiracy thinking posits the political subject as uncertain, at risk, and mistrustful. Unlike the Hobbesian subject who is also beset by forces beyond its control, the subject of conspiracy will not trade its access to truth for security. Consequently, it accepts the likelihood that its connections will remain tenuous. Fragile connections will require supplement. People need to be reassured. Trust no one.

Producing a "We"

In *On Revolution* Hannah Arendt considers America's founding in terms of an originary moment located in the preamble to the Declaration of Independence: "We hold these truths to be self evident. . . ."[32] Reading *On Revolution* as providing an account of the Declaration as a "purely performative speech act," Bonnie Honig explains that for Arendt the declaration of the "We hold" is the source of power in the act of founding; "the act of foundation requires no appeal to a source of authority beyond itself."[33] She argues further that Arendt's emphasis on the pure performativity of the "We hold" comes at the cost of its constative moments, "these truths to be self-evident."[34] To this end, Honig introduces Derrida's interpretation of the Declaration as an ambiguous combination of performative and constative utterances. "For Derrida," she writes, "no signature, promise, performative—no act of foundation—possesses resources adequate to guarantee itself. . . . Each and every one necessarily needs some external systemically illegitimate guarantee to work."[35]

I want to think more about these systemically illegitimate guarantees and how they might inform declarations of independence. To do this, I move out of the preamble and onto the list of grievances, a list that explains why self-evident truths needed to be invoked at all. The Declaration does not create a "we" out of nothing. It calls a "we" into being as those who must resist a conspiracy, as those who share a conspiracy theory. In so doing, the Declaration establishes a terrain of freedom and action outside of politics as usual.

Pauline Maier observes that most modern discussions of the Declaration focus on the first two paragraphs, devoting little serious attention to the charges against the king.[36] In contrast, she argues that the charges were "essential to the Declaration's central purpose," which was "to demonstrate that the King had inflicted on the colonists 'unremitting injuries and usurpations,' all of which had as a 'direct object the establishment of an absolute tyranny.' "[37] The recounting of this history, the charges leveled at the King, includes claims that he refused to pass laws, dissolved representative houses, obstructed the administration of justice, "plundered our seas," "ravaged our coasts," "burnt our towns," excited domestic insurrections, and endeavored to bring on the "inhabitants of our frontiers the merciless Indian savages." The grievances were not just statements of fact introduced to identify specific crimes and injuries. They were part of a political strategy.

Maier notes that today even professional historians would have trouble identifying the precise source of some of the accusations leveled against the king, especially since they were unclear to many already in the eighteenth century. Some events were referred to only obliquely. Others were expressed so ambiguously as to provide only the barest clues as to what Jefferson had in mind. Indeed, a writer at the time thought the American effort to find reasons for separating from Britain "suffered for lack of 'truth and sense.' "[38] "The grievances in the Declaration were not meant to identify," Maier explains, "precisely which event had reconciled Americans to separate nationhood. The grievances in the Declaration served a different purpose—not to explain the Americans' change of heart but to justify revolution by proving that George III was a tyrant."[39] The grievances, for all their imprecision and ambiguity, were strategically deployed in order to establish a new political space, a space of freedom, a space apart from the constraints of politics as usual. They sought to convince those who would hear them—and, as Maier points out, the most common method of proclaiming the Declaration was reading it before large audiences—of a pattern of actions indicative of tyranny, a pattern that today we might think of as a conspiracy.[40]

According to Bernard Bailyn, that there was a conspiratorial pattern to British actions was a common idea at the time. Bailyn argues that the political pamphlets appearing in the years immediately preceding the revolution reflect the conviction that nothing less was afoot than "a deliberate assault launched surreptitiously by plotters against liberty both in England and America."[41] Similarly, Gordon Wood finds "internal decay" to be a predominant image in pre-revolutionary writing: "A poison had entered the nation and was turning the people and the government into 'one mass of corruption.' "[42] Wood notes that by the 1770s most every piece of Whig writing—pamphlet, newspaper, essay, or letter—dwelt on an obsessive fear of conspiracy.[43] For Bailyn and Wood, conspiracy thinking is central to the American founding. Bailyn claims that the dominant elements of revolutionary ideology were fears of corruption and of a ministerial conspiracy.[44] Wood goes even further, arguing that the belief in a ministerial conspiracy against the colonists' liberties was "the only frame of mind with which they could justify and explain their revolution."[45] Conspiracy thinking, far from the paranoid irrationality it would become associated with in pluralist theory, was part of a new science of human affairs, the application of rational principles, the tracing, disclosing, and connecting of motives and events to an ulterior plan. Wood writes:

> The tendency to see events as the result of a calculated plot . . . appears particularly strong in the eighteenth century, a product, it seems, not only of the political realities and assumptions of the age, but of its very enlightenment, a consequence of the popularization of politics and the secularization of knowledge. . . . Enlightened rationalists as well as Calvinist clergy were obsessed with the motives that lay hidden by deceiving, even self-deceiving statements, and they continually sought to penetrate beneath the surface of events in order to find their real significance in the inner hearts of men. Yet in replacing Providence with human motivation as a source of historical explanation, men still felt the need to discover the design, "the grand *plan*," that lay beneath the otherwise incomprehensible jumble of events. Now it seemed possible to men of this enlightened age that they would be able . . . to disclose at last what had always been in darker days "the hidden and . . . uncertain connection of events."[46]

According to this early version of what became known as the Whig conception of history, events were caused by human actions, actions that were understood in terms of motives and intentions, actions that had meaning, especially when placed in connection with one another.

That events could be scientifically analyzed in terms of patterns of meaningful, intentional actions gave a logic to the colonists' demands. It made them, in a word, rational. This was particularly important given that the Americans were hardly an oppressed people. As Wood points out, "They had no crushing imperial shackles to throw off."[47] Nonetheless, armed with a theory of action, the colonists could use the threat of conspiracy to produce a new political space. Bailyn writes: "The fact that the ministerial conspiracy against liberty had risen from corruption was of the utmost importance to the colonists. It gave radical new meaning to their claims: it transformed them from constitutional argument to expressions of a world regenerative creed."[48]

For the colonists, conspiracy theory—a theory that exposed the hidden links among a variety of political acts and concluded that such interconnections were evidence of tyrannical designs—established the conditions for potential political action outside of the available political spaces. The grievances in the Declaration justified moving outside of British law. Distrust of British authority helped produce a new "we," a "we" constituted out of those sharing a fear of corruption and ministerial conspiracy, a "we" hailed in the Declaration as those who might believe that the king was plotting against their liberty, a "we" using its new space of freedom as a site from which to pass judgment on British political actions. Conspiracy theory enabled the colonists to act extra-legally while claiming the name of the law of reason.

"Are you now or have you ever . . ."

The paradox of the public, the deep connection between conspiracy thinking and publicity, has been central to the production of America. Indeed, the work of some major historians of the American revolution demonstrates that conspiracy is installed from the outset in what would be known as the American public. Evoking conspiracy helps to create a new political space. It calls into being a "we" united around the conviction that a despotic plot is underfoot to undermine their freedom.

More than two hundred years later, Americans are still thinking conspiratorially. But it does not mean the same thing. There are different modes of conspiracy, different conspiratorial codings and narratives in American history. Not all conspiracy theories concern themselves with the same enemies, the same fears. In a different time, a different context, the interconnected actions they invoke resonate with a different set of possibilities and fears.

At the time of the founding, worries over conspiracy expressed fears of tyranny and corruption. Linked to the desire for a new political space, they suggested that resistance was possible. Conspiracy thinking, as well as the possibility of resistance, was embedded in the conviction that rational explanations of human behavior were possible, that events were caused by specific, intentional, interconnected actions. This conviction provided the reassurance of truth and rightness necessary to supplement the fragility of political connections produced in the context of a rather difficult-to-justify rebellion.

Today conspiracy suggests a more varied and complex set of anxieties around information, control, access, and credibility. When conspiracy theorists point to intentional actions and plots, to planned events and coordinated activities, many find them hard to believe. The world seems too complicated for planning, for resistance. People can't keep secrets. No group can coordinate its actions to the degree necessary to bring off something like the assassination of JFK or secret experimentation on civilian populations. Now we know that "it's the system." In this setting, nonaction makes more sense than action. Or, the only actions for which there is official political space are those that involve filling out polls or pulling little levers. How action is understood has changed and with it the meaning of conspiracy.

Changes in information networks also affect the meaning of conspiracy. Media are fragmented and disperse. We can get information from websites, newsgroups, chain letters, network news, public access TV, direct mail, magazines, newspapers, and radio. Various players are involved in the funding, production, and distribution of information. Pharmaceutical companies provide free information on new health hazards and the drugs necessary to combat them. Single corporations control numerous magazines. The dispersion of media makes it hard for us to know what to believe, who to trust. The criteria for judgment are no longer clear.[49] Moreover, even as we are inundated with information, there is still plenty that we do not know.[50] What kind of loan programs are available for folks in my income bracket? How many downer cows in the United States have had mad cow disease? Was sarin gas used on Americans who had allegedly defected to Laos during the Vietnam War? There is a lot of information. But it does not completely eliminate the secret. The same explosion of information that makes conspiracy outrageous to some makes it necessary for others.

Representations of rationality have changed. Instead of linked into understandings presumed to be shared, rationality more often than not varies with its context. To be sure, there were different rationalities during the days of the Declaration. Some people worried about witches. Some practiced witchcraft. But for the most part, the homogeneity of the nation, of those who counted as part of the public, was supported by a set of beliefs in the unity of law and nature. Human actions had meaning within this specific context. Our world is too confusing, too unknowable, too complex for design and causality to make sense. Many of us are exposed to different ways of thinking. We saw the O. J. Simpson trial. We have heard the stories of Satanic cults abusing children. And we have heard them from different sides, narrated from within different conceptions of rationality. Again, within conceptions of rationality accepted in and legitimated by the public sphere, conspiracy seems naive, a childish wish for meaning and connection in a complicated world. For those of us who do not try to subsume the conflicts, fragments, and doubts of the information age under a unitary reason, however, conspiracy thinking is simply another option, one with particular resonance given the confusions of late-capitalist technoculture.

For the experts, then, what was considered a rational and scientific way of understanding political events at the time of the Declaration is now a sign of pathology: "In the paranoid's worldview, events do not simply occur; they are deliberately caused by someone. For the paranoid, coincidence does not exist. Everything happens by design."[51] Not only is there no difference between conspiracy thinking and paranoia—indeed, they are symptoms of each other—but the very search for a causal explanation is suspect. For Robert S. Robins and Jerrold M. Post, "One of the distinctive qualities of the paranoid appeal is its reliance on ideas, explanations, and arguments of causality."[52] This is not to say that Robins and Post do not supply causal explanations for conspiracy thinking. They do. And, they do not think of their own explanations as one bit paranoid. These include a sociobiological theory that inscribes a will to paranoia as a natural outcome of evolution and as a basic factor of human psychology, a metaphorical account of paranoia in terms of infection (as bacillus and virus) that "distorts" healthy political responses, and an associative analysis of paranoid thinking with "the logic of the child or primitive people trying to make sense of the incomprehensible."[53] Robins and Post do not try to connect these explanations or make their metaphors consistent. This may be because they think connection itself is pathological.

In technocultural America, only some of us are at liberty to think causally. Causal explanations are the currency of the few. If the uncredentialed attempt to use them, something must be wrong. They must be sick, childish, or attempting to spread infection. At the very least, those who think that there are patterns in politics and that intentional actions stand behind political events must not share in the common sense. What stands behind the critique of conspiracy thinking, then, is a conception of politics as possible only in certain channels, as occupying a specific and limited domain anything outside of which is suspect. Within this domain, action is possible. Outside it, even considering action is pathological. The only permissible response or reaction, it seems, is passivity—or allowing oneself to be interpellated as part of the public that witnesses what happens in the sphere of legitimate politics.[54] After all, revelation has replaced action in what counts as the public sphere. Uncovering the truth is more important than actually doing something. When pundits and pluralists attack conspiracy thinking, they are not aiming for more political involvement or increased political activity. They want action within the parameters defined by elites, action that legitimizes the status quo, that confirms the party system, pays lobbyists, and provides daily soundbites.[55]

Critics of conspiracy theory police the borders of political normality so closely because these borders are actually very difficult to discern. The distinction between public sphere norms and conspiracy thinking is not a stable one. Some versions of conspiracy thinking look like nice clean applications of public sphere ideals. Put somewhat differently, critiques of conspiracy thinking do two things. They produce the normal by excluding conspiracy theory as pathological. At the same time, they normalize paranoia as a predominant logic of the public sphere. The public sphere requires that the secret be uncovered and the "we" of the nation secured.

Critics of conspiracy thinking often point out that those most likely to be "at risk of acquiring the virus" are the "politically disaffected," who have experienced exclusion, degradation, oppression, and marginalization.[56] Richard Hofstadter finds that when people lack access to political processes of bargaining and decisionmaking, their "original conception of the world of power as omnipotent, sinister, and malicious" is confirmed.[57] He does not think, in other words, that these folks might turn to conspiracy theory to explain their exclusion. Instead, he presumes that they were paranoid originally, from the outset, prior to any exclusion. Robins and Post also begin from the idea that belief in conspiracy is misguided. They emphasize the harmfulness of conspiracy thinking, refusing the possibility that it might enable some of those outside the mainstream to create spaces for action, to mobilize, to engage in politics, and to contest their exclusion from the nation's dominant political spheres.[58] Like Robins and Post, Pipes points out the prevalence of conspiracy thinking among African Americans and similarly rejects those political views with "deeply unsettling implications about the existing order."[59] Moreover, he dismisses communism, notions of imperialism, and Latin American studies as paranoid and "conspiracist"—his word for belief in conspiracies that are not true.[60] For Pipes, anything outside the mainstream is conspiracist; yet this very center is produced through the designation of some views as conspiracist. Challenging the status quo, then, is excluded as a political option. The only recourse for the marginalized and disaffected is simply to stop being marginalized, to enter the mainstream, to accept and legitimize the American political system.

Some attacks on conspiracy thinking seem to be attacks on independent or non-institutionalized thinking altogether. In effect admitting to his delegitimation of the voices of the already excluded, Pipes stresses that conspiracy thinkers tend to be self-taught. "This is not the legitimate scholarship produced by academics with university training, membership in professional associations, and social esteem. It is, rather, the mirror world of conspiracism, with its amateur autodidacts who lack institutional affiliation and suffer exclusion from the established institutions."[61] Robins and Post observe that some who join conspiracy-oriented groups seek greater meaning in their lives. But none of these critics explains why one should disparage the efforts of another to find or create meaning. It seems, again, like they are suspicious of any attempts to make sense of the world in ways not authorized in advance by major institutions and worldviews. Only some interpreters are authorized.

That conspiracy thinking's outsider status is the problem becomes all the clearer when one notes the contradictions in accounts of what, exactly, constitutes conspiracy thinking. Pipes claims that conspiracy theories are vague, illogical, and inconsistent. Hofstadter says that they are unambiguous, rationalistic, and consistent. Pipes finds conspiracy thinking in disreputable presses, unaccredited journals, and on the internet. Yet he also acknowledges that reputable publishers and authors may think conspiratorially, especially if they are on the left. He admits that discerning conspiracy thinking is a subjective process. It seems to me that finding the center, the mainstream, is even more subjective.

Some critics think of conspiracy thinking as a style. This is Hofstadter's strategy in his influential essay, "The Paranoid Style in American Politics." An interpretation is conspiracy-minded not because of what it claims, but because of how it is claimed. "What distinguishes the paranoid style is not, then, the absence of verifiable facts . . . but rather the curious leap in imagination that is always made at some critical point in the recital of events."[62] And what makes an interpretation "curious" is its deviation from common knowledge, from "conventional political reasoning," from "the normal political process of bargain and compromise."[63] Robins and Post agree. For them, conspiracy thinking is a distortion, caricature, exaggeration, or parody of the useful, prudent, and sound practices of normal political behavior.[64] Of course, they might be right. Conspiracy thinking may well be an extreme version of the norms of interaction in what is considered the sphere of public politics. But who is doing the considering and why are those the norms that count? Insofar as critics of conspiracy thinking produce the terrain of the normalized political through the exclusion of some forms of political thinking and acting, they seem to create precisely that sphere of predictable, rational, explicable political action—that space occupied by rational wheeler-dealers—they condemn conspiracy theorists for presupposing. The critical accounts of conspiracy thinking prominent in American history and political science since the McCarthy era rely on a notion of political reality that they produce through the demonization of some political movements, styles, and theories as extreme, radical, or paranoid.

Even though their critiques are based in the assumption that the conspiracy thinker is wrong, misguided, deceived, or deceiving, a predominant theme in these attacks is the supposition of truth on the part of the conspiracy thinker. The conspiracy theorist is attacked for believing something to be true that the critic knows is false. This is precisely how the critic is able to discern a distorted belief from an appropriate one. The critic knows that corporate, commercial, financial interests have no significant impact on American politics, say, and this knowledge enables him or her to discover the mistaken beliefs that mark one as a conspiracy thinker.[65] Robins and Post claim that for the conspiracy thinker, "skepticism is treason" and "true belief does not permit question and doubt."[66] This might mean that most ufologists do not count as conspiracy thinkers. The majority of those researching alien abduction and UFOs experience extreme doubt. They often do not believe even themselves. They pursue alternative explanations.[67] In fact, much of the practice of conspiracy thinking involves sifting through volumes of "evidence," debating what fits and what does not, and trying to discern how the events or plots at issue might have taken place. The instability of the facts, the uncertainty of the evidence, are the challenges facing the conspiracy thinker. Far from being treason, skepticism is part of conspiracy thinking.[68]

Finally, critics of conspiracy thinking reproduce precisely that element of conspiracy thinking they find most objectionable: the tendency toward moralism and judgmentalism. Conspiracy theorists are said to rely on a friends/enemies opposition, viewing world history in terms of an ultimate battle between two opposing forces.[69] They refuse to compromise, seeing not error, but evil. For the critic, this refusal is grounds for excluding the conspiracy minded from the political process *in advance*. Since they cannot negotiate, they should not be party to the negotiations constitutive of politics. Hence the critics, too, as they reduce the activities of conspiracy thinkers to questions of judgment, effect the same moralism and judgmentalism they condemn. The critics, having established that politics means compromise and negotiation, block those who might have a different view. In so doing, they set up their own criteria for judgment as the checkpoint for crossing the border from the irrational into the political. In this respect, judging itself becomes the penultimate political act, the act that determines who is one of us and who can reasonably be excluded. The boundaries of the nation, the rationality of the public sphere, depend on revealing and judging those who threaten the basic character of who we are.

Perhaps I overstate my case. After all, must there not be a difference between folks who think that the Trilateral Commission is behind American foreign policy and those fighting the deceptions of the tobacco industry? Isn't it just a little paranoid to link all these together? Yes, it is. But the problem is that this is precisely what is said by those wishing to protect America and Americans from the infections, seductions, and distortions of conspiracy thinking. Those who dismiss conspiracy theory link together fears of the Trilateral Commission with fears of corporate political influence. They link together critical inquiry into the systematic workings of racism, critical exploration of the practices of imperialism and colonialism, with complex and anti-Semitic stories of international bankers. They turn issues of complaint and content into questions of style, participating in the reduction of political actions to disclosure and judgment. In so doing, these politicians, pundits, and political theorists attempt to establish a safe and rational space for politics, for a politics of negotiation and compromise, a politics of the status quo with no room for extremism, radicalism, or rage.

Ironically, even as critics of conspiracy thinking exclude possibilities for radical interrogation of basic political practices and institutions, they include within the political the policies and manipulations of the national security state. For example, people like Buckley and Pipes do not associate cold war mentalities, surveillance of populations, or experiments on civilians with the "virus" of conspiracy thinking. These are not distortions of the usual politics, hence they must be part of rational government, in keeping with the norms of the public sphere. Maybe the most significant difference between conspiracy thinking and legitimate reason is who's calling the shots.

Public Excess

There is at least one more significant difference between conspiracy theory and public sphere theory. Conspiracy theory assumes that no one ("on the inside" or included within the political) can be trusted. Public sphere theory, especially in its Habermasian version, assumes that everyone ("on the inside" or included within the political) can be trusted. Pluralist theories have a Habermasian flavor when they presume that political participants are adversaries (not enemies) who work to compromise (not deceive). They rely on a single, shared political rationality: everyone knows and abides by the same rules of the game. I wonder about the privilege of trust. I wonder about how it can advantage the insiders—those already empowered by histories of racism, sexism, and homophobia. I also wonder why, if everyone can be trusted, those who reason differently must be excluded. Maybe everyone can be trusted because there is so little difference between you and me . . . when I think about you I trust myself.

Political theory, in particular normative models of the public sphere, rarely looks at the mucky complications of popular culture; it rarely considers thinking that deviates from its version of common sense, suspecting neither that what it deems a deviation may well be a reflection, nor that the thinking it excludes from the political is already part of it. The derision of popular excesses by academically legitimized political theory is also part of official lamentations on the state of the nation. Media pundits and professionals work to uncover the hidden secrets haunting the public, secrets that may lurk in the pants, closets, or offices of public leaders. They generate an audience, hailing it as the concerned "we" of the public sphere. Then they condemn it for being interpellated. We see this time and again as trials and events are covered in hushed tones and then talking heads appear to talk about Americans' love of scandal and debased sense of politics.

We can read conspiracy theories for their seductions, trying to figure out how Marilyn Monroe really died, who was behind the assassination of Martin Luther King, Jr., and whether Freemasons rule the world. We can also read them for the way they engage the paradox of the public, the paradox of a totalizing conception of the democratic public produced through the media of the public sphere. If we do so, we might understand how evoking the possibility of a conspiracy that threatens the nation can establish a space behind the national public; how conspiracy theories escape the boundaries of the political and enter a different, albeit risky terrain where action might be possible. Hillary Clinton attempted such an escape when she blamed a vast right-wing conspiracy for her husband's problems. Pre-revolutionary thinkers tried as well when they attributed to the king a pattern of monstrous acts designed to restrict the liberties of the colonists. And, oddly enough, even those who blame Illuminati, Trilateralists, and extraterrestrials for all sorts of imagined crimes are seeking a space of action beyond the limited terrain they have before them. They don't trust a government or a political system that gives them the options of being interpellated as a loyal audience of citizens or engaging in party politics that seem futile at best.

Like conspiracy thinkers, the pluralists and pundits who criticize them also participate in the production of political space, this time the space of what is officially recognized as the political, the space authorized as the nation. Each grapples with the instability of the public national "we" and the boundaries of political space. Compelled by the hidden that underlies conceptions of the public, each seeks to reveal it in its own way. Critics of conspiracy theory reveal the distortions that designate the paranoid, using them to produce the norms and boundaries of the sphere of normal political action. And conspiracy thinkers, employing the same logic, seek to uncover those distortions of the political that reveal its deceptions, those hidden excesses distorting its capacity to function as a site of representation, governance, or freedom.

notes

Jodi Dean: Introduction

I am grateful to Lee Quinby for her patient re-readings of numerous drafts of this introduction and to Larry Grossberg for his helpful, pointed criticism. Thanks also to Alison Shonkwiler for her thoughtful support of this project.

1. See Michael Rogin, *Ronald Reagan: The Movie* (Berkeley: University of California Press, 1987).

2. Sheldon Wolin, "Political Theory as a Vocation," *American Political Science Review* (December 1969): 1078. This essay is generally cited as a key moment in the preservation of normative political theory in the face of the scienticism and behaviorism of American political science in the fifties and sixties. For a history of American political theory as a subfield see, John Gunnell, *The Descent of Political Theory* (Chicago: University of Chicago Press, 1993).

3. Wolin, "Political Theory as a Vocation," 1078.

4. Stuart Hall, "The Emergence of Cultural Studies and the Crisis of the Humanities," *October* 53 (1990): 11, cited in *Cultural Studies*, ed. Lawrence Grossberg, Cary Nelson, and Paula Treichler (New York: Routledge, 1992), 3.

5. Hall, "The Emergence of Cultural Studies," in *Cultural Studies*, 5.

6. Michel Foucault, *Ethics, Subjectivity, and Truth*, ed. Paul Rabinow (New York: New Press, 1997), 114.

7. Ibid.

8. As Akhil Gupta and James Ferguson write in their introduction to *Culture, Power, Place* (Durham, N.C.: Duke University Press, 1997), "All associations of place, people, and culture are social and historical creations to be explained, not given natural facts" (4).

9. The claim I am rejecting here comes from Nancy Fraser, *Justice Interruptus* (New York: Routledge, 1997), 5.

10. William E. Connolly, *The Ethos of Pluralization* (Minneapolis: University of Minnesota Press, 1995), xxi.

11. See Hall, "The Emergence of Cultural Studies," in *Cultural Studies*, 2: "The choice of research practices depends upon the questions that are asked, and the questions that are asked depend on their context."

12. Lee Quinby's work is exemplary in this regard as it links the traditions of millennialist thinking in America with specific enactments of racism, sexism, and homophobia. See *Anti-Apocalypse: Essays in Genealogical Thinking* (Minneapolis: University of Minnesota Press, 1994) and *Millennial Seduction: A Skeptic Confronts Apocalyptic Culture* (Ithaca: Cornell University Press, 1999).

13. John Rawls is the most influential contemporary thinker with respect to these two versions of the liberal project.

14. Ernesto Laclau and Chantal Mouffe's theorization of a discursive structure as "an *articulatory practice* which constitutes and organizes social relations" is helpful here. See *Hegemony and Socialist Strategy* (London: Verso, 1985), 96.

15. Catriona Sandilands, "Is the Personal Always Political? Environmentalism in Arendt's Age of 'The Social,' " in *Organizing Dissent: Contemporary Social Movement in Theory and Practice*, ed. William K. Carroll (Toronto: Garamond Press, 1997), 77. Thanks to Lee Quinby for bringing this to my attention.

16. See Shane Phelan, *Getting Specific: Postmodern Lesbian Politics* (Minneapolis: University of Minnesota Press, 1994). Phelan writes (40), "Getting specific is the prerequisite for a politics that is neither vanguardist nor blandly pluralist, that recognizes differences as important and enduring and difficult and works not to erase or eliminate those differences but to weave the threads that might link us."

17. See Patricia Williams's scenario of privatized response to issues of racial accountability in *The Alchemy of Race and Rights* (Cambridge: Harvard University Press, 1991), 64.

18. Slavoj Žižek, *The Plague of Fantasies* (London: Verso, 1997), 1.

19. Sheldon Wolin, "What Time Is It?" *Theory and Event* 1.1 (1997): paragraph 8.

20. Describing the trials of her interactions with "the leadership of the humanities community," Lynne V. Cheney, former chair of the National Endowment for the Humanities, writes, "Every statement in every text (or not in a text, for that matter) was said to be political, said to be aimed at advancing the interest of the speaker or writer. . . . Politics writ small had become politics written so large that it drove out the possibility of human beings doing anything nonpolitical—such as encouraging the search for truth." *Telling the Truth* (New York: Simon and Schuster, 1995), 15.

21. Amy Gutmann, Introduction to *Multiculturalism and "The Politics of Recognition,"* an essay by Charles Taylor (Princeton: Princeton University Press, 1992), 20.

22. Lee Quinby describes this cynicism as the tendency to "yadayadayada," in "Millennial Civilization and Its Discontents: Terminal Cynicism, Conspiracy Mania, and Avatarism," *Psychohistory Review* (Winter 1999): 1–16.

23. Linda Kintz provides a compelling account of the way that radio personality Rush Limbaugh redeploys cynicism to fuel conservative political passion in *Between Jesus and the Market* (Durham, N.C.: Duke University Press, 1997), 204–13.

24. Mark Shapiro provides an account of conservative activism in "Who's Behind the Culture War," gopher:// gopher.igc.apc.org:70/00/orgs/alternet/demval/cultwars.

25. I am using Connolly's redefinition of fundamentalism "to include the refusal to acknowledge the contestability of your own fundaments or to resist violences in the exclusionary logics of identity in which you are implicated" (xxviii).

26. This quotation is from Paul M. Weyrich's letter of February 16, 1999, in which he concedes the loss of the "culture war" and appeals to conservatives to secede from the barbarism of mainstream "political correctness." He writes that "politics has failed because of the collapse of the culture. The culture we are living in becomes an ever-wider sewer. In truth, I think we are caught up in a cultural collapse of historic proportions, a collapse so great that it simply overwhelms politics."

Available at the Free Congress Foundation website, www.freecongress.org. I'm indebted to Paul Passavant for bringing this to my attention.

27. Explorations of the changed location of the state proceed from a variety of theoretical orientations. See, for example, Claude Lefort, *Democracy and Political Theory* (Minneapolis: University of Minnesota Press, 1988); Michael Shapiro, *Reading the Postmodern Polity* (Minneapolis: University of Minnesota Press, 1991); and Jürgen Habermas, "Three Models of Democracy," *Constellations* 1, 1 (April 1994): 1–10.

28. For an analysis of new social movements as they have targeted civil society, see Jean Cohen and Andrew Arato, *Civil Society and Political Theory* (Cambridge: MIT Press, 1992), chap. 10, and Jodi Dean, *Solidarity of Strangers* (Berkeley: University of California Press, 1996), chaps. 2–3.

29. Wolin, "What Time Is It?" paragraph 2.

30. David Held, ed., *Political Theory Today*, editor's introduction (Stanford: Stanford University Press, 1991), 6.

31. Jeffrey C. Isaac, "The Strange Silence of Political Theory," *Political Theory* 23, 4 (November 1995): 636–52.

32. Thomas L. Dumm, "Strangers and Liberals," *Political Theory* 22, 1 (February 1994): 170–71.

33. Michel Foucault, "The Ethics of Concern for Self as a Practice of Freedom," in *Ethics, Subjectivity and Truth*. My sentence is a paraphrase. Foucault says, "Whereas, if you try to analyze power not on the basis of freedom, strategies, and governmentality, but on the basis of the political institution, you can only conceive of the subject as a subject of law" (300).

34. Michael Sandel, *Liberalism and the Limits of Justice* (Cambridge: Cambridge University Press, 1982), 172–73.

35. See Michael Walzer, *Spheres of Justice* (New York: Basic Books, 1993), and Charles Taylor, *Sources of the Self* (Cambridge: Harvard University Press, 1989).

36. For evidence of the convergence of liberal, communitarian, and New Left political theory, see the symposium edited by Michael Walzer, "The State of Political Theory," *Dissent* (Summer 1989): 337–70.

37. See Frederick M. Dolan, *Allegories of America* (Ithaca: Cornell University Press, 1994), and Frederick M. Dolan and Thomas L. Dumm, eds., *Rhetorical Republics* (Amherst: University of Massachusetts Press, 1993), for the provocative posing of these questions.

38. Martha Nussbaum demonstrates such a preoccupation with newness in her attack on Judith Butler, "The Professor of Parody," *New Republic* (February 22, 1999): 37–45.

William E. Connolly: The Will, Capital Punishment, and Cultural War

A version of this essay appears in *The Killing State: Capital Punishment in Law, Politics, and Culture*, edited by Austin Sarat (New York: Oxford University Press, 1998). It appears here with permission.

1. *The Confessions of St. Augustine*, trans. John K. Ryan (New York: Image Books, 1960), book 8, chapter 9, 196–97.

2. Ibid., 197.

3. Cesare Beccaria, *On Crimes and Punishments*, trans. David Young (New York: Hackett Publishing, 1986), 17.

4. Ibid., 49.

5. Immanuel Kant, *The Metaphysics of Morals*, trans. Mary Gregor (Cambridge: Cambridge University Press, 1991), 141–42.

6. Immanuel Kant, *Religion within the Limits of Reason Alone*, trans. Theodore Greene and Hoyt Hudson (New York: Harper Torchbooks, 1960), 32.

7. Friedrich Nietzsche, *Human All Too Human*, trans. R. J. Hollinger (New York: Cambridge University Press, 1986), 306.

8. Sister Helen Prejean, *Dead Man Walking* (New York: Random House, 1994).

9. Ibid., 236–37.

10. Ibid., 226.

11. James Q. Wilson and Richard J. Herrnstein, *Crime and Human Nature: The Definitive Study of the Causes of Crime* (New York: Simon and Schuster, 1985).

12. Ibid., 505–6.

13. Quoted from V. P. Hans, "Death by Jury," in Norman J. Finkel, *Commonsense Justice: Jurors' Notions of the Law* (Cambridge: Harvard University Press, 1995), 184.

14. Austin Sarat, "Speaking of Death: Narratives of Violence in Capital Trials," 168–69, in Sarat and Thomas R. Kearns, eds., *The Rhetoric of Law* (Ann Arbor: University of Michigan Press, 1994), 135–84.

15. Wendy Brown, in a superb chapter of *States of Injury: Power and Freedom in Late Modernity* (Princeton: Princeton University Press, 1995), titled "Wounded Attachments," explores how the attachments people form to destructive modes of their own subjection can foster profound resentments seeking legitimate outlets. "Insofar as what Nietzsche calls slave morality produces identity in relation to power, insofar as identity rooted in this reaction achieves its moral superiority by reproaching power and action themselves as evil, identity . . . becomes deeply invested in its own impotence, even while it seeks to assuage the pain of its powerlessness through its vengeful moralizing, through its wide distribution of suffering. . . . Indeed, it is more likely to punish and reproach—'punishment is what revenge calls itself— . . .' than to find venues of self-affirming action" (70–71). This book, and in particular this chapter, explores more deeply and persistently the psychology and social mechanisms I am engaging here with respect to capital punishment.

16. William J. Bennett, *The Devaluing of America: The Fight for Our Culture and Our Children* (New York: Simon and Schuster, 1995), 116.

17. Ibid.

18. Ibid., 173.

19. The quotations occur between pages 199 and 202 of Camus's "Reflection on the Guillotine," in *Resistance, Rebellion, and Death*, trans. Justin O'Brien (New York: Vintage Books, 1960).

20. Prejean, *Dead Man Walking*, 156.

21. I suppose that Nietzsche can help on the first front, while thinkers like Arendt and Foucault might help on the second. The problem, for starters, is that few of us are now prepared to show how each front is entangled in the other, and not

too many are prepared to listen to the diagnosis. But it remains important to keep trying.

Lauren Berlant: The Subject of True Feeling

A version of this essay appears in *Cultural Pluralism, Identity Politics, and the Law*, edited by Austin Sarat and Thomas Kearns (Ann Arbor: University of Michigan Press, 1999). It appears here with permission.

1. See, for example, George DeMartino and Stephen Cullenberg, "Beyond the Competitiveness Debate: An Internationalist Agenda," *Social Text* 41 (1994): 11–39.

2. The media attention paid to child labor in the manufacture of the Kathie Lee Gifford clothing line is a case in point. This issue has quickly joined child abuse as an ongoing zone of fascination and (mainly) impotent concern in the political public sphere. See, for a relatively unjaded extended example, Sidney Schamberg, "Six Cents an Hour," *Life* (June 1996): 38–48. For a more general view of the political/media exploitation of the exploited child figure, see McKenzie Wark, "Fresh Maimed Babies: The Uses of Innocence," *Transition* 65 (Spring 1995): 36–47.

3. For more exposition on the ways political cultures that value abstract or universal personhood produce privileged bodies and identities that travel unmarked, unremarkable, and free of structural humiliation, see Lauren Berlant, "National Brands/National Bodies: *Imitation of Life*," in *The Phantom Public Sphere*, ed. Bruce Robbins, (Minneapolis: University of Minnesota Press, 1993), 173–208, and *The Queen of America Goes to Washington City: Essays on Sex and Citizenship* (Durham: Duke University Press, 1997); Richard Dyer, "White," in *The Matter of Images* (New York: Routledge, 1993), 141–63; and Peggy Phelan, *Unmarked: The Politics of Performance* (New York: Routledge, 1993).

4. The essay by Sigmund Freud summarized here is "Mourning and Melancholia," in *General Psychological Theory*, introduction by Philip Rieff (New York: Collier Books, 1963), 164–79.

5. The best work on the civilized barbarism of mourning has been done on AIDS discourse. See Douglas Crimp, "Mourning and Militancy," in *Out There: Marginalization and Contemporary Cultures*, ed. Russell Ferguson, Martha Gever, Trinh T. Minh-Ha, and Cornel West (Cambridge: MIT Press, 1990), and the essays in Douglas Crimp, ed., *AIDS: Cultural Analysis/Cultural Activism* (Cambridge: MIT Press, 1988). Crimp is especially acute on the necessary articulation of sentimentality and politics: because processes of legitimation cannot do without the production of consent, and empathetic misrecognition is one tactic for creating it. The question is how, and at what cost, different kinds of subjects and contexts of empathy are imagined in the struggle for radical social transformation. See also Jeff Nunokowa, "AIDS and the Age of Mourning," *Yale Journal of Criticism* 4, 2 (Spring 1991): 1–12. Judith Butler's work has also been a crucial intertext here, notably its representation of heterosexual melancholia. This opened a space for thinking about the social function of mourning in similar contexts of normative hierarchy where intimacies appear to have to be constructed, not suppressed. See *Gender Trouble* (New York: Routledge, 1990) and *Bodies That Matter* (New York: Routledge, 1993).

6. On the structures and rhetorics of coercive flexibility in transnational times, see David Harvey, *The Condition of Postmodernity* (London: Basil Blackwell, 1989); Roger Rouse, "Thinking through Transnationalism: Notes on the Cultural Politics of Class Relations in the Contemporary United States," *Public Culture* 7 (Winter 1995): 353–402; and Emily Martin, *Flexible Bodies* (Boston: Beacon Press, 1994). On the "bottom line" as a way of describing minority struggle in the United States, see Elizabeth Alexander, " 'Can You Be BLACK and Look at This?': Reading the Rodney King Video(s)," *The Black Public Sphere*, ed. The Black Public Sphere Collective (Chicago: University of Chicago Press, 1995), 81–98.

7. Wendy Brown, "Wounded Attachments," in *The Identity in Question*, ed. John Rajchman (New York: Routledge, 1995), 199–227. See also Brown's excellent "Rights and Identity in Late Modernity: Revisiting the 'Jewish Question,' " in *Identities, Politics, and Rights*, ed. Austin Sarat and Thomas R. Kearns (Ann Arbor: University of Michigan Press, 1995), 85–130.

8. One critic who has not underestimated the hegemonic capacities of state deployments of pain is Elaine Scarry, *The Body in Pain* (New York: Oxford, 1985).

9. On rights talk and normativity see Sarat and Kearns, *Identities, Politics, and Rights*.

10. See Berlant, *Queen of America*. The following paragraphs revise and repeat some arguments from this book. For an essay specifically on scandalized childhood in the contemporary United States, see Marilyn Ivy, "Recovering the Inner Child in Late Twentieth Century America," *Social Text* 37 (1993): 227–52.

11. Nathanson speaks this line in *The Silent Scream* (1984).

12. On cynicism as the citizen's response to state authoritarianism, see Slavoj Žižek, *The Sublime Object of Ideology* (London: Verso, 1989), 11–53.

13. Jean Baudrillard posits banality as the affective dominant of postmodern life: see *In the Shadow of the Silent Majorities . . . Or the End of the Social and Other Essays*, trans. Paul Foss, Paul Patton, and John Johnston (New York: Semiotexte, 1983), and "From the System to the Destiny of Objects," in *The Ecstasy of Communication*, ed. Sylvere Lotringer (New York: Semiotexte, 1987), 77–96. See also Achille Mbembe, "Prosaics of Servitude and Authoritarian Civilities," *Public Culture* 5 (Fall 1992): 123–48; Achille Mbembe and Janet Roitman, "Figures of the Subject in Times of Crisis," *Public Culture* 7 (Winter 1995): 323–52, and Meaghan Morris, "Banality in Cultural Studies," in *Logics of Television: Essays in Cultural Criticism*, ed. Patricia Mellencamp (Bloomington: Indiana University Press, 1990), 14–43.

14. Justice Hugo Black, concurring, *Griswold v. Connecticut* 381 U.S. 479 (1965) at 509.

15. Stephanie Guitton and Peter Irons, eds., *May It Please the Court: Arguments on Abortion* (New York: New Press, 1995), 7.

16. Justice William O. Douglas, Opinion of the Court, *Griswold* at 480.

17. Ibid.

18. Justice Arthur Goldberg, concurring, *Griswold* at 499.

19. I borrow this rhetoric of zoning, and specifically the sense of its relation to the production of normative sexuality, from Lauren Berlant and Michael Warner, "Sex in Public," *Critical Inquiry* 24 (Winter 1998): 547–66.

20. For the Court's account of the Constitutional guarantees that create zones of privacy, see Douglas, *Griswold* at 484.

21. Guitton and Irons, *May It Please the Court*, 7.

22. Douglas, *Griswold* at 485, 486.

23. Ibid. at 484.

24. Justice Blackmun, Opinion of the Court, *Roe v. Wade* 410 U.S. 113 (1973) at 708.

25. Justice Scalia, dissent, *Planned Parenthood v. Casey* at 2876–77.

26. Ibid. Scalia also blasts Justice Blackmun (fn. 2, at 2876) for using a constitutionally meaningless rhetoric of intimacy.

27. A passionate and artful argument about what cases constitute precedent for *Roe* takes place between Justices O'Connor, Kennedy, Souter, and Scalia at 2808–2816 and 2860–2867.

28. Friedrich Nietzsche, *On the Genealogy of Morals*, ed. Walter Kaufmann (New York: Vintage, 1957), 57–96. See also Brown, "Wounded Attachments."

29. Justices O'Connor, Kennedy, and Souter, *Planned Parenthood v. Casey* at 2807.

30. Ibid.

31. Ibid. at 2827.

32. Catharine A. MacKinnon, "Reflections on Law in the Everyday Life of Women," in *Law in Everyday Life*, ed. Austin Sarat and Thomas R. Kearns (Ann Arbor: University of Michigan Press, 1995), 117–18. See also MacKinnon, *Toward a Feminist Theory of the State* (Cambridge: Harvard University Press, 1989), 184–94.

33. *Planned Parenthood v. Casey* at 2829.

34. Mari J. Matsuda, "Looking to the Bottom: Critical Legal Studies and Reparations," in *Critical Race Theory: The Key Writings That Formed the Movement*, ed. Kimberlè Crenshaw, Neil Gotanda, Gary Peller, and Kendall Thomas (New York: The New Press, 1995), 63–80.

35. Critical Legal Studies, critical race theory, radical feminist legal theory, and an emergent body of work in gay and lesbian culture, power, and the law encompass a huge bibliography that cannot be encompassed in a single, omnibus footnote.

36. Robin West, *Narrative, Authority, and Law* (Ann Arbor: University of Michigan Press, 1993).

37. Ibid., 19–20. Much the same kind of respect and critique can be given to Catharine MacKinnon's promotion of juridical reparation on behalf of women's pain under patriarchy. In her work the inner little girl of every woman stands as the true abused self who is denied full citizenship in the United States. See "Live Sex Acts" in Berlant, *Queen of America*.

38. Another instance in which a generic child's nonideological relation to justice is held as the proper index of adult aspiration is to be found in Patricia Williams, *The Alchemy of Race and Rights* (Cambridge: Harvard University Press, 1991), 12, 27.

39. See Lucinda M. Finley, "A Break in the Silence: Including Women's Issues in a Torts Course," *Yale Journal of Law and Feminism* 1 (1989): 41–73.

40. Kendall Thomas, "Beyond the Privacy Principle," in *After Identity: A Reader in Law and Culture*, ed. Dan Danielsen and Karen Engle (New York: Routledge, 1995), 277–93.

41. Brown, "Wounded Attachments," 220–21.

42. See Shoshana Felman and Dori Laub, *Testimony: Crises of Witnessing in Literature, Psychoanalysis, and History* (New York: Routledge, 1992), and Jean-François Lyotard, *The Differend* (Minneapolis: University of Minnesota Press, 1988).

43. Jacques Derrida, "Force of Law: The 'Mystical Foundations of Authority'," in *Deconstruction and the Possibility of Justice*, ed. Drucilla Cornell, Michel Rosenfeld, and David Grey Carlson (New York: Routledge, 1992), 3–67, esp. 61–63.

44. This point is made by Slavoj Žižek, "The Spectre of Ideology," in *Mapping Ideology*, ed. Slavoj Žižek (New York: Routledge, 1994), 17.

Barbara Cruikshank: Cultural Politics

1. Alexis de Tocqueville, *Democracy in America* (New York: Harper and Row, 1969), 373.

2. Ibid., 47.

3. For a chilling tale of just how murderous discourse can be, see Samuel Delany's account of research on AIDS transmission, "The Rhetoric of Sex, the Discourse of Desire," in *Heterotopia: Postmodern Utopias and the Body Politic*, ed. Tobin Siebers (Ann Arbor: University of Michigan Press, 1994). It is important to note that I am not discussing "fighting words" so much as discourses. Judith Butler's book, *Excitable Speech: A Politics of the Performative* (New York: Routledge, 1997), discusses the relation of speech and harm.

4. More commonly, the spark for political theory is understood to follow from disorder. Political theory, then, is written to reconstitute the political order in crisis. See Sheldon Wolin, *Politics and Vision* (Boston: Little, Brown, 1960), 8. For a significantly different and compelling view of political theorizing, see Kirstie McClure, "The Issue of Foundations: Scientized Politics, Political Science, and Feminist Critical Practice," in *Feminists Theorize the Political*, ed. Judith Butler and Joan Scott (New York: Routledge, 1992), 341–68.

5. Niccolò Machiavelli, *The Prince and the Discourses*, trans. C. E. Detmold (New York: Random House, 1950), 168.

6. Francis Fukuyama, *The End of History and the Last Man* (New York: Free Press, 1992).

7. Machiavelli, *The Prince*, 168.

8. Note that it is possible for a great (either good enough or bad enough) man to redeem a people, to bring them back to their roots, according to Machiavelli.

9. Tocqueville, *Democracy in America*, 342.

10. Newt Gingrich, "Remarks by Rep. Newt Gingrich (November 11, 1994)," appendix to the volume, *Contract with America: The Bold Plan by Rep. Newt Gingrich, Rep. Dick Armey, and the House Republicans to Change the Nation*, ed. Ed Gillespie and Bob Schellhas (New York: Random House, 1994).

11. See the recent work of neoconservative Gertrude Himmelfarb, *On Looking into the Abyss: Untimely Thoughts on Culture and Society* (New York: Alfred A. Knopf, 1994).

12. Gingrich, "Remarks," p. 182.

13. Ibid., p. 191.

14. For an account of how white blue-collar workers, largely a secular group, were tied to the rise of the religious right, see William Connolly, *The Ethos of Pluralization* (Minneapolis: University of Minnesota Press, 1995), 109–18.

15. Consider the volatility of abortion politics, for example: clinic bombings, bombastic rhetoric, "stealth campaigns" for local offices, the mass mobilization campaigns of Operation Rescue. All that and, by and in the large, American government remains stable, tinkering here and there with the rights of association and flirting with partial birth abortion legislation.

16. Gingrich, "Remarks," 189–90.

17. Samuel Huntington, *The Crisis of Democracy: Report on the Governability of Democracies to the Trilateral Commission*, ed. Michael Crozier et al. (New York: New York University Press, 1975), 4. More recently, Huntington published *The Clash of Civilizations and the Remaking of World Order* (New York: Simon and Schuster, 1996).

18. Huntington, *Crisis of Democracy*, 7.

19. Robert H. Bork, *Slouching towards Gomorrah: Modern Liberalism and American Decline* (New York: Regan Books/Harper Collins, 1997), 339.

20. Gertrude Himmelfarb, *The De-Moralization of Society: From Victorian Virtues to Modern Values* (New York: Vintage, 1994), 236.

21. Ibid., 239.

22. Ibid., 224.

23. Ibid., 248.

24. James Kurth, "The Post-Modern State," *National Interest* (Summer 1992): 26–35. William Connolly confronts Kurth's fundamentalism in *The Ethos of Pluralization*, 114–18.

25. Kurth, "Post-Modern State," 26–27.

26. Ibid., 30.

27. Ibid., 26.

28. Note that the logic of American exceptionalism rules out the relevance of what I have written to this point because continental political theory is brought to bear upon the context of American politics. Tocqueville has always been an exception to the rule, however, as he himself was an exceptionalist. For the classic theory of American exceptionalism, see Louis Hartz, *The Liberal Tradition in America* (New York: Harcourt Brace, 1955).

29. Daniel Boorstin, *The Genius of American Politics* (Chicago: University of Chicago Press, 1953), 100.

30. Ibid., 184–5.

31. Ibid., 8–9.

32. Ibid., 169.

33. Ibid., 186; emphasis mine.

34. Ibid., 33.

35. Boorstin's way of putting things is derived from Judith Butler's essay, "Contingent Foundations: Feminism and the Question of 'Postmodernism,' " in Butler and Scott, *Feminists Theorize the Political*, 4. If it is inaccurate to put the problem of political theory in this way it is, of course, my own error.

36. Boorstin does cite God as the giver of the given, so to speak, on p. 179. "Why

should we make a five-year plan for ourselves when God seems to have had a thousand-year plan ready-made for us?"

37. Delany, "The Rhetoric of Sex," 266.

38. The phrasing here is taken from William Connolly, *The Terms of Political Discourse* (Princeton: Princeton University Press, 1983).

39. Robert Bork, for example, clings to traditional political wisdom in answer to his own question, "Can democratic government survive?" "There seems no possibility of retrieving democratic government from the grasp of the Supreme Court, which now governs us in the name of the Constitution in ways not remotely contemplated by the framers and ratifiers of that Constitution" (*Slouching towards Gomorrah*, 318).

40. For a full exploration of that possibility, see William Connolly, *The Ethos of Pluralization*.

41. See Judith Butler, "Merely Cultural," *New Left Review* 227 (January/February 1998): 33–44.

42. For an account of what we might expect from political theory, see McClure, "The Issue of Foundations."

George Lipsitz: Academic Politics and Social Change

1. John Dos Passos, "Whom Can We Appeal To?" *New Masses* 6 (August 1930): 8. Quoted in Michael Denning, *The Cultural Front* (New York: Verso, 1996), 179–80.

2. Danny HoSang, "Who's Got the Power? Does Anyone? Many Youth Organizations Try, but Few Succeed," *Third Force* 3, 4 (September/October 1995): 19–23.

3. Ibid., 22.

4. Toni Cade Bambara, "What It Is I Think I'm Doing Anyhow," in *The Writer on Her Work*, ed. Janet Sternburg (New York: W. W. Norton, 1981), 160.

5. John Stauber and Sheldon Rampton, "The Public Relations Industry's Secret War on Activists," *CovertAction Quarterly* 55 (Winter 1995–96): 18–25, 57; Sidney Blumenthal, *The Rise of the Counter-Establishment: From Conservative Ideology to Political Power* (New York: Times Books, 1987); Jerome L. Himmelstein, *To the Right: The Transformation of American Conservatism* (Berkeley: University of California Press, 1990); Alan Crawford, *Thunder on the Right* (New York: Pantheon Books, 1980); Thomas Ferguson and Joel Rogers, *Right Turn: The Decline of the Democrats and the Future of American Politics* (New York: Hill and Wang, 1986); Russ Bellant, *The Coors Connection: How Coors Family Philanthropy Undermines Democratic Pluralism* (Boston: South End, 1991).

6. Jean Stefanic and Richard Delgado, *No Mercy: How Conservative Think Tanks and Foundations Changed America's Social Agenda* (Philadelphia: Temple University Press, 1996).

7. Bambara quoted in Alice A. Deck, "Toni Cade Bambara," in *Black Women in America: An Historical Encyclopedia*, ed. Darlene Clark Hine, Elsa Barkley Brown, and Rosalyn Terborg-Penn (Bloomington: Indiana University Press, 1993), 80.

8. Sidney Plotkin and William E. Scheuerman, *Private Interest, Public Spending: Balanced Budget Conservatism and the Fiscal Crisis* (Boston: South End, 1994).

9. See George Lipsitz, *The Possessive Investment in Whiteness: How White People Profit from Identity Politics* (Philadelphia: Temple University Press, 1998).

10. For evidence about the genuinely radical nature of the civil rights movement see Charles Payne, *I've Got the Light of Freedom: The Organizing Tradition and the Mississippi Freedom Struggle* (Berkeley: University of California Press), 1995, and George Lipsitz, *A Life in the Struggle: Ivory Perry and the Culture of Opposition* (Philadelphia: Temple University Press, 1988, 1995).

11. Angela Davis, "Interview with Lisa Lowe: Reflections on Race, Class, and Gender in the USA," in *The Politics of Culture in the Shadow of Capital*, ed. Lisa Lowe and David Lloyd (Durham, N.C.: Duke University Press, 1997), 303–23.

12. Lisa Lowe, "Work, Immigration, Gender: New Subjects of Cultural Politics," in Lowe and Lloyd, *Politics of Culture in the Shadow of Capital*, 362.

13. George Lipsitz, "The Apotheosis of 'Glory,' Surveying Social History," *Journal of American History* 81, 2 (September 1994): 585–91.

14. Michael Denning, *The Cultural Front* (London: Verso, 1996), 69–70.

15. Ibid., 208, 237, 273, 277, 281.

16. Ibid., 134–35.

17. Glenn Omatsu, "The 'Four Prisons' and the Movements of Liberation: Asian American Activism from the 1960s to the 1990s," in *The State of Asian America: Activism and Resistance in the 1990s*, ed. Karin Aguilar-San Juan (Boston: South End, 1994), 19–69.

18. Laura Pulido, "Multiracial Organizing Among Environmental Justice Activists in Los Angeles," in *Rethinking Los Angeles*, ed. Michael J. Dear, H. Eric Schockman, and Greg Hise (Thousand Oaks, Calif.: Sage, 1996), 171–89; Robert Bullard, "Decision Making," and Clarice E. Gaylord and Elizabeth Bell, "Environmental Justice: A National Priority," both in *Faces of Environmental Racism: Confronting Issues of Global Justice*, ed. Laura Westra and Peter S. Wenz (Lanham, Md.: Rowman and Littlefield, 1995), 3–28, 29–39.

19. Manning Marable, *The Crisis of Color and Democracy: Essays on Race, Class, and Power* (Monroe, Maine: Common Courage Press, 1992).

20. Frantz Fanon, *The Wretched of the Earth* (New York: Grove Press, 1968), 243.

21. Gerry Meraz, "Culture for the Cause," *Urb* 42 (May 1995): 69.

22. C. Ondine Chavoya, "Collaborative Public Art and Multimedia Installation: David Avalos, Louis Hock, and Elizabeth Sisco's 'Welcome to America's Finest Tourist Plantation,' " in *The Ethnic Eye: Latino Media Arts*, ed. Chon Norriega and Ana M. Lopez (Minneapolis: University of Minnesota Press, 1996), 208–27; Michelle Habell-Pallan, "No Cultural Icon," unpublished manuscript, 1995; Tricia Rose, *Black Noise* (Hanover, N.H.: Wesleyan University Press, 1994).

23. Robin D. G. Kelley, *Hammer and Hoe: Alabama Communists during the Great Depression* (Chapel Hill: University of North Carolina Press, 1990) and *Race Rebels: Culture, Politics, and the Black Working Class* (New York: Free Press, 1994); Robert Fisher, *Let the People Decide: Neighborhood Organizing in America* (Boston: Twayne, 1984); David Gutierrez, *Walls and Mirrors* (Berkeley: University of California Press, 1995); Payne, *I've Got the Light of Freedom;* Vicki Ruiz, *Cannery Women, Cannery Lives: Mexican Women, Unionization, and the California Food Processing Industry, 1930–1950* (Albuquerque: University of New Mexico Press, 1987).

Mark Reinhardt: The Song Remains the Same

1. A significant portion of this essay is a revised version of "Look Who's Talking: Political Subjects, Political Objects, and Political Discourse in Contemporary Theory," which appeared in *Political Theory* 23, 4 (November 1995): 689–719, reprinted by permission. My revision and extension owes a debt to the invitation and suggestions of Jodi Dean and to written comments (sometimes resisted here, I regret) on that earlier version sent to me by William Connolly, John Schaar, and Samuel Delany. The epigraph by Delany is from his written response (personal communication, used with permission). The other epigraph comes from Led Zeppelin, "The Song Remains the Same," on *The Houses of the Holy* (WEA/Atlantic, 1994). I thank my colleague James McAllister for his Zeppeliniana.

2. Although, within political science, the boundaries of the territory seem to be familiar and relatively clear-cut, let me specify that by "communitarianism," I mean the work of such thinkers as Michael Sandel, Jean Elshtain, Alasdair MacIntyre, Robert Bellah and his colleagues, and the writers gathered around Amitai Etzioni's journal, *The Responsive Community*. "Liberalism," which covers an exceptionally rich range of thought, is the least developed term in my essay, for I treat it only glancingly; but for my modest purposes here, the analytic philosophical defense of individual rights-as-trumps developed by such thinkers as Dworkin and Rawls is paradigmatic. Cultural studies, which originated as a term of self-description in the 1960s among the neo-Marxist work of the Birmingham school, has obviously become an amorphous catch-all. My own, rather indiosyncratic, sense of how the term can be used within political theory should become apparent as the essay unfolds.

3. The popular press consistently estimated the audience for the chase at ninety to ninety-five million people. According to the Nielsen ratings, the largest television audience for a presidential debate was 80.6 million for 1980's Carter-Reagan debate. *Nielsen Reports* (New York: Nielsen Media Research, 1993), 4.

4. Michael Sandel, *Liberalism and the Limits of Justice* (New York: Oxford University Press, 1982). I think Sandel's move from community to subjectivity is an unusually rigorous and worked-out example of a pervasive, communitarian gesture.

5. Robert Bellah et al., *Habits of the Heart* (Berkeley: University of California Press, 1985).

6. The most prominent recent example of this is Richard Rorty's *Achieving Our Country* (Cambridge: Harvard University Press, 1997), but see also, for instance, Seyla Benhabib's *Situating the Self: Gender, Community, and Postmodernism in Contemporary Ethics* (New York: Routledge, 1992). For a devastating critique of how the term is used by avowed critics of postmodernism, see Judith Butler, "Contingent Foundations: Feminism and the Question of 'Postmodernism,' " in *Feminists Theorize the Political*, ed. Judith Butler and Joan Scott (New York: Routledge, 1992), 3–21.

7. *A Call to Civil Society* (New York: Institute for American Values, 1998). Besides Elshtain, the political and legal theorists among the twenty-four signatories include William Galston, Mary Ann Glendon, and Robert George. The full list ranges across a variety of professions and political orientations (including, for instance both U.S. Senator Joseph Lieberman and theologian/critical theorist Cor-

nel West). Some signs of this internal diversity can be found in the report, yet I think I do it no injustice by characterizing it as a document representing significant tendencies in contemporary communitarian analyses of politics and policy in this country.

8. Ibid., 3–5.

9. Ibid., 6.

10. Ibid., 7, 16.

11. Ibid., 4–5.

12. Proposals 27 through 31 of the report's 41 recommendations concern economic problems and institutions. Most involve moral exhortations for more humane business practices. I find it hard to imagine that other readers will find these particularly substantive or useful. See ibid., 24–25.

13. Ibid., 5.

14. Ibid., 18.

15. Ibid., 20.

16. Ibid., 18.

17. Those looking for a fuller treatment can now consult Jill Locke's recent essay "Hiding for Whom? Obscurity, Dignity, and the Politics of Truth," *Theory & Event* 3:3 (1999). Locke is particularly illuminating on the report's reactionary sex and gender politics, which she persuasively links to the persistent "defense of a fantasy norm of family life" in the work of report author Jean Elshtain. My chapter was written before Locke's excellent article was published.

18. Daniel Bell, *Communitarianism and Its Critics* (New York: Oxford University Press, 1993), 1.

19. Ibid., 1.

20. Ibid., 8–9.

21. Ibid., 63, 100.

22. Ibid., 30–37.

23. Ibid., 90–91.

24. Ibid., 168–69.

25. Ibid., 100–108.

26. Ibid., 210.

27. Ibid., 225.

28. Ibid., 21.

29. Ibid., 180, 181, 202.

30. Not surprisingly, Kymlicka pursues such a restoration, noting both the empirical dubiousness of Bell's account of American understandings of sex, and wondering if shared understandings are the best grounds for gay politics.

31. Bell, *Communitarianism and Its Critics*, 170.

32. Ibid., 170.

Paul A. Passavant: The Governmentality of Discussion

The author acknowledges Tina Mai Chen, Jodi Dean, Peter Fitzpatrick, Gay Seidman, Michael J. Shapiro and John Shovlin for their aid. Responsibility for remaining weaknesses rests with the author.

1. *Young v. American Mini Theatres* 96 S. Ct. 2440 (1976); *Renton v. Playtime Theatres* 106 S. Ct. 925 (1986); *Barnes v. Glen Theatre* 501 U.S. 560 (1991).

2. Susan Sachs, "Civility vs. Civil Liberties," *New York Times* (July 6, 1998): A12.

3. Michel Foucault, "Governmentality," in *The Foucault Effect*, ed. G. Burchell, C. Gordon, and P. Miller (Chicago: University of Chicago Press, 1991), 102.

4. Thomas Dumm, *Democracy and Punishment* (Madison: University of Wisconsin Press, 1987).

5. Michael Warner, "The Mass Public and the Mass Subject," in *Habermas and the Public Sphere*, ed. Craig Calhoun (Cambridge: MIT Press, 1992) 385.

6. Michael Sandel, *Democracy's Discontent* (Cambridge: Harvard University Press, 1996); Mary Ann Glendon, *Rights Talk* (New York: Free Press, 1991).

7. John Stuart Mill, "On Liberty," in *Three Essays*, ed. Richard Wollheim (New York: Oxford University Press 1975), 15–16; "The East India Company's Charter," in *Writings on India*, ed. J. M. Robson, M. Moir, and Z. Moir (Toronto: University of Toronto Press, [1852] 1990), 51.

8. Paul A. Passavant, "A Moral Geography of Liberty: John Stuart Mill and American Free Speech Discourse," *Social and Legal Studies* 5 (1996): 301.

9. Martin Luther King, Jr., quoted in Taylor Branch, *Parting the Waters: America in the King Years, 1954–63* (New York: Simon and Schuster, 1988), 138–39.

10. Ibid., 140. Emphasis mine.

11. See ibid.

12. Amitai Etzioni, *The Spirit of Community* (New York: Crown, 1993); Mary Ann Glendon, *Rights Talk* (New York: Free Press, 1991).

13. See Sandel, *Democracy's Discontent*, 317–51; Robert Bellah et al., *Habits of the Heart* (New York: Harper and Row, 1985).

14. Ernesto Laclau and Chantal Mouffe, *Hegemony and Socialist Strategy* (New York: Verso, 1985).

15. Michel Foucault, "The Subject and Power," *Critical Inquiry* 8 (1982): 782.

16. *Hague v. CIO* 59 S. Ct. 954 (1939). Emphasis mine.

17. Thomas Dumm, *Democracy and Punishment*; Michel Foucault, *Discipline and Punish* (New York: Vintage, 1979).

18. *Bethel School District v. Fraser* 106 S. Ct. 3159 (1986): 3163–64. Internal quotations removed. Emphasis mine.

19. Passavant, "A Moral Geography of Liberty," 313–14.

20. Michel Foucault, *The History of Sexuality* (New York: Vintage, 1990), 139.

21. See also Ann Laura Stoler, *Race and the Education of Desire* (Durham, N.C.: Duke University Press, 1995), chapter 4.

22. Norbert Elias, *The Civilizing Process* (Cambridge: Basil Blackwell, 1994), 156.

23. Cf. ibid., 462–64.

24. George Mosse, *Nationalism and Sexuality* (Madison: University of Wisconsin Press, 1985).

25. Michael Rogin, *Ronald Reagan, The Movie* (Berkeley: University of California Press, 1987).

26. Samuel Huntington, "The Clash of Civilizations?" *Foreign Affairs* 72 (1993): 22.

27. In addition to Cass Sunstein's work cited below, see Bruce Ackerman, *We the People* (Cambridge: Harvard University Press, 1991); Samuel Beer, *To Make a Nation* (Cambridge: Harvard University Press, 1993).

28. Cass Sunstein, *Democracy and the Problem of Free Speech* (New York: Free Press, 1993), 248, xvi. See also Sunstein, *The Partial Constitution* (Cambridge: Harvard University Press, 1993).

29. Sunstein, *Free Speech*, xvii, xx, 164. Sunstein mentions nude dancing at viii, xii, 2, 14, 148, and 164.

30. Beer, *To Make a Nation*, 66, 401–2. Emphasis mine.

31. Walter Bagehot, *Physics and Politics* (New York: Alfred Knopf, 1948), 161, 172. Emphasis mine.

32. See ibid., 128.

33. Ibid., 189.

34. Ibid., 189–90.

35. Ibid., 202–6. Emphasis removed.

36. For a general discussion of the linkages of class, gender, sexuality, race, and urban space, see Anne McClintock, *Imperial Leather: Race, Gender, and Sexuality in the Colonial Contest* (New York: Routledge, 1995).

37. Bagehot, *Physics and Politics*, 122, 201.

38. See also Murray Dry, "Free Speech in Political Philosophy and Its Relation to American Constitutional Law: A Consideration of Mill, Meiklejohn, and Plato," *Constitutional Commentary* 11 (1994): 81; R. George Wright, "A Rationale from J. S. Mill for the Free Speech Clause," *The Supreme Court Review* (1986): 149.

39. Sunstein, *Free Speech*, 7, 164. One might protest that Sunstein's interest in regulating the threats to "civility produced by racial hate speech" (p. 7) cancels out the racial effects of his unqualified use of Bagehot's "government by discussion"; i.e., Sunstein is intentionally not a racist, and is unintentionally associated with the argument of racial progress made by the Social Darwinist Bagehot. While intentions can be significant in certain contexts, I am more interested here in how such cultural texts continue to inform constitutional discourse on questions of reason and value. Moreover, the very fact that certain forms of representation can be accepted unproblematically as constituting our legal reality without us thinking about it is precisely what I put in question here.

40. *Young v. American Mini Theatres* at 2449, 2452; *Jacobellis v. Ohio* 378 U.S. 184 (1964), Warren dissenting at 199.

41. *Roth v. United States* 354 U.S. 476 (1957) 487. Emphasis mine.

42. *Ginzburg v. United States*, 86 SCT. 942 (1966) 948–49. Emphasis mine.

43. *Barnes v. Glen Theatre* is cited in *Adele Buzzetti d/b/a Cozy Cabin and Vanessa Doe v. City of New York et al.* 1998 US App LEXIS 5609 (1998), which upholds the zoning regulations. At the time of this writing, the Supreme Court has not decided *City of Erie v. Pap's A.M.* (No. 98–1161).

44. *Ardery v. The State* 56 Ind. 328 (1877); *Barnes v. Glen Theatre.*

45. *Ardery v. The State*, 329–30. My emphasis.

46. *Miller v. Civil City of South Bend* 904 F. 2d 1081 (7th Cir. 1990) 1089, 1096.

47. Ibid., 1100, 1104.

48. *American Booksellers Ass'n v. Hudnut* 771 F. 2d 323 (1985) 328. Recall, also, that Catharine MacKinnon rejected the framework of obscenity in favor of "pornography." See "Not a Moral Issue," in Catharine MacKinnon, *Feminism Unmodified* (Cambridge: Harvard University Press, 1987).

49. *Miller v. Civil City*, Easterbrook dissenting at 1125, 1131.

Judith Grant: The Cultural Turn in Marxism

1. Richard Rorty, *Achieving Our Country: Leftist Thought in Twentieth-Century America* (Cambridge: Harvard University Press, 1998), 4–7.
2. Ibid., 41.
3. Ibid., 91–92.
4. Ibid., 99.
5. Herbert Marcuse, *One-Dimensional Man* (Boston: Beacon Press, 1964), 3.
6. Ibid., 14.
7. Max Horkheimer and Theodor Adorno, *The Dialectic of Enlightenment*, trans. John Cumming (New York: Continuum, 1990).
8. Martin Jay, *Marxism and Totality: Adventures of a Concept from Lukács to Habermas* (Berkeley: University of California Press, 1984).
9. Karl Marx, "A Manifesto of the Communist Party," in *The Marx-Engels Reader*, ed. Robert Tucker (New York: Norton, 1978), 479.
10. Karl Marx, Introduction to *The Grundrisse*, in *Marx: Later Political Writings*, ed. and trans. Terrell Carver (Cambridge: Cambridge University Press, 1996), 135.
11. Ibid., 137.
12. Ibid., 137.
13. Marx, "Wage, Labour and Capital," in Tucker, *Marx-Engels Reader*, 207.
14. Georg Lukács, *History and Class Consciousness: Studies in Marxist Dialectics*, trans. Rodney Livingstone (Cambridge: MIT Press, 1971), 1.
15. Ibid., 51.
16. Jay, *Marxism and Totality*, 85.
17. Ibid., 103.
18. Friedrich Engels, "Socialism, Utopian and Scientific," in *Communism, Fascism and Democracy*, ed. Carl Cohen (New York: Random House, 1972), 110.
19. V. I. Lenin, "State and Revolution," in *Communism, Fascism, and Democracy*, ed. Cohen, 145.
20. Ibid., 149.
21. Joseph Stalin, "The Foundations of Leninism," in *Communism, Fascism, and Democracy*, ed. Cohen, 159.
22. Rosa Luxemburg, "Democracy and Dictatorship," in *Twentieth Century Political Theory*, ed. Stephen Eric Bronner (New York: Routledge, 1977), 144.
23. Ibid., 145.
24. Theodor Adorno, *Negative Dialectics* (New York: Continuum, 1973), 320. Emphasis mine.
25. Karl Marx, "The Theses on Feuerbach," in Tucker, *Marx-Engels Reader*, 144.
26. Marcuse, *One Dimensional Man*, 61.
27. Theodor Adorno, *Aesthetic Theory*, ed. Gretel Adorno and Rolf Tiedemann, trans. C. Lenhardt (London: Routledge and Kegan Paul, 1984), 196.
28. Marcuse, *One-Dimensional Man*, 63.
29. Walter Benjamin, "The Work of Art in the Age of Mechanical Reproduction," in Benjamin, *Illuminations*, ed. Hannah Arendt (New York: Schocken, 1969), 227.
30. Marcuse, *One-Dimensional Man*, 65.
31. Benjamin, "Work of Art," 231.

32. Fredric Jameson, ed., *Aesthetics and Politics: Debates between Bloch, Lukács, Brecht, Benjamin, Adorno*, ed. Ronald Taylor (New York: Schocken, 1979), 123.

33. Ibid., 125–26.

34. Judith Butler points to a hierarchy among Marxists resulting precisely from this split. She worries that the attempt to assert "real" politics over "superstructural" questions of race and sexuality amounts to a kind of "neo-conservative" Marxism. See Judith Butler, "Merely Culture," *New Left Review* 227 (January/February 1998): 33–45.

35. Walter Benjamin, *Reflections*, ed. and trans. Peter Demetz (New York: Harcourt, Brace, Jovanovich, 1978), 222.

36. Ibid., 229.

37. Adorno, *Aesthetic Theory*, 349–50.

38. Ibid., 350.

39. Richard Wolin, *Walter Benjamin: An Aesthetic of Redemption* (Berkeley: University of California Press, 1994), 59.

40. Ibid., 167.

41. Ibid., 53.

42. Ibid., 126.

43. Fredric Jameson, *Late Marxism* (London: Verso, 1990), 47–48.

Paul Apostolidis: Action or Distraction?

1. See Edwin Diamond and Robert A. Silverman, *White House to Your House: Media and Politics in Virtual America* (Cambridge: MIT Press, 1997), and Robyn Wiegman, "Missiles and Melodrama (Masculinity and the Televisual War)," in *Seeing through the Media: The Persian Gulf War*, ed. Susan Jeffords and Lauren Rabinovitz (New Brunswick: Rutgers University Press, 1994), 171–87.

2. See Tania Modleski, *Feminism without Women: Culture and Criticism in a Postfeminist Age* (New York: Routledge, 1991), and Tricia Rose, *Black Noise: Rap Music and Black Culture in Contemporary America* (Hanover, N.H.: Wesleyan University Press, 1994).

3. For notable recent work along these lines that lacks hook's concern with political practice, see E. Ann Kaplan, *Looking for the Other: Feminism, Film, and the Imperial Gaze* (New York: Routledge, 1997); Fred Pfeil, *White Guys: Studies in Postmodern Domination and Difference* (New York: Verso, 1995); Paul Smith, *Clint Eastwood: A Cultural Production* (Minneapolis: University of Minnesota Press, 1993); and Elizabeth G. Traube, *Dreaming Identities: Class, Gender, and Generation in 1980, Hollywood* (Boulder: Westview, 1992).

4. An account of cultural studies in the United States could easily choose to focus on the literature in any of the following areas: media theory; criticism of art, music, cinema, architecture, and literature; feminist theory; queer theory; critical race theory; Latino/a studies; and some writing on the environment.

5. Lawrence Grossberg, *We Gotta Get Out of This Place: Popular Conservatism and Postmodern Culture* (New York: Routledge, 1992), 21.

6. Grossberg borrows the concept of articulation from the writings of Ernesto Laclau and Stuart Hall, who in turn adapt the notion from Antonio Gramsci.

Grossberg offers the following definition: "Articulation is the production of identity on top of difference, of unities out of fragments, of structures across practices. Articulation links this practice to that effect, this text to that meaning, this meaning to that reality, this experience to those politics. And these links are themselves articulated into larger structures, etc." For Grossberg, articulation thus signifies ideological work in the broadest sense, and is the basic and "continuous" mode of political contestation, (ibid., 54).

7. Ibid., 227–38.

8. Ibid., 271.

9. Ibid., 357.

10. Ibid., 238.

11. Linda Kintz, *Between Jesus and the Market: The Emotions That Matter in Right-Wing America* (Durham, N.C.: Duke University Press, 1997), 57.

12. bell hooks, *Reel to Real: Race, Sex, and Class at the Movies* (New York: Routledge, 1996), 19.

13. Ibid., 22.

14. Ibid., 24.

15. Ibid., 20.

16. Ibid., 3.

17. Ibid., 6.

18. In other writings, hooks has directly engaged the project of elaborating a critical pedagogy, or what she calls "education as the practice of freedom." Her essays on this subject are focused on the interactions of professors and students in the academic realm. Nevertheless, on the basis of these texts, we might reasonably expect that from hooks's perspective a liberating pedagogy of popular culture would be formulated along certain distinctive lines. In particular, it would encourage both leaders and other participants to "share" their personal experiences in ways that enable individual growth, call into question the relationship of authority embedded in the teacher-student relationship, and nourish the fruitful combination of "analytical and experiential" ways of knowing. A critical pedagogy of popular culture would further activate "dialogue" between groups with historically divergent experiences of racism, patriarchy, and capitalism with the aim of unmasking hidden anguish and rage, fostering mutual understanding, and cultivating political solidarity. In light of this earlier work on teaching processes, hooks's analyses of film and her insistence on the "pedagogical" aspect of movies suggest the following questions: How might experiencing and discussing movies uniquely contribute to the development of a critical and political pedagogy? How might films (and watching them) not only furnish a range of texts (and personal experiences) for the "transgressive teacher" to use but also distinctly shape what it means to carry out a liberating pedagogy? (See bell hooks, *Teaching to Transgress: Education as the Practice of Freedom* [New York: Routledge, 1994], especially 7, 21, 47, 70–71, 81, 89, 109).

19. Andrew Ross, *No Respect: Intellectuals & Popular Culture* (New York: Routledge, 1989), 22–23.

20. Ibid., 41.

21. Ibid., 195.

22. Ibid., 197.

23. Ibid., 206–7.

24. By contrast, although Gramsci maintained a purposefully broad notion of who an intellectual might be, in terms of social and institutional position, he nevertheless had a very definite sense of what an intellectual ought to do, namely, to awaken the revolutionary will and consciousness that lay dormant in mass social groups and channel their commitment into concrete organizations (parties) capable of challenging entrenched forces in the state. Precisely these endeavors, for Gramsci, distinguished the *political* agent from one who operated at merely the cultural or economic levels. See Gramsci's distinction between the "various moments or levels" in the "relations of forces" in society, in "The Modern Prince," in *Selections from the Prison Notebooks*, ed. and trans. Quintin Hoare and Geoffrey Nowell Smith (New York: International Publishers, 1971), 175–85.

25. Ross, *No Respect*, 206–7.

26. There are, however, exceptions to this rule. See Jodi Dean, *Aliens in America: Conspiracy Cultures From Outerspace to Cyberspace* (Ithaca: Cornell University Press, 1998); Thomas L. Dumm, *united states* (Ithaca: Cornell University Press, 1994); Anne Norton, *Republic of Signs: Liberal Theory and American Popular Culture* (Chicago: University of Chicago Press, 1993); and Michael Rogin, *Ronald Reagan, The Movie and Other Episodes in Political Demonology* (Berkeley: University of California Press, 1987).

27. Fredric Jameson, *Postmodernism; or, The Cultural Logic of Late Capitalism* (Durham, N.C.: Duke University Press, 1991), 35–38.

28. Ibid., 48.

29. Ibid., 49.

30. Ibid., 38.

31. Anonymous, *Primary Colors: A Novel of Politics* (New York: Random House, 1996).

32. Counterposed to her is Fat Willie's daughter, who is literally seduced by Stanton and afterwards claims that she is pregnant with Stanton's child-although Stanton is not the only possible father. She too, however, is positioned as a threatening outsider-figure by virtue of the fact that her paternity accusation threatens to sabotage Stanton's candidacy. With this character, moreover, the film engages in the most crass stereotyping: the one teenage black girl in the movie behaves promiscuously and gets pregnant out of wedlock.

33. hooks's theory furthermore encourages us to question the film's representations of lesbians and gay men in the characters of Holden and Picker. In a dynamic that parallels the other-ing of Burton's first partner, the viewer's commitment to care about Stanton-style politics requires the rejection of these characters' wishes for the radical transformation of political life. Thus, the hope for a genuine alternative to the new conservatism is stigmatized as pathological by its association with these self-destructive figures, while in turn the embrace of Stantonism is linked to hostility toward gays and lesbians.

34. Berlant elaborates that "a radical social theory of sexual citizenship in the United States must not aspire to reoccupy the dead identities of privacy, or name the innocence of youth as the index of adult practice and knowledge, or nationalize sexuality or sex as the central mode of self-legitimation or public identity-making." For precisely these ideological practices have become central to the legiti-

mation of capitalism and the state today, as is illustrated by the *Griswold v. Connecticut* and *Bowers v. Hardwick* Supreme Court decisions as well as battles in the 1990s over projects funded by the National Endowment for the Arts. Lauren Berlant, *The Queen of America Goes to Washington City: Essays on Sex and Citizenship* (Durham, N.C.: Duke University Press, 1997), 55–81; see especially 80–81.

35. For a specific account of the new right's mobilization that focuses on the cooperative activities of leaders on a variety of different strategic fronts and among a multitude of organizations, see Sara Diamond, *Roads to Dominion: Right-Wing Movements and Political Power in the United States* (New York: Guilford Press, 1995). The politics of new-right culture need not only be understood in purely strategic terms, however. Aesthetic or compositional tensions within new right culture can also be interpreted as unintentionally expressing and contesting broader social contradictions. See my analysis of *Focus on the Family's* radio broadcasts in the context of post-Fordism in *Stations of the Cross: Adorno and Christian Right Radio* (Durham, N.C.: Duke University Press, forthcoming in 2000).

Linda Zerilli: Democracy and National Fantasy

I wish to thank Bonnie Honig, Gregor Gnädig, and George Shulman, and, especially, my research assistant, Laurie Naranch, for their comments on this essay.

1. Consider the political practice of naming national symbols in the age of global culture. As Richard Blum observes, "The statue was variously known as the 'goddess of democracy' (*minzhu nushen*), the 'spirit of democracy' (*minzhu zhishen*), the 'goddess of the nation' (*minzunushen*), and the 'goddess of liberty' (*ziyou nushen*). . . . The statue's final appellation—Goddess of Democracy—appears to have emerged as an unplanned afterthought. According to one participant in the project, the name was blurted out spontaneously by a student craftsman on May 30, in response to a television interviewer's question. The name stuck." Richard Blum, *Burying Mao: Chinese Politics in the Age of Deng Xiaoping* (Princeton: Princeton University Press, 1996), 273.

2. Neil Kottler, "The Statue of Liberty as Idea, Symbol, and Historical Presence," in *Making a Universal Symbol: The Statue of Liberty Revisited*, ed. Wilton S. Dillon and Neil Kottler (Washington, D.C.: Smithsonian Institution Press, 1994), 4–5.

3. See "Beijing Reports Arrest of 11 Protesters," *New York Times*, May 31, 1989; "Chinese Students, in About-Face, Will Continue Occupying Square," *New York Times*, May 30, 1989; Scott Simmie and Bob Nixon, *Tiananmen Square* (Vancouver: Douglas and McIntyre, 1990), 158–59.

4. "Chinese Students, in About-Face, Will Continue Occupying Square."

5. Tsao Hsingyan Lian, "A Beijing Chronicle," in *Making a Universal Symbol: The Statue of Liberty Revisited*, 104–5.

6. I thank Bonnie Honig for her formulation of this point.

7. Hannah Arendt, *On Revolution* (New York: Viking, 1965), 207, 206, 183.

8. Hannah Arendt, "The Concept of History," in *Between Past and Future: Eight Exercises in Political Thought* (New York: Penguin, 1968), 64. What Arendt objects to in the modern concept of history is the reduction of the singularity of the deed

to the engulfing notion of process, without which the deed is nothing. She is therefore critical of both "Tocqueville's and Marx's generalizations, especially their conviction that revolution had been the result of an irresistible force rather than the outcome of specific deeds and events" (64, 259).

9. As Arendt explains this uneasy relationship, the Founders confronted a problem that "seemed unsolvable: if foundation was the aim and the end of revolution, then the revolutionary spirit was not merely the spirit of beginning something new but of starting something permanent and enduring; a lasting institution, embodying this spirit and encouraging it to new achievements, would be self-defeating. From which it unfortunately seems to follow that nothing threatens the very achievements of revolution more dangerously and more acutely than the very spirit which has brought them about. Should freedom, in its most exalted sense as freedom to act, be the price to be paid for foundation?" *On Revolution*, 235.

10. Arendt cites as an exception Jefferson's plans for the ward system through which counties would be subdivided into "small republics," allowing "every man in the State" to become "an acting member of the Common government, transacting in person a great portion of its rights and duties, subordinate indeed, yet important, and entirely within his competence." The ward system, as Arendt observes, was intended to combat political passivity and in this way keep alive the spirit of democratic invention but within an institutional framework. Crucially important to Jefferson's vision was the insightful recognition that it was only by breaking up the people as a mass that they would be moved to participate in public affairs and to do so in ways that were consistent with the durability of the republic. "Hence, the ward system was not meant to strengthen the power of the many but the power of 'every one' within the limits of his competence." *On Revolution*, 257.

11. Slavoj Žižek, *Tarrying with the Negative: Kant, Hegel, and the Critique of Ideology* (Durham, N.C.: Duke University Press, 1993), 200.

12. Mary J. Shapiro, *Gateway to Liberty: The Story of the Statue of Liberty and Ellis Island* (New York: Vintage, 1986), 65.

13. Marina Warner, *Monuments and Maidens: The Allegory of the Female Form* (London: Weidenfeld and Nicholson, 1985), 12.

14. June Hardgrove, "The American Fundraising Campaign," in *Liberty: The French-American Statue in Art and History*, ed. Pierre Provoyeur and June Hardgrove (New York: Perennial, 1986), 156.

15. John Higham, *From Boundlessness to Consolidation: The Transformation of American Culture, 1848–1860* (Ann Arbor: William L. Clements Library, 1969), 18.

16. Quoted in Robert H. Byer, "Words, Monuments, Beholders: The Visual Arts in Hawthorne's *The Marble Faun*," in *American Iconology*, ed. David C. Miller (New Haven: Yale University Press, 1993), 164. In the context of the deep social divisions that characterized America in the late nineteenth century, the notion that visual language was superior to verbal language took on a renewed appeal that echoed the earlier view of men like Webster, who saw in Bunker Hill the power of signs that "were silent, but awful," all the more meaningful for never being spoken (166). Monumental signs were felt to be superior in this sense because they presumably escaped the contests over meaning which, in the view of men like Webster, plagued the written and spoken word. It was as if monuments could set-

tle public debate by offering the same object of perception that would furnish the final arbitration for every possible misunderstanding. As Byer argues, Webster's view of monuments as symbols and rituals of national unity came under attack by writers such as Emerson and Hawthorne.

17. Ibid., 170.

18. Lauren Berlant, *The Anatomy of National Fantasy: Hawthorne, Utopia, and Everyday Life* (Chicago: University of Chicago Press, 1991), 23.

19. *World*, March 16, 1885. Quoted in Shapiro, *Gateway to Liberty*, 49–50.

20. Pulitzer was not the first to publish these names, but his list was popular and broad rather than elitist and narrow.

21. Philippe Roger, "The Edifying Edifice," in Provoyeur and Hardgrove, *Liberty: The French-American Statue in Art and History*, 272.

22. Quoted in Christian Blanchet and Bertrand Dard, *Statue of Liberty: The First Hundred Years*, trans. Bernard A. Weisberger (New York: American Heritage Press, 1985), 178.

23. Anne McClintock, *Imperial Leather: Race, Gender, and Sexuality in the Colonial Contest* (New York: Routledge, 1995), 59.

24. Emma Lazarus's famous poem, "The New Colossus," which was written to raise funds for the pedestal and which now occupies a prominent place on the front door to the monument, was neither read nor mentioned at the dedication ceremony in 1886. It was not until 1903 that the plaque bearing her poem was discreetly installed on the second floor inside, where it attracted little attention. An 1886 proposal for an entry station for immigrants on Bedloe Island received numerous complaints—Bartholdi himself called it "a monstrous plan." The fiftieth anniversary of the statue in 1936 repeated the traditional motifs of the 1886 dedication, stressing Franco-American friendship and liberty as an abstract idea.

25. John Higham, *Send These to Me: Jews and Other Immigrants in Urban America* (Baltimore: Johns Hopkins University Press, 1975), 81.

26. Bonnie Honig, *No Place Like Home: Democracy and the Politics of Foreignness* (Princeton: Princeton University Press, 2000).

27. This theme of liberation from slavery was eventually and quite explicitly dropped from Bartholdi's "Liberty Enlightening the World." Bartholdi eliminated the broken chains and Phyrigian cap that had historically served to symbolize the emergence from slavery, partly to fend off objections from Southerners in his decade-long effort to raise funds for the project.

28. Quoted in Blanchet and Dard, *Statue of Liberty: The First Hundred Years*, 121.

29. Žižek, *Tarrying with the Negative*, 195, 196.

30. Alexis de Tocqueville, *Democracy in America*, trans. George Laurence, ed. J. P. Mayer (New York: Anchor, 1969), 469.

31. Quoted in Pierre Provoyeur, "Bartholdi and the Colossal Tradition," in Provoyeur and Hardgrove, *Liberty: The French-American Statue in Art and History*, 64.

32. Pierre Provoyeur, "Artistic Problems," in Provoyeur and Hardgrove, *Liberty: The French-American Statue in Art and History*, 98.

33. Kaja Silverman, "Liberty, Maternity, Commodification," in *The Point of Theory*, ed. Mieke Bal and Inge B. Hoer (New York: Continuum, 1994), 22.

34. Quoted in Provoyeur, "Artistic Problems," 96.

35. Silverman, "Liberty, Maternity, Commodification," 21. This rationalism and

control has to be squared with another feature of the statue, a feature it shares with Eiffel's Tower—its utter uselessness. To borrow Roland Barthes's account of the tower, the Statue of Liberty must escape reason by virtue of its sheer inutility—and this in an age that could not endure a useless object. Not unlike Eiffel—who tried to contain the scandal of uselessness by offering up the tower for aerodynamic measurements, radio, electric research, and meteorological observations—Bartholdi made similar gestures of utility. But all his utilitarian excuses, as Barthes writes of Eiffel's, are nothing compared to the great imaginary function of the monument, its sheer capacity to provoke fantasy. Roland Barthes, "The Eiffel Tower," in *The Eiffel Tower and Other Essays* (New York: Hill and Wang, 1979).

36. I am indebted to Bonnie Honig for her account of the original taking of power that is featured in democratic origin stories.

37. Kathleen Chevalier, quoted in Kottler, "The Statue of Liberty as Idea, Symbol, and Historical Presence," 36.

38. Richard H. Schneider, *Freedom's Holy Light* (New York: Thomas Nelson Publishers, 1985), 6, 15. Another odd aspect of this homecoming narrative is Schneider's momentary sense that the statue had been replaced by a smaller model. It may seem astonishing to think that a monument of this size, which took two decades to build and install, could be dismantled, stored in a secure location, and replaced by a copy. But my account of the statue shows that the original has not been thinkable without the copy.

39. When we look at this image of Wincherly we should recall that the feminist disruption of one political mythology (woman as symbol but not citizen) is also the consolidation of another (white women as guardians of the nation). The National American Women's Suffrage Association, for example, made powerful use of anti-immigrant and racist sentiment to argue for the female franchise on the basis of moral difference articulated in terms of both femininity and whiteness.

40. One might consider in connection with the Davis image an 1884 image by Thomas Worth called "Liberty Frightenin' the World," that also features a black woman as liberty but with a significantly different racialized political meaning. More recent appropriations of the statue include a 1975 image that appeared on the back cover of *Mad* magazine, of Ms. Liberty holding a bra in her hand, and a 1997 full-page advertisement in the *New York Times* using the statue to announce that "gay and lesbian values are American values."

41. Walter Benjamin, "The Task of the Translator," in *Illuminations* (New York: Schocken Books, 1969), 73; Jacques Derrida, "Des Tours de Babel," in *Difference in Translation*, ed. Joseph Graham (Ithaca: Cornell University Press, 1985), 180, 188.

42. *New York Times*, April 18, 1996, B2.

43. Žižek, *Tarrying with the Negative*, 200.

Priscilla Wald: Imagined Immunities

I am grateful to the University of Washington for a Royalty Research Fund grant that allowed me relief from teaching in spring 1998, during which time I completed a significant amount of the research and writing of this essay. I also wish to thank audiences at the University of Maryland, Purdue University, and the Institute for the Study of American Culture at Dartmouth College (summer 1998) for extremely helpful responses to this work. My deep gratitude as well to Dale Bauer, Amy Kaplan, and Jodi Dean and to the members of my writing groups at the University of Washington: Christine Di Stefano, Angela Ginorio, Susan Glenn, Caroline Chung Simpson, Shirley Yee, Ann Anagnost, Lucy Jarosz, Susan Jeffords, Victoria Lawson, Lorna Rhodes, and Laurie Sears for their attentive and astute comments on a draft of this essay. And to Betsy Klimasmith and Gretchen Murphy for their superb research assistance.

1. These are recurring images and can be found, in various incarnations, in a number of works. The monkey is from the film *Outbreak;* the speeding car is from the television movie *The Stand* (based on Stephen King's best-selling novel); the lab technician is such a common image at this point that the sources range from journalistic and other nonfictional accounts of contagious disease to fictional sources; and the persuasive adolescent is an HIV carrier from an episode of the television show *Law and Order* (the show was about efforts to prosecute the carrier for the spread of HIV).

2. See Robert Lawson-Peebles, *Landscape and Written Expression in Revolutionary America: The World Turned Upside Down* (Cambridge: Cambridge University Press, 1988), 39.

3. Although Soper alerted the medical community to her existence in 1907, she was not dubbed "Typhoid Mary" until 1908. On "Typhoid Mary," see Judith Walzer Leavitt, *Typhoid Mary: Captive to the Public's Health* (Boston: Beacon Press, 1996); Andrew Mendelsohn, "False 'Typhoid Mary' Strikes Again: The Social and the Scientific in the Making of Modern Public Health," *Isis* 86 (1995): 268–77; and Kraut, 96–104. On the story of "Typhoid Mary" as a carrier narrative, see my "Cultures and Carriers: 'Typhoid Mary' and the Science of Social Control," *Social Text* 52/53, 15.3 and 4 (Fall/Winter 1997): 181–214.

4. Heather Schell and Lisa Lynch have both convincingly documented how the politics of a period find expression in accounts of emerging viruses and pandemics. I build on this work as I examine the mutual impact of scientific theories and discoveries about contagion and ideas about the relationships that constitute community at times of major demographic shifts in the United States. See Shell, "Outburst! A Chilling True Story about Emerging-Virus Narratives and the Pandemic Social Change," *Configurations* 5.1 (Winter 1997): 93–133, and Lynch, "The Neo/Bio/Colonial Hot Zone: African Viruses, American Fairytales," *International Journal of Cultural Studies*, forthcoming.

5. Nancy Tomes makes similar use of Anderson's concept in *The Gospel of Germs: Men, Women, and the Microbe in American Life* (Cambridge: Harvard University Press, 1986), 7.

6. Benedict Anderson, *Imagined Communities: Reflections on the Origins and Spread of Nationalism*, rev. ed. (London: Verso, 1991), 6.

7. Ibid., 6–7.

8. Ibid., 7.

9. Etienne Balibar, "The Nation Form: History and Ideology," trans. Chris Turner, in Etienne Balibar and Immanuel Wallerstein, *Race, Nation, Class: Ambiguous Identities* (London: Verso, 1991), 86–106, 93.

10. Ibid., 93.
11. Ibid., 96.
12. Here I am exploring further an idea I first suggested in my discussion of the Gettysburg Address in *Constituting Americans: Cultural Anxiety and Narrative Form* (Durham, N.C.: Duke University Press, 1995).
13. Alan M. Kraut, *Silent/Travelers: Germs, Genes, and the "Immigrant Menace"* (Baltimore: Johns Hopkins University Press, 1994), 3.
14. See Bruno Latour, *The Pasteurization of France* (Cambridge: Harvard University Press, 1988).
15. Edward Alsworth Ross, *Social Control: A Survey of the Foundations of Order* (New York: Macmillan, 1901).
16. Jacob A. Riis, *How the Other Half Lives: Studies among the Tenements of New York* (New York: Dover Publications, 1971), 88. Originally published in 1890, this is a reprint of the 1901 Scribner's Sons' edition.
17. Correspondence, Barrett Wendell to Horace Kallen, cited in Kallen, "Democracy Versus the Melting-Pot: A Study of American Nationality," *Nation* 100 (February 18 and 25, 1915): 190–94, 217–20, 219.
18. J. Snowman in Louis Wirth, *The Ghetto* (Chicago: University of Chicago Press, 1928) 68–69.
19. On the shift in ideas about immunity (especially in relation to personhood), see Emily Martin, *Flexible Bodies: Tracking Immunity in American Culture from the Days of Polio to the Age of AIDS* (Boston: Beacon Press, 1994). Although my own discussion of immunity is in a different context from Martin's, I have found this work useful in theorizing the concept.
20. William H. McNeill, *Plagues and Peoples* (New York: Doubleday, 1976), 130.
21. See Terra Ziporyn, *Disease in the Popular American Press* (Westport, Conn.: Greenwood Press, 1988), 8.
22. Correspondence, Ezra Pound to William Carlos Williams, cited in Williams, prologue, *Kora in Hell: Improvisations* (Boston: Four Seas Company, 1920), 13–14.
23. Daniel Sargent, "Professor Wendell and the Philosophers," in *Essays in Memory of Barrett Wendell by His Assistants* (Cambridge: Harvard University Press, 1926), 11–20.
24. Tomes, *Gospel of Germs*, 92.
25. Patrick Lynch, *Carriers* (New York: Berkley Publishing Group, 1996), 351.
26. For a discussion of the earliest epidemiological maps, see Mary Poovey's treatment of Edwin Chadwick in *Making a Social Body: British Cultural Formation, 1830–1864* (Chicago: University of Chicago Press, 1995), esp. 117–20. As Poovey suggests, the epidemiologist creates a narrative through the mapping of the disease. Maps, as Anderson notes, constitute important images through which to imagine community.
27. Richard Preston, *The Hot Zone* (New York: Anchor Books Doubleday, 1994), 16. Portions of this book were originally published in *The New Yorker*, and this edition was reprinted from a hardcover published by Random House in 1994.
28. Ibid., 19.
29. Stephen King, *The Stand* (New York: Signet, 1991), 67.
30. One section of the exhibit *Epidemic! The World of Infectious Disease*, featured at

New York City's Museum of Natural History in 1999, was aptly entitled "It's a Small World." This exhibit, and its accompanying lecture series and film festival, again attests to the popular fascination with this material.

31. Preston, *Hot Zone*, 78.

32. Arno Karlen, *Man and Microbes: Disease and Plagues in History and Modern Times* (New York: Simon and Schuster, 1996), 63.

33. Lynch, *Carriers*, 71.

34. McNeill, *Plagues and People*, 199.

35. Gina Kolata, "Scientists See a Mysterious Similarity in a Pair of Deadly Plagues," *New York Times*, May 26, 1998, B9–B10. The hypothesis, originally published in the *American Journal of Human Genetics*, was subsequently refuted. For an extended discussion of the hypothesis and its media coverage, see my forthcoming essay, "Future Perfect: Grammar, Genes, and Geography."

36. There is a striking *difference* between the communities that form emotionally in response to a disease and the communities to which a disease biologically gives rise. The latter is not typically the concern of those who are suffering from a disease. This potential link between diseases, however, does form an interesting scientific analogue to the metaphorical links evoked repeatedly both in fiction and nonfiction. Bubonic plague, for example, serves as a point of reference for someone living through an epidemic (or the fear of one), and, as many writers have noted, the HIV virus seems to have sparked interest in what Laurie Garrett calls "the coming plague." See Laurie Garrett, *The Coming Plague: Newly Emerging Diseases in a World Out of Balance* (New York: Farrar, Straus and Giroux, 1994).

In general, although AIDS narratives share some features with other stories of carriers and contagion, the specifics of that disease, including the length of its incubation (making it difficult to track), the relative difficulty of its transmission and the activist education that has arisen in response to it require a much more detailed and nuanced discussion than I could give it in this essay. It is a question I will consider in the larger manuscript of which this essay is a part.

37. Anderson, *Imagined Communities*, 5.

38. Ibid., 163.

39. Robin Cook, *Invasion* (New York: Berkley Publishing Group, 1997), 238.

40. Ibid., 117.

41. Ibid., 285.

42. Ibid., 125; ellipsis in text.

43. Ibid., 263.

44. Ibid., 266.

45. Ibid., 267.

46. Ibid., 282.

47. Ibid., 252.

48. Lynch, *Carriers*, 12. I say aptly named because of the association of the name Rhodes with colonialism in Africa. The point is that westerners should not be in the jungle because of dangers to the west.

49. Ibid., 370; ellipsis added.

50. Ibid., 366.

51. Ibid., 346.

52. Richard M. Krause, Foreword to *Emerging Viruses*, ed. Stephen S. Morse (New York: Oxford University Press, 1993), xvii–xix, xvii.

53. Lynch, *Carriers*, 422.

George Shulman: Race and the Romance of American Nationalism

I wish to thank Peter Euben, Victoria Hattam, and Michael Rogin for their insightful comments on earlier drafts.

1. Richard Rorty, *Achieving Our Country* (Cambridge: Harvard University Press, 1998), 10, 22, 29. Since pragmatism needs cultural consensus, Rorty promotes civic religiosity, but this public faith cannot be subjected to the critical irony he makes a private virtue and attacks in "cultural politics."

2. Ibid., 11–14. Baldwin consistently mocked what Rorty calls American "civic religion." Also, Rorty dedicates his book to Irving Howe, who attacked Baldwin (and Ellison) for not writing "social protest" novels, which indicates the reasons Baldwin faulted the left Rorty recovers.

3. By this reading, democracy subverts hierarchy and fixity in favor of the chosen, the hybrid, the plural, and the fluid. My trouble with this romance is its two assumptions: that "melting" the fixed is simply emancipatory, and that democracy can exist without stable markers. Perhaps fluidity poses its own problems; perhaps certain markers are a condition of democracy or of any possibility. But which, when, and why?

4. Karl Marx, "The Class Struggles in France," in *Surveys From Exile*, ed. David Fernbach (New York: Vintage, 1974), 60; Alexis de Tocqueville, *Democracy in America*, vol. 2 (New York: Vintage, 1945), chaps. 17–18.

5. To sense the disparity between these two explanations, contrast the worlds evoked in C. Wright Mills, *The Power Elite* (London: Oxford, 1956), and Ralph Ellison's *Invisible Man* (New York: Signet, 1947), or the recent movies *Bulworth* and the *Truman Show*. In fact, "mass" society is produced partly by an exclusionary color line, so that conformity relates to norms of whiteness, and individualism and its vicissitudes are symbolized racially.

6. Michael Rogin, *Blackface/White Noise*, (Berkeley: University of California, 1996), 23–27. See also Richard Slotkin, *Regeneration through Violence* (Middletown: Wesleyan University Press, 1973).

7. All quoted passages are in "Letter from Birmingham City Jail," collected in *A Testament of Hope: The Essential Writings and Speeches of Martin Luther King Jr.*, ed. James M. Washington (New York: HarperCollins, 1986).

8. To say it harshly, there is no Aristotelian or Machiavellian dimension in King's thought about politics. But the issue is complex because King was supremely politic in the way he built coalitions, used moral suasion, and wielded other kinds of power. Moreover, could an "agonistic" politics avoid legitimizing white supremacy? For a politics that emerges by criticizing the dream of formal equality, self-evidence, and transcendent principles, see Kimberle Crenshaw, "Reel Time/Real Justice," in Robert Gooding-Williams, *Reading Rodney King/Reading Urban Uprising* (New York: Routledge, 1993).

9. On the other hand, Morrison says black people "signify benevolence, harm-

less and servile guardianship, and endless love," in "Introduction: Friday on the Potomac," *Race-ing Justice/En-gendering Power*, ed. Toni Morrison (New York: Pantheon, 1992), xv.

10. As part of this cultural politics, most variants of black nationalism and Afrocentrism narrate stories of rebirth that overcome self-hatred by recovering an identity untainted by white supremacy and America. See Paul Gilroy, *The Black Atlantic* (Cambridge: Harvard University Press, 1993).

11. The images of Tom and Aunt Jemima suggest how white need and black subordination underwrite a white assertion whose desire and violence are projected onto the other (savage) image. See James Baldwin, "Many Thousands Gone" and "Everybody's Protest Novel," in *Notes of a Native Son* (New York: Bantam, 1955).

12. For Williams, Daniel Boone showed what European immigrants had yet to do: "There must be a wedding. But . . . only he saw the prototype of it all, the native savage. To Boone the Indian was his greatest master. Not for himself surely to be an Indian . . . but the reverse: to be *himself* in a new world, Indianlike." Williams (and D. H. Lawrence) praise an identificatory "wedding" with "the native savage," for experiences of "ecstasy" and "regenerative violence" kill off an old culture ruled by resentment. Restoring the European self to what it had split off, Williams models an "American" culture both "new" and "noble" because "native." But to heirs like Rogin and Slotkin, Williams repeats the tradition of the winners: identification is the prelude to murder not marriage. See William Carlos Williams, *In the American Grain* (New York: New Directions, 1925), 130–39.

13. Norman Mailer, *The Presidential Papers* (New York: Berkeley Medallion, 1963), 38.

14. Ibid., 39, 40. Recall D. H. Lawrence: "The essential American soul is hard, isolate, stoic, and a killer. . . . When this man breaks from static isolation and makes a new movement, then look out, something will be happening," *Classic Studies in American Literature* (New York: Viking, [1923] 1964), 63.

15. Ibid., 39–40.

16. Ibid., 210.

17. Ibid., 210, 59. The mythic language of frontiers, outlaws, masculine potency, and regenerative encounters with danger and violence were crucial justifications of every imperial endeavor in American history, and were voiced by JFK to justify anti-communism and counter-insurgency warfare at the same time that Mailer is writing. Mailer opposed the Vietnam War very early on, but continued to invoke and tried to redeem the language of regenerative violence and frontiers. In his view, the war betrayed the meaning of those myths, which had to be turned inward, to foster more conflict amongst voices within the self and groups in society.

18. Norman Mailer, "The White Negro," in *Advertisements for Myself* (Cambridge: Harvard University Press, [1959] 1992), 343, 339.

19. Ibid., 340–41.

20. Ibid., 346.

21. Ibid., 340, 356.

22. Mailer, *Presidential Papers*, 25–26.

23. Roth quoted in Michael Rogin, "On the Jewish Question," *Democracy* 3, 2 (Spring 1983): 105.

24. James Baldwin, "The Black Boy Looks at the White Boy" collected in James

Baldwin, *Nobody Knows My Name* (New York: Beacon, 1961). Not coincidentally, Eldridge Cleaver praises Mailer and viciously attacks Baldwin in *Soul on Ice* (New York: Dell, 1968).

25. James Baldwin, "Stranger in the Village," in *Notes of a Native Son* (New York: Bantam, 1964), 145; *The Fire Next Time* (New York: Dell, 1962), 125–26.

26. See the illuminating essay by Lawrie Balfour, " 'A Most Disagreeable Mirror'/Race Consciousness as Double Consciousness," in *Political Theory* 26, no. 2 (June 1998): 346–69.

27. Baldwin, *The Fire Next Time*, 129.

28. Baldwin, "Stranger in the Village," 148.

29. The legacy of white supremacy is completely negative for whites, but not for blacks: they see through and know what whites deny. If they are not crushed or twisted by oppression, but learn to face both the worst that life can bring and the Bigger in their brains, they are less ruled by fear, and become the only bearers of nobility and tragic spirit in American culture.

30. Baldwin, "Many Thousands Gone," in *Notes of a Native Son*, 34.

31. Baldwin, "White Man's Guilt," in *The Price of the Ticket* (New York: St. Martin's Press, 1985), 410.

32. Perhaps the American Nietzsche is not Emerson, who denies the power of history, but Baldwin, who democratizes a Nietzschean ethos, partly by confronting the resentment of weakness Nietzsche projects onto "slaves," and partly by seeking to return white culture to "life" or the dionysian.

33. Baldwin, "Many Thousands Gone," 13.

34. Baldwin writes: "The only way he [the white] can be released from the Negro's tyrannical power over him is to consent, in effect, to become part of that suffering and dancing country that he now watches wistfully from the heights of his lonely power and, armed with spiritual traveller's checks, visits surreptitiously after dark." *The Fire Next Time*, 129.

35. Baldwin, "In Search of a Majority," in *The Price of the Ticket*, 235. In the early fifties, Perry Miller voices the "existential" view that action creates and precedes identity: the essence of "American character" is that identity is "achieved rather than given." But Miller excludes "negroes" by associating them with instinct not invention. See "The Shaping of American Character" in *Nature's Nation* (Boston: Belknap Press, 1967). Responding in effect and maybe in fact, Baldwin and Ralph Ellison subvert white supremacy by making blacks "Americans" in Miller's sense: uprooting from a given identity has compelled them to "achieve" an identity, and like Europeans, by taking on and wearing a mask, that is, by appropriation. Any achieved identity is thus marked by impurity (now called hybridity). But Baldwin and Ellison also show that acts of masking and appropriation are not equivalent. Indeed, it is the very flux and uncertainty of such a society that drives anxious whites to impose racialized identities.

36. Baldwin, *The Fire Next Time*, 19, 131, 140.

37. On de-reifying nationhood, see Joan Wallach Scott, "After History?" *Common Knowledge* 5, no. 3 (Winter 1996).

38. Perhaps, though, my diction and claim about "contest" is like his about white supremacy: these are less arguments we justify with evidence, though to some degree we do, but visions of life so fundamental they must be "accepted" as self-ev-

ident, and serve as the ground for any argument and evidence. Shifting *these* is the greatest political act, often silent and enacted by poets.

39. Baldwin, "In Search of a Majority," 233.

Aida A. Hozic: Making of the Unwanted Colonies

1. "U Acquires 'Zlata's Diary,' " *Daily Variety*, February 2, 1994, p. 1.

2. In February 1997, Phil Alden Robinson's dreams to make a film about Sarajevo finally started to materialize. With Universal Pictures and Steven Spielberg's DreamWorks Studio as co-producers, the film acquired a new title—*The Age of Aquarius*—and a new storyline. According to *Daily Variety*, Robinson "amalgamated" his own experiences in Bosnia and *Zlata's Diary* into "a drama that casts [Harrison] Ford as a mercenary who ferries food and weapons to war-torn countries, selling them for profit. He falls in love with a Bosnian woman in a country plagued by political turmoil, murder and ethnic cleansing" (*Daily Variety*, March 21, 1997). Ford's counterpart was supposed to be British actress Kristin Scott Thomas, the star of the Oscar-winning film *The English Patient*. However, at the end of 1997, citing an exorbitant budget and geopolitical problems, Universal Pictures pulled out of *The Age of Aquarius*. The future of the film, whose shooting was supposed to start in April of 1998, remains uncertain.

3. The transformation of Sarajevo into a spectacle did not go unnoticed in Sarajevo itself. The city's trapped residents were bewildered by, and often quite cynical about, numerous celebrity visitors who used the war as the vehicle for their own self-promotion. Reflecting this sentiment, Sanjin Jukic, an artist from Sarajevo, created a multimedia installation called "Sarajevo Ghetto Spectacle," which toured the world with the exhibit *Witnesses of Existence*, organized by gallery OBALA in the midst of the war. (The photo of Jukic's work also appeared in a long photo-article from Sarajevo in the September 1993 issue of *The Face*.)

4. Mike Edwards, "Central Africa's Cycle of Violence," *National Geographic*, June 1997, 124–33.

5. See Martin Shaw, *Civil Society and Media in Global Crises* (London: Pinter, 1996).

6. For an overview of these debates see Johanna Neuman, *Lights, Camera, War* (New York: St. Martin's Press, 1995), and materials from two conferences sponsored by the U.S. Institute of Peace: *Managing Chaos* (November 30–December 1, 1994) and *Virtual Diplomacy* (April 1–2, 1997). Extensive literature on the Gulf War also covers many of these issues. See, for example, W. Lance Bennett and David L. Paletz, eds., *Taken by Storm: The Media, Public Opinion, and U.S. Foreign Policy* (Chicago: University of Chicago Press, 1994); Robert E. Denton, Jr., ed., *The Media and the Persian Gulf War* (Westport, Conn.: Praeger, 1993); William V. Kennedy, *The Military and the Media* (New York: Praeger, 1993); Hamid Mowlana, George Gerbner, and Herbert I. Schiller, eds., *Triumph of the Image* (Boulder: Westview Press, 1992).

7. See Jean Baudrillard, *The Gulf War Did Not Take Place* (Bloomington: Indiana University Press, 1995).

8. In one of the first long reports from the Yugoslav battlefields, P. J. O'Rourke wrote in *Rolling Stone*: "I drove to Bihac with London Times reporter Ed Gorman,

BBC reporter Bob Simpson and a Croatian translator, Sonja, who pretended to be Serbian when we were stopped by Serbian soldiers. It was easy for Sonja to pretend to be Serbian because Serbs and Croats are so much alike that the only way they can tell each other apart is by religion. And most of them aren't religious. So the difference between Serbs and Croats is that Serbs don't go to eastern Orthodox services and the Croats don't attend mass. And the difference between Serbs and Muslims is that five times a day Serbs don't pray to Mecca." See "Gang Bang Bang," *Rolling Stone*, January 7, 1993, pp. 41ff.

9. On indeterminacy of ethnic violence, not just visual, see Arjun Appadurai's text "Dead Certainty: Ethnic Violence in the Era of Globalization," *Public Culture* 10:2 (1998): 225–47.

10. Thomas L. Friedman, writing about violence in Africa in the *New York Times*, says explicitly: "There is Bosnia envy here. Gen. J. M. Inieger, commander of the Nigerian peacekeepers, says the only way to heal Liberia is for Nigerian forces to occupy the whole country. But that would mean Nigeria increasing its force from 7,000 to 18,000 men, which would require $135 million. 'That is what NATO spends in a few days in Bosnia,' complains General Inieger. 'But no one wants to pay for peacekeeping in Liberia.' 'It is because we are Africans, not Europeans,' says Liberian newspaper publisher Sando Moore. 'People say: "They are Africans; let them kill each other." ' " See Thomas L. Friedman, "Heart of Darkness," *New York Times*, January 21, 1996, sec. 4, p. 15.

11. Thomas Keenan, "Introduction ('like a museum')," in Alexander Garcia Düttmann, Werner Hamacher, John G. Hanhardt, Thomas Keenan, Friedrich Kittler, Gyan Prakash, Andrew Ross, and Kristin Ross, *The End(s) of the Museum (Els limits del museu)* (Barcelona: Fundació Antoni Tàpies, 1996), 22.

12. Friedman, "Heart of Darkness," 18.

13. *Nightline*, ABC News, November 10, 1993. The special report, *Mostar: The Death of a City*, and its motto, "Let it not be said that we did not know," subsequently became a part of the exhibit "Faces of Sorrow" sponsored by *Time* magazine and the United Nations. The exhibit was also displayed at Simon Wiesenthal's Museum of Tolerance in Los Angeles, the U.S. Holocaust Museum in Washington, D.C., and is still displayed on the web at: http://www.i3tele.com/photoperspectives/facesofsorrow/html/exhibition.html

14. "Winter Olympics from Sarajevo will be a lavish TV spectacle," *Christian Science Monitor*, January 18, 1984, 20.

15. "Going Out in Style," *Christian Science Monitor*, February 27, 1984, p. 52.

16. "Sarajevo 'Gets Sober' from Olympic High, but Hardly Somber," *Washington Post*, April 15, 1983.

17. "Bosnia Takes On the World," *Economist*, February 4, 1984, 50.

18. "Deep in Bosnian Forest, a Host City is Transformed," *New York Times*, July 24, 1983, sec. 5, p. 1.

19. Ibid., 1.

20. Susan Woodward views this excessive co-dependence with the Yugoslav military as one of the main reasons for the war in Bosnia. "Even in the 1980s," writes Woodward, "when the army was being substantially downsized, 40 to 55 percent of the Bosnian economy was tied to military industries; 50 to 55 percent of its in-

dustry was federally mandated investment for that reason; and 40,000 people were employed directly in military production. Sixty to 80 percent of the army's physical assets (armaments factories, supply routes, airfields, mines and basic raw materials, stockpiles, training schools, oil depots) were located in Bosnia-Herzegovina. On the eve of the war, 68 percent of the federal army's 140,000 troops were stationed in the republic. To the extent that the Yugoslav army was fighting a war for its own integrity and state, it could not easily be a neutral party in Bosnia-Herzegovina or abandon its own economic foundation." See Woodward, *Balkan Tragedy* (Washington, D.C.: Brookings Institute, 1995), 259.

21. Ibid., 236.

22. Joan Copjec, *Read My Desire* (Cambridge, Mass.: MIT Press, 1994).

23. Stuart Hall, "When Was the Post-Colonial? Thinking at the Limit," in *The Post-Colonial Question*, ed. Iain Chambers and Lidia Curti (London: Routledge, 1996), 257.

24. Bart Moore-Gilbert identifies this conflict between cultural and economic interpretations of colonialism as the conflict between "postcolonial theory" and "postcolonial criticism." If the proponents of the theory, such as Said, Bhabha, or Spivak—despite important differences among them—mostly focus on issues of representation, postcolonial critics (Aijaz Ahmad, Abdul JanMohamed, Ketu Katarak, Arif Dirlik) continue to stress material realities (and brutalities) of colonialism and blame the theorists for obfuscating such issues. See Bart Moore-Gilbert, *Postcolonial Theory* (London: Verso, 1997). Political economists in the strict sense do not even go as far as to engage in a dialogue with either postcolonial theorists or critics. As Jeffrey Frieden notes (without any irony), "Most controversy [among political economists] over colonialism and foreign investment revolves around the simple question whether economic considerations were important to colonial imperialism or not." See Jeffrey Frieden, "International Investment and Colonial Control: A New Interpretation," *International Organization*, 48, no. 4 (Fall 1994): 562. This kind of denial of economic foundations in imperial projects would seem problematic even to the most literal of the literary critics.

25. Laura Mulvey describes the fetishism as the gaze that refuses to see. "While curiosity is a compulsive desire to see and to know, to investigate something secret, fetishism is born out of a refusal to see, a refusal to accept the difference the female body represents for the male. These complex series of turning away, of covering over, not of the eyes but of understanding, of fixating on a substitute object to hold the gaze, leave the female body as an enigma and threat, condemned to return as a symbol of anxiety while simultaneously being transformed into its own screen in representation." See *Fetishism and Curiosity* (Bloomington: Indiana University Press, 1996), 64.

26. Frieden, "International Investment and Colonial Control."

27. Homi Bhabha, "The Other Question," in *Contemporary Postcolonial Theory*, ed. Padmini Mongia (London: Arnold, 1996).

28. The critical divide between the "Holy Trinity" of postcolonial studies—Edward Said, Homi Bhabha, and Gyatari Spivak—and their disciples still runs along the subject-object fault line. Said is, somewhat unjustly, criticized for endowing the colonizer with absolute power and, in turn, for denying agency to colonial sub-

jects; the *other*, for Said, is mostly a construct of colonial imagination. See *Orientalism* (Harmondsworth: Penguin, 1978) and *Culture and Imperialism* (New York: Knopf, 1993). In contrast, Bhabha's concept of "hybridity" blurs the boundaries between colonizers and the colonized, self and the *other*, and, particularly, attempts to fracture a unified and authoritative vision of the former. At the same time, however, Bhabha also relates "hybridity" to movements of culture and capital, to unstable (both in terms of power and in terms of location) positions of colonizers and their subjects due to migration, refugee flows, and transnational movements. See *Location of Culture* (London: Routledge, 1994). Spivak, finally, deconstructs the notion of a sovereign subaltern subject yet frequently describes the subaltern as the "wholly *other*" located beyond the colonizer's frame of reference, unknown and unknowable within the Western system of knowledge. For Spivak, the first step toward comprehending the *other* involves its radical un-imagining. See *In Other Worlds* (London: Routledge, 1987) and Donna Landry and Gerald MacLean, eds., *The Spivak Reader* (London: Routledge, 1995). Nonetheless, all three authors, albeit not without tensions and contradictions, continue to view identities, location, culture, and power as co-determined; the friction that I am trying to address here views this co-determinacy as problematic.

29. The term "myth of the ethnic conflict" was borrowed from John Bowen's article "The Myth of Global Ethnic Conflict," *Journal of Democracy* 7:4 (1996): 3–14. The article was brought to my attention by Catherine and David Newbury, whose own work on Rwanda is a continuous struggle against the persistence of such myths in the West.

30. Spivak, in particular, has been critical of the confluence of interest and desire in Deleuze's and Foucault's writings. See "Can the Subaltern Speak? Speculations on Widow Sacrifice," in *Marxism and the Interpretation of Culture*, ed. Cary Nelson and Lawrence Grossberg (London: Macmillan, 1987), 271–313.

31. Robert J. C. Young, *Colonial Desire* (London: Routledge, 1995), 181.

32. Gilles Deleuze and Felix Guattari, *Anti-Oedipus* (Minneapolis: University of Minnesota Press, 1983).

33. Ibid., 182.

34. Ibid., 26.

35. Young, *Colonial Desire*, 170, 172.

36. Larry Grossberg, "The Space of Culture, The Power of Space," in Chambers and Curti, *Post-Colonial Question*, 169–88.

37. Peter Maas, *Love Thy Neighbor* (New York: Alfred A. Knopf, 1996), 146.

38. Arjun Appadurai, *Modernity at Large* (Minneapolis: University of Minnesota Press, 1996).

39. Jeffrey Winters, *Power in Motion* (Ithaca: Cornell University Press, 1996).

40. *Development Co-operation: DAC Report 1995* (Paris: OECD, 1996) 65.

41. Following the collapse of the Asian financial markets, IMF has expanded the scope of its surveillance to include broader range of institutional measures, effectively placing both politics and economics of its member countries under its control. See *IMF Survey Supplement on the Fund* (September 1998) at http://www.imf.org/external/pubs/ft/survey/sup0998/06.htm for a detailed description of IMF's surveillance objectives. For a critique of panoptical capitalism,

see Stephen Gill, "Finance, Production, and Panopticism" in his edited volume *Globalization, Democratization, and Multilateralism* (London: St. Martin's Press, 1997) and Kevin Robins and Frank Webster "Cybernetic Capitalism: Information, Technology, Everyday Life" in Vincent Mosco and Janet Wasko, eds., *The Political Economy of Information* (Madison: University of Wisconsin Press, 1988).

Kathleen Stewart: Real American Dreams (Can Be Nightmares)

I am grateful for comments on versions of this paper from Begona Aretxaga, Lauren Berlant, Donald Brenneis, Ann Cvetkovich, Steven Feld, Edmund Gordon, Susan Harding, Charles Hale, Diane Losche, Rosalind Morris, Gretchen Ritter, and Michael Taussig and for the opportunity to present it at the University of California, Santa Cruz, Department of Anthropology, Columbia University, Department of Anthropology, the University of Texas, Austin, Department of Anthropology, and Yale University's Center for Agrarian Studies.

1. Michael Taussig, *The Nervous System* (New York: Routledge, 1992).

2. See Miriam Hansen, Foreword to Oskar Negt and Alexander Kluge, *Public Sphere and Experience: Toward an Analysis of the Bourgeois and Proletarian Public Sphere*, trans. Peter Labanyi, Jamie Owen Daniel, and Assenka Oksiloff (Minneapolis: University of Minnesota Press, 1993), ix–xli. Hansen describes the proletarian public sphere not as an empirical category but as "a category of negation in both a critical and a utopian sense, referring to the fragmentation of human labor and existence and its dialectical opposite, the practical negation of existing conditions in their totality" (xxxi). "The concept of a proletarian public sphere could be constructed, discursively, from its systematic negation, that is, from hegemonic efforts to suppress, fragment, delegitimize, or assimilate any public formation that suggests an alternative, autonomous organization of experience" (xxxii).

3. For discussions of deepening class inequalities in the 1980s and 1990s, see Berch Berberoglu, *The Legacy of Empire: Economic Decline and Class Polarization in the United States*, trans. Mark Poster (St. Louis: Telos Press, 1992); Samuel Bowles, David M. Gordon, and Thomas Weisskopf, *After the Waste Land: A Democratic Economics for the Year 2000* (Armonk, N.Y.: M. E. Sharpe, 1990); Sheldon Danzinger and Peter Gottschalk, *America Unequal* (New York: Russell Sage Foundation, and Cambridge: Harvard University Press, 1995); Matt Wray and Annalee Newitz, eds., *White Trash: Race and Class in America* (New York: Routledge, 1997); and I. Susser, "The Construction of Poverty and Homelessness in U.S. Cities," *Annual Reviews in Anthropology* 25 (1996): 411–35.

4. See, for instance, Osha Gray Davidson, *Broken Heartland: The Rise of America's Rural Ghetto* (New York: Duncan and Sweet, 1992); Cynthia Duncan, ed., *Rural Poverty in America* (New York: Auburn House, 1992); Janet Fitchen, *Poverty in Rural America: A Case Study* (Boulder: Westview Press, 1981); and Yvonne Vissing, *Out of Sight, Out of Mind: Homeless Children and Families in Small-Town America* (Lexington: University Press of Kentucky, 1996).

5. I take class to be not a pre-given set of interests but a formation based on a struggle in three dimensions: economic, political and symbolic. In *Cultural Studies and Cultural Value* (Oxford: Clarendon Press, 1995), James Frow puts it this way:

"It is a question of discursive *representation* of interests, of calculation and hypothesis. There is no class essence and there are no unified class actors, founded in the objectivity of social interest: there are, however, processes of class formation, without absolute origin or telos, with definite discursive conditions, and played out through particular institutional forms and balances of power, through calculations and miscalculations, through desires and fears and fantasies" (111).

6. See, for instance, Philippe Bourgois, *In Search of Respect: Selling Crack in El Barrio* (Cambridge: Cambridge University Press, 1995); Jay Macleod, *Ain't No Makin' It: Aspirations and Attainment in a Low-Income Neighborhood* (Boulder: Westview Press, 1995); Katherine S. Newman, *Falling from Grace: The Experience of Downward Mobility in the American Middle Class* (New York: Vintage, 1989); Roger Rouse, "Thinking through Transnationalism: Notes on the Cultural Politics of Class Relations in the Contemporary United States," *Public Culture* 7, 2 (1995): 353–402; Studs Terkel, *The Great Divide: Second Thoughts on the American Dream* (New York: Pantheon Books, 1988); and Elizabeth Traube, *Dreaming Identities* (Boulder: Westview, 1992).

7. Hansen, "Foreword," xxxviii.

8. For discussions of counterpublics see Geoff Eley, "Nations, Publics and Political Cultures: Placing Habermas in the Nineteenth Century," in *Habermas and the Public Sphere*, ed. Craig Calhoun (Cambridge: MIT Press, 1992), 289–339; Nancy Frazer, "Rethinking the Public Sphere: A Contribution to the Critique of Actually Existing Democracy," *Social Text* 25/26 (1990): 57; Hansen, "Foreword"; and Mary Ryan, *Women in Public: Between Banners and Ballots, 1825–1880* (Baltimore: Johns Hopkins University Press, 1990). Hansen describes counterpublics as publics based not on natural communities and a language of authenticity, homogeneity, and continuity but on the admission of discursive struggle ("Foreword," xxxvi).

9. See Wendy Brown, *States of Injury: Power and Freedom in Late Modernity* (Princeton: Princeton University Press, 1995).

10. Jürgen Habermas's theory of the public sphere, in *The Structural Transformation of the Public Sphere: An Inquiry into a Category of Bourgeois Society*, trans. Thomas Burger (Cambridge: MIT Press, 1989), has been widely critiqued on these grounds. See, especially, Craig Calhoun, ed., *Habermas and the Public Sphere* (Cambridge: MIT Press, 1992); and Bruce Robbins, ed., *The Phantom Public Sphere* (Minneapolis: University of Minnesota Press, 1993).

11. Michael Warner delineates this desire for publicity or publicness itself and the fashioning of its forms of expression in transformations of public culture in "The Mass Public and the Mass Subject," in Calhoun, *Habermas and the Public Sphere*, 377–401.

12. Lauren Berlant, *The Queen of America Goes to Washington City* (Durham, N.C.: Duke University Press, 1997); Hal Foster, "Death in America," *October* 75 (Winter 1996): 37–59; Mark Seltzer, "Wound Culture: Trauma in the Pathological Public Sphere," *October* 80 (1997): 3–26; and Michael Warner, "Mass Public."

13. Susan Buck-Morss, "Aesthetics/Anaesthetics," *New Formations* (1993): 123–43; Marilyn Ivy, "Have You Seen Me? Recovering the Inner Child in Late Twentieth-Century America," *Social Text* 37 (1993): 227–52.

14. For discussions of the political culture of class and its political unconscious see, Pierre Bourdieu, *Distinction: A Social Critique of the Judgement of Taste*, trans. Richard Nice (Cambridge: Harvard University Press, 1984); Bourgois, *In Search of*

Respect; Michel de Certeau, *The Practice of Everyday Life*, trans. Steven Randall (Berkeley: University of California Press, 1984); Jonas Frykman and Orvar Lofgren, *Culture Builders: A Historical Anthropology of Middle-Class Life*, trans. Alan Crozier (New Brunswick: Rutgers University Press, 1987); Paul Gilroy, *"There Ain't No Black in the Union Jack": The Cultural Politics of Race and Nation* (Chicago: University of Chicago Press, 1991); John Hartigan, "Reading Trash: Deliverance and the Poetics of White Trash," *Visual Anthropology Review* 8,2 (1992): 8–15; Dick Hebdige, *Hiding in the Light: On Images and Things* (New York: Routledge, 1988); Fredric Jameson, *The Political Unconscious: Narrative as a Socially Symbolic Act* (Ithaca: Cornell University Press, 1981); Donald Lowe, *History of Bourgeois Perception* (Chicago: University of Chicago Press, 1982); Toby Miller, *The Well-Tempered Self: Citizenship, Culture, and the Postmodern Subject* (Baltimore: Johns Hopkins University Press, 1993); Peter Stallybrass and Allon White, *The Politics and Poetics of Transgression* (Ithaca: Cornell University Press, 1986); Kathleen Stewart, "Nostalgia: a Polemic," *Cultural Anthropology* 3, no. 3 (1988): 227–41, and *A Space on the Side of the Road: Cultural Poetics in an "Other" America* (Princeton: Princeton University Press, 1996); Susan Stewart, *On Longing: Narratives of the Miniature, the Gigantic, the Souvenir, the Collection* (Baltimore: Johns Hopkins University Press, 1984); and Paul Willis, *Learning to Labor: How Working-Class Kids Get Working-Class Jobs* (New York: Columbia University Press, 1981).

15. Marie-Helene Huet, *Monstrous Imagination* (Cambridge: Harvard University Press, 1993). For discussions of the cultural politics of monstrosity, see also Jeffrey Jerome Cohen, ed., *Monster Theory* (Minneapolis: University of Minnesota Press, 1996); and Judith Halberstam, *Skin Shows: Gothic Horror and the Technology of Monsters* (Durham, N.C.: Duke University Press, 1995).

16. I lived in the coal-mining camps and hollers of southwestern West Virginia for two continuous years of fieldwork, 1980 through 1982, and during shorter periods of time in the years since.

17. "Coal camps" is a local term for the remnants of coal-mining company towns built, largely, between 1880 and 1930. Most of them were disbanded as company towns in the 1950s when the mines were mechanized, and three quarters of miners were disemployed, as mass diasporic migrations ensued. The houses and company stores and movie theaters were sold to individual familes or, often, left to ruin.

18. Maurice Blanchot theorizes the everyday as aporia: "The everyday is the inaccessible to which we have always already had access" (17), and "the everyday breaks down structures and undoes forms, even while ceaselessly regathering itself behind the form whose ruin it has insensibly brought about" (20). "Everyday Speech," *Everyday Life*, ed. Alice Kaplan and Kristin Ross, *Yale French Studies* 73 (1987).

19. Guy Debord argues that the "awareness of the profound richness and energy abandoned in everyday life is inseparable from awareness of the poverty of the dominant organization of this life" (71). "Perspectives for Conscious Alterations in Everyday Life," in *Situationist International Anthology*, ed. and trans. Ken Knabb (Berkeley: Bureau of Public Secrets, 1981), 68–75.

20. Berlant, *Queen of America;* Brown, *States of Injury;* Foster, "Death of America"; Seltzer, "Wound Culture"; and Warner, "Mass Public," all note moments of

the emergence or eruption of publicness in contemporary U.S. culture in an arena of spectacularized accident, trauma, or wound.

21. Dick Hebdige, *Subculture: The Meaning of Style* (London: Routledge, 1979).

22. Jacques Lacan, *Ecrits*, trans. A. Sheridan (New York: Norton, 1977).

23. See Jean-François Lyotard, *The Postmodern Condition: A Report on Knowledge*, trans. Geoff Bennington and Brian Massumi (Minneapolis: University of Minnesota Press, 1985); and Slavoj Žižek, *Looking Awry: An Introduction to Jacques Lacan through Popular Culture* (Cambridge: MIT Press, 1995).

24. See Avery Gordon, *Ghostly Matters: Haunting and the Sociological Imagination* (Minneapolis: University of Minnesota Press, 1997); and Marilyn Ivy, *Discourses of the Vanishing: Modernity, Phantasm, Japan* (Chicago: University of Chicago Press, 1995).

25. Michael Taussig, "Tactility and Distraction" *Cultural Anthropology* 6,2 (1991): 147–53, and Michael Taussig, *Mimesis and Alterity: A Particular History of the Senses* (New York: Routledge, 1993).

26. Walter Benjamin, "A Small History of Photography," in *One-Way Street and Other Writings*, trans. Edmund Jephcott and E. Shorter (London: New Left Books, 1979), 243.

27. Walter Benjamin, "Surrealism: The Last Snapshot of the European Intelligentsia," in *Reflections: Essays, Aphorisms, Autobiographical Writings*, ed. Peter Demetz, trans. Edmund Jephcott (New York: Harcourt Brace Jovanovich, 1978), 177–92.

28. Steven Shaviro, "Bodies of Fear: The Films of David Cronenberg," in *The Politics of Everyday Fear*, ed. Brian Massumi (Minneapolis: University of Minnesota Press, 1993), 31.

29. Raymond Williams, *Marxism and Literature* (Oxford: Oxford University Press, 1977), 130.

30. Gordon, *Ghostly Matters*, 210.

31. Jean-Luc Nancy, *The Inoperative Community*, ed. Peter Connor, trans. Peter Connor, Lisa Garbus, Michael Holand, and Simona Sawhey (Minneapolis: University of Minnesota Press, 1991).

32. See Avital Ronnell, "Trauma TV: Twelve Steps Beyond the Pleasure Principle," in *Finitude's Score: Essays for the End of the Millennium* (Lincoln: University of Nebraska Press, 1994); and Warner, "Mass Public."

Thomas L. Dumm: Wild Things

A version of this essay appears in *A Politics of the Ordinary* (New York: New York University Press, 1999). It appears here with permission.

1. That conference, "Modern Communication and the Disappearance of Art and Politics," resulted in an edited volume that contains Baudrillard's "Transpolitics, Transsexuality, Transaesthetics," as well as a useful response by Ron Silliman, "What Do Cyborgs Want? (Paris, Suburb of the Twentieth Century)," which together provoked the event I describe below. See William Stearn and William Chaloupka, eds., *Jean Baudrillard: The Disappearance of Art and Politics* (New York: St. Martin's Press, 1992), 9–26, 27–37.

2. *Baudrillard*, "Transpolitics," 26.

3. On the writing and early recording history of "Wild Thing" see Chip Taylor, "Rough Mix: How I Wrote 'Wild Thing,' " *Musician* 16 (March 1996).

4. For a sustained analysis of the relationship of beer to the bloodiness of fascism, see Klaus Theweleit, *Male Fantasies, Volume 1: Women, Floods, Bodies, History*, trans. Stephen Conway, in collaboration with Erica Carter and Chris Turner (Minneapolis: University of Minnesota Press, 1987).

5. On Thoreau and resignation, see Thomas L. Dumm, "Resignation," *Critical Inquiry* (Fall 1998).

6. Jane Bennett, *Thoreau's Nature: Ethics, Politics, and the Wild* (Thousand Oaks, Calif.: Sage Publications, 1994), 3.

7. Nicholson utters these lines in the 1995 melodramatic film directed by Rob Reiner, also starring Demi Moore and Tom Cruise, *A Few Good Men*. The question of being able to handle the truth is deeply evocative of a passage of analysis in Stanley Cavell's essay on the relationship of Emerson's thought to Nietzsche and Heidegger, "Aversive Thinking," where the idea of *hand*someness, clutching, and grasping are all brought into play in relationship to thinking about the humanity of truth. See Stanley Cavell, *Conditions Handsome and Unhandsome: The Constitution of Emersonian Perfectionism* (Chicago: University of Chicago Press, 1990), 38.

8. For a report, see David S. Bennahum, "Just Gaming: Three Days in the Desert with Jean Baudrillard, DJ Spooky, and the Chance Band," *Lingua Franca* (February 1997): 59–63.

9. One important example of what I am calling mediated uncanniness is Marjorie Garber's tour de force, "Jell-O," in Marjorie Garber and Rebecca Walkowitz, eds., *Secret Agents: The Rosenberg Case, McCarthyism and Fifties America* (New York: Routledge, 1995). In that essay, Garber connects the phrase Harry Gold is reported to have said when he handed over a ripped Jell-O box as his sign, "Benny sent me," to the prosaic but eerie fact that Jell-O was the sponsor of the *Jack Benny Program* on the radio at that time. This is eerie in the sense that the guilt of Julius Rosenberg hinged on the fact that Gold came from Julius, not from Benny, and the reconstruction of the phrase became a matter of contestation throughout the spy trial. Such a mediated uncanniness in this case might serve as an exemplary proof, though whether it would be sustained in a court of law is another question.

10. Stanley Cavell, *In Quest of the Ordinary: Lines of Skepticism and Romanticism* (Chicago: University of Chicago Press, 1988), especially "Emerson, Coleridge, Kant," and Cavell, *Conditions Handsome and Unhandsome*, especially "Aversive Thinking."

11. Elinor Ostrom, "A Behavioral Approach to the Rational Choice Theory of Collective Action: Presidential Address, American Political Science Association, 1997," *American Political Science Review* 92,1 (March 1998): 18.

12. Jean Baudrillard, *Simulations*, trans. Paul Foss, Paul Patton, and Philip Beitchman (New York: Semiotext(e), 1983), 13.

13. Ralph Waldo Emerson, "The American Scholar," in *Emerson: Essays and Lectures*, ed. Joel Porte (New York: Library of America, 1983), 58.

14. Michel Foucault, "The Masked Philosopher," in *The Essential Works of Michel*

Foucault, Vol. 1, Ethics, Subjectivity, and Truth, ed. Paul Rabinow (New York: New Press, 1997), 323; Jacques Derrida, *Specters of Marx: The State of the Debt, the Work of Mourning, & the New International*, trans. Peggy Kamuf (New York: Routledge, 1994); Stanley Cavell, *Contesting Tears: The Hollywood Melodrama of the Unknown Woman* (Chicago: University of Chicago Press, 1996); Judith Butler, *Gender Trouble: Feminism and the Subversion of Identity* (New York: Routledge, 1990); Gilles Deleuze and Felix Guatarri, *Kafka: Toward a Minor Literature*, trans. Dana Polan (Minneapolis: University of Minnesota Press, 1986); and William E. Connolly, *The Ethos of Pluralization* (Minneapolis: University of Minnesota Press, 1996), for examples. As many know, these are only examples culled from large and distinctive bodies of work. But a gesture is a gesture.

15. The comparison of the ordinary, the normalized, and the eventful is a subject I take up in *A Politics of the Ordinary* (New York: New York University Press, 1999).

Michael J. Shapiro: The Politics of the "Family"

1. Erich Auerbach, "Odysseus' Scar," in *Mimesis*, trans. Willard R. Trask (Princeton: Princeton University Press, 1953), 10.

2. Ibid., 15.

3. The Palestinian filmmaker Elias Suileman appreciates this aspect of old men's stories. In his *Chronicle of a Disappearance*, there is a comparable story, told by an old grandfather. His story about his life in the Turkish army frustrates his listeners, who want to learn something about what Turkey was like at the turn of the century. Instead, his narration is a wholly self-absorbed account of how one day he avoided the bad army food and ate a satisfying meal he bought from a street vendor. Each time the story is solicited—with the hope of more local detail—the narration remains focused on the details of his meal.

4. The expression is the title of Jean-François Lyotard's *Libidinal Economy*, trans. Iain Hamilton Grant (Bloomington: Indiana University Press, 1993). While the English translation of Freud's concept of *Besetzung* is "cathexesis" in the *Standard Edition*, in French, it has been translated as *investissement*, doubtless encouraging French critical thinkers to inter-articulate economic and sexual discourses.

5. See Jonathan Rosenbaum, "A Gun up Your Ass: An Interview with Jim Jarmusch," *Cineaste* 22,2 (1996): 23.

6. This remark is made by Jonathan Rosenbaum, ibid., 20.

7. Gilles Deleuze, *Cinema* 2, trans. Hugh Tomlinson and Robert Galeta (London: Athlone, 1989), 24.

8. Ibid., 23.

9. Ibid., 127.

10. Ibid., 129.

11. As Richard Slotkin has pointed out, by the eighteenth century more regionally developed stories displaced the biblical version of America's expansion. The significant icons were no longer virtuous, self-sacrificing Puritans but heroic adventurers and Indian fighters. Summarizing this shift, he says: "In the American mythogenesis the founding fathers were not those eighteenth century gentlemen

who composed a nation at Philadelphia. Rather, they were those who . . . tore violently a nation from the implacable and opulent wilderness—the rogues, adventurers, and land-boomers; the Indian fighters, traders, missionaries, explorers, and hunters who killed and were killed until they had mastered the wilderness." *Regeneration through Violence: The Mythology of the American Frontier, 1600–1860* (Middletown, Conn.: Wesleyan University Press, 1973), 4.

12. Gilles Deleuze and Felix Guattari, *A Thousand Plateaus*, trans. Brian Massumi (Minneapolis: University of Minnesota Press, 1987), 385.

13. Ibid., 386.

14. Ibid., 380.

15. The quotation belongs to Partha Chatterjee, whose treatment of civil society in the thought of Hegel has influenced my discussion here. See Partha Chatterjee, "A Response to Taylor's Modes of Civil Society," *Public Culture* 3,1 (Fall 1990), 123.

16. G. W. F. Hegel, *Philosophy of Right*, trans. T. M. Knox (London: Oxford University Press, 1945), 148.

17. Ibid.

18. Ibid., 154.

19. Ibid., 161.

20. Ibid., 155.

21. Etienne Balibar, "Ambiguous Universality," *Differences* 7,1 (Spring 1995): 56.

22. Ibid., 58–59.

23. See Jean-Luc Nancy, *The Birth to Presence*, trans. B. Holmes et al. (Stanford: Stanford University Press, 1993), 143–66.

24. In Jacques Donzelot's *The Policing of Families*, trans. Robert Hurley (New York: Pantheon, 1979), a genealogical treatment of the co-emergence of "society" and the modern family is explicitly proposed as a "critique of political reason," 8.

25. Ibid., 7.

26. Ibid.

27. Ibid., 25.

28. Ibid., 225.

29. Ibid., 227.

30. See for example Michel Foucault, *The History of Sexuality*, trans. Robert Hurley (New York: Pantheon, 1978).

31. See George Mosse, *Nationalism and Sexuality* (New York: Howard Fertig, 1985).

32. William Bennett and C. Deloris Tucker, "Smut-Free Stores," *New York Times*, December 9, 1996, A15.

33. Ibid.

34. Katha Pollit makes a similar argument in her analysis of Dan Quayle's attack on the "Murphy Brown" television sitom, in "Why I Hate 'Family Values' (Let Me Count the Ways)," *Nation*, July 27, 1992, p. 94.

35. On this issue see Mosse, *Nationalism and Sexuality*.

36. This process is described by Norbert Elias, *The Civilizing Process*, trans. Edmund Jephcott (New York: Blackwell, 1994), 22ff.

37. Mosse, *Nationalism and Sexuality*, 53.

38. Noel Burch, "Spatial and Temporal Articulations," in *Theory of Film Practice*, trans. Helen Lane (New York: Praeger, 1973), 17.

39. Even the L. L. Bean catalogue, for example, romanticizes an American home that is "cozy and unbroken," a place with people who are "mostly married, with car pools and mortgages and aging parents"; it is a world with "no room for the confusion about sex roles that currently besets the rest of our society." Holly Brubach, "Mail-Order America," *New York Times Magazine*, November 11, 1993, 58.

40. Nancy Fraser, "After the Family Wage: Gender Equity and the Welfare State," *Political Theory* 2, no. 4 (November, 1994): 591.

41. Ibid., 597.

42. Sade was of course much more doctrinal than Jack Horner. This is not the place to map the positions and enigmas in Sadean thought and stagings. The primary parallel is their shared resistance to official strictures on sexuality and their encouragement of singularity (best articulated in Sade's "Philosophy in the Bedroom"). I address myself to Sadean thought more extensively in Michael J. Shapiro, *Reading "Adam Smith": Desire, History, and Value* (Newbury Park, Calif.: Sage, 1993), 116–32.

43. Jonathan Crary, "Unbinding Vision: Manet and the Attentive Observer in the Late Nineteenth Century," in Leo Charney and Vanessa R. Schwartz, eds., *Cinema and the Invention of Modern Life* (Berkeley: University of California Press, 1995), 46–71.

44. Jean-Luc Nancy, *The Sense of the World*, trans. Jeffrey S. Librett (Minneapolis: University of Minnesota Press, 1997), 93.

45. For an elaboration of this position see Jean Luc Nancy, *The Inoperative Community*, trans. Peter Connor, Lisa Garbus, Michael Holland, and Simona Sawhney (Minneapolis: University of Minnesota Press, 1991).

Jodi Dean: Declarations of Independence

I owe special thanks to Colleen McDonough for her research assistance. Thanks also to Justin Oberman for sharing with me his knowledge of the Illuminati and to Meredith Maslich and Dawn Rooth for their work on the Clintons, Monica Lewinsky, and Kenneth Starr. I'm indebted to Larry Haapanen for his bibliography of conspiracy theories. Bill Chaloupka, Iva Deutchman, Tom Dumm, Paul Passavant, Lee Quinby, and Alison Shonk-wiler provided helpful suggestions on an earlier draft of this essay. A version of this paper was presented to the seminar on cultural studies at Union College, and I'm grateful to the participants for their provocative engagement with the text. These include Lori Marso, Hyungji Park, Andy Feffer, Catharine Womack, Bonnie McDonald, Gail Donaldson, William Garcia, and Sarah Henry.

1. Quote available at http://home.att.net/~joserojas/conspiracy.html.

2. Philip Weiss, "The Clinton Haters," *New York Times Magazine*, February 23, 1997.

3. Found at http://www.geocities.com/Pentagon/2783/lewinsky.html.

4. William F. Buckley, "Are You a Right-Wing Conspirator?" *National Review*, February 23, 1998, 62–63. I am indebted to Dawn Rooth for bringing this article to my attention.

5. Howard Krutz, "Clintons Long Under Siege by Conservative Detractors," *Washington Post*, January 28, 1998, A1, 20. I am indebted to Meredith Maslich for bringing this article to my attention.

6. In *Political Paranoia: The Psychopolitics of Hatred* (New Haven: Yale University Press, 1997), Robert S. Robins and Jerrold M. Post argue that a sign of political paranoia is viewing political rivals as enemies. Moreover, the predominant metaphor they use for conspiracy thinking and paranoia (which they equate) is that of virus spreading infection. See 23, 47.

7. Daniel Pipes, *Conspiracy* (New York: Free Press, 1997), 49.

8. I take the concept of interpellation from Louis Althusser, "Ideology and Ideological State Apparatuses," in *Lenin and Philosophy*, trans. Ben Brewster (New York: Monthly Review Press, 1971), 170–86. I want to distance myself, however, from Althusser's focus on ideology by linking interpellation with the more deliberate and self-conscious actions of those who are able to use media to create audiences, opinions, and publics. Although the content of the subject position into which one is interpellated is never fixed (and, indeed, here interpellation is connected with refiguration), PR and entertainment culture remind us daily of the effort that goes into the production of distinct groups and publics: the "cool" who need Nikes, the "insecure" who need special scents and deodorizers, and so forth.

9. In a defense of liberal pluralism, Edward Shils similarly linked publicity and secrecy in the 1950s. See *The Torment of Secrecy: The Background and Consequences of American Security Policies* (Glencoe, Ill.: Free Press, 1956).

10. See Laura J. Gurak, *Persuasion and Privacy in Cyberspace: The Online Protests over Lotus Marketplace and the Clipper Chip* (New Haven: Yale University Press, 1997).

11. Wendy M. Grossman writes, "Many Net surfers don't realize it, but the average Web site can tell what browser you're using, what domain you're coming from, and what type of computer and operating system you're using as well as what pages you've looked at and for how long. A lot of Web sites put this information into a small bit of text called a 'cookie' and store it on your hard drive, to streamline your next visit to their site, which some people feel is an invasion of privacy." *net.wars* (New York: New York University Press, 1997), 188.

12. Paul Rabinow, ed., *The Foucault Reader* (New York: Pantheon Books, 1984), 316.

13. Michel Foucault, *Discipline and Punish*, trans. Alan Sheridan (New York: Vintage Books, 1979).

14. See Lauren Berlant's account of the privatization of the national political in *The Queen of America Goes to Washington City* (Durham, N.C.: Duke University Press, 1997).

15. Thomas L. Dumm, *united states* (Ithaca: Cornell University Press, 1994), 108.

16. Jürgen Habermas, *The Structural Transformation of the Public Sphere*, trans. Thomas Burger (Cambridge: MIT Press, 1989), 4.

17. Ibid., 35.

18. Eve Kosofsky Sedgwick writes: "Paranoia is characterized by placing, in practice, an extraordinary stress on the efficacy of knowledge per se—knowledge in the form of exposure. . . . Paranoia for all its vaunted suspicion acts as though its work would be accomplished if only it could finally, this time, somehow get its story truly known." "Paranoid Reading and Reparative Reading; or, You're So Paranoid, You Probably Think This Introduction Is About You," in *Novel Gazing: Queer Readings in Fiction*, ed. Eve Kosofsky Sedgwick (Durham: Duke University Press, 1997), 17. I am indebted to Peter Knight for bringing this essay to my attention.

19. For an example of the outrage that can be expressed over the line being crossed, see Frederick Crews, "The Mindsnatchers," *New York Review of Books*, June 25, 1998, 14ff.

20. For a more thorough discussion of Sagan, Hopkins, and the politics of authorization at work in denunciations of ufology, see my *Aliens in America: Conspiracy Cultures from Outerspace to Cyberspace* (Ithaca: Cornell University Press, 1998).

21. See David H. Bennett, *The Party of Fear: From Nativist Movements to the New Right in America History* (New York: Vintage Books, 1990); Richard Hofstadter, *The Paranoid Style in American Politics and Other Essays* (Cambridge: Harvard University Press, [1952] 1996); George Johnson, *Architects of Fear: Conspiracy Theories and Paranoia in American Politics* (Los Angeles: Jeremy P. Tarcher, 1983); Seymour Martin Lipset and Earl Raab, *The Politics of Unreason: Right-Wing Extremism in America, 1790–1970* (New York: Harper and Row, 1970); and the contributions to *Conspiracy: The Fear of Subversion in American History*, eds. Richard O. Curry and Thomas M. Brown (New York: Holt, Rinehart, and Winston, 1972).

22. Michael Rogin, *Ronald Reagan, The Movie, and Other Episodes in Political Demonology* (Berkeley: University of California Press, 1987).

23. Ibid., 284.

24. See Rogin's analysis of the realist and symbolic approaches to political demonology prominent in American political science during the 1950s, ibid., 272–300.

25. William E. Connolly, *The Ethos of Pluralization* (Minneapolis: University of Minnesota Press, 1995), xiii–xvi.

26. Lipset and Raab, *Politics of Unreason*, 6.

27. Pipes, *Conspiracy*, 38.

28. Rogin, *Ronald Reagan, The Movie*, 278.

29. This is not a new criticism. Theories of pluralism have coexisted with their critiques. For example, in a critical analysis rooted in political realism, E. E. Schattschneider writes, "The flaw in the pluralist heaven is that the heavenly chorus sings with a strong upperclass accent. Probably about 90 percent of the people cannot get into the pressure system." *The Semi-Sovereign People: A Realist's View of Democracy in America* (Hinsdale, Ill.: Dryden Press, 1960), 35. I am indebted to Iva Deutchman for bringing this to my attention.

30. Lipset and Raab, *Politics of Unreason*, 6.

31. I am indebted to Paul Passavant for making this clear to me.

32. Hannah Arendt, *On Revolution* (London: Penguin Books, 1963).

33. Bonnie Honig, *Political Theory and the Displacement of Politics* (Ithaca: Cornell University Press, 1993), 101.

34. The distinction between performative and constative sentences is a distinction between doing something and saying something. Performatives are themselves actions (I promise, I agree). Constatives describe or report something to be the case. As Honig's critique of Arendt makes clear, there are sentences that do both at the same time (We hold). See J. L. Austin, *How To Do Things with Words* (Cambridge: Harvard University Press, [1962] 1975).

35. Honig, *Political Theory and the Displacement of Politics*, 106.

36. Pauline Maier, *American Scripture: Making the Declaration of Independence* (New York: Alfred A. Knopf, 1997), 123.

37. Ibid., 105.

38. Ibid., 106.

39. Ibid., 115.

40. Ibid., 156.

41. Bernard Bailyn, *The Ideological Origins of the American Revolution* (Cambridge: Harvard University Press, 1972), 95.

42. Gordon S. Wood, *The Creation of the American Republic, 1776–1787* (New York: Norton, 1972), 32.

43. Ibid., 39.

44. Bailyn, *Ideological Origins of the American Revolution*, 144.

45. Wood, *Creation of the American Republic*, 40.

46. Ibid., 40–41.

47. Ibid., 3.

48. Bailyn, *Ideological Origins of the American Revolution*, 138.

49. For a more thorough discussion of the problem of judgment in late capitalist technoculture, see my *Aliens in America*. I am indebted to Tom Dumm for pushing me to think further about the changes in representations of rationality.

50. See William Wresch, *Disconnected: Have and Have-nots in the Information Age* (New Brunswick: Rutgers University Press, 1996).

51. Robins and Post, *Political Paranoia*, 8. See also Pipes, *Conspiracy*, 44.

52. Robins and Post, *Political Paranoia*, 42.

53. Ibid., 9.

54. See Dean, *Aliens in America*, chap. 2.

55. As Richard Hofstadter writes, "He [the paranoid] does not see social conflict as something to be mediated and compromised in the manner of the working politician." *Paranoid Style in American Politics*, 31.

56. Robins and Post employ the virus metaphor, *Political Paranoia*, 61; Pipes, *Conspiracy*, 2.

57. Hofstadter, *Paranoid Style in American Politics*, 39.

58. Indeed, Robins and Post go so far as to take Patricia Turner to task for failing to condemn paranoia in her excellent study of rumor in some African-American communities; *Political Paranoia*, 64. See Patricia A. Turner, *I Heard It through the Grapevine: Rumor in African-American Culture* (Berkeley: University of California Press, 1994).

59. Pipes, *Conspiracy*, 183.

60. Ibid., 163.

61. Ibid., 33.

62. Hofstadter, *Paranoid Style in American Politics*, 37.

63. Ibid., 5, 39.

64. Robins and Post, *Political Paranoia*, 18–19.

65. For an example, see Pipes, *Conspiracy*, chapter 8.

66. Robins and Post, *Political Paranoia*, 95.

67. See Dean, *Aliens in America*. See also Diana Tumminia, "How Prophecy Never Fails: Interpretive Reason in a Flying Saucer Group," *Sociology of Religion* 59,2 (1998): 157–70. Tumminia argues that working through failure, skepticism, and disbelief enabled the Unarius Academy of Science to strengthen the bonds among group members. They pursued a process of "collaborative reinvention" in the face of the failure of the Space Brothers to return as expected.

68. For an alternative account of the relationship between conspiracy, skepticism, and paranoia, see Lee Quinby, *Millennial Seduction: A Skeptic Confronts Apocalyptic Culture* (Ithaca: Cornell University Press, 1999).

69. Hofstadter, *Paranoid Style in American Politics*, 31.

contributors

PAUL APOSTOLIDIS teaches political theory and United States politics at Whitman College in Walla Walla, Washington. He is the author of *Stations of the Cross: Adorno and Christian Right Radio*, forthcoming in 2000 from Duke University Press. His current projects examine the politics of Christian right popular culture and Latinos and gentrification.

LAUREN BERLANT teaches at the University of Chicago. She is author of *The Anatomy of National Fantasy: Hawthorne, Utopia, and Everyday Life* (University of Chicago Press, 1991) and *The Queen of America Goes to Washington City: Essays on Sex and Citizenship* (Duke University Press, 1997), and editor of a special issue of *Critical Inquiry* (of which she is a co-editor) on intimacy (Winter 1998).

WILLIAM E. CONNOLLY teaches political theory at Johns Hopkins University, where he is Professor and Chair. His most recent books include *Why I'm Not a Secularist* (University of Minnesota Press, 1999) and *The Ethos of Pluralization* (University of Minnesota Press, 1995).

BARBARA CRUIKSHANK teaches political theory at the University of Massachusetts and is the author of *The Will to Empower: Democratic Citizens and Other Subjects* (Cornell University Press, 1999).

JODI DEAN teaches political and cultural theory at Hobart and William Smith Colleges, where she is an associate professor of political science. She edited *Feminism and the New Democracy: Resiting the Political* (Sage, 1997). She is the author of *Solidarity of Strangers: Feminism after Identity Politics* (University of California Press, 1996) and *Aliens in America: Conspiracy Cultures from Outerspace to Cyberspace* (Cornell University Press, 1998).

THOMAS L. DUMM is a professor of political science at Amherst College and coeditor of the online journal of political theory, *Theory & Event*. His books include *Democracy and Punishment* (University of Wisconsin Press, 1987), *united states* (Cornell University Press, 1994), *Michel Foucault and the Politics of Freedom* (Sage, 1996), and *A Politics of the Ordinary* (New York University Press, 1999).

JUDITH GRANT is an associate professor of political science at the University of Southern California in Los Angeles. She specializes in nineteenth- and twentieth-century social and political theory. She is the author of *Fundamental Feminism* (Routledge, 1993) and *Dworkin and MacKinnon* (forthcoming, Sage, 2000). For more information see http: / / wwwrcf.usc.edu / ~judithg /.

AIDA A. HOZIC writes (mostly but not only) about the political economy of media and culture industries. She is currently teaching in the Politics Department at Ithaca College. A recipient of a John D. and Catherine T. MacArthur Research and Writing Grant for the project on "unwanted colonies," she will be at Cornell in 2000–2001.

GEORGE LIPSITZ is professor of ethnic studies at the University of California, San Diego. His publications include *The Possessive Investment in Whiteness: How White People Profit from Identity Politics* (Temple University Press, 1998), *A Life in Struggle: Ivory Perry and the Politics of Opposition* (Temple University Press, 1995), *Dangerous Crossroads* (Verso, 1994), *Rainbow at Midnight* (University of Illinois Press, 1994), *Sidewalks of St. Louis* (University of Missouri Press, 1991), and *Time Passages* (University of Minnesota Press, 1990).

PAUL A. PASSAVANT is assistant professor of political science at Hobart and William Smith Colleges. He has authored essays on rights, culture, and free speech.

MARK REINHARDT teaches political theory and American Studies at Williams College. He is author of *The Art of Being Free: Taking Liberties with Tocqueville, Marx, and Arendt* (Cornell University Press, 1997), and is currently writing a book about fugitive slaves and antebellum political culture.

MICHAEL J. SHAPIRO is professor of political science at the University of Hawaii. His most recent books include *Violent Cartographies: Mapping Cultures of War* (University of Minnesota Press, 1997) and *Cinematic Political Thought* (New York University Press, 1999).

GEORGE SHULMAN teaches political thought and American Studies at the Gallatin School of New York University. He was recently awarded an NEH fellowship to complete his second book, *Prophecy and Redemption in American Political Culture*.

KATHLEEN STEWART teaches cultural anthropology at the University of Texas, Austin. She is the author of *A Space on the Side of the Road: Cultural Poetics in an "Other" America* (Princeton University Press, 1996). She is currently completing a book called *The Private Life of Public Culture*, which takes up themes of abjection, trauma, and public culture in the United States. She is also working on a third book project based on fieldwork in Las Vegas that tracks the meanings of risk culture, master-planned communities, and working-class political imaginaries.

PRISCILLA WALD teaches in the English department at Duke University. She is the author of *Constituting Americans: Cultural Anxiety and Narrative Form* (Duke University Press, 1995) and is currently at work on a manuscript about contagion and Americanism.

LINDA ZERILLI is professor of political science at Northwestern University. She is the author of *Signifying Woman: Culture and Chaos in Rousseau, Burke, and Mill* (Cornell University Press, 1994).

index